# The Public Relations Strategic Toolkit

*The Public Relations Strategic Toolkit* provides a structured approach to understanding public relations and corporate communications. The focus is on professional skills development as well as approaches that are widely recognised as 'best practice'. Original methods are considered alongside well-established procedures to ensure the changing requirements of contemporary practice are reflected.

Split into four parts covering the public relations profession, strategic planning, corporate communication and stakeholder engagement, this textbook covers everything involved in the critical practice of public relations in an accessible manner. Features include:

- definitions of key terms
- contemporary case studies
- insight from practitioners
- handy checklists
- practical activities and assignments.

Covering the practicalities of using traditional and social media as well as international considerations, ethics and PR within contexts from politics to charities, this guide gives you all the critical and practical skills you need to introduce you to a career in public relations.

**Alison Theaker** has thirty years' experience in public relations and taught public relations and integrated marketing communications in the UK and the USA. She is the author of bestselling textbooks *The Public Relations Handbook* (2012) and *Effective Media Relations* (2005). She is an elected Fellow of the Chartered Institute of Public Relations (CIPR) and was its first Head of Education and Training. She has addressed conferences in the UK, USA and Australia about the future of the industry, developing teams and improving writing skills. She is now a PR coach for small businesses, running her own consultancy, The Spark (www.thesparkuk.com), as well as being an accredited action learning facilitator.

**Heather Yaxley** is a hybrid public relations practitioner–academic, with over twenty-five years' experience working in-house and as a consultant. She is a CIPR Fellow and Accredited Practitioner as well as an honorary member and director of the Motor Industry Public Affairs Association Ltd. A lecturer at Bournemouth University, where she is studying for a Ph.D., Heather is also course director for the CIPR qualifications with Cambridge Marketing Colleges. She established Applause Consultancy in 2000 and has worked with clients including Nissan, Bentley Motors, Coca-Cola, npower renewables, Tata and General Motors. She is a PR pioneer in social media and can be found as Greenbanana in Twitter and other social networks.

# The Public Relations Strategic Toolkit

An essential guide to successful public relations practice

Alison Theaker and Heather Yaxley

Routledge
Taylor & Francis Group

LONDON AND NEW YORK

First published 2013
by Routledge
2 Park Square, Milton Park, Abingdon, Oxon OX14 4RN

Simultaneously published in the USA and Canada
by Routledge
711 Third Avenue, New York, NY 10017

*Routledge is an imprint of the Taylor & Francis Group, an informa business*

*British Library Cataloguing in Publication Data*
A catalogue record for this book is available from the British Library

*Library of Congress Cataloging in Publication Data*
Theaker, Alison.
  The public relations strategic toolkit: an essential guide to successful
  public relations practice/Alison Theaker and Heather Yaxley. –
  1st ed.
  p. cm.
  Includes bibliographical references and index.
  1. Corporations – Public relations. 2. Business communication.
  I. Yaxley, Heather, 1971– II. Title.
  HD59.T4744 2012                                      659.2 – dc23
  2012006225


ISBN: 978-0-415-67647-2 (hbk)
ISBN: 978-0-415-67648-9 (pbk)
ISBN: 978-0-203-14365-0 (ebk)

Typeset in Helvetica Neue and Avant Garde
by Florence Production Ltd, Stoodleigh, Devon

MIX
Paper from
responsible sources

FSC
www.fsc.org   FSC® C004839            Printed and bound in Great Britain by the MPG Books Group

# Contents

# Figures

# Tables

# Foreword

This book is intended to be a 'how to' book with brains for public relations practitioners, students and others interested in this fascinating field. So while it includes theoretical concepts and discussions about the nature of public relations, it is also full of examples of real-life practice.

When we were discussing how *The PR Strategic Toolkit* would be different from its sister book, *The Public Relations Handbook*, we were clear that we wanted it to be of use to practitioners, not just those studying for a PR qualification. At the same time, we wanted this book to be underpinned by thinking and knowledge derived from our experiences of PR as academics, educators, practitioners and consultants.

We both believe that theory improves practice, but it is not the whole story. Our aim is to consider what is involved in contemporary PR work from the perspective of understanding why certain strategies, tactics and practices are undertaken and how they can be improved.

Although we have co-authored this book, its contents reflect our individual areas of knowledge, experience and interest. We agreed the structure and scope of the content and then undertook production of sections and chapters independently.

Part I: The profession – draws on Alison Theaker's considerable expertise gained working in the UK, US and Australia. It ranges from the difficult task of defining PR to looking at what practitioners do, as well as the role of professional bodies and the question of professionalisation and issues affecting the development of public relations.

Part II: Public relations – planning reflects Heather Yaxley's interest in ensuring public relations work is considered and credible. She presents practical guidance, with handy checklists and useful activities, covering the strategic planning process from research through implementation to reporting. Her framework acknowledges the complex reality of PR practice and challenges traditional linear models of planning.

Part III: Corporate communications – features chapters by Alison and Heather examining six key areas of public relations. The chapters combine the authors' familiarity of theoretical and practical know-how with insight from their contacts and case studies, which they feel offer useful examples of contemporary PR practice.

Part IV: Stakeholder engagement – looks at connecting with key groups whose actions have a strategic effect on organisations. In these chapters, Alison and Heather consider methods, issues and opportunities facing those working in more specialist areas. A variety of practitioners share their experiences and insight is offered to be of particular relevance to those new to these areas.

Each chapter is set out in a similar way, with a Check Point outlining its objectives and an End Point reviewing the key points. Within the work, you will find Talking Points flagging up issues for debate, Reading Points with links to other sources and Action Points, which connect to practice.

Illustrations, figures, tables and diagrams help you connect the ideas presented to your own work.

The approach throughout the book aims to be thought-provoking, with questions about, and challenges to, accepted procedures, while championing flexible, reflective practice and engagement with new developments. We do not seek to be prescriptive, and encourage practitioners, and students, to examine our work with an open and inquiring mind. Our intention is to stimulate you to think, even if you disagree with our perspectives.

While presenting our own opinions, *The PR Strategic Toolkit* draws on ideas, models and concepts that are explored in academic and practitioner literature. We are grateful to all those who have contributed directly or indirectly to this book, most particularly, those who shared their own stories.

Thanks go also to our families, friends and others who have inspired or challenged our thinking about public relations.

# Acknowledgements

## TABLES

1.1 P. Kotler and W. Mindak (1978) 'Marketing and Public Relations', *Journal of Marketing* by American Marketing Association; American Marketing Society; National Association of Marketing Teachers Copyright. Reproduced with permission of American Marketing Association via Copyright Clearance Center

2.1 Adapted from Cornelissen, J. (2008) *Corporate Communications: a guide to theory and practice*, London: Sage

2.2 Johanna Fawkes (2012), 'What is Public Relations?' in Alison Theaker, *The Public Relations Handbook,* 4th edition, Abingdon: Routledge

2.3 Alison Theaker

3.1 Johanna Fawkes and Ralph Tench (2005) 'Public Relations Education in the UK'

14.1 T. Cannon (1992), *Corporate Responsibility*, London: Pitman

14.2 Heather Yaxley (2009), http://greenbanana.info/career/2011/12/05/the-social-dimension-of-csr/

19.1 Used by permission of Sue Dewhurst and Liam FitzPatrick

20.1 Heather Yaxley

## FIGURES

5.1 Heather Yaxley

5.2 Heather Yaxley

6.1 Based on Saunders, M., Lewis, P. and Thornhill, A. (2002), *Research Methods for Business Students,* 2nd edition. Harlow: FT/Prentice Hall

7.1 Adapted from Anderson, F.W., Hadley, L., Rockland, D. and Weiner, M. (1999), *Guidelines for Setting Measurable Public Relations Objectives: an update*, Gainesville, FL: Institute for Public Relations

| | |
|---|---|
| 7.2 | Heather Yaxley |
| 7.3 | Heather Yaxley |
| 7.4 | Heather Yaxley |
| 8.1 | Heather Yaxley |
| 8.2 | Heather Yaxley |
| 8.3 | Heather Yaxley |
| 8.4 | Heather Yaxley |
| 8.5 | Heather Yaxley |
| 8.6 | Heather Yaxley |
| 9.1 | Adapted from Covey, S.R. (1989), *The Seven Habits of Highly Effective People: restoring the character ethic,* London: Simon & Schuster |
| 9.2 | Heather Yaxley |
| 9.3 | Heather Yaxley |
| 10.1 | Adapted from Overview of the Valid Metrics Framework (2012), proposed by AMEC |
| 10.2 | Heather Yaxley |
| 11.1 | Courtesy of Plymouth University |
| 11.2 | Courtesy of Plymouth University |
| 11.3 | Courtesy of the Devon Air Ambulance Trust |
| 11.4 | Courtesy of the Devon Air Ambulance Trust |
| 11.5 | Courtesy of the Devon Air Ambulance Trust |
| 12.1 | Courtesy of Crealy Rocks |
| 12.2 | Courtesy of the *Express and Echo* |
| 12.3 | Courtesy of Claire Crawley, StartPoint PR |
| 14.1 | Courtesy of Venus |
| 14.2 | Courtesy of Venus |
| 14.3 | Courtesy of Venus |
| 14.4 | Courtesy of Pennywell Farm |
| 15.1 | Courtesy of David Evans |
| 15.2a | Courtesy of Apeiron Communication |
| 15.2b | Courtesy of Apeiron Communication |
| 17.1 | Heather Yaxley |
| 17.2 | Heather Yaxley |
| 19.1 | Courtesy of Severn Trent Water |
| 19.2 | Courtesy of Freshfields Bruckhaus Deringer LLP |
| 19.3 | Courtesy of Freshfields Bruckhaus Deringer LLP |
| 20.1 | Heather Yaxley |
| 20.2 | Heather Yaxley |
| 20.3 | Heather Yaxley |
| 21.1 | Courtesy of the Environment Agency |
| 21.2 | Courtesy of Westward Housing Group |
| 22.1 | Courtesy of Sally Hurst |
| 22.2 | Courtesy of Langage Farm |
| 22.3 | Courtesy of Lis Anderson, JBP PR |

# Part I

# The profession

# Introduction

## Alison Theaker

When I started in PR practice in 1982, I was not aware of the range of textbooks available to me that might have helped me perform my job better. Indeed, I was surprised to find a whole shelf of them in the library when I started as the first lecturer on the new BA in Public Relations at the then Leeds Polytechnic (now Leeds Metropolitan University).

One of the questions that I was asked at interview was, 'What is the difference between education and training?'

Experience and training is good, but by definition they are looking at what has gone before. They are valuable but not the whole story. Education, using theory to try and see why something worked on a deeper level, is vital in enabling us to apply the lessons of experience. It gives us more ways of looking beneath the surface of what happened to us, a variety of lenses through which to view an event. It allows us to use different language when we talk to board members, we can see that we may have been using communication or management theory without being aware of it. We can be critical of our profession and so we can change it. It gives us more tools than just learning on the job. Taking time out to examine our own practice also means we can become objective about what works.

The competence of practitioners was raised in a Department of Trade and Industry (DTI) study in 2003, and is what the many qualifications in PR are trying to address. Any profession will always be judged by the few who don't fulfil the required standards rather than the many who do. However, the willingness of more and more graduates to enter PR, the expansion of both academic and professional courses in the discipline, the ever growing body of knowledge coming from practitioners and academics willing to look at the theory underpinning their practice shows the increased willingness of PR to be reflective.

This first section starts by introducing public relations and looking at some different definitions. Traditionally, this has been a difficult area for practitioners, as everyone seems to have their own idea of what public relations is. By comparing PR to other related professions and business functions such as advertising, marketing and journalism, the picture hopefully gets clearer.

The second chapter investigates exactly what PR practitioners do, looking at the various roles they might play in an organisation, as well as listing the tasks that they perform. This is built on in Chapter 3, which gives an overview of the PR industry in the UK and looks at the various professional bodies that are striving to improve the reputation of public relations.

Finally, the section is completed with a look at the question of professionalisation and issues affecting the development of public relations. Several prominent academics and practitioners have been asked for their views on the challenges facing the industry in the next five years.

CHAPTER 1

# What is public relations?

## *Alison Theaker*

This chapter provides an introduction to public relations and outlines its relationship to journalism, marketing, advertising, promotion and publicity. Practical examples are included to show what PR does and how it works in organisations.

## CHECK POINT

After reading this chapter, you should be able to:

* compare various definitions of public relations;
* assess criticisms of public relations;
* distinguish public relations from journalism, marketing, and advertising.

## DEFINITIONS

What are your initial impressions of public relations? Perhaps you think it is about organising parties, promoting pop bands, getting press coverage and launching exciting new products. Or maybe you believe it's all about politics – writing speeches, announcing new policies, handling awkward questions or 'spinning' difficult situations. Clearly there are different views of what public relations is – which is why it is important to consider definitions, identify areas of debate and look to establish a common understanding.

Grunig and Hunt (1984) believe Dorman Eaton, a lawyer, was the first to use the term 'public relations' in addressing the Yale Law School on 'The Public Relations and Duties of the Legal Profession' in 1882. The meaning – looking out for the welfare of the public – was reflected by Theodore Vail, president of the American Telephone and Telegraph Co. in the theme of the company's annual report in 1908. How does this use reflect usage of the term today?

In 1976, Rex Harlow gathered 472 definitions of public relations and many hundreds more have been proposed subsequently. Faced with so many opinions, you may feel that John Marston's 1963 view of PR is still true today: 'a brotherhood of some 100,000 whose common bond is its profession and whose common woe is that no two of them can ever quite agree on what that profession is' (cited in Hutton 1999). Indeed, there is robust debate over whether PR is indeed a profession (L'Etang and Pieczka 2006a).

Some definitions of public relations are positivist; that is they are based on explaining what is involved in the practice of public relations, or what it achieves within organisations. Others are normative and state a vision of what PR should be. Any difference between positivist and normative definitions reveals disagreements about whether the reality of PR lives up to the ideals or aspirations for its practice.

Definitions are also useful in clarifying what public relations is not; distinguishing it from other functions where there may be some confusion. It is important to remember that those who present definitions are putting across their own view of what PR is, should be or is not. They are seeking to persuade, not simply explain or inform. A definition also needs to be put into a social context, since meaning may change over time or be culturally dependent. This can be seen when reviewing different definitions or views of public relations:

- Public relations is a distinctive management function which helps establish and maintain mutual lines of communication, understanding, acceptance and cooperation between an organisation and its publics; involves the management of problems or issues; helps management to keep informed on and responsive to public opinion; defines and emphasises the responsibility of management to serve the public interest; helps management keep abreast of and effectively utilise change, serving as an early warning system to help anticipate trends; and uses research and ethical communication techniques as its principal tools. Quoted in Wilcox *et al.* (2003: 7).
- Public relations is the art and social science of analysing trends, predicting their consequences, counselling organisation's leadership, and implementing

planned programs of action which will serve both the organisation's and the public interest. Quoted in Wilcox *et al.* (2003: 5).

- Public relations helps our complex, pluralistic society to reach decisions and function more effectively by contributing to mutual understanding among groups and institutions. It serves to bring private and public policies into harmony. Quoted in Wilcox *et al.* (2003: 6).

- Public relations is the management of communications between an organisation and its publics. Grunig and Hunt (1984).

- Public relations is about reputation – the result of what you do, what you say and what others say about you. Public relations is the discipline which looks after reputation, with the aim of earning understanding and support and influencing opinion and behaviour. It is the planned and sustained effort to establish and maintain goodwill and mutual understanding between an organisation and its publics. Quoted in Fawkes (2012a: 5).

- Public relations is about managing strategic relationships. Hutton (1999).

- Public relations is an old and noble profession, essential for the preservation of an open society. Verčič (2004).

- Public relations is about building and managing relationships. Our role is to assemble and navigate the complex and ambiguous relationships required to operate either as an organisation or as individuals living and working in our fragmenting environment. Arrow (2008).

- Public relations is the occupation responsible for the management of organisational relationships and reputation. It encompasses issues management, public affairs, corporate communications, stakeholder relations, risk communication and corporate social responsibility (CSR). Public relations operates on behalf of many different types of organisation both at the governmental and corporate level, to small business and voluntary sectors. Public relations arises at points of societal change and resistance. L'Etang (2009).

PR practitioners:

- participate in defining organisational values, principles, strategies, policies and processes;

- apply social networking, research skills and tools to interpret stakeholders' and society's expectations as a basis for decisions;

- deliver timely analysis and recommendations for an effective governance of stakeholder relationships by enhancing transparency, trustworthy behaviour, authentic and verifiable representation, thus sustaining the organisation's 'licence to operate';

- create an internal listening culture, an open system that allows the organisation to anticipate, adapt and respond. *Stockholm Accords* (2010).

**ACTION POINT**

■ What do you think is the purpose of these definitions or views of public relations?

■ Are they positivist and/or normative?

■ Which clarify your understanding?

■ In what way do they distinguish PR from other functions?

■ Do you agree or disagree with the viewpoints expressed?

The key elements of PR involve being able to convey information in an appropriate way to a specific public – which may include announcing news, narrating stories or engaging in discussion – in order to build relationships that help achieve relevant aims and objectives.

There are three considerations of the word 'public' that are relevant to understanding public relations:

1    In sociology, 'public' relates to a community or group of people who have something in common, for example, an interest or activity. Sometimes the phrase 'general public' is used to indicate everyone, which is so broad that, according to Cutlip *et al.* (2000: 383) 'there simply is no such thing'. This indicates that communications should normally engage with more defined categories of people. PR practice doesn't necessarily mean engaging directly with the public; it often involves indirect methods of communications (such as through the media), although the end goal may be to influence a particular public.

2    The views of a population can be determined as 'public opinion'. This is researched using surveys of a sample of people whose individual views, attitudes, and beliefs about a particular topic or question are then aggregated. Unless a census of everyone in the population is taken, sampling needs to ensure the results of the survey can be generalised. Such surveys emphasise a combined opinion; specifically of the majority of respondents, which may hide significant variation of opinion among a public. PR activities are sometimes intended to sway 'public opinion', especially where this is thought to be influential, for example on government policy.

3    The term 'public' can be seen as the opposite of private. However, not all PR activities are undertaken in the public domain. Interpersonal communications and building relationships with individuals can be important elements of the PR function. This meaning of public does relate to being well known as in 'public figures', making something public, or being 'in the public eye'. It also has a connection to 'news publication' and 'publicity', which are considered below.

# CRITICISMS

Course leader Suzanne Fitzgerald at Rowan University in New Jersey, US recently asked her students to find out popular definitions of PR, and one came up with 'Public relations is perfuming manure'. This analogy is not unique. Moloney (2000: 23) quotes a former group editor of PR Week, Steven Farish, as stating: 'you would be hard pushed to find an industry which is as gleefully vilified as the noble profession of public relations – otherwise known as "the latrine of parasitic misinformation" as it was dubbed by *The Guardian*.'

**READING POINT**

■ The concept of a 'public' and how PR practitioners identify specific groups is considered in Chapter 6.

It is not unusual to see criticism of PR and its practitioners, particularly by the media. Bryan Appleyard, a respected journalist wrote in the *Sunday Times* (2003): 'Truth has been destroyed by public relations executives, or "scum" as we like to call them.' PR has been accused of contributing to a decline of journalism into 'churnalism' (Davies 2008) as media become reliant on press releases and pseudo-events. Suzanne Moore called PR 'that industry made of nothingness' (2011).

Public relations has also been called 'spin', a pejorative term focusing on presenting selective information or lying. An ethics debate organised by *PR Week* in 2007 concluded with practitioners voting against the motion that 'PR has a duty to tell the truth'. Others equate public relations to propaganda (see Kill Jill case study on pp. 10–12).

The term 'PR disaster' (defined as 'anything that could catalyse embarrassing or negative publicity for any given organisation', McCusker 2006b: 311) implies that practitioners are responsible when issues have not been addressed effectively and dismisses a strategic role for the function in crisis management. Indeed, attempts to explain an organisation's position may be labelled as a 'PR exercise' (defined as 'a situation of communication with no substance within it', Green 2007: 215).

PR practitioners are accused of being 'invisible persuaders' (Mitchie 1998) and its use by organisations is exposed by critics such as Stauber and Rampton (2004) and Miller and Dinan (2008) as seeking to subvert society in favour of those with power, and the money to employ skilful PR counsel. L'Etang (1996: 105) sees PR as 'necessarily partisan and intrinsically undemocratic' reflecting that practitioners are employed to represent their paymasters in the best way possible.

Public impressions of those working in public relations are likely to be informed by high-profile publicists and spin doctors featured in television programmes, movies or in the media. Such fictional and real-life characters are often portrayed in a negative light and consequently serve as poor role models for PR practice.

On the one hand, there's the cliché of PR bunnies (Frolich and Peters 2007), attractive young women working in the fashion, beauty, or music industries. Typecast in

*The Devil Wears Prada*, *Sex in the City* or *Absolutely Fabulous*, they organise celebrity launches, secure reality television shows for their clients, chat to journalists, enjoy long lunches and drink champagne with handsome men in the best nightclubs.

The other image is the Machiavellian male PR media-manipulator, who will do whatever it takes to promote his clients or protect their reputation. This type of PR practitioner is generally placed at the heart of government or in the boardroom, advising senior executives in crisis situations to adopt clever, but morally dubious, strategies or bullying journalists into doing things their way. In the movies, you'll find him in *Wag the Dog* or *Thank you for Smoking* and on television in *Absolute Power* or *West Wing*.

Most public relations work in reality is less glamorous and more ethical. But its key elements can be found in these extreme stereotypes. Generally, PR practitioners are involved in communicating and building relationships on behalf of organisations (in the private, public or not-for-profit sectors) or individuals (such as celebrities). To do this, they work with the media and other influencers, produce communications materials, organise events and manage responses to emerging problems.

This explanation presents a benign or neutral perspective of PR, and arguably it is not the function itself that causes issues, but its usage by those with either good or negative ends in mind.

## ACTION POINT

In 2008, the Scottish Government and Healthier Scotland ran a high-profile billboard campaign using posters and video, offering viewers the choice to 'Kill Jill: Yes or No'. The 'No' option was connected to the web address for organ donation, with the message: 'If you register online to be a donor you could save a life. If you don't you won't.' The campaign aimed to increase the number of registered organ donors in Scotland. At the time, one person in Scotland died each week through the lack of an organ for transplant.

This campaign was criticised strongly by law professor Hugh McLachlan in the *Scotsman*. His main issue was that the campaign was funded by the Scottish Government. He classified the campaign as propaganda rather than information.

> Information is different from propaganda. Propagandists want us to think feel and act in particular ways ... If the Scottish Government and Health Scotland really wanted to give us information rather than propaganda ... they would tell us what the absolute as well as the relative risks are.

He also pointed out that there was a difference between actually killing someone and 'refraining from doing something that might have postponed his or her death.' Finally he stated, 'Political parties, pressure groups and individual people are entitled to ply the public with propaganda. The state, its agents and agencies are not.'

Unsurprisingly, the article caused a lively debate on the Scotsman's website. Don Smith, who claimed responsibility for creating the advert felt that he had 'contributed to something positive and worthwhile'. He suggested that such advertising was a 'powerful tool for promoting positive social change,' and that lives would be saved as a result of the campaign.

Giles Moffat (2008) added, 'Brands influence choice, so why should social marketing not? Especially when the majority believe the cause to be good, moral, just and beneficial to society?' He continued, 'There's nothing wrong with social marketing campaigns emphasising a point of view if they are founded in belief and conviction that they are doing the right thing.' This last point caused Hugh McLachlan to respond, 'There certainly is if the state funds and promotes it.'

In 2009, the number of donors on the register rose to a ten-year high. Possibly spurred on by this success, the Scottish Government ran a £500,000 campaign in February 2010, called 'Spare Clare'. Reported in the *Daily Record* (2010), the campaign was backed by liver transplant recipient Claire Riley, who said:

> Being given the gift of life has allowed me to live a full life, free of pain and anxiety. I have been able to go on and have a family of my own. I now have two young sons and no longer lie on the couch unable to move from tiredness – I can play and have fun with my wonderful children like any other healthy, happy mother. This year's campaign encourages Scots to think if they would 'Spare Clare – Yes or No?' As a Claire who has been spared, I can only urge people to give the gift of life. Just ask yourself one question– if your friend, family member or work colleague needed an organ, would you want them spared?

O'Shaughnessy (1996) sought to distinguish social marketing and social propaganda. He felt that the main characteristic of the former was that it was a deliberate intent to influence or manipulate attitudes for the benefit of the source of the information rather than that of the recipient. It could show explicit bias and be based on lies and deception. He says, 'Propaganda simplifies and exaggerates: it is often propelled by a clear, purposive and coherent ideology.'

Social marketing on the other hand contains an emphasis on customers and should be based on 'some research defined conception of audience wants'. O'Shaughnessy suggested this approach would mean that the message would not be framed in an antagonistic way, but presented more ambivalently and assuming that the audience would therefore make up their own minds. He also recognised that most social marketing agrees with a government agenda, and often sought to change the behaviour of the victim rather than deal with the cause of the problem.

■ Given these conflicting viewpoints, and bearing in mind the definitions presented above, do you think that the 'Kill Jill' and 'Spare Clare' campaigns are social propaganda, social marketing or public relations?

## DIFFERENCES FROM OTHER MANAGEMENT DISCIPLINES

PR uses a variety of techniques and overlaps with other areas of management. In an effort to further define PR, we will now look at some of these and contrast and compare what each function involves.

## Marketing

Public relations and marketing are often seen as adversarial, although it may just be that they pursue similar goals in different ways. Marketeers tend to see PR as a subordinate part of their armoury of tools, and indeed businesses reinforce this by the organisation of their communications functions. Public relations practitioners often see marketing as part of their remit, for they believe it is primarily concerned with selling products to consumers. All organisations have a need for public relations, but not all are involved in marketing. The Fire Service carries out community and media relations, but does not try to convince people to start more fires and so use their services more. They may 'market' safety advice and the availability of the service, however.

The Chartered Institute of Marketing (2011) defines marketing as: 'The management process responsible for identifying, anticipating and satisfying consumer requirements profitably.' This puts marketing clearly in the arena of creating sales, while PR has a broader, reputational remit.

What is clear is that public relations and marketing should ideally be corporate allies, working together for common goals. Kitchen (1997: 227–234) surveyed

**TABLE 1.1 Spheres of responsibility for marketing and PR**

| Marketing | Marketing Public Relations | Public Relations |
|---|---|---|
| Market Assessment | Image Assessment | Publications |
| Customer Segmentation | Customer Satisfaction | Events |
| Product Development | Surveys | News |
| Pricing | Media Strategy | Community Relations |
| Distribution | Corporate Advertising | Identity Media |
| Servicing | Employee Attitudes | Lobbying |
| Sales Force | Atmospherics | Social Investments |
| Sales Promotion | | |
| Product Advertising | | |

marketing and PR personnel in the UK. PR was viewed as important for marketing support by the marketeers, while PR executives saw this as a minor area and viewed issues management, employee communications and corporate communications as their priorities. However, there was general agreement that PR was part of integrated marketing communications.

Kitchen suggests that while there is 'a significant relationship between corporate public relations and marketing public relations', the focus of each is different. Marketing aims to create exchanges with consumers and uses PR tools to that end. Public relations on the other hand aims to 'create and maintain mutually beneficial relations with publics who could impact on business success' (Kitchen 1997: 234). So while the marketing team may create special offers and sales promotions, PR people will be seeking media coverage and arranging launch events.

Kotler and Mindak (1978) suggested the model below to illustrate the relationship between the three disciplines of marketing, marketing public relations and public relations.

# Advertising

The Institute of Practitioners in Advertising's definition of advertising is: 'Advertising presents the most persuasive possible selling message to the right prospects for the product or service at the lowest possible cost' (quoted in Fawkes 2012a: 12). While advertising is clearly about increasing sales, as we have seen above, PR aims to increase understanding. While advertising buys space or airtime to put across a message which is controlled by the organisation paying for the advert, PR practitioners give newsworthy information to journalists to persuade them to mention products and services in editorial pages or programmes. Once the information is given to the media, they can report it in whatever fashion they like, or choose not to report it at all.

Sometimes, however, an organisation might buy space to put across a general message about its environmental credentials or community involvement. This is known as corporate advertising and is more likely to be written by the PR department. A good clue is whether an advert would aim to get the recipient to buy something or not.

An advertorial or advertising feature is another area of overlap. They often appear in magazines and while the space is bought, just like an ad, it is filled with text and images similar to the surrounding editorial. While consumers can differentiate between adverts, advertorial and editorial, the advertorial gives the organisation complete control over the content while aiming to make it look more like independent article.

Advertising works best when it is repeated often, as this reinforces its messages. Ries suggested that PR worked best when launching a product, with advertising used to support continued sales (Ries and Ries 2002).

## Journalism

Ivy Ledbetter Lee is credited as being one of the first American pioneers of public relations. An ex-journalist, his Declaration of Principles in 1906 stated that:

> Our plan is, frankly and openly, on behalf of the business concerns and public institutions to supply to the press and public of the United States prompt and accurate information which it is of interest and value to the public to know about.
>
> (Grunig and Hunt 1984: 33)

At first sight this may not seem dissimilar to the NUJ's Code of Conduct (NUJ 2011), which declares that a journalist 'Strives to ensure that information disseminated is honestly conveyed, accurate and fair.' Why then is the relationship between journalists and PR practitioners fraught with tension? Gregory (2006) suggested that 'It is the power of public relations that journalists fear, not its weakness. That is one reason why they mock it.'

The Free Dictionary (2011) (www.thefreedictionary.com/journalism) defines journalism simply as 'The collecting, writing, editing, and presenting of news or news articles in newspapers and magazines and in radio and television broadcasts'. However, the instutionalisation of the 'freedom of the press' in Western democracies gives an added weight to journalistic reporting. The implication is that the media reports an objective version of the truth, while PR practitioners who are employed by organisations or clients can never be impartial. Journalists need PR practitioners to respond to their requests for information and are motivated by getting a good story. The press officer, on the other hand, is invested in presenting their organisation in the most favourable light possible. The PR practitioner may also wish the journalist to report on their organisation to give an added credence or third party endorsement to its actions.

Before Lee's Principles, the traditional approach to the media by business was to suppress all unfavourable information. The advent of social media and citizen journalism has rendered that approach even more untenable. Journalists will continue to hunt out newsworthy stories and PR practitioners will continue to present the most positive account of their organisation.

## END POINT

This chapter has shown that academics and practitioners continue to try and define public relations, but that despite many efforts there is no single accepted definition. This presents a problem as its main ideas are easily adopted by marketing, human resources or other elements in an organisation. However, the main elements of PR are generally agreed to focus on it being a management function, and that it involves communication between an organisation and its publics. Public relations is a growing field and makes a considerable contribution to the economy. This Toolkit aims to explore the elements of public relations and to provide clear guidance on successful techniques and practices used in the industry today.

CHAPTER 2

# What do PR practitioners do?

*Alison Theaker*

This chapter examines the roles of PR practitioners and looks at what they need to be good at.

## CHECK POINT

After reading this chapter, you should know:

- what the main tasks involved in day-to-day public relations are;
- what research has found PR practitioners actually do;
- the differences between working in-house for a specific organisation and in a consultancy.

## PUBLIC RELATIONS ROLES

Glen Broom (1982) looked at what public relations practitioners did and formulated them into four dominant roles (Table 2.1). He suggested that there was one technician role and three closely related managerial functions.

Working with David Dozier, Broom (1995) later suggested that these roles could be reduced to two more general categories of technician and manager. The technician focused on technical, tactical tasks such as writing, editing, production of materials, maintaining contacts and issuing press releases. The communication

**TABLE 2.1 Broom's four practitioner roles (adapted from Cornelissen 2008)**

| Role | Characteristics |
| --- | --- |
| Communication Technician | Carries out communication programmes. Preparing and producing communication materials. Not part of the management team. |
| Expert Prescriber | The authority on communication problems and their solutions. While can be part of the management team, is often regarded as the 'expert' so that the other members are generally passive. |
| Communication Facilitator | A go-between, liaising between the organisation and its stakeholders. A boundary-spanner, conveying organisational views externally and publics' views internally. |
| Problem-Solving Facilitator | Collaborates with other managers to define and solve communication problems. More likely to play an active part in strategic decision making for the organisation. |

manager, on the other hand, is more likely to participate in management decisions, advise on the implications of policy decisions with regard to public reaction, social responsibility, and evaluate the results of communication programmes. In real life, it is rare to find a practitioner who simply fulfils one or other of these roles exclusively, as all may perform elements of both. It is helpful though to consider whether the work is predominantly one or the other.

## Public relations tasks

Public relations practitioners communicate with many different publics or audiences, in many different ways. Table 2.2 provides a guide to the main activities practitioners are involved with.

What does this look like in practice? The following case studies give some accounts of the experiences of people working in the industry.

## What do practitioners do? The research perspective

Researchers DeSanto and Moss (2004) recorded what PR managers actually did. They carried out interviews with practitioners in the UK and US and found that managers spent most of their time in meetings, both internal (UK, 16 per cent of time; US, 24 per cent) and external (UK, 31 per cent; US, 15 per cent). One fifth of managers' time was taken up by administration tasks, while troubleshooting took up 7 per cent of UK managers' time and 15 per cent in the US. Only 10 per cent of PR managers' time was spent in planning. While some of the respondents were members of the top management team and were taken seriously, most had little involvement in policy-making within organisations.

**TABLE 2.2 A rough guide to the main activities in public relations**

| Public relations activity | Explanation | Examples |
|---|---|---|
| Internal communications | Communicating with employees | In-house newsletter, suggestion boxes |
| Corporate PR | Communicating on behalf of whole organisation, not goods or services | Annual reports, conferences, ethical statements, visual identity, images |
| Media relations | Communicating with journalists; specialists; and editors from local, national, international and trade media, including newspapers, magazines, radio, TV and web-based communication | Press releases, photocalls, video news releases, off-the-record briefings, press events |
| Business to business | Communicating with other organisations, e.g. suppliers, retailers | Exhibitions, trade events, newsletters |
| Public affairs | Communicating with opinion formers (e.g. local/national politicians), monitoring political environment | Presentations, briefings, private meetings, public speeches |
| Community relations/ corporate social responsibility | Communicating with local community, elected representatives, headteachers, etc. | Exhibitions, presentations, letters, meetings, sports activities and other sponsorship |
| Investor relations | Communicating with financial organisations/individuals | Newsletters, briefings, events |
| Strategic communication | ID and analysis of situation, problem and solutions to further organisational goals | Researching, planning and executing a campaign to improve ethical reputation of organisation |
| Issues management | Monitoring political, social, economic and technological environment | Considering effect of US economy on UK organisation |
| Crisis management | Communicating clear messages in fast-changing situation or emergency | Dealing with media after major rail crash on behalf of police, hospital or local authority |
| Copywriting | Writing for different audiences to high standards of literacy | Press releases, newsletters, web pages, annual reports |
| Publications management | Overseeing print/media processes, often using new technology | Leaflets, internal magazines, websites |
| Events management, exhibitions | Organisation of complex events, exhibitions | Annual conference, press launch, trade shows |

Source: Fawkes (2012a)

**ACTION POINT**

# A DAY IN THE LIFE OF A MARKETING AND PR ASSISTANT

As well as the administrative responsibilities of being a marketing assistant, I am also used as a PR resource for the business. A usual day amalgamates the complexities of media monitoring, press release writing and distribution to client liaison, media database expanding and networking for new opportunities.

Media monitoring is the most important part of the day, this is usually the first task undertaken. This involves getting the local papers and checking for client coverage. This time is also used to pinpoint any competitive coverage on behalf of our clients to highlight any areas of opportunity in which our clients can gain press coverage and stay competitive.

If coverage has not been successful, I will form a media report of all channels submitted to and feedback received, if necessary, from media contacts as to why it has not been covered if applicable.

Clippings are extracted from the papers and filed into client folders to keep a record of coverage, but also to measure the estimated value of the coverage. Searching for coverage online is just as important.

It is also my job to inform our clients when they receive press coverage.

Compiling press releases (as and when they come up) usually starts with a telephone call or a website feedback form from the client. The next stage in this process is to call up and take an initial brief from the client, as well as arranging a suitable time to meet them to carry out an interview and take a press shot.

The next part in the process is to research about the client, to combine with the client interview in order to write the release. Before sending the release back to the client for amendments I would usually send the release to a colleague to be checked over for content analysis and structure. This will then be sent back to the client for amendments and final approval.

While this is happening a media list is formed for the client using both online and offline channels. Usually the media list will compile 80 per cent of the same media contacts. The other 20 per cent is made up of industry specific publications that would pick the release up. It is our job to make sure that we have reached out to the correct audience.

Each client will have their own media list depending on what field, area or sector they are in.

On approval of the release, it is then distributed. This can sometimes take from ten minutes to up to one hour to complete this process. The time it takes depends on how many media channels you are submitting to. Online channels require much of this time due to the complexity of the distribution websites.

Following up on a release involves a telephone call a day to two days after release to those you have submitted to, checking that they have everything they require, but also used as a subtle reminder that you would like coverage.

I have learnt so far that . . .

- PR is not simply about press release writing and distribution.
- To be successful in the current economic climate, you need to form a relationship with the business editors (not just through email).
- A telephone conversation to introduce yourself, and an understanding of what each editor would like to be sent, as well as thanking them for previous coverage goes a long way to enhancing your reputation with editors.

Additional tasks completed in the day include:

- searching for new business opportunities through tender websites;
- attending networking events to uphold the reputation of the company externally;
- being the first point of contact for all client enquiries.

*Samantha Langridge graduated from the University College Plymouth St Mark and St John in 2008 with a Public Relations with Management degree. She is currently working as a marketing and PR assistant with CODE (Company of Designers England Limited) Marketing and Communications. CODE specialises in marketing strategy and planning, online marketing and website design, design for marketing communications and PR and reputation management.*

## ACTION POINT

## A DAY IN THE LIFE OF A CONSULTANCY DIRECTOR

I run a small public relations agency in Cornwall and, with fifteen clients currently on the books, a varied range of day-to-day activities is always guaranteed.

I've worked in the public relations industry for about twenty years, with another seven spent as a freelance feature writer for national newspapers and magazines. That journalistic experience – when I covered everything from battle of the beauty queen stories to parenting, policing, education, defence, gardening and property issues – stood me in very good stead for what I do now. Not just because it gave me a good understanding of the pitching process but because my clients come from a broad range of industries and have very different needs.

We used to handle a lot of public sector work for the Skills Funding Agency, the National Apprenticeship Service, the NHS and various universities and colleges across the South West. What we did for them was largely about profile building and reputation enhancement – developing strategies, producing publications, collating responses to media enquiries, managing events, writing press releases and building up databases of case studies. To start with the sign-off protocols involved meant progress was often relatively slow but, as funding cuts became imminent, there was a noticeable change in gear. Our work for the National Apprenticeship Service, for example, was expected to have a direct impact on employer and apprentice recruitment and that, from our point of view, was far more satisfying.

Our current clients are all from the private and charitable sectors. In the majority of cases, they expect what we do to impact on their bottom line – increasing visitor numbers for instance. South Crofty Mine is different. They've been a client for seven years and our activities with them have been much more about community and stakeholder engagement and changing perceptions.

*Sue Bradbury, Director, SBPR*

Several surveys have asked practitioners what they do. Despite Genasi's (CEBR 2005) claim that public relations had 'Developed well beyond traditional media work,' 70 per cent of in-house and 48 per cent of consultancy work was then concerned with media relations. Bowden Green (2006) carried out research into how CIPR members in the south-west of England practised PR. He found that two-thirds of them regarded PR as projecting favourable messages through managing relationships with the media.

While the 2006 *PR Week* Survey found that practitioners were working more hours (Johnson 2007), and the CEBR study in 2005 had found that a quarter of practitioners worked over 48 hours per week, it was questionable whether these long hours were productive. Research by Time Act Solutions with fifty agencies found that they were spending a staggering 45 per cent of their time on account management and reporting back, but less than 20 per cent on media relations – the main task recorded. Strategic counsel took up 0.6 per cent of their time. They seemed to be spending more time getting authorised than actually doing the job. While smaller agencies seemed to be more efficient, spending 42 per cent of time on media relations plus 15 per cent on writing press releases, still only 4 per cent was spent on counselling clients. This does not give a picture of an industry engaged in board level activity (Gray 2006b).

Research carried out for *PR Week UK* by Brands2Life also found a disparity between theory and practice. Senior communications people rated customers as their most important stakeholders, then employees and the media. However, media relations was ranked as the most time-consuming task, followed by corporate communications and then internal communications (Bashford 2006).

The EUPRERA research project, European Communication Monitor (Tench and Yeomans 2009), sampled 1,524 communications professionals, across thirty-seven different European countries. Three quarters of them felt they were taken seriously by senior management, with 64 per cent involved in decision-making. Most important disciplines were marketing/brand management, corporate communications, crisis/issue management, investor relations and public affairs/lobbying. However, practitioners were still mainly reliant on media monitoring to assess their effectiveness. The CIPR's 2010 benchmarking study found that growth was expected in online reputation management, crisis management and internal communications. Sponsorship and events management were expected to decline. While members were broadly comfortable with their knowledge of social media, 23 per cent admitted that their knowledge was limited. Media relations continued to be the most time consuming task in both in-house (78 per cent) and consultancy (88 per cent). Strategy development and planning were the next main functions in consultancy, with internal communications and strategy development in-house.

Zerfass *et al.* (2010) updated the European Communication Monitor and found that while over 70 per cent thought communications were more important since the recession, only 22 per cent had actually gained resources and 37 per cent had lost resources. Media relations with print journalists was expected to decrease by 9.5 per cent but actually increased by 5.2 per cent from 2007 to 2010. The growth of use of online channels was overestimated, as social media had been expected to rise by 41 per cent, but actually only increased by 15 per cent. Less than one-third of organisations had implemented guidelines for social media communications. Evaluation still relied heavily on media response and internet/intranet usage. Only a quarter were tracking the impact of communications on financial strategic targets.

Arrow (2009) complained, 'Even the most professional of practitioners is still implementing regurgitated values, set elsewhere in the organisation.' Despite the high hopes expressed in the industry, the picture painted above still seems to be of an industry that continues to focus on tactical rather than strategic thinking, with media relations still regarded as the core activity.

The *PR Census* (Gorkana 2011) commissioned by *PR Week* found that general media relations was still the main function of 21 per cent of practitioners. While online communications was included by 78 per cent of professionals, only 2 per cent regarded it as their main function. Media relations strategy planning, communications strategy development and writing articles and newsletters were the other task in the top five.

## Where do they do it?

Again, the lines of demarcation as to the environment in which practitioners operate largely tends to split into two arenas. One is referred to as in-house, where you would be employed by a company to carry out its communications. Most practitioners in the UK, 82 per cent, work in-house. (CEBR 2005). The other would be to work in a public relations consultancy, where you would be employed by the agency but would perform communications tasks for a variety of clients. Some also work as independent consultants or freelancers. Consultancies range from full-service agencies, which might also provide research, advertising and marketing as well as public relations, to specialist agencies that might focus on a particular industry, such as construction or manufacturing, or on PR for particular groups, such as

**READING POINT**

■ Tench and Yeomans (2009) suggest looking at adverts for public relations jobs to see what employers are looking for. This will give an idea of what skills employers are looking for, whether that is technical knowledge or personal qualities, and what experience and qualifications. Relevant publications include *The Guardian* and Independent Media sections and *PR Week*. It may also be useful to look at the websites of PR consultancies where possible jobs may also be included.

**TABLE 2.3 Advantages and disadvantages of in-house and consultancy PR functions**

|  | In-house public relations function | Public relations consultancy |
|---|---|---|
| **Advantages** | Dedicated PR professional<br>Intimate knowledge of organisation<br>Usually less expensive<br>Contacts within company<br>Can perform many different tasks | Experience of working for several clients<br>Employed only when needed<br>Objective viewpoint<br>May have specialised contacts |
| **Disadvantages** | Have to be paid full time<br>Can get too close to the company view<br>May not be regarded highly by management | May not always be available<br>More expensive to use |

young people or ethnic minorities, or a particular element such as internal communication or financial PR.

A freelance practitioner may be employed by either an in-house department or a consultancy to work on specific contracts, whether because of their specialist skills or to cope with peaks in demand or staff absence.

## Overload

It also seems to be an accepted stereotype that practitioners work long hours and are always on call for their clients. A blog post on *PR Daily* in early 2011 listed '42 more signs you work in PR'. The list included the following:

- Your Blackberry sleeps with you every night. Your better half does not.
- You no longer count calories – just your re-tweets.
- Your home number is on your office voicemail.
- You've heard all the lines about sleep: 'Sleep is overrated.'
- Every Friday around 17:00 you think, 'This could be crisis time!'
- You're afraid to go more than 15 minutes without checking Twitter/Facebook/news feeds to make sure you're not missing anything.

These contributions by PR practitioners themselves seem to indicate that they support the need to be seen to be working longer and harder than anyone else, ready to jump when their clients contact them. Would the same list have been produced by a group of lawyers?

**TALKING POINT**

## WHAT SKILLS ARE NEEDED TO WORK IN PR?

Caroline Shepherd (2011) undertook research as part of her undergraduate PR degree at the University of Central Lancashire (UCLAN) to investigate what skills were needed to enable PR graduates to get jobs in the industry. She was inspired by conflicting views on whether a degree in PR was a necessary prerequisite for working in the industry. Many commentators stated that employers valued experience of the work as more important than gaining a degree in PR, although she cited Public Relations Consultants Association (PRCA) research from 2009 that found that 70 per cent of PR leaders thought a university degree was more important now than fifteen years ago.

The majority of her fifty respondents had a PR or media degree, with others having Journalism or English degrees and only one not having a degree at all. Two thirds felt that they had learnt more from their placement year or work experience than from their degree, but nearly half stated that they would not be where they were without their degree. Only one respondent, a mature student, felt that their degree had taught them nothing at all. While working in education, this was a frustrating perception among students that experience taught more than what was learned in the classroom. As Anne Gregory has said, 'Experience is about looking backward at what you have done, while education is about looking forward and how you do things.' It is interesting to see that while experience was rated more highly, a significant proportion of respondents recognised that their degree had been instrumental in getting them the job they were in.

An article on *PR Daily* by Becky Johns (2011) reviewed the responses to a question posted on Twitter about whether a high GPA (Grade Point Average) at college was really important. Johns responded that a high grade was not an indication of how someone would perform in the working world, and while she advised students to: 'Take your classes seriously. Do the work. Show up and learn something,' she concluded that, 'the GPA you achieve in college doesn't matter.' She suggested an alternative list of things that mattered more:

- Knowing how you learn – whether by seeing, hearing, writing or practising, this knowledge is useful in learning things in the workplace.

- Applying theory to real life situations – being able to apply information in new situations.

- Time management – learning to meet deadlines, tackle to-do lists and still have something of a social life.

- Relevant professional experience – using jobs, internships, student and volunteer projects to show that you can do the work.

- A portfolio – keeping samples of work to show prospective employers.

- The ability to give and receive feedback – learning to accept praise and criticism will help in the workplace as well as with collaborating with others.

- Presentation skills – knowing how to convey ideas clearly.

- Writing skills – these are used in everything from reports to pitches to emails. Many students leave college lacking solid writing ability.

- Your network – who you know is more important than what you know, so get into the habit of meeting new people. You are most likely to find jobs through your network.

Cornelissen (2008) reported some comments from practitioners on the qualities needed in communications. Qualities included: personality, lateral thinking, creativity, common sense, being persuasive in writing and verbally, being able to write a press release, sense of humour, interpersonal skills in building relationships. He also included results of a UK survey which found that communication skills (verbal communication, writing, editing) and personal characteristics (integrity, influence, persuasion, diplomacy, critical judgement) were at the top of the list. Other competences were enthusiasm, confidence, reflection and learning from previous experience, intuition and problem solving.

What other areas of work stress that experience is more important than qualifications? Would you feel happy having surgery from a surgeon who did not have an academic qualification but had just practised for years? What does this preoccupation say about the confidence of public relations practitioners in what they do?

However, not all who work in PR advise on being available 24:7. PR lecturer and consultant Kirk Hazlett (2011b), while admitting that he has a full-time job and a part-time one as well as consulting on the side, recommends the need to take 'me time': 'Walk in the sunshine, eat ice cream, and relax.' He mentions this as the solution for 'impending burnout' and suggests that it enables one to return to work recharged with renewed energy and determination.

## END POINT

Having reviewed some of the research done to try and quantify and codify the work that PR practitioners do, this chapter has suggested that there are four different roles that PR practitioners carry out, with two major categories of technician and manager. PR involves communicating with different audiences in a variety of ways and despite a desire to be seen as a strategic communicator, most PR practitioners spend most of their time dealing with the media. PR is carried out in-house, in a consultancy or freelance, and skills and experience are regarded more highly than academic qualifications.

# CHAPTER 3

# The PR industry and careers in it

*Alison Theaker*

This chapter gives an overview of the PR industry, its development and future trends.

## CHECK POINT

This chapter includes:

- an overview of the development of the industry;
- a review of the main professional bodies;
- information on entry routes;
- a discussion on professional development;
- practical guidance and advice from practitioners for those wanting to work in the industry;
- different sectors of the industry.

## THE PUBLIC RELATIONS INDUSTRY

The latest estimates are that there about 61,600 people working in public relations in the UK and that PR has a turnover of about £7.5 billion, according to a survey by *PR Week* (2011). Although only 1,300 responses were received, the information gained was added to government, ONS and data from PR Week's own reports to create the *PR Census* (Gorkana 2011).

The *Census* confirmed that the majority – 64 per cent – of the industry was female and also white British – 84 per cent. Only 20 per cent of the industry was over forty-five years of age. The average annual salary was £48,000, ranging from £21,500 for an account executive in a consultancy to £49,000 for an in-house communications director. In addition, the majority of the industry in the UK was concentrated in Greater London, with 51 per cent. Only 4 per cent worked in Scotland, Northern Ireland and the Channel Islands. Interestingly, while 6 per cent of practitioners work in the North East and Yorkshire, and the same in the North West, average salary in the former is £50,587, the highest outside London, and in the latter only £33,094, the UK's lowest (Bussey 2011).

## HISTORY OF PR

So how did public relations begin? American academics James Grunig and Todd Hunt (1984) looked at the origins of the PR industry in the US and classified PR practice into four types. These four models have created much debate, and form a good foundation for discussion of later ideas.

Grunig and Hunt called the first era of PR history the press agentry or publicity model. It relates to the period from 1875 to 1900, when businesses used stunts to promote their products. They cited showman Phineas Barnum as an example of someone who didn't let the truth get in the way of a good story, and who used many tricks to get his events covered for free in the papers. They suggested that this philosophy of faking stories to get coverage is at the root of journalists' antipathy towards present day PR.

Next came the public information model, which Grunig and Hunt credit to Ivy Ledbetter Lee, originally a journalist who set up a PR agency, which prided itself on giving accurate information to the papers. His belief was that providing information to reporters to enable them to do their job was more productive than suppressing news about a company. He is also thought to be one of the first to use the press handout or press release, a staple of today's PR. The major difference in this model was the emphasis on telling the truth. Both these models are essentially one-way methods of communication, where the organisation sends out information it wants the public to know.

With the advent of the First World War, propaganda was used to persuade people to support the war effort. Edward Bernays worked in the Creel Committee on Public Information and experienced how communications were used. He was also a nephew of Sigmund Freud and became interested in his ideas on psychology. Bernays felt that psychological theory could be used to promote commercial interests and worked as a freelance press agent. He claimed to have invented the term 'public relations counsel.' Grunig and Hunt called Bernays' methods two-way asymmetrical communication, because it included the use of research to find out what the public thought and took this into account. Often this meant that Bernays used what he found that the public liked about an organisation and emphasised this in its communications. He orchestrated a famous stunt on behalf of Lucky Strike cigarettes based on psychological research into why women did not smoke in public. This showed that cigarettes represented male power, which meant that women were less likely to smoke. He organised a group of debutantes to light up cigarettes during the New York Parade, and presented this to the media as lighting 'Torches for Freedom.' Women smoking was thus linked to being more independent. While this model of PR includes two-way communications, even Grunig and Hunt state that the practitioner is merely 'telling management what the public will accept. They do not tell management how to please the public'.

The fourth model is the one that has caused most controversy. Named two-way symmetrical communications and devised by American academics Cutlip and Center (Grunig and Hunt 1984: 42), this defined PR as 'the communication and interpretation of ideas and information to the publics of an institution; the communication and interpretation of information, ideas and opinions from those publics to the institution in an effort to bring the two into harmonious adjustment.' Subsequent research by Grunig and others added the notion of 'excellent communications', where this two-way model was presented as an ideal way of practising PR. It implies that the organisation will change its policies not just its communications as a result of learning about public opinion. PR practitioners are then seen as 'boundary spanners', presenting the views of an organisation and its publics to each other. Several academics such as L'Etang have queried whether this is in fact possible in practice, as the practitioner will surely always work on behalf of the organisation which pays them. The advent of the internet and social media has been heralded by some as the dawning of the age of true two-way communications as it makes an organisation's actions more transparent. The rapid spread of opinions through the web and on Facebook and Twitter have meant that organisations now have to pay more attention to such opinions.

While these models were originally put forward after an examination of the historical development of PR in the US, it was not found to be a linear progression. Indeed, Grunig and Hunt suggested that all four models were still practised in a variety of situations. Also, they were only linked to the US profession. Others, such as L'Etang, have studied the history of PR in the UK, where the industry had its beginnings in public sector public relations. PR in the UK has therefore more of an underlying emphasis on public interest.

Are these models of any use to current practitioners, especially as they have been shown to be flawed? Yes and no. It is true that practitioners do practice a variety of methods depending on the situation, and that PR has changed from using mainly one-way communications telling people what an organisation wants them to hear, to being more concerned with developing relationships and having conversations with the publics their organisations are affected by. As more academics and practitioners start to reflect on and examine practice, diverse models of PR can be developed that do not focus on a US-centric view and which take into account practitioners that do not fit into the four models above.

**TALKING POINT**

**Based on a paper she presented at the 2nd International History of Public Relations Conference in 2011, Heather Yaxley reflects on the background to careers in PR.**

## THINKING ABOUT CAREERS IN PUBLIC RELATIONS

Opportunities to work in public relations have existed for over a century, when jobs were distinguished as press agents, publicists and public relations counsel in order of prestige and salary. By the mid-twentieth century, many companies and public sector organisations employed PR practitioners and external agencies, primarily to handle media relations although opportunities also existed to work within internal communications and community relations. Senior manager roles were increasingly common having responsibility for large teams in many cases.

The occupation was male dominated until the 1980s, and women are largely absent in the early history. Exceptions are Constance Hope, author of *Publicity is Broccoli,* who ran her own New York agency from the 1930s and Doris Fleischman (working with her famous husband, Edward Bernays) who offered guidance for women seeking a career in PR in the 1935 publication: *An Outline of Careers for Women*.

Despite the growth of PR as an occupation, women tended to be employed in junior roles or female-oriented industries until the 1990s. Despite subsequently taking on senior positions across the board, the 2011 *PR Census* (Gorkana 2011) shows discrepancy in terms of gender representation and reward at the highest level.

PR has been argued as an emerging profession since its earliest days, although it is still possible to gain employment and career progression without any specialist qualification or even experience in the field. There is no defined career development or pathway as is evident in established professions.

An emphasis on craft skills (particularly writing and media relations) focuses attention on technical roles, which are seen as a path to management in the PR literature, job adverts and in the training programmes and qualifications offered by the professional bodies.

Hierarchical structures do exist within larger PR agencies and in-house teams. However, many practitioners are self employed or work in small organisations where there are few if any opportunities for career progression. It is also common for non-specialists to enter the field in senior roles (notably former journalists) which challenges the concept of a specific career ladder in PR. Similarly, digital PR developments have offered the chance for many younger practitioners to leapfrog older colleagues who have been less willing or able to take advantage of new opportunities.

There are also questions over the jurisdiction of PR with marketing and other associated disciplines blurring the career paths open to practitioners. The openness of the occupation means it tends to expand and contract quickly, making it responsive to economic and other social pressures. These present opportunities and threats to those seeking to build a career in PR.

In many ways, PR reflects a prototype modern entrepreneurial career. It is a flexible and adaptable occupation where personal circumstances and interests can be accommodated by the variety of opportunities available. It lacks a formal, controlled, career framework meaning practitioners need to be empowered in the management of their own careers.

## Professional bodies

The PRCA is the trade body for consultancies in the UK, and members are companies rather than individuals. It opened membership up to in-house teams in late 2009, and freelancers in 2010. It has 235 agency members, and in excess of fifty in-house teams, and represents a total of 8,000 practitioners. The CIPR is the association for individual practitioners and has over 9,500 members. The professional bodies together only account for less than 30 per cent of practitioners. Requirements for qualifications and professional and ethical behaviours can only apply to association members.

Other influential professional bodies include the Public Relations Society of America (PRSA), which with 21,000 members is the largest association of individual practitioners in the world.

There are also several international bodies. The IPRA (International Public Relations Association) was founded in 1955 with only fifteen members in five countries. Small by national association criteria, the organisation represents around 1,000 members in 100 countries. The Confédération Européenne de Relations Publiques (CERP) has fifteen member organisations including the CIPR. The PRCA is also a member of the International Communications Consultants Organisation (ICCO) which has 1,400 member companies in twenty-eight countries. There is also the Global Alliance of Public Relations and Communications Management (GA) and the World Public Relations Forum.

# Getting in

The PR industry has had an uneasy relationship with academic qualifications, with many declaring that experience is the best way to gain entry to the profession. With the drive of the Institute towards Chartered status, practitioners needed to show that they were qualified to do the work and approving academic and professional courses became a major plank of the case for such status.

The first PR courses were offered in the US. Josef Wright introduced one at the University of Illinois in 1920 and Edwards Bernays taught one in the Journalism department of the New York University School of Commerce, Accounts and Finance in the 1930s. The 1981 Commission on Public Relations Education recommended that the content of undergraduate and postgraduate courses should include mass communications, PR theories, media relations techniques, research methodology, case studies, work placements and PR management (Cutlip *et al.* 2000: 150). A further commission in 1987 added ethics, law and evaluation to the list (IPRA 1990). The Public Relations Education Commission set up by the PRSA in 1999, added business context, finance, communication theory and a supervised work placement in practice (Commission of PR Education 1999). The International Public Relations Association (IPRA) published guidelines for PR education in 1990, advising that, 'public relations courses should be taught by individuals with a sound experience and understanding of both the academic and professional aspects of the field' (IPRA 1990). The suggested curriculum became more and more crowded.

The CIPR approved six courses in 1989, including vocational, undergraduate, post-graduate and Masters programmes in the UK. The number of approved courses has since risen to thirty-five BA programmes and twenty Masters provided at thirty institutions. (A list of approved courses is available at www.cipr.co.uk.) In 1998, the CIPR also introduced its own qualifications, the Advanced Certificate and Diploma, which provide a part-time route to qualification for those who are already working in the profession and who are unable to return to full-time education. The PRCA has also introduced its own qualifications, a Foundation, Advanced Certificate and Diploma. Each course is modular in structure and the emphasis is on practical skills.

There are still many in the industry who do not have a relevant qualification, although there are few who do not have any qualifications at all. Some consultancies or in-house departments have a specifically designed graduate training scheme in public relations, but often training tends to be ad hoc.

Academic courses have to walk an uneasy tightrope between developing general graduate skills and satisfying a critical industry that does not always understand

**TABLE 3.1 Ranking of discipline topics by employers**

| Subject | % |
| --- | --- |
| 1  Writing skills | 86 |
| 2  Media relations | 81 |
| 3  Public relations practice | 80 |
| 4  One-year work placements | 64 |
| 5  Media practice | 51 |
| 6  Live projects for external clients | 40 |
| 7  Journalism | 40 |
| 8  Media analysis | 40 |
| 9  Internal communications | 34 |
| 10  Business principles | 31 |
| 11  Public relations theory | 30 |

Source: Tench and Fawkes (2005) cited in Fawkes (2012a)

the constraints of academic standards. The table above shows the results of UK research that shows which skills were valued by employers.

*PR Week* published the results of a survey of ninety-six in-house PR practitioners in August 2011 which asked what skills were needed now and in the next five years. The top five current skills essentially stayed the same, with the addition of ability to work with social media and technology which shot to the top of the list. The other attributes were essentially personal qualities rather than skills – creative and strategic thinking; charismatic personality and good networker; flexibility to adapt to clients' needs; articulate and persuasive communicator – as well as knowledge of the industry. The supporting article appeared to largely ignore these findings, as apart from digital skills, practitioners were advised that commercial acumen, international experience, work on integrated campaign and traditional skills such as building media contacts were key (Magee 2011b).

An online discussion started by US lecturer Rob Brown in 2011 on LinkedIn asked what five things should be taught in a basic PR course. Suggestions included 'Know your audience is the golden rule,' and several advised using good and bad examples of PR practice to show what PR involved. Others stressed that PR was not just the use of media relations and social media but encompassed crisis communications, government and investor relations, event planning and speech writing. Pleas for good writing skills were repeated, as was an awareness of cultural differences in a global industry.

Having taught PR at undergraduate and graduate level over fifteen years in the UK and US, I would agree with many of these. Writing skills are important whatever industry you are in, and however you communicate. Knowing how to gather information and craft a convincing argument is also important. Convincing students on either side of the pond that they need help to improve their writing is another matter. Researching this in the US, UK and Australia, I found that teaching writing as an integral part of the subject and setting aside a significant proportion of marks was the only way to motivate students to take the time to redraft their work rather than just submitting their first attempt.

I also feel that teaching the broader spectrum of PR rather than concentrating on media relations is vital. Unfortunately the industry, while making noise about wanting strategic thinking, tends to concentrate on whether first job candidates can write a press release or not.

One US student on a fifteen-week *Introduction to PR Principles* said, 'I've never done any PR before. I want to know all about it and whether I should go for a career in the industry.' As courses become more modularised and students can pick and mix from one-semester options, there has become more demand for this kind of instant gratification.

Kirk Hazlett, professor at Curry College, MA, advises that, 'getting a job is a job in itself' (2011a). His students are enabled to take an internship in their final semester. After making sure that their CV and cover letter is professionally presented, networking is the next step. 'Nearly three-quarters of all job openings are never posted,' says Hazlett, 'They're filled through referrals.' (See Amy Hurn's experience on p. 37.) Arik Hanson, principal of ACH Communications in Minnesota agreed in his post about a PRSA panel event about successful job searching. He suggested creative ways to get noticed in the application process, including one candidate who compared herself to the many Disney princesses. He felt the most powerful thing was to start a blog to improve visibility in the now commonplace Google search on candidates. It also gives prospective employees the chance to show off those all-important writing skills.

Andrew Cave (2011) looked at the qualities required from corporate communicators. While companies may once have wanted former journalists, he revealed that the most sought after backgrounds were now from government and regulators, with higher levels of financial and technological know-how. Organisations were having to deal with a greater range of stakeholders, including NGOs, activists and online networks. There was now more emphasis on integrated communications campaigns and understanding the big picture. Finally, a much more central role for internal communications meant that corporate communications directors had to adopt a more joined up approach to internal and external messages.

Several practitioners were asked if they had any advice for those wishing to enter the industry. Below is a selection:

## WANT A CAREER IN PR?

Pay your dues. When you are first starting off in a career in PR, you really need to ring-fence a few years just for gaining good, hardworking, unglamorous experience. Get your head down and slog, rather than thinking about the glory. If you get genuine experience early on, you'll have a solid foundation to build on when the bigger, more exciting opportunities come along.

Be nice to people. It is the right thing to do. And people will remember you later in your career. PR is about managing relationships. Build relationships with journalists – not just for the story you are currently working on but for longer term benefits. Same goes for clients and colleagues – and not just the marketing director. Where will the most junior member of staff that you deal be in five years' time?

Take a risk! In PR, if you risk nothing, you win nothing. Don't be afraid of big ideas, however new you are to the industry. Back your own thoughts and beliefs and you will get noticed. Big, crazy, outlandish ideas often pave the way to killer concepts that are more realistic.

Read . . . a lot! Read PR text books and industry publications, read biographies for media and PR people and borrow ideas that you can put in your own words. You are not expected to know everything when you first join the profession but your proactive ideas are what will set you apart. Consider studying PR at undergraduate and postgraduate courses.

Do work you are proud of, at the highest level you are allowed to. If it is writing a press release, make it your best. As soon as you can, enter PR industry awards. The process of entering them will help you evaluate what you are proud of and how to communicate this to other people.

*Justin McKeown, Founder and Director, Mission Agency Ltd, which provides communications consultancy and training for brands, corporates, public sector bodies and charities.*

## New entrants: the top seven qualities required

1   Common sense – the thing about common sense is that it is not very common! Trust your instincts but double check before acting.

2   Empathy – but don't take it personally. You need to have the sales-man's ability to be enthusiastic and persuasive, very sensitive to client or journalist nuances but a skin tougher than an unripe avocado.

3   The ability to write quickly, well and accurately.

4   Excellent organisational skills.

5   See the big picture but pay attention to details. You must focus on the goal at all times and not get sidetracked, while being flexible enough to integrate opportunities that meet your aims.

6   Worry enough to ensure you have thought of all the pitfalls, do your best to ensure they don't happen, then set about minimising the consequences if you cannot guarantee to prevent them.

7   Try to do relevant work – at university, college or in your spare time. It will give you an advantage over those who don't – and network constantly on and offline, keeping your own goal in mind.

*Claire Moran, Managing Director, The Forge Public Relations*

## It's not just what you know . . .

I started university with one clear strategic goal: to achieve a first-class honours degree in my specialist subject, Public Relations. I also started with something a bit different to other young undergraduates – one year's work experience. Here is my story of not only obtaining a first but also gaining multiple employment offers from all over the UK before I had finished my degree, let alone graduated!

I initially took a gap year to travel but my travel plans fell through. I also needed money. The hunt was on to find work experience. Working for free is a good way to get your feet under the table but it's not one I agree with. Luckily, all three agencies that I worked with agreed to pay me.

After three weeks at Formedia, a full-service agency, I was offered a full-time job as a PR Assistant in 2007. This was down to timing and (dare I say it) some talent. After just nine months in the role I was promoted to account manager. So far, so good.

In late 2008, one of Formedia's clients approached me with an employment offer based solely on their experience of working with me. At a CIPR event, Janet Street Porter said you should always have more than three things on the go at any one time. It is advice that has stayed with me and really helped improve my employability. Taking part in business competitions, placements, freelance work as well as university and working meant that the job offers came flooding in (great when salary negotiations start!).

I've recently been headhunted again – this time by two different employers and again for jobs that were not advertised. In my opinion, if you set yourself apart from the competition you don't need to waste time or stress on job applications. I got the first that I always wanted but that isn't what got me the job offers. Focus on what's important and always strive to be the best you can be. Good luck!

*After graduating in 2009, Amy Hurn is now Head of Marketing for Natterbox Ltd. Natterbox offers cloud-based voice services that integrates voice communications with business's CRM systems.*

## Professional development

In April 2000 the CIPR introduced Developing Excellence, a continuous professional development (CPD) scheme. This scheme, while voluntary, aims to encourage members to continue their development. This was a major element of the Institute's successful bid for Chartered status.

Four suggested levels of development were devised:

- Level 1 PR executive
- Level 2 account manager or PR officer
- Level 3 account director or head of department
- Level 4 board member, managing director, chief executive.

Particular skills were included at each level, and all CIPR workshops carried an indication of their level.

With the introduction of Chartered Practitioner status, including an emphasis on preparing a short dissertation and defending this in front of a panel of experts, Accredited Practitioner became a simpler process. Credits were given for completion of the CIPR's qualifications and training courses. There was also a 'fast track' option available to gain the 180 points required within twelve months rather than three years. Having been involved in the development of the original scheme, this seems to downgrade the requirements needed to a one-off achievement, rather than the emphasis on continual development. It's still about time spent doing different activities, rather than assessing whether this makes someone better at their job. Like the PRSA model of an exam to gain extra status, this only measures someone's expertise at one moment in time. With the rapid pace of change in the industry this

- Would making membership of the one of the professional bodies compulsory improve the quality of PR advice available to clients? Studies in countries where this is the case found that it was very difficult to enforce as there were so many different job titles in the field. In addition, infringement of the law was not actively pursued, with few prosecutions. It also did not tackle the issue of competence.

- Would making all members of such bodies at least sign up to the CPD scheme be an improvement? How could the schemes be made more robust? How does PR compare with professions such as law and medicine where CPD is compulsory to practise?

- If networking seems to be the most important skill in getting a job, how do your own skills in this area stack up? Have you gained jobs through responding to adverts or by using your own contacts?

does not really address the issue of needing to take part in life-long learning. The PRCA also launched a programme of skills-focused training in 2008. Like the CIPR scheme, it is voluntary and only affects its members.

An online discussion started by Beth Okun, PR spokesperson at the Gwinnett Medical Centre in Georgia in August 2011, examined the benefits of gaining the PRSA Accreditation. While some practitioners felt undergoing the process demonstrated their commitment to the industry, several responded that it made no difference to their clients. Even though the CIPR promised to educate employers about the need to ask for professional body membership, specific qualifications and Accredited or Chartered status, most advertised jobs in PR do not include it in their job specifications.

## Sectors and specialisms

PR is practised in all kinds of organisations, and most use the same tools and techniques. However, as the industry has developed, various areas of expertise have emerged. Practitioners working in the same industry have formed special groups, such as MIPAA, which provides support for those working in the motor industry. The CIPR lists various sectoral groups, which members can join to network with those with common interests. Currently these are:

- construction and property – in-house and agency professionals in construction, residential and commercial property, architecture, building services, housebuilding, structural and civil engineering;
- corporate and financial – practitioners within the city and industry;

- education and skills;
- fifth estate – anyone working within the not-for-profit sector;
- public affairs – professionals who interact with government, the EU and devolved parliaments and assemblies;
- health and medical – includes NHS, private healthcare, health insurance and the pharmaceutical industry. Also those who deal with patients groups, health charities and medical research;
- science, technology, engineering and mathematics;
- international – for members working in-house or in a consultancy in an international context, or who want to develop their career in this direction;
- local public services – members in local government, health, housing and education;
- marketing communications.

There is another group, which is called sectoral, although it relates to a particular specialism in PR rather than a specific industry. CIPR Inside provides a forum to share ideas and practices for those who work in internal communication.

PR agencies also split their areas of specialism into different sectors. Grayling sets out six divisions of expertise. Some of these relate to categories similar to the CIPR, such as healthcare and pharmaceutical; financial and professional services; consumer; and government and public sector. However, they also add energy, environment and industry, which cover cement and steel manufacturing, mining, oil, gas, electricity and alternative energies. Their clients include government departments, corporates and NGOs globally. Grayling also has a technology, telecoms and media division which offers a full range of media relations and marketing communications to clients in this competitive industry.

There has also been academic research into growing areas of PR activity. One such is litigation public relations, investigated by Beke (2011). This is about 'managing the communications process during any legal dispute . . . so as to affect the outcome or its impact on the client's overall reputation' (Haggerty, in Beke 2011). Beke suggests that this area of PR developed in the US, but has changed when it migrated to the UK as a result of the different legal traditions of the two countries. With the growth of litigation and the growth of media interest in prominent disputes, legal teams have increasingly used PR support.

Public affairs has attracted media attention since the 1990s when MPs were found to be offering themselves on a consultancy basis to lobbying firms. Hearings by the Committee on Standards in Public Life unearthed concerns about the ethics of elected representatives being paid to advise those who wished to change or prevent legislation. The CIPR, PRCA and the Association of Professional Political Consultants (APPC) all revised their codes of practice. McGrath (2011) looked at how lobbying was regarded in the nineteenth and twentieth centuries, to see how its current reputation evolved.

Garsten and Howard (2011) have also investigated how practitioners have differentiated the services they offer by stressing specialist and sector expertise. They list consumer, business to business, media relations, digital communications, CSR, internal communications, investor and government relations. Indeed, this textbook follows a similar approach in splitting public relations into such specialisms in Parts 3 and 4. Garsten and Howard examined how these specialisms have developed over the past twenty-five years to try and provide insights into how they might evolve in the future.

The 2011 PR *Census* listed sectors where consultancies tended to get the majority of their work from. Within the private sector, the most demanding sectors were technology; consumer services, media and marketing; general business services; financial services and food, beverages and tobacco. On the in-house side, the majority of practitioners worked in charity/not for profit; public sector agency; and local government, the areas from which consultancies got the least work.

## END POINT

This chapter has summarised historical models of public relations and shown that there are several models for how PR might be practised. These models continue to create debate and to be compared against real-world examples. The main professional bodies have been reviewed alongside a variety of ways that people can gain access to work in PR. Practitioner views on the skills needed show that there is no one right way to succeed. Valued qualities such as determination and creativity might be exactly the ones needed to take the industry forward so that practitioners may act in a more professional way. Some of these themes will be revisited in Chapter 4.

# Professionalism and trends in PR

*Alison Theaker*

PR has always had an uneasy relationship with the concept of professionalism. Some practitioners have even declared that they do not see it in this way. At other times, the pursuit of professionalism just seems like a way for PR people to gain respect or even just charge more for their services.

## CHECK POINT

This chapter will examine:

- what makes a profession?
- what controls exists to govern public relations?
- what issues are affecting the development of the industry?

## DEFINING A PROFESSION

The *Concise Oxford Dictionary*'s definition of profession is 'a vocation or calling, especially one that involves some branch of advanced learning or science'. Originally, the professions were law and medicine, and were practised by the sons of wealthy landowners after they had been to Oxford or Cambridge universities. Later, specialised knowledge became the basis for entry (Cutlip *et al.* 2000). Some of the characteristics of a profession are:

- an underlying cognitive base;
- practitioners;
- a disciplinary organisation;
- induction, training and licensing of members;
- rewards and sanctions for members;
- a code of ethics and accountability;
- quality assurance;
- the ability to ensure high standards of remuneration.

(Elton 1993: 137)

The establishment of professional bodies worldwide has led to the introduction of codes of conduct and calls for regulation. Grunig and Hunt (1984: 4) put forward the view that 'True professionals possess a body of knowledge and have mastered communication techniques that are not known by the average citizen'.

L'Etang and Pieczka (2006a) suggest that professionalisation is a simply a way to improve occupational standing and win social approval.

The Global Alliance of Public Relations Associations, founded in 2000, agreed principles which stated that a profession's characteristics included:

- mastery of a particular intellectual skill through education and training;
- acceptance of duties to a broader society than merely one's clients or employers;
- objectivity;
- high standards of conduct and performance.

The declaration also pledged the Alliance members to conduct themselves with 'integrity, truth, accuracy, fairness and responsibility to our clients, our client publics and to an informed society'.

In January 2003, the IPR was awarded DTI funding to conduct a best practice overview of the UK PR industry. The objectives of the study were both to spotlight best practice and to show how public relations contributed to the national economy and the competitiveness of British industry internationally. In early 2005, the IPR was awarded its Royal Charter and became the Chartered Institute of Public Relations.

However, Cornelissen (2008) suggests that an occupation will be seen as a profession only when it is socially valued as such. Public relations still has some way to go to achieve this. Corporate Watch even suggests: 'There is a considerable body of evidence . . . to suggest that modern public relations practices are having a . . . deleterious impact on the democratic process.' It goes on to list the achievements of the industry as putting 'a positive spin on disasters', undermining 'citizens' campaigns', gaining 'public support for conducting warfare' and changing 'public perception of repressive regimes'. The PR department is said to provide 'a line of defence . . . to prevent information from slipping out' (www.corporatewatch. org.uk/profiles/pr_industry).

The Global Alliance continues to promote the debate of professional standards in PR. In 2010, the Stockholm Accords were published. These Accords put forward recommendations for the governance, management and sustainability of organ-isations and indicated how PR professionals contributed to the communicative organisation. Also in 2010, the 2nd Summit on Measurement set out the *Barcelona Principles*. They are mainly concerned with good practice in demonstrating the effectiveness of PR, but emphasise the importance of goal setting and measurement (CIPR 2011a).

# DEFINING THE PRACTICE

A Delphi survey was undertaken in 2000 to attempt to draw up a common European definition of PR but it concluded that 'it is difficult to find any pattern in the naming of the field'. It did suggest that there were four characteristics of European public relations:

- reflective – analysing standards in society to enable the organisation to adjust its own standards;
- managerial – developing plans and maintaining relationships with publics;
- operational – carrying out communication plans;
- educational – helping the members of the organisation to become effective communicators (van Ruler and Verčič 2002).

Cornelissen (2008) suggests that 'the development of the body of knowledge is the crucial plank in the field's quest for professional status'.

# CODES OF PRACTICE

The CIPR Code of Conduct, updated after a major consultation in 2000, covers members' practice of PR: how the practitioner deals with the media, the public, employers, clients and colleagues. The Code emphasises 'honest and proper regard for the public interest, reliable and accurate information'. The member is required to 'maintain the highest standards of professional endeavour, integrity, confidentiality, financial propriety and personal conduct' and to bring neither the Institute nor the profession into disrepute. Professional activities must be conducted with 'honest and responsible regard for the public interest', and any conflicts of interest must be declared to clients as soon as they arise. Members must 'deal honestly and fairly in business' and 'never knowingly mislead clients, employers, colleagues and fellow professionals about the nature of representation'.

Members are expected to 'take all reasonable care to ensure employment best practice', which includes 'giving no cause for complaint of unfair discrimination', and safeguard confidences. Members must also be aware of legislation and regulation in all countries where they practise. Maintaining professional standards specifically encourages members to undertake the Institute's CPD programme and to encourage employees and colleagues to become members also. The Code sets out a highly detailed process governing complaints relating to professional conduct.

The PRCA's Professional Charter covers similar ground. The Charter covers negotiation of terms and stresses the need for accuracy, openness about interests and regard to the public interest. The PRCA has specific codes which relate to investor relations, healthcare and parliamentary advice, which are in addition to the provisions of the Professional Charter. Those in investor relations deal with price-sensitive information and healthcare professionals have to be aware of legislation and make sure balanced and accurate information is given.

The Global Alliance's 2009 Annual Report stated that 'a majority' of members had filed the necessary certification to standardise their codes of ethics. Minimum elements that must be included are:

- an obligation to protect and enhance the profession;
- to be informed about practices which ensure ethical conduct;
- to actively pursue professional development;
- to define what public relations can and cannot accomplish;
- to counsel members on ethical decision-making;
- a requirement that members observe the recommendations of the Protocol.

Clauses on advocacy, honesty, integrity, expertise and loyalty are also required.

Despite these ideals, such bodies have no legal teeth. Codes can only affect members of these bodies, and even then then are unable to force compliance – their only punishment is to expel the offender from membership.

# CREDIBILITY OF PRACTITIONERS

'Honesty begins at home. It is synonymous with trust and trust is the lubricant that makes our practice function.' Despite this aspiration, John Budd (1994: 5) relates the example of Hill and Knowlton chief, Robert Dilenschneider, who in 1988 warned against:

twisting the facts 'a little'; unquestionably doing the unquestionable thing; ducking the truth, doing anything you knew 'in your bones' was wrong. Two years later [he] . . . advocates an array of highly questionable stratagems . . . publicly attack the competitor; steal his best people; insert Quislings into his ranks; and pre-empt his access to the media.

The conduct and regulation of lobbyists has been constantly debated in the media. Back in 1956, Tim Traverse Healey warned that 'the further development of public relations depends on the confidence of the community in the integrity of our practitioners' (quoted in Budd 1994: 4). In 1997 a number of MPs lost their seats as a result of revelations in the media that some firms had allegedly been involved in paying them to raise questions in the House, and Ian Greer Associates, a long-standing firm of lobbyists, was forced out of business. Subsequently, Labour aide Derek Draper, was accused of boasting that he could secure access to ministers for those who wanted to make their case. He was forced to resign. A media frenzy about 'spin doctors' and lobbyists resulted in calls for more regulation and slurs cast upon public relations practitioners of all kinds, not just those engaged in public affairs.

In October 1994, the then Prime Minister, John Major, set up the Committee on Standards in Public Life under Lord Nolan. The Committee continued under the Labour government with Lord Neill as chair, and the IPR also gave evidence to the Wicks Committee on how to help clarity in political communication. Despite all this time spent in such committees, the nature of lobbying continues to be debated. Public affairs practitioners now have an extensive code which relates to their conduct towards MPs and clients. The UK Public Affairs Council (UKPAC) initially comprised the PRCA (which ceased membership in 2011), CIPR and APPC.

PR possesses several of the prerequisites to be considered a profession, and the professional bodies show a clear desire to address the issues of entry, training and conduct of practitioners. They recognise that in order to achieve this, they must get the message across about ethical and professional working standards. The problem, ironically in an industry that prides itself on the ability of its practitioners

**READING POINT**

■ Kathy Fitzpatrick and Carolyn Bronstein put forward the case for responsible advocacy in *Ethics in Public Relations* (Fitzpatrick 2006; Fitzpatrick and Bronstein 2006). It is useful to compare their approach with Tony Harcup's examination of a related profession which is often critical of PR practitioners, in *The Ethical Journalist* (Harcup 2007).

to communicate, is one of getting the message across to the relevant stakeholders in business. In February 2007, in the *PR Week* ethics debate, the motion 'PR has a duty to tell the truth' was defeated. The motion had been opposed by Max Clifford. The editor, Danny Rogers, paradoxically commented, 'the fact that PR people admit they need to lie occasionally is a sign of growing honesty and confidence in what they do' (2007). This hardly helps the case for professionalism.

## TALKING POINT

## DIVERSITY

The CIPR (2009) benchmarking report found the majority (65 per cent) of the 1,940 respondents were female, but that 30 per cent of male respondents held boardroom positions, compared to 18 per cent of their female counterparts. Edwards (2010) reports that although 12 per cent of the adult working population in the UK is from black and minority ethnic groups (BAME), only 1 per cent of public relations practitioners is from these groups.

Avril Lee, UK CEO for Ketchum Pleon, was interviewed by *PR Week* (Cartmell 2011a) and quoted as saying:

> I don't believe the industry reflects the wider society we are in . . . It's not right and it's not good for business. If we get more diverse talent the work can only improve. If we don't have these people how can we understand these groups?

The *PR Census* (Gorkana 2011) found that there had been little progress since the CIPR report. The majority (64 per cent) of the industry was still female. Only 2 per cent came from black Caribbean, African or British backgrounds however.

How many black PR practitioners do you know? Are there any in your company? Why is the PR industry not attractive to people from ethnic minorities? Is it a problem that the industry does not reflect the ethnic mix of the UK population?

## FUTURE ISSUES

Several studies have examined issues that will affect the development of public relations in the future. Theaker (2012) reflected that the reputation of the industry itself continued to concern practitioners. This is especially ironic given that PR is responsible for the reputation of its clients.

Dealing with new channels of communication and social media is another common topic. However, Zerfass *et al*. (2010) found that less than one third of organisations had implemented guidelines for social media communications and that many practitioners thought that open dialogue posed a threat.

Richard Edelman, CEO of Edelman, the world's largest privately owned PR agency, spoke at the 2011 PRSA Leadership Rally. His main theme was trust. 'We operate in a world without trust . . . People see everything as spin and lies.' He believed that PR had the power to build trust. However, he felt that while PR was best equipped to deal with complex communications, practitioners from different disciplines, especially advertising, were competing for this position (Woodward 2011).

Ogilvy PR Australia's CEO, Kieran Moore, declared that, 'the age of spin . . . is now dead.' He was announcing agency research, which suggested that PR's most significant role in 2021 would be strategic thinking and planning. The majority of respondents (76 per cent) felt that the term 'PR' would be dropped in the next decade (Digital Market Asia 2011).

A series of meetings were held with CIPR regional groups in the UK in 2011 to discuss possible future developments to 2020. The Wessex group felt that a successful future would involve a respected practice led by a strong professional body. However, the most likely scenario suggested that PR would continue to be misunderstood and that citizen control over communications would increase. Thus there remained a need for a better definition of what PR practice was meant to achieve, allied to a need to improve approaches to evaluation (White 2011).

The 2011 Communication Director's survey (Murphy 2011) revealed that integrating communications across the organisation was the major challenge for respondents. Because of the rise of social media, audiences are able to access information from several sources so communications must be consistent. This increased the need for new ideas, but directors felt that these most often came from advertising agencies, underlining Edelman's point above.

Finally, *PR Week* (Rogers 2011) spoke to the CEOs of the five largest agency groups: Omnicom, WPP, Interpublic, Publicis and Havas. The issues that they were concerned about were: digital media; brand management; hiring and developing talent; globalisation; and social media and CSR. Digital media enables more precise targeting of audiences, but also means that consumers can act against brands that they feel are invading their privacy. Brand management is becoming more complex because consumers can get impressions from several sources, especially from each other. Developing talent is a challenge for the industry. Sir Martin Sorrell of WPP said, 'Our industry is notorious for not developing talent but nicking it . . . We don't recruit people very well, we don't assess them very well, we don't give feedback very well.' John Wren of Omnicom put forward the Omnicom University as a way to try and improve this. New markets are developing globally, especially Asia, Latin America, Africa and the Middle East, and Central and Eastern Europe. Social media has also meant a growing interest in CSR, and David Jones of Havas felt that 'If companies are not socially responsible, the digitally empowered consumer will punish them'.

## ACTION POINT

**Several eminent practitioners and academics were asked what they felt were the main issues that the PR industry was facing. Their replies are included below:**

In the future, public relations professionals are going to have to be more aware of the overall context in which their organisations operate. According to the World Economic Forum (WEF) there are five principal drivers that are making a major impact on the world and organisations. These are time *compression, complexity, interconnectivity* of issues, *interdependence* in the global village and a shift in *context* – power is shifting from the west to the east and from the north to the south. Following the first truly global crisis, the economic catastrophe of 2008, in part the result of these drivers eliding, means that governments are unable to supply answers or deal with some of the major issues that are currently facing the world such as the potential for inter-generational conflict and the social impacts of the recession. In the meantime longer-term issues such as climate change and the impact on water supplies, health problems, mass migration and so on are in some cases being put on the back burner, but are still there adding to the complexity of the context in which we operate as professionals. These complex and multi-faceted or 'wicked' problems in turn affect organisation and the way they need to interact with the world and their stakeholders. The barriers between the economic, social, technological and political spheres are breaking down and organisations can no longer isolate themselves from being involved in these wider concerns. The WEF concludes that it is only by acting 'together' that there is a sustainable future. This provides a major opportunity for public relations. Contextual and communicative intelligence will be the new gold. Understanding, interpreting and interacting with a world of growing complexity will be a skill that will be highly prized by senior managers in the future. This has always been our role, and it will be vital for organisational survival in the future.

*Professor Anne Gregory PhD, Director, Centre for Public Relations Studies, Leeds Business School, Leeds Metropolitan University*

We are living in the most exciting and challenging time in the history of the public relations profession. We are experiencing a shift in the role of PR. Yesterday, it was about being both *reactive* and *proactive*. Today, it's about being *interactive* – building and nurturing a wide network of relationships, with less time to generate our own content, and a greater need to *influence* content generated by others. More than ever, it's about communication without control.

With this shift come new battles about the boundaries of public relations. Always a topic of debate, this challenge will accelerate in the years to come. Be prepared for more incursions onto 'our' turf from advertising firms, digital agencies, management consultants, trainers and others.

We are dealing with publics who are more sophisticated, sceptical and demanding. External publics are seeking more transparency and more authentic engagement with the organisations we represent; and internal publics are demanding smarter, sharper measurement of the value of public relations.

With these challenges come a series of interconnected opportunities:

First, we must elevate the role of public relations through advocacy – enhancing our profession's relevance to modern organisations and their stakeholders. This was a key goal of the Global Alliance in facilitating the Stockholm Accords in 2010.

Second, through the Global Alliance and other international networks, we have to continue to share knowledge and best practices across borders, and gradually work toward higher and more consistent standards in public relations education, credentialing, ethics, measurement and overall practice.

Third, we must sharpen the skills of public relations professionals – enhancing their literacy in business, public policy and the behavioural sciences.

These are compelling opportunities. Never has there been a greater need for public relations in the public interest – to help bring about economic recovery, political freedom, technological advancement and social justice.

Through global collaboration, I am confident that our profession will prove equal to the task.

*Daniel Tisch, APR, Fellow, Canadian Public Relations Society.*
*Chair, Global Alliance for Public Relations and Communication*
*Management*

Following a half decade of prolonged crisis and global turmoils, we (at least in the West) have reviewed, absorbed and learned to live with different expectations, knowing very well that the younger generations will not even remember 'how it used to be'.

From the perspective of how public, social and private organisations and society will develop their relationships between themselves and with others, it is necessary for public relations professionals to articulate and 'own' the 'value network' and the 'communicative organisation' concepts that in 2010 were among the principal conceptual pillars of the Stockholm Accords.

A 'value network' approach to strategy implies that the societal value of any organisation lies in the quality of relationships among participants to an undefined and fuzzy number of internal/external networks, as well as among the networks themselves.

A 'communicative organisation' approach to management implies its embeddedness in a framework where all actions and behaviours are communicative, and being communicative, for any organisation, is an essential and horizontal part of its sustainability policy vis-à-vis the quest to reinforce its licence to operate.

Also, as more and more organisations will be required by external pressures, by laws, by voluntary norms to develop integrated reporting, public relations professionals need to acquire competencies and tools to fully align and integrate internal/external/mandatory/voluntary reporting and stakeholder engagement processes, including all marketing, safety, environmental, and public relations/affairs activities.

The implication is a full organisation overhaul that transforms the organisation in a Janus-like infographic profile, where material values and immaterial values totally integrate into the communicative organisation.

*Toni Muzi Falconi, Director Methodos (Italy), adjunct professor of global relations at NYU (USA) and of public relations at the Vatican's LUMSA University (Rome).*

It has been estimated that reputation accounts for much as much as 30 to 70 per cent of the gap between the book value and market capitalization of most companies.

The value tied to corporate reputation is something that public relations professionals have long understood. But as Arthur W. Page noted, the public's perception of an organisation is determined 90 per cent by what it does and 10 per cent by what it says.

So, at a time when faith in business and government institutions is waning, and the reputations of even the most venerable brands are at constant risk, corporate communications is emerging as an essential skill set for C-level executives (professional job titles that begins with 'C,' e.g. Chief Executive Officer (CEO) Chief Operational Officer (COO), Chief Financial Officer (CFO)) in the twenty-first century.

A survey of 204 American business leaders (vice president and above) conducted in September 2011 by the PRSA underscores these new realities. It found that 93 per cent of business leaders now believe public relations is just as important to their companies as other forms of communication, including advertising and marketing.

And, the responsibility for communicating effectively is not confined solely to public relations departments and agencies. Nearly all the business leaders surveyed (97 per cent) said that CEOs themselves should understand the role of corporate reputation management. An even higher number (98 per cent) said it's also important for C-level executives to have a working knowledge of basic public relations skills.

Despite acknowledging public relations' importance, nine out of ten business leaders (94 per cent) surveyed admitted that the senior executives within their companies needed additional training in core communication disciplines, such as reputation management and corporate communication.

This is one reason why nearly all the business leaders surveyed (98 per cent) believe that business schools should incorporate instruction on corporate communications and reputation management strategy into Masters of Business Administration (MBA) curricula.

Making strategic communication a focus of MBA programs in the future, therefore, not only will make an enormous contribution to the practice of public relations, it also will contribute to the sound business practices to which Arthur Page alluded.

*Arthur Yann, Vice President, Public Relations, The Public Relations Society of America*

From the PRCA/*PR Week* 2011 Census, we know that even during the recession, our industry grew – both in financial value, and in number of people employed. That growth follows the pattern of certainly the last twenty years, arguably longer. And there is no reason to presume that this growth will not continue into the future.

The challenge and the opportunity therefore is not about the numbers. It's more about the quality. We are not like law or accountancy – and the obsession with becoming so is futile and also betrays rather a lack of self-confidence. There simply are no barriers to entry. Anybody with a phone and a laptop can set themselves up, and looking at some of the people in our industry who have done so, we are clearly all the better for it. So creating artificial barriers to entry will not work. Instead, we need, in my view, to emphasise two natural dividing lines that play to our strengths – ethical standards and professional standards. And to make those lines crystal clear.

We need far more effectively to differentiate between those who subscribe to codes of conduct, and those who do not. Between those who meet independent audits of the quality of their service, and those who do not. Between those who declare who they work for, and are happy to be judged by the company they keep, and those who prefer to keep such things hidden. I believe the PRCA makes such distinctions, but that we are by no means alone in doing so, and that we all could certainly do so better.

As well as the need to distinguish on grounds of ethics and professional skill, there lies of course the territorial issue – who 'owns' social media and the like. Who does the CEO turn to for advice? But those are second tier issues – get the ethics and the professionalism right, and they will follow naturally.

*Francis Ingham, PRCA Chief Executive*

Public relations (perhaps for the first time) it is truly doing what it says on the tin. We have unprecedented opportunities to relate to and engage directly with 'the public' in interactive and transformative ways. In a period of huge advances in communication technologies, two key shifts have emerged.

The first of these is the rapidity with which reputation-shaping news and opinion can spread across the globe and the shortened timescales for responding to and engaging with stakeholders and opinion formers. To excel in this environment, public relations practitioners have to be highly informed and plugged into their organisations at a senior and strategic level in order to respond quickly and effectively when issues emerge. And if they are really good, they should have developed the tools to see these issues coming and to pre-act rather than react.

The second key shift is the convergence of communications disciplines – both internal and external. A perfect storm of financial pressures, flatter organisational structures and digital communications has blurred the lines between traditional disciplines including public relations, marketing and employee engagement and put the focus squarely on ROI. Pitches for fully integrated campaigns are being contested by agencies who may not previously have considered themselves as competitors and in-house, that all important place at the strategy table is a prize with more than the Communications Director's name on it.

Add to this the proposition that there is now no distinction between an internal and an external audience and you can see why tensions have arisen as to who owns the message. So PR practitioners are working in a faster paced and more competitive environment and that's a challenge. But what an opportunity also to demonstrate the value of the skills that we have developed and honed over the last seventy or so years. When reputations can be lost in the time it takes to type 140 characters and the effect on the bottom line can be catastrophic, where better to go for well thought through strategic advice than to the PR profession?

*Jane Wilson, Chief Executive Officer, Chartered Institute of Public Relations*

## END POINT

The discussion of whether public relations can be, or desires to be, a profession, continues worldwide. In a presentation to the Public Relations Institute of Australia in 2007, I suggested that the answers to the questions, 'Can PR ever be a profession?' and 'Does it matter?' would be 'No' and 'No'. I do not feel that PR will ever have the same gravitas as law or medicine, but that while clients and organisations continue to see the benefits of using PR counsel to communicate their aims and value, that it should not worry PR practitioners. That is not to say that I condone 'unprofessional' behaviour, nor denigrate the efforts of the global PR community to agree on good practice guidelines. It is healthy that we reflect on practice and strive to improve it. The opinions in the last section show that academics, practitioners and professional organisations are addressing these questions on an international scale.

# Part II

# Public relations planning

# Introduction

*Heather Yaxley*

This section presents planning as a professional approach to public relations strategy. It reflects a need for PR objectives and activities to be derived from, and support, the wider organisational strategy and be consistent with the mission, vision and goals set by senior management.

An organisation may have a formal process of planning, with a hierarchy of plans whereby functional and operational plans are developed from a main strategic plan. Organisations often undertake an annual planning process, including establishing budgets. Within this process, the PR department establishes a functional plan detailing its purpose, resourcing and priorities. The head of public relations determines operational plans to be integrated with other functions, such as marketing and HR. Specific campaign plans are then required for projects undertaken. Consultancies may also be briefed on developing campaign plans.

This process is thorough – and time-consuming. It reflects a rational approach to management whereby matters can be predicted and controlled. Yet, logical planning seems to contrast with the spontaneous flexibility of day-to-day operations in a busy PR function. Too often plans, if prepared, are forgotten, or only reviewed and amended as part of the next cycle of planning.

This section of *The PR Strategic Toolkit* takes a pragmatic approach to planning. It encourages an adaptive process, whereby flexibility is built into plans to allow for emerging developments, a partnership perspective of PR and a proactive stance in identifying and benefiting from new opportunities. It also encourages dynamic issues management recognising the role of public relations in managing risk and crisis situations (Chapter 13).

While stages in professional planning are considered in the next six chapters, these do not constitute a rigid set of procedures, or recommended best practices, to be followed without question. Plans must be contingent (dependent) on external and internal situations rather than implying a single solution regardless of the nature of the organisation, its PR resource or the circumstances it faces. Indeed, this section aims to equip practitioners with practical tools (from research to evaluation) to be used as necessary in planning a range of PR programmes.

This section is intended to underpin other chapters in *The PR Strategic Toolkit* where specialist application or engagement with particular publics is required. The Appendix contains supplementary materials, including checklists and pro-forma documents, which practitioners are encouraged to adapt for their own purposes.

The framework presented in this section reflects the two key aspects of plans identified by Mintzberg (1994):

1 action planning (strategies and programs) – management decisions to inform behaviour;
2 performance controls (budget and objectives) – assess results of behaviour undertaken.

PR practice has focused traditionally more on action than control, but the necessity to achieve specific objectives within agreed budgets is a fundamental aspect of professional planning and should not be ignored. It is a challenge to be both goal-directed and activity-focused, but without a clear purpose, PR actions run the risk of being superficial, disparate and undervalued. At the same time, a scientific approach that focuses primarily on the end direction and budget constraints without the ideas, inspiration and creativity required to determine effective solutions loses the art of public relations.

Integrating the two aspects of planning acknowledges that public relations is involved primarily with intangibles, such as reputation, relationships and communications. Although the processes involved can be defined and controlled to some extent, the outcomes of PR activities may be harder to pin down. This does not excuse the failure to determine objectives and undertake evaluation seen all too often in PR practice. For example, no more than a veneer of planning is evident in many published campaign case studies.

In preparing this section, various PR planning models have been reviewed. The basic structure of these (indeed, any management planning process) is reflected in the following chapters:

Chapter 5 – Situational analysis focuses on research skills, tools and techniques that enable PR practitioners to gain insight into organisations, issues and opportunities.

Chapter 6 – Understanding public psychology brings in theories, concepts and methods that provide knowledge based on undertaking quantitative and qualitative research.

Chapter 7 – Setting objectives provides a detailed consideration of practical approaches, alongside a critique of common problems and errors.

Chapter 8 – Strategic campaign execution tackles the implementation stage at the heart of all PR planning models. As well as creativity and tactics, a strategic approach is emphasised and what is meant by a PR strategy is explained. A framework for developing narratives (from a dialogic perspective) is presented alongside tips on pitching and gaining approval for ideas.

Chapter 9 – Budgeting and resourcing offers a straightforward approach that even maths-phobic PR practitioners can adopt. It looks at identifying required resources, determining costs, presenting budgets and other skills required in performance control management.

Chapter 10 – Monitoring and evaluation is presented at the end of the section, but needs to be entwined throughout the planning process. The chapter presents an ongoing, iterative approach to guiding and adapting plans through the implementation phase. In this way it differs from planning models that imply an objective can be set, actions undertaken and success evaluated. Although it is vital to know where you are heading, planning should allow for the end goal to be reviewed and redirected if necessary.

The structure of the section follows the simple RACE approach of Research, Action, Communication and Evaluation (Marston 1963, cited by Smith 2005). However, it reflects the philosophy of Baines *et al.* (2004) that planning steps are not necessarily followed in order; they may be undertaken simultaneously or revisited during the process.

Planning is ultimately about what can be done with the available time, money and resources, rather than what is ideal or desirable. Over-promising and under-delivering undermines professional PR practice and is avoided by a realistic approach that does not claim to be low cost, or free. Certainly much can be done using public relations without big budgets, but cutting corners or skimping on the time and effort required to plan is a false economy. Organisations gain real value employing public relations strategies wisely; this section seeks to guide practitioners in achieving that aim.

# CHAPTER 5

# Situational analysis

## Heather Yaxley

This chapter provides an understanding of the research skills, tools and techniques that enable PR practitioners to gain insight into organisations, issues and opportunities.

## CHECK POINT

After reading this chapter, you should be able to:

- adopt a knowledge management approach to public relations;
- apply research skills, tools and techniques to inform PR activities.

## KNOWLEDGE MANAGEMENT

Van Ruler *et al*. (2008: 1) argue a focus on informal, ad-hoc research in public relations is harmful to 'its prestige and its status'. For public relations to act as a strategic function, it needs to demonstrate competency in analysing issues and opportunities in order to recommend responses that contribute towards the achievement of organisational goals. The knowledge base of PR practitioners will not be respected if it is based predominantly on personal experience, intuition, common sense, methodologically weak research or habitual practice. It is important to be able to explain and justify why a course of action is recommended, not simply to detail how to execute it.

Organisations increasingly recognise the value of knowledge as a strategic resource (Zack 2002) with computer systems enabling information to be recorded and analysed to provide intelligence upon which decisions can be made. From a public relations perspective, knowledge management includes consideration of the social capital inherent in the organisation's relationships. This suggests, for example, the traditional PR contact book has strategic value if developed into an intelligent contact management system (compliant with data protection legislation).

A Public Relations Information System Management (PRISM) approach is presented in Figure 5.1. This concept incorporates objective, quantitative data (e.g. statistics regarding media contact), and subjective, qualitative information (e.g. narrative analysis of media reporting). It advocates looking beyond organisational boundaries as knowledge is increasingly co-constructed via the internet (Phillips and Young

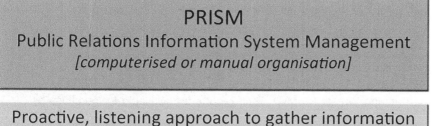

FIGURE 5.1 Public Relations Information System Management (PRISM)

2009). A partnership approach based on listening is suggested rather than using research as 'surveillance' (L'Etang 2008: 86) whereby organisations seek to exert power over those being monitored.

Ihlen (2009) draws on Bourdieu's typology of capital in the context of public relations. This is useful for reflection on the value of the organisation's PRISM knowledge base (Figure 5.2).

Knowledge management systems should be designed around the needs of the PR function (and where relevant, the wider organisation, including senior management) for timely, relevant information to guide decision-making and address matters that arise. It should include secondary (existing) and primary (commissioned) research undertaken internally and externally, on a specific and/or continuous basis.

The starting point is existing information within the PR function, followed by information collected elsewhere in the organisation (e.g. market research). Collaboration with other functions is a cost-effective option for primary research.

**ACTION POINT**

Media relations services provided by car manufacturers in the UK are researched on an annual basis by Ipsos MORI and the Guild of Motoring Writers (GoMW). Their reports are available for purchase by those who have participated.

The Ipsos MORI survey has been running since 1976. It involves face-to-face audit of views of 70 selected journalists, which can be tailored for individual companies. It claims to help PR practitioners to:

- understand motoring journalists' disposition to organisations and how PR can shape it;
- benchmark against competitors;
- evaluate the effectiveness of communications and media relations;
- gain insight into topical issues affecting organisations;
- pinpoint areas for improvement and plan future communications and media relations strategies.

The annual GoMW survey was introduced in 1997. It is undertaken by Motoring Research and claims to be an important benchmark for the industry. Opinions of the 400 strong membership of the Guild are sought, with claims of a response rate over 50 per cent, the majority of whom are happy to have their views attributed. The top three rated manufacturer PR functions are announced annually.

■ How useful would feedback from journalists be as part of an organisation's PRISM approach?

■ What are the benefits and drawbacks of surveys?

**Economic PR capital**
- Records of resources (budget, staffing, tools, collateral materials) available to the PR function to achieve the organization's communicative and relationship objectives

**Knowledge PR capital**
- Cultural/informational capital possessed by individuals within the PR function (e.g. 'professional knowledge, verbal facility, or general cultural awareness' Ihlen 2009: 72). This could be determined, monitored and managed in conjunction with the organization's HR procedures, e.g.: appraisals, training and CPD

- Repositories of knowledge within the PR function, such as libraries, publications, reports, image and video archives, media coverage, historical records, etc

- Procedural knowledge, for example, of financial or political processes, or how traditional and online media operate

- Human and information sources of knowledge within the organization, such as professional standing, sector expertise, opinion leadership and competent spokespeople

- Knowledge of networks supporting co-orientation, alliance building and other PR strategies

**Social PR capital**
- Patterns of relationships maintained by the PR function and the wider organization. These occur at the individual, functional and organisational levels. Capital includes the size of direct network, plus indirect relationships accessible through it

- Evaluation of exchange and communal (Grunig 2001) relationships. Covey (1989: 55) states human assets are pivotal as 'people control physical and financial assets'. He also discusses building trust within relationships as an 'Emotional Bank Account' (p. 188) which further implies capital balances can be created and maintained

- Level of 'investment' (conscious or unconscious) put into building relationships, particularly by the PR function, plus indicators such as contact records

- Formal and informal obligations in relationships. These may only be realised in the long term and reflect a level of risk in terms of the return on investment made (Ihlen 2009). Social capital is necessary to achieve some outcomes and in these circumstances, it has to be 'well-established' (Ihlen 2009: 74) before any return can be realised. This can be considered in the case of CSR

- Tangible benefits, e.g. reduced costs or organisational advantage. For example, PR's role in internal communications may increase productivity by enhancing relationships between employees and management

- Knowledge capital may be accessed through the established network of relationships, and also transferred by the organization to others in the network, thereby enhancing social capital

- Comparative information regarding similar organizations enables benchmarking

- Symbolic capital, such as reputation for being knowledgeable or well-connected is inherent in social capital and can be obtained through knowledge capital. Other elements of reputation, such as credibility or legitimacy can also be determined through analysis of relationships. Ihlen (2009) advocates qualitative analysis of symbolic capital. He argues (p.76) that it is 'easier to secure symbolic capital through cultural capital than through economic capital'. That is, it is harder to buy a good reputation!

**FIGURE 5.2** Capital value within Public Relations Information System Management (PRISM)

Commercial services are also available to support construction of a PRISM structure. Freitag and Quesinberry Stokes (2009) detail the following media-related service providers:

- news and information distribution networks – maintain media database information;
- media monitoring companies – provide media directories, 'clippings' services, broadcast transcripts, and statistical-analysis reports;
- software providers – offer the above services and systems 'for managing public relations functions such as organising and cataloguing collateral materials, managing contacts, monitoring legislative issues, and coordinating compliance reporting' (p. 27);
- broadcast specialists – produce and co-ordinate relevant materials, organise tours and training.

A PRISM set-up need not be complicated or expensive to create and maintain. Existing systems and procedures can be integrated within a more holistic knowledge management approach. What is important is that information is not left to stagnate. Phillips and Young (2009: 76) claim 'the half-life of knowledge is becoming shorter' but knowledgeable people are a valued asset. In addition to recording existing knowledge, the PR function needs to interrogate, analyse, and interpret data to create new knowledge.

Stacey (2003) argues new knowledge is often tacit and needs to be translated from its location in someone's head into an explicit form. He says knowledge is diffused between members of a team though mimicry and a process of 'discussion, dialogue and disagreement' (p. 164). Phillips and Young (2009) believe collaboration should be extended outside the organisation's boundaries, albeit while recognising the importance of protecting vital information. They advocate PR should develop 'transparency policies' (p. 77), which supports it as a strategic bridging function within organisations (Kim and Ni 2010).

## UNDERTAKING RESEARCH

In order to adopt the PRISM approach, or gain insight as the first step in planning PR campaigns, it is important to understand the basic components of research.

Watson and Noble (2007) identify the first stage of PR planning as analysing the problem, which Cutlip et al. (2000) explain as understanding what is happening now. CIPR (2011c) suggests gaining input from analysing existing data, conducting original research, auditing the organisation's communications, as well as benchmarking and reviewing the client/management brief. A comprehensive checklist of information required in a PR brief is available in the Appendix on p. 332.

# Formative research

The purpose of initial research is to provide sufficient context to enable reflection on the nature and causes of the situation to be addressed by a PR campaign. Smith (2005) recommends formative research should analyse the:

1 situation (problem or opportunity facing the organisation)
2 organisation
3 publics (Chapter 6).

Analysis starts with an orderly investigative process of fact finding, which can also be used to monitor and adjust action plans as required. Cutlip *et al.* (2000) advise a process that involves:

- a searching look backward – history of the organisation and the problem;
- a wide look around – publics' opinion about the organisation;
- a deep look inside – character, personality of the organisation;
- a long, long look ahead – contribution to mission, forces affecting future success.

Research can be descriptive (what, when, where and who) or explanatory (why and how). It may involve quantitative data that can be counted or measured (e.g. opinion polls) or qualitative information (e.g. stakeholder views).

Sufficient understanding may be obtained solely via existing (secondary) sources or original (primary) research may need to be commissioned (surveys, observation, focus groups, etc.). Primary data will be more up to date and tailored to the specific requirements, but will be more costly, time consuming and may require expert skills and resources to acquire.

**ACTION POINT**

Secondary sources include: meeting records, books, newspapers, magazines, multimedia materials, online and social media, census studies, published reports, statistics, academic journals, historical data, media usage information, lifestyle studies (e.g. http://kantar media-tgigb.com/), organisational surveys (e.g. consumer or employee), online surveys (e.g. www.yougov.co.uk) and government data (www.direct.gov.uk).

- Identify an issue or organisation in the news and review secondary sources to gain a deeper understanding.
- What methods were used to originate the data found?
- What insight have you gained and how did you analyse the information?

## Primary research

If existing data does not provide enough understanding, primary research may need to be undertaken. This can be done in-house, although professional research companies offer expertise in constructing objectives and questions, determining suitable methodologies, undertaking research and analysing results.

Egan (2007) presents a linear research process:

1   set research objectives

2   define research problem

3   assess the value of the research (in order to justify required resources)

4   construct the research proposal (see Appendix, p. 333, for checklist)

5   agree data collection method(s)

6   specify measurement technique(s)

7   select sample

8   collect data

9   analyse results

10   produce final report.

## Internet research

Online sources provide easy and often free access to an enormous volume of information. As well as secondary data, primary research can be undertaken using social media and online tools. Blythe (2006) warns the advantages of online research are offset by concerns over validity and credibility. PR practitioners should remember all data (whether sourced online or by other means) need to be reviewed to provide intelligent insight.

## ANALYSIS

Information obtained by research needs to be interpreted to provide meaning that can inform decision-making. Data must be prioritised, reviewed, edited and key aspects identified. This should involve an objective process, or at least, bias or subjectivity needs to be acknowledged if it cannot be avoided. Any limitations on the data, such as time dependency, need to be considered.

As part of their 'boundary spanning' role, PR managers should provide insight into issues that could impact on the organisation to determine appropriate responses. This involves environmental scanning, scenario planning, trend forecasting and information analysis.

TALKING
POINT

## SEMANTIC WEB AND BEYOND

Yu (2007) explains how traditionally search engines, such as Google, create an index of keywords by trawling everything online using spider software. Various algorithms are then used to order the information provided when someone undertakes a search. Such 'syntactic web' searches do not offer any interpretation of results without human intervention (Breitman *et al.* 2007: 4). This means care is needed when relying on search engines to generate research data; particularly as people tend to look only at the top few results (Phillips and Young 2009).

Evolution of the internet led to the concept of the semantic web in 2001 and 'the advent of social machines' (Hendler and Berners-Lee 2010: 156) supporting the development of wiki technology and social media. Macnamara (2010: 269) explains the semantic web is constructed using 'sophisticated data language' enabling searches based on concepts and descriptions rather than keywords. This means video content, for example, becomes searchable, although Macnamara suggested crowd-sourcing may be required to code the vast amount of information available online.

Another development for online search is the ability of new technologies, 'recommendation engines' (Macnamara, 2010: 270) to learn and remember information about users. This means data found is personalised which has implications for conducting research using the internet.

Hendler and Berners-Lee (2010: 157) argue for further advances to 'allow the virtually unlimited interaction of the Web of people'. They envisage 'new kinds of social machines that will provide people, individually and collectively, with the ability to immerse themselves in the accumulated knowledge and the constant interactions of humankind'. This future involves empowering people whose interactions contribute towards a global information space, rather than them passively receiving information created by others.

How do you use the internet to undertake research? Compare the results provided by using different search engines. What are the implications of the development of the semantic web, recommendation engines and interpersonal interaction for building a PR knowledge management system?

## Scanning and forecasting

Johnson *et al.* (2005: 230) recommend 'constant but thin' attention should be paid to changes in the organisation's environment. Scanning is inherent in PR operations (e.g. media monitoring) but should be formalised within a PRISM approach to enable tracking of trends, changes and emerging issues. Regular reports can then be generated as a professional outcome from this aspect of the PR knowledge base.

Environmental scanning involves gathering and processing information in order to identify and monitor issues that may affect the achievement of the organisation's aims. Sung (2007) advocates a formal environmental scanning process, which enables the PR function to provide 'an early warning system' to management (Moss and Warnaby 1997: 61). Environmental scanning helps improve understanding of an issue and facilitates scenario planning.

Scenario planning is a useful method of strategic thinking (Van der Heijden 2011). It involves envisioning possible future situations that can be evaluated and compared. PR practitioners tend to take a short-term focus, so scenario planning enables them to contribute towards longer-term strategic decision-making (Sung 2007). The process of considering possible outcomes helps address uncertainties (Chapter 13). Scenario planning should be undertaken in partnership with other functions in the organisation, and external publics (where feasible). As a 'collective and learning process' (Sung 2007: 191) it can be used to assist knowledge transfer between the PR function and these other parties.

Trend forecasting identifies current issues and extrapolates these on the basis of previous experience or statistical predictions. It could be used to create a 'most likely' scenario or investigate how uncertainties could affect the future. One key question in trend forecasting is 'what if?' to allow creative answers to emerge. Historical data and trends may, or may not, help predict the future; disruptive thinking may be required to challenge the idea of continuity.

Gap analysis involves considering variation between the existing and desired situation. Koenig (2003: 297) specifies the need to focus on what is most important rather than easiest to address. Once the nature of any disparity is identified, its significance can be determined and action taken to close the gap, if appropriate. A gap analysis can be used in conjunction with other tools such as a cultural web (Chapter 19) or stakeholder mapping (Chapter 6) which can be plotted for the current and ideal scenarios.

Forcefield analysis identifies factors that support or counter proposed changes, allowing reflection on how aspects supporting change can be reinforced and those countering it can be overcome (Johnson *et al.* 2005). The nature and magnitude of the identified forces need to be assessed and a cost–benefit analysis undertaken to determine the value of taking action.

**ACTION POINT**

CIPR has used scenario planning to guide its future strategic direction. The Future of PR 2020 research initiative led by Dr Jon White involved a series of scenario planning meetings in 2011 with members of the Institute's regional and special interest groups. See the study's full report at: www.cipr.co.uk/sites/default/files/PRpercent202020percent20 Finalpercent20Report_0.pdf

■ How useful do you feel scenario planning is in determining the future of public relations?

■ In what way can the findings be used to inform CIPR's activities?

■ What information was used by to inform reflections on possible scenarios?

■ What other methods could have been used?

■ Can you apply the other analytic tools discussed in this chapter to the Future of PR 2020 project?

Predicting what may happen in the future may involve human reflection or computer modelling. Gregory (2012: 67) states 'information is power' although Pieczka (2006: 350) cautions against the belief that information creates a clearer picture, arguing any process needs 'to take account of human sense-making strategies'. This emphasises forecasting is an interpretive rather than a deductive process.

# PESTEL analysis

This is a mapping tool reviewing the findings obtained by environmental scanning. It is used to evaluate the impact of Political, Economic, Socio-cultural, Technological, Environmental and Legal issues. A PESTEL analysis can be used at a big-picture (macro) level, or to examine a specific issue (micro level). As with risk analysis (Chapter 13), the likelihood of any incidents occurring and their potential consequences need to be determined. A numerical or other indicator could be used. For example, arrows could be included to identify trends, with plus/minus symbols indicating possible impact.

A checklist for undertaking a PESTEL analysis is provided in the Appendix on pp. 335–337. The first step is to determine salient issues, with additional secondary or primary research used to identify less obvious matters. Many sources of data can be used (media coverage, internal knowledge, external reports, etc.) but analysis requires answering the question 'so what?' to understand the implications for the particular situation.

Inter-relationships between various factors in the PESTEL analysis need to be considered. However, the main aim of the analysis is to consider critical issues rather than worry about the 'right' box in which to include a particular factor. It is important to use evidence in reflecting on issues and note reference sources to facilitate reporting to management and for future reference.

## SWOT analysis

Insight from a PESTEL analysis can be reviewed using a SWOT analysis (see the SWOT checklist in the Appendix, p. 337). This considers internal capabilities (strengths and weaknesses) as well as key issues facing the organisation (opportunities and threats) as a basis for developing responses. Objective data and reflection is required to avoid any over-confidence in assessing the organisation's competencies. In this way, the PR practitioner needs to enact Holtzhausen's (2002: 77) concept of the organisational activist prepared to stand up in the face of 'the normative discourse of corporate management'. When reviewing issues it is important to separate those where action is possible from those where the organisation has no control. In other cases, counsel may be that PR activities are not an appropriate response and/or the organisation needs to change its policies and practices.

## Corporate communications audit

Undertaking a communications audit enables the PR function to analyse different sources of information. According to Grunig and Hunt (1984) an audit should be receiver-oriented to determine whether information has been received, understood or acted on.

A checklist for undertaking a communications audit is provided in the Appendix (pp. 338–339). An audit provides insight into the process and content of communications (distribution and feedback). It should review data relating to channels, target audiences and key messages. Communications may be categorised in terms of being direct/mediated, one-way/two-way, level of technological sophistication, ownership of channel, source/control of information, involvement of the audience, reach, cost per impression, key challenges to effectiveness, etc. Research may be undertaken routinely or conducted for specific campaigns.

## Content analysis

The content of communications (including media coverage) can be analysed using quantitative and qualitative methods (see Appendix). A framework should be used to categorise factual data (title, edition, date, etc. for a newspaper cutting) and methods of analysis (e.g. rating as positive/neutral/negative). A deductive counting system within pre-determined categories (e.g. brand mention) could be used or a more in-depth, exploratory approach (inductive) developed to identify themes and look for meaning within the data. Coding of articles may be undertaken by humans or computerised.

Macnamara (2005) proposes a media analysis model to consider:

- issues – strategic insight and intelligence into issues/trends reported in the media;

ACTION
POINT

In the 1970s, the International Communications Association (ICA) undertook a longitudinal study as a model for organisational communication audits (Goldhaber and Krivonos 1977). The model analysed communication networks and experiences. Audiences were asked to rate communication vehicles on the following scales:

| | | |
|---|---|---|
| Not useful | to | Very useful |
| Inaccurate | to | Accurate |
| Ineffective | to | Very effective |
| Untimely | to | Timely |
| Dishonest | to | Honest |

Respondents were asked to comment on their needs and media preferences; satisfaction with amount of information received; method of communication; ability to understand that information and preferred method of communication.

All current communication vehicles were assessed for usefulness, actual use, accuracy, timeliness, comprehensiveness and perceived effectiveness. Factors relating to trust and honesty were included if required. Other factors were determined from initial exploratory interviews with select stakeholders.

■ How useful do you think this approach would be for understanding views towards the organisation and situations it faces?

■ What are the problems and benefits of such research?

- client – evaluate effectiveness of media relations and PR for the particular organisation in terms of what is being reported;
- sources – strategic insight and intelligence into other sources in media, such as competitors;
- public – evaluate messages reaching target audiences – share of voice, impact on opinion.

Analysis has three steps:

1 select the media form/genre;
2 select issues/investigation period;
3 sample content (census, random, purposive, quota, stratified composite).

It is important to consider if any sample of materials being analysed is representative and replicable, or selected for other, more purposeful reasons. For example, relating to a critical incident or issue.

Fawkes (2012b) notes discourse analysis as a supplement to media content analysis. This involves looking at the meaning of language as well as subjective experience and the context and social rules governing specific narrative use.

# OUTCOME OF ANALYTICAL PROCESS

Cutlip *et al.* (2000: 347) describe the situation analysis as 'the unabridged collection about everything that is known about the situation, its history, forces operating on it and those involved or affected internally and externally'. (This latter aspect is considered in Chapter 6.)

The PR manager needs to summarise the findings of the research and analytical tools to produce a problem statement or insight report to be presented as intelligence to management or used to inform campaign development.

## Intelligence summary

A succinct summary should include statements regarding:

- the initial problem/opportunity that research has sought to examine;
- an overview of the research methodology and sources used;
- key findings and an interpretation of these;
- identification of any limitations and need for any additional research;
- insight gained into the problem/opportunity that PR activities need to address;
- appendices containing further detail, list of sources, etc.

This summary will be supplemented by the outcome of research into publics (Chapter 6). It should help inform objectives and other aspects of the PR plan. However, it should not include suggestions relating to how the issue will be addressed. Iterative research should be undertaken where feasible during the implementation phase. An update report that adds new knowledge can then be produced. In addition, research, reflection and results of any PR activities undertaken should be added to the knowledge management database.

It is particularly important when presenting the outcome of analysis that a logical and considered approach is undertaken. While providing a concise overview (executive report) which clarifies the context, key findings and main issues to be addressed (problem statement), the source and detail of research undertaken should be available for reference to demonstrate a robustness of methodological approach.

# END POINT

A knowledge management approach to public relations is suggested to establish a PRISM structure comprising a comprehensive intelligence resource. The value of PR to the organisation is underpinned by the economic, knowledge and social capital this approach offers.

As well as providing continuous intelligence, research is the first step in PR planning. It enables information to be obtained in relation to problems or opportunities facing organisations. Analysis of the situation and the organisation needs to be undertaken (alongside analysis of publics – Chapter 6) using existing and original information (where necessary). A range of tools are available to PR practitioners to support their strategic role as 'boundary-spanners'. An organisational activist approach is recommended to ensure frank and objective reporting to management of the issues identified.

# Understanding public psychology

*Heather Yaxley*

This chapter considers theories and concepts originating in the field of psychology and outlines methods to research and analyse stakeholders and publics.

## CHECK POINT

After reading this chapter, you should be able to:

*   relate public psychology to the PR strategic planning process;
*   understand how to segment stakeholders and publics for research purposes;
*   consider a variety of research methods to gain insight into the attitudes and behaviour of stakeholders and publics.

## PSYCHOLOGY AND PUBLIC RELATIONS

White (2000: 148) suggests PR is applied psychology because it concerns 'the way people think, feel and behave'. In the 1920s, PR counsel Edward Bernays drew on 'a hodgepodge built from various modern psychological theories' (Ewen 1998: 169). For example, his 'Torches of Freedom' campaign challenged the taboo on women smoking by using Freud's ideas of penis envy to associate cigarettes with a challenge to male power.

Interest in psychology by government and other organisations continues to be based on a belief that by analysing human cognitions people can be made to behave in certain ways (see Kill Jill example, Chapter 1). In reality, psychology is more complicated than this 'black box' concept implies.

In terms of planning, Smith (2005) includes analysis of publics in the formative research phase. Other models, such as Gregory's 10-step planning framework (2000), place publics later in the process, after setting objectives. She acknowledges, however, the need to understand the stakeholder point of view as a starting point.

## Empathetic listening

Cutlip *et al.* (2000: 344) state: 'effective public relations starts with listening' and recommend systematic research to obtain 'reliable feedback'. Covey (1989: 237) advocates the principle: 'seek first to understand, then to be understood', which is achieved by 'empathetic listening' (p. 240).

Listening and understanding relate to research and analysis of stakeholders and publics within the PR strategic planning process. Recognising the perspectives of those with whom we seek to communicate, influence, build relationships or co-orientate demonstrates a proactive, 'diagnose before you prescribe' approach, which Covey says is 'the mark of all true professionals' (1989: 243).

## Learning theories

Theories looking at how behaviour is acquired or changed assume a predictable relationship between a stimulus and a response (Bettinghaus and Cody 1994). Social learning theories suggest people acquire mental rules relating to positive or negative outcomes which reinforce their behavioural responses. Psychologists, therefore, study the formation of attitudes (learned evaluations), beliefs (subjective expectations) and values (guiding principles) and their relationship to behaviour. These and other relevant cognitive aspects can be researched within the PR planning process.

## Relationship theories

Socio-psychological theories investigate how people interact with others. They cover concepts such as credibility, social norms, social exchange, trust, loyalty, conflict, co-operation and co-orientation. Despite emergence of a relational perspective of PR in the 1990s (Jahansoozi 2006), there has been limited consideration of methods for researching and understanding socio-psychological aspects within the planning process.

Rather than providing insight into group psychology, the use of opinion polls aggregates individual opinions, while focus groups offer in-depth, qualitative information primarily to generate ideas or assess concepts (Edmunds 2000). Participant selection tends to be based on matching relevant demographic or other criteria rather than interpersonal relationships. The extent to which participants constitute a public is therefore questionable.

Jahansoozi (2006) notes the need to establish baseline measures of knowledge between an organisation and publics. She cites surveys of 'individual members of the public' (p. 88) used to determine variables relating to co-orientation (e.g. similarity and mutual understanding of views). However, the wider complexities of organisational-public relationships, inter-public relationships and the impact of inter-organisation relationships (Chapter 20) have received little attention.

A Public Relations Field Dynamics (PRFD) method for measuring and tracking 'the dynamics of multipublic formation, evolution, and interaction' has been used by Springston and Keyton (2001: 117). Using the SYMLOG (System for the Multiple Level Observation of Groups) approach, they researched a series of dimensions, with individual responses mapped to reflect group perceptions.

Social psychologist, Donelson R. Forsyth, has studied group dynamics extensively believing that 'to understand people, we must understand their groups' (2009: 2). He confirms groups influence members' actions, thoughts and feelings. As well as group cohesion, Forsyth considers entitativity (perceived unity), which indicates people may appear to be a group when they are not (or vice versa). The characteristics of a group that can be researched are stated (p. 12) as:

> Interaction: Groups create, organise, and sustain relationship and task interactions among members.
>
> Goals: Groups have instrumental purposes, for they facilitate the achievement of aims or outcomes sought by the members.
>
> Interdependence: Group members depend on one another, in that each member influences and is influenced by each other member.
>
> Structure: Groups are organised, with each individual connected lo others in a pattern of relationships, roles, and norms.
>
> Unity: Groups are cohesive social arrangements of individuals that perceivers, in some cases, consider to be unified wholes.

The potential existence of a 'group mind' (different to summation of individual cognitions) suggests a need to understand psychology of the group itself. For example, group norms may vary from each member's personal standard, but be agreed by them. Janis (1972) identifies 'groupthink' where seeking consensus overrides dissent and consideration of other options.

## SEGMENTATION

Penn (2007: xii) claims 'the one-size-fits-all approach to the world is dead'. In PR, failure to differentiate the heterogeneous population into homogenous segments reflects an aggregation strategy (the traditional approach to mass media relations). Cutlip *et al.* (2000: 245) argue against the concept of the 'general public' saying PR practitioners should identify and define specific publics and establish the nature of their relationship to the organisation or issue/opportunity to be addressed. A segmentation checklist is provided in the Appendix on pp. 340–341.

Segmentation strategies are evident in interpersonal and targeted media communications, while media fragmentation and technological developments further support a move towards more focused communications. There are several ways in which populations can be segmented.

## Demographics

Demographic segmentation is based on specific or multiple personal characteristics such as: age, gender, family size, income, occupation, education, religion, ethnicity and nationality. Although a relatively easy and popular method, categories can be broad and offer limited psychological understanding.

Socio-economic segmentation combines education, income and occupation characteristics (Pickton and Broderick 2005). The traditional six-class system (based on the occupation of the head of household) is evident in ABC1 media circulation data (www.abc.org.uk), indicating advertisers' preference to reach those in the top three categories:

A   higher managerial, administrative and professional

B   intermediate managerial, administrative and professional

C1  supervisory or clerical and junior managerial, administrative and professional.

The other classes (C2: skilled manual; D: semi-skilled and unskilled manual; and E: casual labourers, state pensioners, the unemployed) are traditionally less attractive to advertisers.

Life stage segmentation combines marital status and family size. Segments reflect changes traditionally experienced over time (e.g. Single, Newly weds (no children), Full nest (with sub-stages depending on age of children), Empty nest (children left home), Retired, Solitary survivor) although they do not reflect the diversity, complexity, dynamism and pluralism of modern society.

## Geographics

Geographic segmentation is based on the area where someone lives, works, shops or other relevant behaviour. Various levels can be used; e.g. society, continent, country, region, town, or postcode. For example, Peter *et al.* (1999) suggest Western societies are increasingly concerned with health and fitness.

Another option segments by nature of the area; e.g. coastal, country, urban, while terms such as Third World and BRIC (Brazil, Russia, India and China) are used to describe areas similar in economic development terms. In media relations, geographic segmentation may reflect reach or distribution; e.g. BBC Local offers forty-four English websites.

Geographic segmentation is relevant for International PR (Chapter 15), although increased globalisation (including travel and internet technology) affects its value.

## Geodemographics

Demographic and geographic information are combined to reflect the idiom: birds of a feather flock together. ACORN (a Classification of Residential Neighbour-hoods) groups UK neighbourhoods, postcodes and consumer households into five categories, seventeen groups and fifty-six types (www.caci.co.uk/acorn-classification.aspx). It signifies those living in geographic areas with similar demographic and social characteristics tend to share common lifestyles and patterns of buying behaviour. ACORN uses variables from the government population census undertaken every ten years.

**ACTION POINT**

## UPMYSTREET (www.upmystreet.com)

Upmystreet offers snapshots of ACORN profiles. For example, typical residents of the Norwich postcode NR2 4LW are suburban, privately renting professionals (ACORN Type 19). They are in their twenties and early thirties, well educated and building professional/managerial careers. Comfortable with using the internet in all aspects of their life, they prefer long-haul holidays and enjoy sport and exercise. They spend their money on clothes and eating out. Interested in current affairs, they tend to read broadsheet newspapers.

- Check the profile of residents for a town or postcode that you know.
- How well does this reflect your existing knowledge of the area's residents?
- In what ways could this knowledge be useful in planning a PR campaign?

## Stakeholders

Freeman and McVea (2005: 192) state, 'a stakeholder approach to strategic manage-ment, suggests that managers must formulate and implement processes which satisfy all and only those groups who have a stake in the business'. From a corporate communications perspective, Bernstein (1984: 93) identifies nine 'separate but not discrete' groups: internal, local, influential groups, trade, government, media, financial, customer and general public.

At a broader level, stakeholders can be divided into internal or external, or more narrowly using demographic, geographic and other variables. Internal stakeholders could be segmented by occupation, department, location, grade level, union membership, length of service, for example.

Gregory (2009: 185) confirms practitioners should 'move from the general to the particular' when segmenting. She details a circular model to map stakeholders with those with the highest stake placed nearer the centre. Prioritising may depend on the nature of the issue being addressed. For example, Johnson *et al.* (2005) identify three types of external stakeholders: economic, socio/political and technological.

A power/interest matrix (Johnson *et al.* 2005: 181) creates four segments according to the extent to which stakeholders 'impress their expectations' on the organisation and 'whether they have the power to do so':

- high power and high interest: key players; keep informed and satisfied;
- high power and low interest: keep satisfied;
- low power and high interest: keep informed;
- low power and low interest: require minimal effort.

Mapping should be based on research, although some assumptions could be made. It is important to recognise variation within stakeholder groups and any interaction which could affect group behaviour or indicate a need to consider relationships within or between groups.

Stakeholder mapping can be used as a dynamic tool as part of the planning approach with gap analysis used to consider action required to move from an existing to desired position for a specific issue.

## Behaviour

In marketing, behavioural segmentation generally relates to aspects of the purchasing process or usage. Within public relations, Grunig and Hunt (1984: 144) relate a 'behavioural molecule' with publics detecting, discussing and organising to do something about issues.

Originating from socio-psychological theory (Vasquez and Taylor 2001), the situational theory presented by Grunig and Hunt (1984) proposes four categories depending on cognitive or behavioural connection to an issue:

- nonpublic – not affected by an issue;
- latent – affected but not aware;
- aware – detect an issue but not taken any action;
- active – discussed the issue or taken other action.

Grunig and Hunt (1984: 160) suggest using survey interviews to categorise people in relation to issues. They identify four 'patterns of publics':

- active on all issues;
- apathetic on all issues;
- active only on issues that involve nearly everyone in the population;
- active on single-issues.

Active publics can be segmented (Grunig and Hunt 1984) into those who seek or process information once a problem has been recognised. Participation segments can be determined (e.g. whether someone comments using Twitter or joins a Facebook group). Media usage and preference is another useful way of segmenting publics for PR campaigns.

Segmentation could consider the level of engagement an individual or group has with the organisation. For example, contact and support could be plotted on an axis of friend–foe. The Fair Fuel UK campaign (Chapter 17) identified over 150 parliamentarians actively supporting its campaign, who could be further segmented by the nature of this support to indicate a level of 'friendship'.

## Psychographics

Psychographic segmentation groups people according to their cognitive characteristics, for example:

- attitudes – learned evaluations (e.g. favourable or unfavourable) which protect self-image;
- opinions – judgements which are narrower and less rigid than attitudes;
- beliefs – subjective expectations;
- values – guiding principles;
- interests – matters about which someone is curious or concerned;
- lifestyle – activities, interests and opinions (AIO) which reflect attitudes and values;
- motivations – reasons for behaving in a particular way;
- self-esteem – evaluation of self; feelings of personal worth or confidence.

This type of segmentation is necessary for PR practitioners addressing situations where cognitive (awareness/knowledge) or affective (attitude/preference) change may be sought. For example, PR initiatives to encourage older people to use the internet could segment by attitudes towards technology, beliefs about the costs of using computers or personal interests (e.g. wish to be in contact with family members who live overseas). Patterns of characteristics can be summarised in typologies; for example Technophobes or Silver Surfers.

ACTION POINT

## A PORTRAIT OF GENERATION NEXT

Pew Research Center (2010) noted similarities in the values, attitudes, behaviour and demographic characteristics of Americans termed the Millennial generation (born in 1980s and 1990s). Its study (www.pew research.org/millennials) found members of this generation are 'confident, self-expressive, liberal, upbeat and open to change', as well as 'more ethnically and racially diverse than older adults; less religious, less likely to have served in the military, and on track to become the most educated generation in American history' (p. 1).

Digital technology and social media are important to Millennials, who multi-task using hand-held gadgets. Three-quarters reported a social networking profile and one in five had posted a personal video online. Nearly four in ten have a tattoo and a similar percentage have piercings other than in the earlobe. Politically, two-thirds supported Obama for President in 2008.

However, Fields and Robbins (2008) state, 'you have to communicate one way to one type of teenager (jock, computer geek, emo, goth, party animal, Calvinist), but then you have to communicate a completely different way to another type of teenager (surfer, headbanger, gangsta, spelling-bee freak, polka lover).'

A subculture segment is 'identified by its political or artistic views, race, sexual orientation or other values . . . often expressed visually by the way in which members dress and the symbols they use' (Ambrose and Harris 2007: 228). Subcultures may reflect musical genres (B-boy, Grunger and Techno), class (Chav), lifestyle/political view (Bohemian, Gayskin), and activities/interests (Gamer, Nerd, Otaku).

■ How useful do you think generational studies are for those working in public relations?
■ What is the value in identifying subcultures within this age group?
■ Are you familiar with the typologies listed and how do you feel they could be researched for PR campaigns?

Although segmentation is important, groups must have sufficient homogeneity to be useful, recognisable and accessible. This is particularly relevant when undertaking research to inform PR activities.

## Individuals, groups and organisations

Groups can be segmented using demographic, geographic and other approaches discussed above. They could also be analysed by purpose (e.g. interest or pressure groups), motivation of those joining, relationship to the organisation, etc.

Segmenting organisations is useful for B2B public relations (Chapter 20), where broad categories can be used, e.g.:

- industry sector (e.g. UK Standard Industrial Classification);
- geographic location or presence (e.g. national, multinational or international);
- number of employees (small-medium enterprises (SMEs) defined as under 250 employees);
- financial data (e.g. profitability, turnover, size of budget, membership of FTSE100 index).

Psychographic and behavioural characteristics of organisations and groups as entities can be analysed, along with their reputation. For example, employee satisfaction ratings or environmental performance may be relevant criteria.

# RESEARCH METHODS

Research needs to be undertaken routinely or for specific campaigns. It is important to establish baseline data to inform PR campaigns, particularly when seeking to address cognitive (thinking) or affective (feeling) objectives. This will include factual information relating to publics, e.g. size, location, demographic composition or behaviour of relevant segments.

The most common methods (surveys and interviews) involve individual participants; although groups or organisations can be researched using the following methods (Forsyth 2009):

- observation (covert, overt or participation);
- self-reporting (including sociometry; a way of measuring relationship patterns);
- case studies (including action research; validating theory through practical application);
- correlational studies (seek patterns of relationships between variables).

## Secondary data

As part of operational management, organisations maintain records containing factual, psychographic and behavioural information regarding customers, employees and other stakeholders. Such data can be linked to the PRISM structure discussed in Chapter 5.

Many external sources of data on attitudes and behaviour exist. For example, the National Centre for Social Research (www.natcen.ac.uk) publishes the British Social

Attitudes survey (www.britsocat.com) tracking changing attitudes to social, economic, political and moral issues.

Secondary sources may provide raw data or published summaries. Such research has been conducted for a particular purpose and could be outdated. Nevertheless, it is low cost and relatively easy to access. Raw data offers the opportunity for new analysis.

# Primary research

Where existing information is inadequate or not available, original research may be undertaken. It can be used to improve understanding of publics in relation to issues or opportunities facing an organisation, or inform communications activities e.g. communication preferences, probable responses, etc. The cost and time investment is offset by ensuring PR resources are used effectively with greater likelihood of success in achieving strategic objectives.

Saunders *et al.* (2000: 85) present a research process 'onion' enabling suitable methods of research to be considered (Figure 6.1).

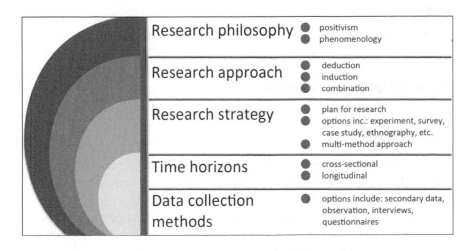

**FIGURE 6.1** Research process

Based on Saunders *et al.* (2000)

## *Research philosophy*

- Positivist – assumes a scientific, objective perspective that seeks generalisations from research.

- Phenomenological – assumes a social-scientific, subjective, perspective that recognises complexity and uniqueness of people and experiences being researched.

### Research approach

- Deductive – tests hypotheses, seeks to determine causal relationships between variables.
- Inductive – builds knowledge, explores reasoning, understands context and meaning.
- Combinative – adopts deductive and inductive approaches.

### Research strategy

- Plan for the research including objectives, questions, sources, constraints, rationale.
- Options include: experiment; survey; case study; grounded theory; ethnography; action research; cross-sectional and longitudinal studies; exploratory, descriptive and explanatory studies.
- Multi-method approach – employment of different methods to extend the value of the study, enable triangulation (increase reliability of data), reduce limitations.

### Time horizons

- Cross-sectional – undertaken at a particular time.
- Longitudinal – undertaken over a long period of time.

### Data collection methods

- Wide range of options including secondary data, observation, interviews, questionnaires.

Key considerations include ethical aspects of designing, conducting and analysing research; credibility of findings and avoiding assumptions or errors in logic. Chapter 5 outlined the benefits of using research specialists. Such expertise is particularly useful when undertaking complex or important research; it also provides independence, which can be important if findings are published. A research brief checklist can be found in the Appendix.

## Sampling issues

A census researches everyone within a population (or segment). Unless this group is small and everyone within it can be accessed, a sample of participants will need to be identified. There are two main ways of sampling (Saunders *et al.* 2000):

1   *Probability sampling*

Used where conclusions will be drawn for the entire population from the results. A population list is required to ensure everyone has an equal chance of selection. If this is not possible, a sampling frame must be determined. For example, a full list of employees could be obtained and a probability sample taken from this. Alternatively, an email list could be used as the sampling frame, although it will omit employees without computer access.

2   *Non-probability sampling*

Various techniques rely on subjective judgement to select participants. These include:

- quota – participants selected using key variables, e.g. if researching PR practitioners, the PR Census (Gorkana 2011) suggests a quota of six females to four males;
- purposive – based on a specific reason, e.g. select typical or exceptional participants;
- snowball – uses a network approach to identifying participants;
- self-selection – voluntary participants;
- convenience – anyone who is available.

## *Response rates*

Hill and Alexander (2006) identify discrepancies between different methods of data collection and a tendency for low response rates to reflect a bias towards those with high levels of involvement (positive or negative). They cite (p. 106) 'a rule of thumb in the research industry is that a response rate above 50 per cent is sufficient to minimize the problem of non-response bias' and urge caution with rates under 20 per cent.

# Surveys

PR practitioners use questionnaires to measure awareness, knowledge, beliefs, attitudes and behaviour (Szondi and Theilmann 2009). However, surveys rely on closed questions which prevent exploration of reasons or meaning. Answers may also reflect what is salient (easily recalled) rather than most important or truthful.

Polls research individual views on issues, which are aggregated to indicate the opinion of a population. Although Brettschneider (2008) confirms the popularity of opinion polls within news reporting, surveys have greater value to PR practitioners than simply gaining media coverage.

Surveys can be self-administered or use an interviewer. Collection methods include: online, telephone, face-to-face, email, postal and delivery and collection. Research can be commissioned by the organisation or questions can be submitted to an existing omnibus survey. Surveys use standardised questions, which could seek factual, evaluative, information, or self-perception responses (Grunig and Hunt 1984). Types of questions include (Saunders *et al.* 2000):

- List – choice of prompted responses. May offer a dichotomous choice (e.g. yes/no, agree/disagree) or multiple choice (list of answers). Don't know, unsure or other options can be included.

- Category – respondents select one response from a list of options, e.g. how often they undertake a particular behaviour.

- Ranking – respondents order their answers as an indication of importance.

- Scale or rating – evaluate attitudes or beliefs by asking respondents to indicate how strongly they agree or disagree with a statement.

- Quantity – requires numerical answers.

- Grid – lists questions in rows with responses indicated across columns.

- Open questions – respondents answer in their own words. These are more common in interviews, but can be included in surveys for exploratory purposes. People tend to skip questions requiring extensive reflection. Time is required to analyse and interpret narrative.

Responses can be coded to produce statistical data such as totals, averages and frequencies. Data can be investigated using cross-tabulations, factor analysis and other calculations to identify trends, correlations and so forth. Results can be presented using tables, charts, graphs and infographics.

**ACTION POINT**

## REPUTATION ANALYSIS

Fortune magazine's list of America's most admired companies asks executives and analysts to rate companies in their industry on eight attributes: quality of products/services; innovativeness; value as a long-term investment; financial soundness; ability to attract, develop and retain talent; community responsibility; use of corporate assets; quality of management.

Since 2006, the Reputation Institute (www.reputationinstitute.com) has interviewed over 85,000 consumers in 41 countries using a standardised measurement system to rate more than 2,500 of the world's largest companies. The results generate a 'RepTrak Pulse' score of 0 to 100, representing an average measure of people's feelings (reputation) for a company.

■ How useful do you think league tables are in understanding the reputation of organisations?

■ What evidence do respondents use in forming their opinions?

■ How can the information be used by PR practitioners in developing plans?

# Qualitative methods

Qualitative research provides a depth of understanding, particularly important when investigating complex communicative relationships and behaviour (Daymon and Holloway 2010). This approach tends to be time-consuming and focus on a select, small number of participants or cases where rich information can be gained. Qualitative research produces insight into individual, subjective experiences rather than statistical or representative data. The researcher is seeking meaning and plays an active role in generating, recording and interpreting results.

The interview (individual or focus group) is the most well-known qualitative research method. Themes or open questions are used as prompts to gain considered responses. Follow-up and probing questions test understanding and add further depth. Interviews can be undertaken face to face, by telephone or online. Video or audio recording is helpful to obtain a full record which can be transcribed to facilitate analysis.

Qualitative analysis should look for themes, similarity/differences and meaning in data. A coding structure can be prepared in advance or a more exploratory approach taken whereby a framework emerges during the analytical process.

**ACTION POINT**

## ANALYSING CORPORATE CULTURE

Schein (1991) recommends researching corporate culture using a focus group of motivated individuals asked to identify relevant cultural artefacts. Spontaneous and prompted responses are analysed to identify shared underlying assumptions. The Cultural Web (Johnson *et al.* 2005) offers a useful framework of categories for research (Chapter 19). Observational research and documentary analysis can be used. Diaries and other forms of self-reflection enable researchers and participants to record and analyse thoughts and experiences. For example, Raz (2003) undertook observational research at Tokyo Disneyland, as well as individual interviews and focus groups. He then reflected on the findings.

■ Using either your own organisation or one that you can visit, use a variety of qualitative methods to gain insight into its culture.

■ Consider issues involved in undertaking observational research and how findings can be analysed.

■ Review your findings using the Cultural Web tool.

# Motivational research

Most research involves a rational thought process, so more creative methods are required to uncover subconscious or hidden motivations that reflect emotional impulses.

Psychoanalyst, Ernest Dichter (1986) believed asking direct questions produced unhelpful answers and sought to put the research problem into a larger frame of reference. Among his famous campaigns was one for Ivory soap where he inter-viewed 100 people regarding their bathing habits. He did not ask why they used soap but discovered a Saturday night bath ritual among women going out looking for romance. This led to the concept of freshness being used in the successful campaign. Dichter believed the researcher's role is to interpret public behaviour as people are unaware why they do things. By talking about experiences, a proposition can be developed which is then validated by quantitative research.

Csíkszentmihályi and Rochberg-Halton (1981: x) examined 'the role of objects in people's definition of who they are, or who they have been, or who they wish to become'. They proposed the emotion evoked by objects is symbolic of attitudes. An example is seen in an episode of *Frasier*, when the lead character replaces an old recliner chair belonging to his father who, becoming upset, shares memories illustrating the chair's sentimental value. By interviewing people about their homes and cherished objects, Csikszentmihalyi and Rochberg-Halton sought to infer attitudes and motivations.

The Zaltman Metaphor-Elicitation Technique (ZMET) seeks to determine mental models of cognitions and emotions that motivate people. It uses visual imagery as research stimuli by asking participants to collect a set of pictures that represent their thoughts and feelings about a topic of interest. Zaltman (cited by Pink 1998) claims:

> A lot goes on in our minds that we're not aware of. Most of what influences what we say and do occurs below the level of awareness. That's why we need new techniques: to get at hidden knowledge – to get at what people don't know they know.

Interviews involve a series of steps that get participants to talk about their selected images. The discussion looks for key ideas, themes and concepts evident in the imagery and narrative. Findings are linked to seven 'deep metaphors' said to be unconscious concepts that reflect physical, moral, social, aesthetic, or psychological ideas. ZMET then uses resulting metaphors to develop imagery or language for communication campaigns.

## END POINT

Cognitive, affective and behavioural understanding of public psychology forms part of the formative research phase of the PR strategic planning process. A range of approaches enable relevant groups of stakeholders and publics to be identified. Statistical data regarding publics can be obtained using surveys. Qualitative methods provide deeper understanding although the researcher then needs to take a more interpretive role to use findings to inform PR campaigns.

Resulting insight into public psychology can be included in the concise research overview (executive report) discussed in Chapter 5.

# CHAPTER 7

# Setting objectives

*Heather Yaxley*

This chapter seeks to address a traditional weakness in the underpinnings of PR activities with a focus on practical approaches, and a critique of common problems, in relation to objective setting.

## CHECK POINT

After reading this chapter, you should be able to:

- understand the role of objectives in PR strategic planning;
- apply practical approaches to set objectives;
- avoid common problems in setting objectives.

## MANAGEMENT BY OBJECTIVES (MBO)

Drucker introduced the term Management by Objectives (MBO) in 1954 (Greenwood 1981: 161), conceiving objectives as 'the core of the structure of a discipline of managing'. MBO was proposed as way of improving the effectiveness and motivation of management.

Objectives specify desired results, emphasising an important connection with monitoring and evaluation (Chapter 10). They provide direction to motivate achievement and should be linked to an organisation's appraisal system.

The overview to Part II discussed a formal process of planning which involves defining the organisation's purpose and key objectives, with functional and operational objectives derived to support these. Criticisms of this hierarchical approach include:

- There are limitations to a top-down, rational approach to management, e.g. impression of control that may not be possible or desirable in reality.
- PR's role is presented as implementing strategy to achieve objectives (which have both been determined at the highest level), rather than contributing towards their construction as part of the senior management.
- Little regard is paid to matters arising that necessitate a more flexible and adaptive approach.
- Setting objectives in isolation of the needs/opinions of stakeholders or any relationships between them and the organisation.
- It is argued that many people are action-oriented rather than goal-driven.
- Resource and other constraints impact on ability to achieve established objectives.
- Objectives frequently lack any foundation in research and may not be achievable or appropriate.
- The value of intuition and expertise of those undertaking specific roles within the organisation is downplayed.

## OBJECTIVES WITHIN STRATEGIC PR PLANS

Most planning models (including those within PR literature) place objective setting after a situational audit. This connects them to formative research (Chapters 5 and 6). The process should be iterative rather than one-way as consideration of objectives may raise a need for additional research.

Objectives answer the question: where do we need to be? At the department level, they establish the purpose and direction of PR within the organisation, with objectives for members of the department underpinning individual roles. Performance standards are required for each key objective to facilitate ongoing monitoring of achievements.

PR objectives need to align with those of other relevant functions within the organisation or with external partners as appropriate. Strategic alignment does not mean PR should be merged with other functions. Indeed, ensuring integration throughout the organisation requires PR to be more than a sub-set of marketing both strategically and in terms of its wider remit.

The PR function needs to determine a set of operational and specific campaign plans, each with their own objectives. Drawing on the formative research phase, objectives can be set to address issues or opportunities relating to particular publics.

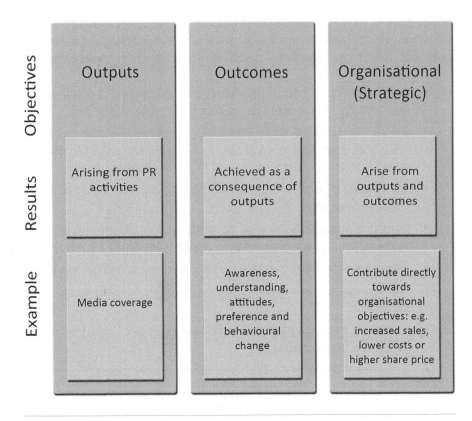

FIGURE 7.1 Illustration of objectives and results

Briefs for external suppliers (including PR consultancies) should detail result-oriented objectives (see Appendix, pp. 348–349).

Figure 7.1 distinguishes objectives by the nature of the result achieved. It should not be presumed output objectives will deliver outcomes or strategic results. For example, media coverage does not indicate sales have been achieved.

Objective setting is not always explicitly evident in models proposing strategic responsibility for PR. It is important to recognise the role of public relations in determining strategic objectives as part of the senior management team, as well as how its activities contribute directly towards achieving organisational objectives.

## UNDERSTANDING OBJECTIVES

Consider the saying: 'If you don't know where you are going, any road will take you there.' Organisations, and PR practitioners, need to know where they are going and consequently plan how they will arrive at the destination. Objectives need to specify the end result, not describe the journey.

Grunig and Hunt (1984) relate objectives to reasons why an organisation needs public relations, how it contributes to organisational effectiveness and the value its activities deliver. Objectives help explain the possible and actual impact of PR. Cutlip *et al.* (2000) state objectives provide:

- focus and direction for developing strategies and tactics;
- guidance and motivation in implementing programmes;
- outcome criteria for assessing progress and impact.

Anderson *et al.* (1999: 5) specify six reasons for 'setting clear, concise and measurable objectives':

- to create a structure to prioritise, clarifying the focus and sequence of strategy and tactics;
- to reduce the potential for disputes before, during, and after the program;
- to focus resources to drive performance and efficiency, providing a sense of purpose that enables tactics and resources to be concentrated where they have most impact;
- to identify areas for prescriptive change and continual improvement; tracking performance against properly set objectives allows for corrective action, or positive adjustments;
- to support evaluation by making it easier to determine if the PR activities meet or exceed expectations;
- to support the business case for PR by linking its objective to the business objective.

Setting PR objectives may involve a process that is either:

proactive – based on the results of a situational analysis; or

reactive – responding to a decision taken (inside or outside the organisation).

Consultancies, and those working in-house as PR technicians rather than managers, are commonly given objectives to achieve. This may be unproblematic if the objectives indicate an issue or opportunity to be addressed. PR practitioners still need to analyse the situation and agree realistic objectives for identified publics and activities. Objectives need to be set for entire programmes and individual projects as well as at the strategic and tactical level (Gregory 2000).

## Task/process objectives

Grunig and Hunt (1984) criticise PR practitioners for focusing on processes (number of releases distributed, schedule for annual report, tactics to handle an immediate crisis) instead of effects (what the release, report or other tactics aim to achieve, such as increased knowledge, acceptance of decisions or a behavioural change). Examples of process or task objectives are:

- to write a press release by 30 June;
- to generate twelve cuttings by 31 July.

Task/process objectives describe activities, but do not consider what value they deliver. For example, whether an article was read, understood, changed opinions or stimulated action. They can help steer what needs to be done, making them useful for monitoring planning and implementation, but not as a measure of outcome. Outcome objectives are required before determining relevant tactics and setting task/process objectives (Chapter 8).

## Outcome objectives

To demonstrate effectiveness, objectives must be outcome oriented – i.e. specify results to be achieved. Cutlip *et al.* (2000) propose three levels of objectives and a choice of direction for the intended outcome (Figure 7.2).

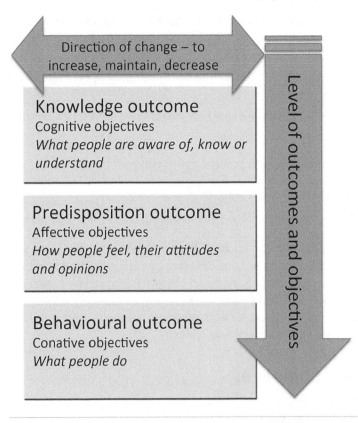

FIGURE 7.2 Matrix detailing level and direction of objectives

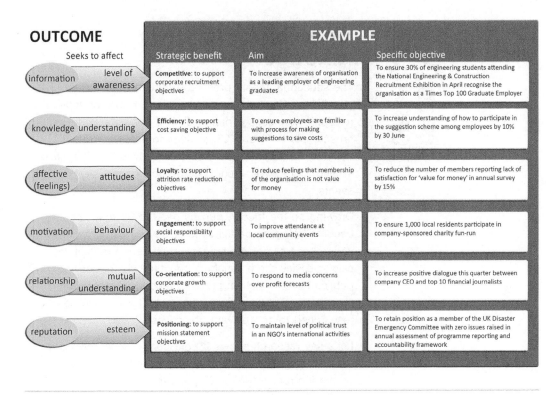

**FIGURE 7.3** Types of outcome objectives

This matrix suggests all PR objectives are persuasive, seeking to influence what others know, feel or do. If organisations wish to co-orientate or build relationships with publics (e.g. adopt a two-way symmetrical communications strategy), PR objectives must reflect a less persuasive intent. Objectives could be agreed or co-constructed using a process of discussion rather than each party seeking to achieve separate objectives. Such objectives need to reflect measures by which the relationship or outcome of the symmetrical discussion can be assessed. Figure 7.3 considers examples of outcome objectives, separating awareness from knowledge and adding relationship and reputation objectives.

Each of the cases in Figure 7.3 reflects only part of the process of achieving a strategic benefit. For example, increasing awareness of an organisation as a top employer will not automatically achieve the competitive benefit of recruiting the best engineering graduates. This highlights the importance of the situational analysis: was a lack of awareness identified as a problem in achieving recruitment objectives? If so, then the suggested objective would be an appropriate first step. At the same time, awareness lacks ambition as an objective for the exhibition, where knowledge, attitudes, behaviour, mutual understanding and esteem could also be improved.

**ACTION POINT**

# SITUATIONAL THEORY IN PRACTICE

The situational theory presented by Grunig and Hunt (1984) identifies publics may be latent, aware or active in relation to an issue (Chapter 6). The company used as an example in Figure 7.3, seeking to achieve strategic benefits via social responsibility objectives, has identified a need to improve attendance at local community events.

Drawing on the theory, publics need to be motivated to become active as participants or advocates of the event (in the case of opinion leaders, such as the media). It also specifies three variables affecting whether or not publics become active: problem recognition, constraint recognition and level of involvement. These could be researched to set relevant objectives.

Let's say research shows 60 per cent of local residents do not recognise problems facing the charity supported by the fun-run. A further 20 per cent recognise the needs of the charity, but feel constrained from participating in the fun-run. Among those unaware of the charity's challenges, 10 per cent have concerns about participating. In addition, 5 per cent of residents do not feel a personal connection to the charity or the event. This data indicates where problem recognition, constraints and personal involvement need to be addressed and enable sub-objectives to be set to increase awareness, change attitudes, improve knowledge or make a personal connection to the charity. These may need to be achieved in order to deliver the overall PR campaign objective to ensure 1,000 local residents participate in the company-sponsored charity fun-run.

This example demonstrates PR plans often need to go beyond communication. Ensuring residents are able to participate in the fun-run involves considering, and where necessary removing, potential barriers relating to the nature of the event, ease of signing-up, relevance of the charity being supported and so forth.

**ACTION POINT**

## PASSIVE SMOKING AND CHILDREN CONCERNS

A report by the Royal College of Physicians, *Passive Smoking and Children* (2010), claimed passive smoking is a major hazard to over 2 million children. Key health problems were reported to generate over 300,000 UK GP consultations, about 9,500 hospital admissions and a cost to the NHS of about £23.3 million.

Qualitative research by the University of Liverpool (2004: v) used focus groups to explore parents' smoking behaviour, including 'the role of knowledge and lay beliefs about the nature and risks of passive smoking to children'. The study found:

- Limited knowledge, with a belief that coughs are relatively minor and many parents unconvinced of a link to exposure to tobacco smoke.

- High awareness of the association between cot death and exposing newborn babies to smoke; three-quarters of parents smoked in their homes and cited difficulties in leaving young children to go outside.

- Parents relied on their existing knowledge and experiences as much as official information.

- Resistance to smoking cessation indicated rejection of messages about children's health.

■ What type of objectives do you feel would be relevant for any PR health campaign to address this issue? Is lack of awareness or knowledge the cause of parents' smoking behaviour?

■ Would an initial objective to increase the percentage of parents who know they should not smoke around their children by 50 per cent before the summer holidays be reasonable?

■ Would a hierarchy of effects approach be feasible for objectives?

■ Why might those already aware of the dangers continue to smoke?

■ Would a behavioural objective to reduce number of parents smoking in front of their children by 10 per cent within twelve months be reasonable?

The complex relationship between types of objectives needs careful consideration. Developing a clear rationale that explains the reasoning behind determining objectives is recommended.

## Hierarchy of effects

The concept of levels of objectives suggests inter-related steps towards achieving an ultimate goal. It proposes a rational psychological process, e.g. a need to increase awareness before altering attitudes; alter attitudes before changing behaviour. In the classic 'Torches of Freedom' campaign, Bernays needed to make smoking cigarettes acceptable for women before changing their behaviour.

This reflects a persuasive model which asserts people move through a linear sequence of steps. Walser (2004) dates the concept to the 1898 St. Elmo Lewis AIDA model (Awareness, Interest, Decision, Action). Modern usage is traced by Parvanta *et al.* (2011) to Lavidge and Steiner in 1961, who outlined six steps: awareness and knowledge (cognitive); liking and preference (affective); and conviction and purchase (conative). In 1969, McGuire conceived an effects hierarchy for information processing involving attention, comprehension, retention, and behaviour (cited by Rodgers *et al.* 2008).

Such models are simplistic, do not reflect the reality of much decision-making or recognise other psychological theories. The cases considered above illustrate PR practitioners should not presume that increasing awareness will automatically change behaviour. Likewise, participating in a fun-run could raise the charity's profile rather than interest preceding action. Such decisions could also be based on an emotional reaction rather than a logical thought process.

## SETTING OBJECTIVES

Pickton and Broderick (2005: 420) state: 'objective setting is not an easy task', particularly for those who are unfamiliar with the exercise. They suggest referring to past experience and previous activities to determine what is achievable and realistic.

## SMART objectives

To return to the analogy of a journey, vague objectives would be of limited help. What is needed is, at least, a specific destination and time of arrival. Likewise, it is useful for objectives to follow the acronym SMART (Figure 7.4).

## Quantitative and qualitative objectives

Figure 7.3 indicated types of quantitative measures that can be set. For example: to decrease the number of members reporting lack of satisfaction for value for money in annual survey by 15 per cent.

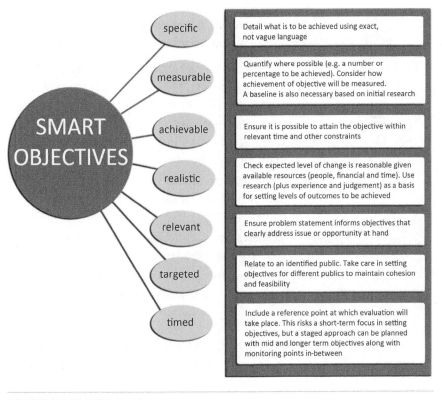

**FIGURE 7.4** SMART objectives

In some circumstances, objectives need to be measured using qualitative methods (Chapter 6). For example: to improve feedback from motoring journalists in the MORI and Guild survey interviews (Chapter 5).

Johnson *et al.* (2005) argue an objective may be important but 'become absurd if it has to be expressed in measurable terms', using the example of achieving a reputational leadership position. However, it is possible for public relations practitioners to develop 'skill in appraising intangible factors', which Batchelor (1938: 30) likens to the analytical abilities of engineers.

## Objectives and publics

In setting PR objectives, it is important to consider publics who need to be engaged as specifically as possible. Chapter 6 discussed the importance of segmentation and research to gain an understanding of publics that can be used to set objectives. The research process can also be used to set qualitative and quantitative objectives.

**Review the following examples of objectives to determine which can be addressed by PR activities:**

- to increase the percentage of the electorate who know how to vote by 10 per cent, two weeks prior to the election date;

- to maintain the number of adults (aged 18–50) who feel eating five fruit or vegetables a day is good for you, over the next twelve months;

- Tto reduce the number of cars parked illegally in spaces reserved for disabled drivers to zero, by 31 December;

- to ensure no local residents object during the planning application process for a new factory;

- to improve recognition among politicians of the organisation as a leading employer.

■ Which are SMART?

■ Do they suggest quantitative or qualitative outcomes?

■ How could they be improved?

## MINDSET OBJECTIVES

One way of looking at objectives is to consider the mindset or psychology of a specific public.

■ Current mindset – what does the specific public currently think, feel or do in relation to the organisation, industry sector, product, trends or issue identified within the problem or opportunity statement?

■ Desired mindset – what is the required outcome; i.e. what you want the specific public to think, feel or do in relation to the problem/opportunity?

# Getting agreement for objectives

Seitel (1998) states that good objectives should stand up to the following questions:

- Do they clearly describe the end result expected?
- Are they understandable to everyone in the organisation?
- Do they list a firm completion date?
- Are they realistic, attainable and measurable?
- Are they consistent with management's objectives?

Being able to answer such questions is important in ensuring that objectives can be agreed with senior management or other partners in the PR programme.

# PROBLEMS

Various problems with understanding and setting objectives are discussed in this chapter. Gregory (2000) lists the following barriers affecting successful achievement of objectives:

- problems resulting from lack of capability of the PR function to carry out required activities;
- financial constraints;
- time issues – internal and external, including unforeseen matters that may arise;
- issues experienced in the decision-making process;
- difficulties arising with support mechanisms including the organisation's administrative and physical infrastructure;
- challenges relating to the specific public;
- problems caused by socio-cultural differences.

# Normative objectives

The problem with normative objectives is that they suggest a common standard that should be achieved by PR activities. For example, a company may expect media releases to generate a specific response rate, reflecting a measure that is common in direct marketing. Although a calculation could be made on the basis of previous experience and set as a future target, this is pretty meaningless. Determining a PR standard result is difficult given the importance of ensuring campaigns reflect the particular needs of an organisation, the issues and opportunities it faces and the specific nature of relevant publics.

## Competitive objectives

The marketing concept of share of voice may be used to set a competitive objective for PR activities (Watson and Noble 2007). The Institute of Practitioners in Advertising (2009) identified correlation between share of voice and share of market, although it is not apparent this applies to editorial coverage. A competitive focus is evident in social media, for example where objectives are set for number of Twitter followers or social media influence ratings (Chapter 16). A problem is in demonstrating such competitive objectives deliver strategic benefits.

## Idealistic objectives

Organisations may experience difficulties if they set idealistic objectives indicating the end result they would like to achieve. Their aspirations may be significantly different to what is realistic. Gregory (2000) criticises the PR industry for over-promising through a lack of understanding of what activities can actually achieve. This emphasises the need for accurate monitoring and evaluation of outcomes, which can be referenced when setting future objectives.

## Stretch objectives

Fung *et al.* (2008: 109) state: stretch objectives seek to push people 'to do more than they think is possible'. They argue this encourages more innovative solutions. If these are viewed simply as motivational objectives, a stretch approach may be useful, but could set unrealistic expectations or prove demoralising if impossible to achieve.

## Inflexible objectives

It may seem strange to suggest objectives need to be flexible. However, it would be dogmatic and unrealistic to ignore any need for adaptation, particularly if the organisation is open to feedback within its PR operations.

## Objective overload

Practitioners may try to do too much, with too many objectives presented for what can be achieved with the resources available. Likewise, a long list of hierarchical objectives may prove overambitious. Another issue is trying to target every stakeholder (Chapter 6) rather than setting priorities for the primary opportunity or issue that has been identified.

## Lack of benchmarks for objectives

Cutlip *et al.* (2000) confirm that without benchmark data judgement will dominate in setting outcome objectives. This can present problems for PR practitioners if management set unrealistic objectives. Being able to present management with reliable research data is more likely to influence them to accept more realistic, relevant and achievable objectives.

## BAD EXAMPLES

**ACTION POINT**

■ Review examples of objectives for campaigns in trade publications, textbooks and PR awards.
■ How well do you think they reflect the recommendations in this chapter?
■ Do they reflect 'good' objectives and how could they be evaluated?
■ How do the objectives stated relate to the campaign and measures of success that are indicated?

One problem with published examples of campaigns is that they are intended to reflect good practice. The impression is given that the cases were 100 per cent successful.

■ Can you find any examples which are reflexive and discuss what went wrong with a campaign?
■ Is there any recognition of a need to adapt either the campaign or the objectives that were initially set?

## END POINT

Objectives are vital within PR strategic planning to ensure resources can be used effectively and specific outcomes achieved. They need be focused on problems or opportunities (identified from research) that affect the organisation and specific publics. Setting objectives is not an easy process, with many possible problems that can be encountered, including a tendency to over-promise and a lack of a reflexive approach in real-world examples within published PR campaigns. Consideration of relevant quantitative and qualitative methods of evaluating objectives ensures public relations is able to offer strategic value to organisations.

# CHAPTER 8

# Strategic campaign execution

*Heather Yaxley*

This chapter reviews the implementation stage at the heart of all PR planning models. It considers creativity and tactics within a strategic framework. PR strategies are explained alongside narrative development (from a dialogic perspective). Finally tips are presented for pitching and gaining approval for ideas.

## CHECK POINT

After reading this chapter, you should be able to:

- develop campaign strategies and narrative approaches;
- identify relevant campaign execution tools;
- secure approval for campaign ideas.

Throughout this book a comprehensive set of tools, strategies and techniques has been presented and critiqued. This chapter complements that expert focus with an overview of the key components of strategic campaign execution. It considers three areas:

1   campaign strategy – methodology underpinning activities;

2   narrative approaches – methodology underpinning communication;

3   campaign tools – methods by which the strategy is executed. Cutlip *et al.* (2000) identify two aspects involved in implementing public relations strategy:

- action component – what needs to be done;
- communication component – what needs to be said.

This phase of the planning process considers: how (strategy) the organisation should achieve its PR objectives (Chapter 7), and what it should do and say (tactics), with regard to particular publics (Chapter 6), in response to the issues and opportunities identified from a situational analysis (Chapter 5).

It involves:

- generating and considering possible strategic actions and responses;
- determining a relevant creative theme (Watson and Noble 2007);
- building a narrative structure including messages and dialogic responses;
- identifying a cohesive programme of communication tactics and activities.

The campaign cannot be executed without considering the costs and resources necessary to implement the plan (Chapter 9) and how it will be monitored and evaluated (Chapter 10).

# 1 CAMPAIGN STRATEGIES

Within the planning framework, campaign strategies need to be considered before detailing tactical aspects. Strategy is often confused with tactics. PR practitioners find it easy to think immediately of the tactical things they could do to address a problem or achieve an objective; but lack an overall, strategic approach. A clear strategy provides a framework for choosing tactics to achieve the required objectives:

- Strategy – is the overall game plan, the overarching idea, concept or approach that explains how the objective will be achieved.
- Tactics – are actions undertaken within the strategic framework at the operational level, i.e. actual events, media activities and communication methods used to implement the strategy.

Proactive strategies are developed to address issues and opportunities; reactive strategies respond to unanticipated circumstances.

Given many PR campaigns seek to achieve behaviour change objectives, psychological theories can be used to inform strategies. Figure 8.1 provides examples and a decision-making process.

## STRATEGY STATEMENT

Wilcox and Cameron (2006: 162) state: 'a strategy statement describes how, in concept, an objective is to be achieved, providing guidelines and themes for the overall program.' The strategy statement provides a rationale for the tactics.

The strategic statement for the UK government's Public Health Responsibility Deal is 'to tap into the potential for businesses and other organisations to improve public health and tackle health inequalities through their influence over food, alcohol, physical activity and health in the workplace'. The government believed a responsibility strategy requiring commercial partners to pledge action would be faster and more effective than adopting a regulatory strategy.

In terms of communications, the government has embraced the concept of a nudge strategy. John *et al.* (2008: 9) explain: 'Nudge is about giving information and social cues so as to help people do positive things for themselves and society.' Kelly (2011) says nudge reflects a libertarian paternalism philosophy and draws on behavioural economics and social psychology. It utilises the concepts of social norms, social contagion, peripheral processing (see Figure 8.1) and framing messages to make certain behaviours more salient.

The book, *Nudge: Improving Decisions about Health, Wealth and Happiness*, by Richard Thaler and Cass Sunstein (2008) reflects the trend for popular psychology-based books such as Gladwell's *The Tipping Point* and Levitt's *Freakonomics*. Such books employ theories and anecdotal case studies to propose ways to change social behaviour. Are you familiar with these or similar titles? How useful are they in informing your understanding of public relations? Why might government base its strategies on the ideas in these books?

## Creative campaign concepts

Gregory (2000) explains public relations strategy can be presented as an approach (e.g. publicity campaign), a conceptual proposition (e.g. thought leadership) or a creative idea (e.g. the Child Bereavement Charity's Mother's Day Campaign).

PR practitioners face considerable competition to be heard; creativity concepts offer a way to stand out, as well as providing cohesion and consistency across

Elaboration Likelihood Model: Petty and Cacioppo (1986) identified two methods by which people adopt messages: central and peripheral processing. The central method requires rational elaboration of messages; the peripheral route reflects an emotional reaction involving little thought.
**Strategy:** An emotional strategy could use shock (drawing on peripheral processing) to reach latent publics who are unaware of an issue. Rational arguments using scientific data and evidence (requiring central processing) could be used to reach aware publics and make them active in seeking information.
**Example:** The Department of Health Quit Smoking campaign uses an emotional strategy (real children asking their parents to stop smoking), supported by a rational strategy (factual information on how to get help to stop smoking).

**Theory of reasoned action:** Fishbein and Ajzen (1980) identified behavioural intention is affected by attitudes towards a behaviour and the subjective norm (motivation to comply with others).
**Strategy:** An endorsement strategy could seek to alter someone's attitudes by focusing on involvement with a reference group.
**Example:** The Royal National Lifeboat Institution (RNLI) used a peer group endorsement strategy to change attitudes with its 'Mystery Packages' YouTube campaign.

**Cognitive dissonance:** Festinger's (1957) concept argues people seek to maintain consistency in the perceptions they hold.
**Strategy:** A co-orientation strategy could align the attitudes of publics and the organization in relation to an issue they both care about. Leadership or CSR strategies could be adopted.
**Example:** Marks & Spencer adopted a Key Opinion Leader (KOL) position with its Plan A sustainability (CSR) strategy.

**FIGURE 8.1** PR strategies and decision-making process

communications. A creative concept should be given an identity, which helps ensure it is memorable (easy to recall) and remarkable (worthy of discussion).

A creative concept embodies the campaign strategy and is more than a list of tactical ideas. Moriarty (1997: 555) says, 'the brilliant creative concept involves what some experts have called the Creative Leap' represented by a 'Big Idea', which needs to be presented in 'an exciting new way'. The creative concept enables the strategy statement to be transformed into an engaging narrative. Ideally, it will become closely associated with an organisation or issue, yet remain adaptable over time.

**ACTION POINT**

## MACMILLAN CANCER SUPPORT WORLD'S BIGGEST COFFEE MORNING

Following a successful coffee morning event by a local fundraising committee in 1990, the charity adopted the simple, yet effective idea in 1991. Since then it has raised over £60 million in total. The idea offers flexibility enabling supporters to adapt the coffee morning concept locally. It has also accommodated record attempts (e.g. the highest and deepest coffee mornings) and attracted corporate partners and celebrity ambassadors.

The basic rules of creativity are to have an open mind, involve different perspectives, generate numerous ideas, record all suggestions, avoid early evaluation and not to be dismissive of previous solutions. Creative concepts should be:

- relevant – review against research, objectives and strategy;
- appropriate – reflecting the organisation's culture and cognisant of its publics' sensitivities;
- simple – readily explained to others and easily implemented;
- compelling – securing buy-in from internal and external stakeholders;
- surprising – cutting through the clutter of other communication activities.

Smith (2005: 13) advocates 'effective creativity', highlighting outcomes should not be forgotten in the enthusiasm of a novel idea. He argues research and creativity are complementary, with research able to inform the creative process and validating ideas.

**ACTION POINT**

## PUBLICITY STUNTS

Creativity is most evident at the tactical level of public relations with stunts used to attract media attention. Taylor Herring (2009) presents a Publicity Stunt Hall Of Fame with ideas including the Olympic torch relay (introduced in 1936), the Women's Institute naked calendar (1999), Tourism Queensland's Best Job in the World (2009) and Lego's model of Obama's inauguration (2008). Beyond securing media coverage, ideas need to ensure the client and its message is recalled, not just the stunt.

Social media offers the opportunity to extend the reach and longevity of an idea beyond traditional media coverage. The Will It Blend (http://willit blend.com/) YouTube videos featuring the BlendTec CEO have become a long-lived sensation attracting over 65 million views, increasing brand recognition, building a reputation for durability and generating sales.

Viral campaigns depend on organic word of mouth to be successful, and trying too hard to be funny or edgy can backfire. Organisations need to be prepared for the irreverent treatment of ideas online. Spoof YouTube videos, Twitter jokes and ironic Facebook groups are frequently used to poke fun at big brand initiatives, albeit often with affection.

Sometimes this offers opportunities for brands. For example, in 2006, the EepyBird videos of geysers created by mixing Coca Cola with Mentos mints became a worldwide sensation, increasing sales of both brands, which quickly realised the value of supporting the initiative.

# Evaluating creativity

Creativity involves more than new ideas, which 'are only part of the equation. Execution is just as important' (Isaacson 2011: 98). It is likely more than one idea will be generated and knowing which to adopt is a matter of judgement. This should be based on a rational decision-making process (Figure 8.2).

Issue
Opportunity
Objectives

Ideas generation process:
imagination, brainstorming,
modelling, 'What if?' question
snowball groups,word/object
prompt, scenario forecasting, etc.

Techniques to achieve a paradigm shift and
create new ideas: Instant response, reconceptualise the
issue/opportunity, big picture and detail perspectives, change the
operational parameters, co-create with others, apply thinking models
(intuition, logic, etc.)

ideas - ideas - ideas - ideas - ideas - ideas - ideas

Ideas review process: gradual process to nurture, select
and test using instinct, research, costings analysis,
originality test, etc.

Techniques to develop ideas, ensure
core concept is protected, gain
agreement, identify implementation
and risk factors, etc.

Implement
preferred
idea

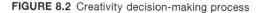

**FIGURE 8.2** Creativity decision-making process

## 2 NARRATIVE APPROACHES

Alongside the campaign strategy, a strong narrative approach is required. This provides a framework for determining what needs to be communicated within a campaign.

Narrative mediates human experience enabling thoughts, attitudes, values and meaning to be expressed through communications. It is a broader concept than key messages, which tend to reflect slogans, headlines and other statements. Key messages are part of the communication component, rather than its entirety as is implied by many PR planning models.

Figure 8.3 illustrates the three core aspects to consider in developing a narrative approach. These aspects need to be researched and considered as part of the communicative element of strategic plans. They also need to be connected to the campaign objectives (Chapter 7) and resources available (Chapter 9).

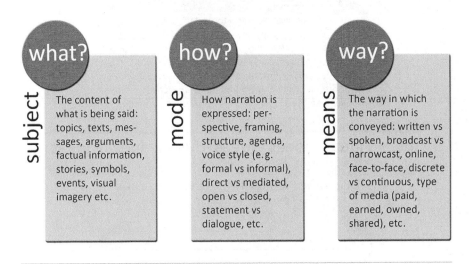

**subject** what? The content of what is being said: topics, texts, messages, arguments, factual information, stories, symbols, events, visual imagery etc.

**mode** how? How narration is expressed: perspective, framing, structure, agenda, voice style (e.g. formal vs informal), direct vs mediated, open vs closed, statement vs dialogue, etc.

**means** way? The way in which the narration is conveyed: written vs spoken, broadcast vs narrowcast, online, face-to-face, discrete vs continuous, type of media (paid, earned, owned, shared), etc.

**FIGURE 8.3** Core aspects of a narrative approach to public relations

The narrative approach for any campaign needs to be derived from the narrative position of the organisation. This should include how communications are managed and organised, authority levels, procedures and so forth. The narrative position will draw on the organisation's brand profile and corporate principles (Figure 8.4). The organisation's style guide should inform the narrative position, or be informed by it if one doesn't exist. The narrative approach, position and style guide should be part of the PRISM discussed in Chapter 5.

**brand profile**
- Brand overview, strategy and distinctive position
- Brand attributes (emotional and rational) and identity
- Mission, purpose, vision, key objectives (and achievements)

**organisational reputation**
- Organisational principles, values and recognised qualities
- Brand promise and deliverables (brand capital/equity)
- Historical and contemporary narrative (internal and external perceptions)
- Relationship and connections with stakeholders/publics (advocacy, preference, credibility)

**narrative position**
- Functional and hierarchical communication responsibilities
- Communication processes and procedures (including style guidelines)
- Programme (timing, content) of communication activities
- Communication assets

**narrative approach**
- Organisational voice and personality
- Distinctive style of communications
- Narrative subject, mode and means

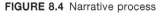

**FIGURE 8.4** Narrative process

# Shaping narrative

The narrative approach needs to be distilled into concise, clear and engaging communications. It needs to be shaped into a framework for production of written and multi-media materials, and participation in dialogue or conversations. Construction needs to reflect natural, human language rather than the corporate speak of key messages. The purpose is to guide thinking and understanding, not rigid use of slick slogans or defensive position statements.

Traditionally, a key message approach (also reflected in message grids or a message house) involved creating consistent statements comprised of pre-determined words, phrases and/or sentences, which could be monitored as outputs of successful communication. This reflects a transmission approach to communications. That is, the focus is on what the organisation wants to say, rather than ensuring others understand, gain a positive impression or empathise with the communications.

It is helpful to determine the priority point(s) that need to be understood, and identify examples, imagery, facts and other ways in which a story can be illustrated, remembered and accepted. PR practitioners need to be the architect of the design and construction of this narrative framework. Their role is to plan communications that are shaped by purpose and context, while allowing flexibility in application within the framework. This is illustrated in Figure 8.5 with a template for shaping narrative in the Appendix.

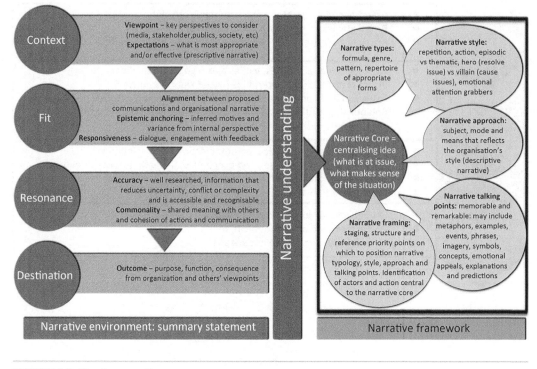

**FIGURE 8.5** Shaping narrative

## Memes

The campaign narrative approach can draw on the concept of a meme, proposed by biologist Professor Richard Dawkins (Green 2010). A meme is a cognitive concept involving transmission of cultural information between humans. It is 'an idea that behaves like a virus – that moves through a population, taking hold in each person it infects' (Gladwell 2000). It is applied to information that possesses the dynamic potential to be spread between individuals. From a PR perspective, this means narrative needs to be memorable and replicable, i.e. easily passed on by word of mouth. The concept emphasises that organisations need to avoid jargon and language that is difficult to recall or repeat.

Green (2010) highlights three aspects of a meme proposed by Dawkins:

- longevity – the meme must survive, to be remembered, recalled and transmitted;
- coherence – the meme has the strength to replicate itself, sticking in someone's head even against their will;
- copyability – others must be able to make a cognitive copy of the meme (although it may not be identical to the original).

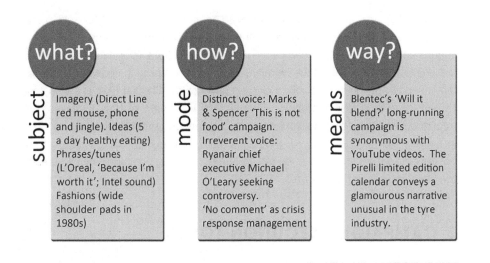

| **what?** subject | **how?** mode | **way?** means |
| --- | --- | --- |
| Imagery (Direct Line red mouse, phone and jingle). Ideas (5 a day healthy eating) Phrases/tunes (L'Oreal, 'Because I'm worth it'; Intel sound) Fashions (wide shoulder pads in 1980s) | Distinct voice: Marks & Spencer 'This is not food' campaign. Irreverent voice: Ryanair chief executive Michael O'Leary seeking controversy. 'No comment' as crisis response management | Blentec's 'Will it blend?' long-running campaign is synonymous with YouTube videos. The Pirelli limited edition calendar conveys a glamourous narrative unusual in the tyre industry. |

**FIGURE 8.6** Narrative approach and memes

**ACTION POINT**

The Royal Wedding of Prince William and Catherine Middleton in 2011 generated several memes. One internet trend was the 'Frowning Flower Girl' image of three-year-old Grace Van Cutsem introduced into various amusing situations. Another was a video of a verger doing a cartwheel in Westminster Abbey, which became a YouTube sensation. Princesses Eugenie and Beatrice had their outfits spoofed as the stepsisters of Disney's Cinderella, with thousands of Photoshop images of Princess Beatrice's hat, which raised over £81,000 for charity when sold on eBay. Finally, interest in chief bridesmaid Pippa Middleton's bottom saw a Facebook group in its honour attract almost 250,000 likes.

These illustrate Moloney's point (2006: 144) that brands 'attract public attention in ways that are not always welcome to their constructors. Sometimes they are connected to popular culture in ironic, creative ways and are transformed into counter-cultural icons'.

■ Can you recall these memes?
■ Why do you think people adapt and transmit the memes?
■ How can these ideas be related to creating a narrative approach?
■ What are the implications of such subversion of news stories for PR practitioners?

Green (2010) argues PR practitioners need to make communications coherent, copyable and robust to benefit from the features of a meme. Stories, slogans, images and brand identities can be strong forms of cultural information. To enable these and other elements of the narrative approach to harness the power of memes, they need to hook into the public's existing psychology (Chapter 6). It is also useful to consider the diffusion process (Chapter 16) in respect of how ideas spread throughout society. PR practitioners can produce meme-friendly communications, in formats that facilitate easy distribution (Figure 8.6), but cannot guarantee they will become viral. It should also be remembered that once communications spread, they take on a life of their own.

## 3 CAMPAIGN EXECUTION TOOLS

The campaign strategy and narrative approach provide guidance to implement what needs to be said and done. Appropriate tools and tactics need to be deployed in a responsive and responsible manner to achieve the campaign objectives and measurable outcomes. Tools, techniques and tactics are considered throughout *The PR Strategic Toolkit* providing expert insight into the effectiveness of various options. A checklist and decision-making guidelines are included in the Appendix on pp. 342–344.

Gregory (2000) suggests two tests for tactics:

- Appropriateness – Will they reach the target publics? Will they have the right impact? Are they credible and influential? Do they suit the message? Are they compatible with other communication devices the organisation is using?
- Deliverability – Can they be implemented successfully, within the budget and required timescale? Are the right people available to implement them?

Chapter 9 details methods for determining a timeframe, costs and resources to execute a planned programme of tactics.

### Health and safety

Campaign plans need to consider legislation constraints including health and safety issues. This may involve compliance with existing policies or contractual arrangements; ensuring adequate public liability insurance is in place; training and documenting procedures. At times, constraints may need to be overcome for the successful implementation of tactics. This requires professional negotiation and possibly revision or adaptation of plans.

# SECURING APPROVAL

All the work involved in research, setting objectives, developing a strategy, building a narrative framework and preparing a programme of tactics will be wasted without securing approval to implement the plan.

In addition to understanding the validity of recommendations, decision-makers need to understand how they relate to organisational objectives, integrate with other functions and have an operational impact. For example, plans may involve action outside the PR function's remit to address problems or maximise opportunities. They may also require support of external partners, suppliers, stakeholders or publics, which needs to be detailed within the report.

Discussion with managers while developing the plan can be a useful way of engaging them and understanding what they are looking for. In general, senior managers are persuaded by arguments that draw on evidence (logic), imagination (creativity) and understanding (theory).

## Evidence

The use of evidence – research, statistics and other analysis – shows a logical and intelligent basis for your campaign. Ensure evidence is credible and presented in a coherent and considered way. Creative elements need to be supported by proof of viability and likely success rather than just being clever. Feedback from a focus group, for example, would be helpful insight into public reception of ideas and narrative elements.

## Imagination

As discussed above, a campaign concept provides cohesion for proposed ideas. An imaginative campaign strategy, narrative and/or individual tactics must be clearly connected to achieving the required objectives. When proposing original or unusual ideas, it is important to acknowledge potential risks and how these can be minimised. A risk management checklist can be found in the Appendix on p. 349.

Ideas need to be presented in a way that enables the management to visualise their impact. Ensure mock-ups of any visuals are executed professionally and feed-back from research is also clearly understandable.

## Understanding

Use of theoretical concepts and models demonstrate a body of evidence supports suggestions, although care needs to be taken to avoid unfamiliar academic terms. Showing appropriate use of tools and studies in developing recommendations demonstrates intelligence and builds the credibility of plans.

## Campaign proposals

Campaign plans may be produced as a written report or a presentation. Organisations may have specific requirements for the style and content of proposals, such as a one-page summary, a detailed report (including supporting evidence), credentials and details of previous experience (in the case of a consultancy pitch document) or samples of specific tasks or tactics to be undertaken within the campaign.

The proposal needs to detail next steps or dates by which a decision should be made. Murray and White (2004) note concern among senior executives that PR practitioners do not demonstrate 'a good enough "radar" for emerging issues'. These authors urge practitioners to articulate more clearly to CEOs their strategic role. This underlines the importance of using research and analysis to provide intelligent insight into issues and opportunities affecting the organisation.

A report or presentation should demonstrate recommendations are both goal-directed and activity-focused. It is normally a good idea to structure a plan chronologically reflecting inductive reasoning. This is a process whereby a rational argument is built leading to recommendations and conclusions. Research and analysis would start the report to highlight understanding and insight into the situation. That would lead on to specific objectives, strategy and tactics before detailing required resources, method of evaluation and a summary of the recommendations at the end of the report.

Given the pressures on management time, it is likely that such a structured report will be preceded by an executive summary that presents a stand-alone overview of the entire campaign, which could be referenced in isolation of the more detailed report.

The key to a successful report is to ensure that essential information can be easily found, with appendices, references and sources noted for further information if it is required. If presenting an action plan (rather than a campaign proposal), it should include details of tasks to be executed alongside responsibilities and deadlines by which they should be completed. Contingency plans may also be included to anticipate events that may occur and enable a 'plan B' to be followed.

Presentation needs to be professional, with high-quality materials reflecting the standard of work involved. The proposal may be an initial recommendation subject to change on the basis of management feedback or additional research. The impact of any changes needs to be understood, particularly on budget and required outcomes. Consultancies need to be clear over issues of intellectual property and confidentiality.

Approval is likely to involve a process of discussion, and additional information or responses to questions may be required. This may require adaption of initial recommendations; although the implications of such accommodation need to be understood. There are also times where proposals may challenge existing practices or management's expectations. Presenting a situation using informed, rather than emotional, arguments is more likely to be successful.

To gain support from members of senior management, knowledge of their challenges, requirements, psychology and interests can be used to ensure the proposal is an effective form of communication. This is an important opportunity to build strong professional relationships and identify ways to engage key influencers in the work of public relations.

## END POINT

Campaign strategies and narrative approaches offer a structured method for considering the actions and communications that need to be executed to achieve strategic objectives. A rational decision-making approach is recommended, alongside recognition of the need for creative approaches. This combination of evidence, imagination and understanding underpins campaign proposals to ensure executive approval of recommendations.

# Budgeting and resourcing

*Heather Yaxley*

This chapter provides a straightforward approach to budgeting and resourcing including identifying requirements, determining costs, presenting financial reports and other skills required in performance control management.

## CHECK POINT

After reading this chapter, you should be able to:

- take a practical management approach to planning budgets and resource requirements;
- understand the process of performance control reporting.

## HUMAN RESOURCE PLANNING AND MANAGEMENT

Practical management of campaigns requires allocation of human resources to undertake the agreed action plan. Activities may be undertaken by a permanent internal PR function, or an external resource (freelance or consultancy) providing strategic or operational support.

When looking to execute a campaign, the nature of work involved needs to be considered. The capability of any internal PR function to plan, manage and execute the project should be assessed alongside requirements to manage routine operations. If the campaign cannot be handled internally, consultancy resource will be sought.

Roles and responsibilities need to be determined and built into the detailed planning process.

# Consultancy resource

External PR support offers expertise and additional human resources. A consultancy may be contracted to provide:

- strategic advice;
- execution of programmes (independently or alongside in-house teams);
- retained PR services (with a monthly fee) at an agreed level;
- ad-hoc or routine project work.

Organisations may appoint consultancies for one-off projects, develop long-term relationships or maintain a roster of consultancies for specific purposes or used on rota.

A detailed PR brief (see Appendix, p. 332) specifies requirements of a campaign (including specific objectives) prior to agreement of a proposal/quote and an official contract. Details of the agreed programme of work, budget, resources and so forth are set out in a contract, alongside financial paperwork (such as purchase orders enabling prompt invoicing). Even when long-standing relationships exist, this professional approach helps avoid misunderstanding and minimise risk (Chapter 13).

When responding to a client brief, a PR consultancy will identify the team undertaking the project, drawing on appropriate levels of knowledge, experience and skills. The team may comprise an account manager (primary client contact), a number of executives and support personnel (full- or part-time to the campaign), plus specialists and experts for specific projects. The consultancy manages the campaign, regularly updating the client on progress. Status reports (see Appendix, p. 345) detail work undertaken and budget allocation. Consultancies may outsource key functions (e.g. media planning, multi-media production, new media/web design) or have the internal resources to undertake these.

The cost of employing a consultancy is based on the time dedicated to the account or project. Personnel are charged at an hourly or daily rate, with the team completing time sheets to monitor how long is spent on individual tasks. This is not simply to ensure that clients are charged accurately, but it enables performance to be monitored. Budgets are calculated on the basis of forecasting time required (which is likely to be based on previous records). Clients may quote a fixed cost, based on an estimated or specific time involvement. Should the nature of the project change, consultancies should review the plan or budget (or both) with the client.

The client–consultancy relationship can be a fractious one. This is most notable in respect of consultancy claims of over-servicing accounts and client counter-claims of exaggerating billable time or under-delivering on promised results. Pieczka (2006) highlights a third perspective, that of consultancy personnel who experience a long-hours culture without paid overtime. This is evident in the results of the *PR Census* (Gorkana 2011) and debate in the industry regarding paid internships (Cartmell 2011b).

Consultancies also charge for additional services including costs of materials, phone calls, travel costs and other expenses. A markup may be charged on bought-in costs, subject to agreement with the client. This normally reflects the accounting consequence (and possible risk) of the consultancy making payments on behalf of clients.

## In-house resource

Even if the campaign is to be executed in-house, human resource requirements need to be determined. Appropriate staff and skill sets need to be identified with work on the project scheduled alongside other responsibilities. It can be useful to consider an hourly cost for internal staff in order to make comparisons against the costs of external resources.

The cost of maintaining an internal resource includes salaries, fixed costs involved in providing a professional working environment, plus costs of training, holiday entitlement and other employee benefits. Charges for equipment (computers, telephones and so on) as well as postage, photocopying, travel and other ongoing costs may be hidden within the accountancy process, but are still met by the organisation. Some organisations cross-charge for PR support provided to other departments (acting as an internal consultancy). The PR function may also be charged if it utilises other personnel or internal services.

## Time management

Working in PR requires multi-tasking – which means having good time management, administrative and prioritising skills. In some organisations, even when working at a senior level, the PR practitioner may not have additional staff and be required to implement rather than just plan activities. Research by Moss *et al.* (2004) reveals most senior managers retain personal responsibility for important elements of technical craft work, such as writing speeches for senior executives or handling highly critical/sensitive tasks such as releasing financial information.

Covey (1989) provides a useful matrix plotting tasks in relation to urgency and importance, which is helpful in looking at time management and workload in PR (Figure 9.1).

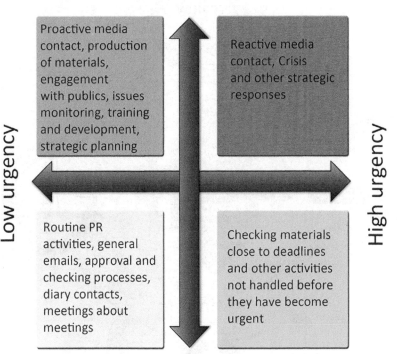

## High importance

Proactive media contact, production of materials, engagement with publics, issues monitoring, training and development, strategic planning

Reactive media contact, Crisis and other strategic responses

Low urgency

High urgency

Routine PR activities, general emails, approval and checking processes, diary contacts, meetings about meetings

Checking materials close to deadlines and other activities not handled before they have become urgent

## Low importance

**FIGURE 9.1** Time management matrix

Based on Covey (1989)

# Time planning

Any campaign will comprise a series of activities that need to be scheduled. This requires assessment of how long such tasks will take to be planned and implemented, as well as the required skills to undertake the allocated activities.

The timescale within which the PR campaign is to be executed can affect resource requirements. For example, if a situation is urgent, additional human and financial resource may be necessary. If there is sufficient time to plan ahead, it may be possible to deliver a campaign with fewer people or more efficient use of resource. Figure 9.2 details considerations involved in developing a timeframe for a campaign.

Mapping the tasks to be undertaken enables consideration of human resource requirements, the deadlines of external suppliers and internal approval processes. It also provides a sanity check on the detailed programme of activities in terms of

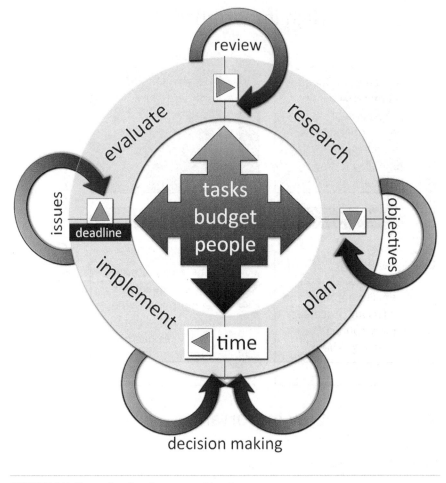

**FIGURE 9.2** Campaign timeframe considerations

its feasibility. If too many tasks have been proposed within a short period of time, additional resource may be required or the campaign may need to be revised. A flexible approach is necessary as it is likely circumstances will arise and affect the planned schedule, even if it has been accurately mapped.

Roles and responsibilities need to be allocated for individual tasks with deadlines that are monitored during the planning and implementation stages (see Appendix).

In determining a suitable campaign or programme of work, the manager needs to have a clear understanding of time availability and what is achievable before any fixed deadlines. Any campaign will comprise a series of activities that need to be scheduled and this requires reflection on how long such tasks need to be planned and implemented. It is necessary also to consider the skills and experience of the people undertaking the allocated activities.

It is important to establish priorities and ensure that time is managed in relation to achieving specific targets. Recognition of key outcomes and how a task will be evaluated is also important in determining how best to allocate time. Where other people or organisations are involved in a campaign, their time management also needs to be considered. Where aspects of the campaign are outsourced or approval is required from management, a reasonable allowance of time, including contingency, needs to be determined.

In order to understand the amount of time required for a task to be undertaken, previous experience can be used as an indicator. Detailed time-diaries, such as those used in consultancies, can be very useful for planning purposes. It is important also to maintain accurate files for previous projects as these can provide a helpful guide to future activities. Other people who have undertaken similar activities or published examples of case studies may also be consulted. Aspects such as meetings, travel, status reports, administration and routine communications on any activity need to be built into plans. Time also needs to be allowed for research, analysis, planning, securing agreement from management, evaluation and a final review of outcomes.

## Critical path analysis

This process considers which elements of a campaign take the longest time and so affect when the project can be completed. It also enables reflection on which tasks are dependent on the completion of others and which can be undertaken simultaneously. It will be necessary to factor in constraints of external resources (e.g. suppliers' deadlines) and available internal resources (who is able to undertake various tasks). Decisions about use of resource and what can be achieved in a particular timeframe or to meet a deadline can then be made. Computer systems such as Microsoft Project enable tasks to be planned, resources considered and progress monitored. Tools such as a GANTT chart or PERT can be helpful in planning complex tasks (see Appendix, p. 346).

## Project calendars

Another option is to map out tasks and key deadlines on a project calendar (see Appendix, p. 346). This can be particularly helpful for larger campaigns or those with a longer timeframe (e.g. annual plans). A timetable of activities by date enables a clear visual picture of the scope of the project to be understood and any conflicts or potential resource constraints identified at an early stage. Peaks in activity may highlight the need to plan for additional resources. Holidays and other personal and ongoing departmental commitments can be factored into the plan.

## BUDGETING

Resource and time are two key elements in effective campaign management, alongside cost control. These three elements need to be considered alongside the scope and quality requirements (Wysocki 2011) for the campaign. Figure 9.3 illustrates the relationships between these five aspects. Requirements in one or more of these will impact on other aspects indicating a need to determine the ideal balance, as well as the consequences of issues that are likely to arise.

A financial budget may be presented as a fixed element of a campaign, particularly in the current economic climate. Indeed, cuts may have been made year-on-year with expectations of delivering the same results for lower investment.

The budget needs to include the cost of people resources as discussed above. Some organisations have a formal procurement process whereby consultancies (and other suppliers) need to be approved prior to work being undertaken. Quotes for services are used in building a budget. The cost of PR consultancies varies significantly, depending on factors including size, expertise and location, as well as the level and competency of personnel undertaking the campaign. Bought-in goods

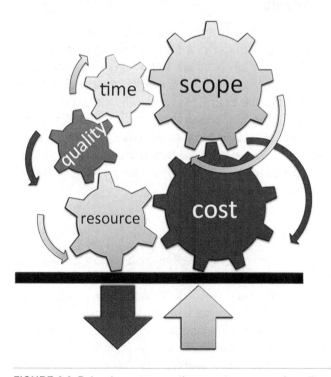

**FIGURE 9.3** Balancing resource, time, cost, scope and quality

and services may include print and design costs for materials, audio-visual services, external suppliers (on retainer or project basis), event organisation, photography, staging, hospitality, travel, etc.

Budgeting to the penny is not advisable since it is unlikely that cost predictions will be 100 per cent accurate at the outset, although reasonable estimates are possible. Rather than adding a certain percentage figure to a budget to allow for contingencies (unexpected or unforeseen costs), clients/managers expect to be consulted on any additional costs as they arise. If these can be anticipated, the proposal should set out the options enabling clients to plan accordingly.

The budget may be affected by the time available to plan and execute the campaign. If time is short, premium prices may be charged. This can be built into the critical path analysis and clients/managers informed in status reports of the implications of any slippage.

Some budget areas may be covered by overall or departmental costs depending on how the financial resources are determined by the individual organisation. Costs such as postage, stationery, etc. may be covered on a corporate basis; an 'overhead' charge may be placed on the department or coding used to recharge exact costs. The cost of expenses incurred by internal personnel also needs to be calculated.

# Control processes

When planning a budget, it is important to consider control processes, which are likely to also be a budget item (e.g. evaluation). Cole (2004) outlines the key steps in establishing a budget control system:

- Forecasts – statements that determine probable costs and other relevant data.
- Budgets – based on the analysis of previous experiences that include any income generation and variable, fixed or capital costs.
- Departmental and corporate budgets – managers are required to produce overall departmental budgets, beyond those for specific campaigns or purposes. These are fed into overall corporate budgets, which take account of the organisation's total income and expenditure, profit objectives and so on.
- Period budget statements – these inform management about performance against targets in relation to relevant periods of time and specify costs incurred and accruals (costs for which invoices have not been received).
- Action required – if any issues are identified in relation to budgets, action will be required to resolve such problems.

Cutlip *et al.* (2000) suggest three useful guidelines:

- knowing the exact cost of what is required in undertaking the activities;
- communicating the budget in terms of what it costs to achieve specific results;
- using computer programmes (spreadsheets) to track costs of individual projects matching actual against projected.

## Methods of setting budgets

Budget planning involves securing agreement on costs required to execute proposed action to achieve specific objectives. Different organisations have different approaches to setting budgets:

- Arbitrarily – a budget figure is allocated without any analysis.
- All you can afford – the organisation decides what it can afford to spend on PR. This may be arbitrary or related to surplus over expenses.
- Historical basis – a figure is allocated relating to what has previously been spent.
- Competitive necessity – the PR budget is set in relation to the standard in the industry or to address a competitive weakness/opportunity.
- Percentage of income – PR budgets may be agreed as a certain percentage of sales income (or fund-raising income in the case of charities) or in relation to the marketing budget.
- Experiment and testing – the budget may be allocated dependent on proving its effectiveness.
- Modelling and simulation – there may be a formula used to predict the required budget.
- Situation driven – the budget may be allocated according to a particular situation, such as to support launch of a new product.
- Objective and task – this is the best approach in terms of determining what needs to be done to achieve the objective. There will obviously be constraints according to what the organisation can afford and the strategic relevance of the activities.

Setting a budget may seem complex but it is a simple matter of determining what needs to be done and researching what it will cost. This is an iterative process as the costs calculated may raise questions about the planned activities and either the plan or the budget needs to be amended.

# Presenting budgets

Organisations may have budget forms and systems that need to be followed. In general, easy to understand tables are used (normally spreadsheets) where costs are specified for individual tasks and an overall cost is calculated (see Appendix, p. 348). Within a campaign proposal, the key elements of the budget would be detailed and managers could expect to be questioned on both the overall figure and specific items. Sufficient detail is necessary to ensure managers understand the financial and resource implications of recommendations. Additional detail would be included in campaign plans, with an operational budget used to track ongoing and final expenditure.

Proposals need to include budgets that reflect the level of expenditure advised by the client, or if no budget was set, it needs to be reasonable for the anticipated results. Detailed explanation can be included to clarify specific aspects or outline options that can be determined before proceeding.

As well as ensuring that any budget takes account of all the tasks included within the plan (including research and evaluation costs), it needs to be sanity checked in relation to the objectives that are to be achieved. Simple calculations such as a cost per head to attend an event can be made. In addition, brand standards of the organisation need to be factored to ensure that budgets are commensurate. For example, the Royal Bank of Scotland reduced its corporate hospitality budget by 90 per cent in 2011, reflecting expectations of a state-owned rather than public sector organisation.

Any campaign needs to be reviewed to consider whether the objectives could have been achieved at a lower cost to ensure that ideas proposed are not disproportionate in terms of return on investment.

# PERFORMANCE CONTROL REPORTING

The management of campaigns and programmes of work involves an understanding of time planning and allocation of budgets and human resources. This requires organisational skills and an ability to produce effective plans to enable others to work efficiently and effectively on tasks. In addition, PR planning and management involves control and reporting of standards of performance and the achievement of desired outcomes.

Management information systems enable reports to be produced, utilising quantitative and qualitative data from a variety of sources. As discussed in Chapter 5, PRISM can be used to inform management decision-making. The strategic campaign planning and execution process outlined in Part II includes documents and information which can be included in the PRISM approach and support ongoing management.

The five elements of effective campaign management (Figure 9.2) need to be monitored and reported, with consideration made of the impact of any variation from plans.

## Human resource

The performance of individuals (whether in-house, consultants or other suppliers) needs to be monitored, controlled and reported. Meetings and status reports are used to monitor progress within the campaign. If a project management system is being used, the consequences of any variance in human resource performance can be considered in respect of impact on finances, time management, etc. In addition, regular team reviews, including official appraisal systems, enable individual perform-ance to be assessed and corrective action implemented. Acknowledgement of achievements is a key component of personnel performance management.

Individuals should also be encouraged to monitor their own performance as part of a proactive career management strategy. As discussed in Chapter 16, some organisations are using gamification systems to motivate personnel through sugges-tion schemes and appraisal programmes.

## Time

Time management has been discussed earlier in this chapter. Monitoring progress on a timely basis, using critical path analysis and project calendars is recommended. In addition, updating daily task plans and monitoring any slippage is a useful monitoring approach. Close management of suppliers, particularly those with whom there is no existing relationship, is important. Printers, for example, are notorious at missing deadlines. Contracts can include penalty clauses to help minimise the risk of slippage, or at least help manage the financial consequences.

## Cost

Performance control reporting includes review of monthly (or more frequent) financial statements of proposed and actual expenditure. Controls on finances also need to indicate where action is required and determine return on investment made.

## Scope

Monitoring and managing the scope of the planned campaign involves determining progress towards achieving the specified objectives. Reports should be produced to determine the attainment of specific deliverables or milestones in a campaign. Remedial action can be identified to accommodate any problems incurred. Adjust-ment where necessary of the objectives can be made or other elements of the plan altered as appropriate.

## Quality

Standards of performance can also evaluate the quality of work undertaken. Any issues or problems arising need to be addressed (Chapter 13).

## Reporting

As well as producing reports to monitor progress of a campaign, regular reporting to management is recommended to demonstrate a professional approach for PR management. Simple one-page documents conveying key indicators could be produced (see Appendix, p. 345). It is important to be open and honest regarding any problems or issues that have been experienced, with implications and solutions outlined.

## PRACTICAL MANAGEMENT CONSIDERATIONS

Although there are many valid reasons to take a planned approach to public relations, it may not be feasible or possible to adhere to such processes in all circumstances. Practical limitations and considerations include:

- Real world complexity: The process of planning may create an illusion of control by focusing on a set of steps to be undertaken. The complexity of actually executing plans is a reminder of the importance of an adaptive approach where flexibility needs to be built in to plans to accommodate changes in the internal or external environment.

- Partnership effects: The planning approach largely focuses on actions for a particular organisation, but the actions and objectives of stakeholders and publics need to be considered. This is to be considered particularly when undertaking campaigns in partnership with others, seeking to build relationships or engage in two-way communications. Involving others in the planning process and considering the impact of their actions is advised.

- Unforeseen circumstances: Some circumstances cannot be anticipated when decisions are made, or things may not go to plan. Risk, issues and crisis management (Chapter 13) should be undertaken, especially for any campaigns that are of significant strategic importance.

- Intended vs. realised strategy: Mintzberg and Waters (1985, cited by Henry 2008) distinguish between the intended strategy (the one chosen for the campaign) and the realised strategy (the one actually carried out). This reflects an adaptive approach, where managers use experience and learning to develop and implement an emergent strategy (which becomes the realised strategy). It is important to recognise such developments and identify factors that affected execution of the intended strategy. There may have been inherent problems with the original proposed strategy or other reasons offering lessons to be learned for future planning.

- Limitations: Planning is ultimately about what can be done with the available time, money and resources, rather than what is ideal or desirable. If the problems discussed in Chapter 7 regarding objective setting have not been avoided, PR activities would not have been able to achieve the unrealistic aims set for them. The plan may also have been compromised by cuts or issues emerging that affected the time, money and resources that were foreseen during the initial planning stage.

- Lack of planning: In the case of routine or ad-hoc opportunities, PR activities may not warrant a full plan as discussed in this section. The principles of thinking before acting remain important and the consequences of failing to plan can be surprising impactful, even resulting in crisis situations.

- Irrationality: Practitioners may prefer to rely on experience and knowledge, to act intuitively without a rigorous process of research or planning. Instincts can be useful, but could reflect irrationality and be a faulty guide to future behaviour. Feelings and gut instinct are not always the most reliable, or professional approach to good management.

- Zeitgeist: Changes in society, cultural considerations (especially for international or localised campaigns) and timing issues can have an impact on the implementation of campaigns. It is possible that plans can be hugely successful sometimes and an absolute failure another time owing to factors that may seem to be entirely outside our control, and simply reflect a changing zeitgeist.

## END POINT

An organised approach enables management of five key elements of campaign plans: human resources, budgets, time, scope and quality. Information management systems and processes help to predict, monitor and report on each element. The successful implementation of plans to achieve the required objectives can still be affected by a number of practical considerations, emphasising the importance of an adaptive approach.

# CHAPTER 10

# Monitoring and evaluation

*Heather Yaxley*

This chapter presents an ongoing, iterative approach to monitoring and evaluation. It supports formative guidance and adaptation of plans through the implementation phase rather than a rigid approach of final assessment.

## CHECK POINT

After reading this chapter, you should be able to:

- identify recent developments in PR evaluation;
- understand the value of pre-emptive, formative and summative evaluation in strategic PR management;
- adopt a practical approach to monitor and evaluate PR campaigns.

## DEVELOPMENT OF PR EVALUATION

Almost every PR textbook describes evaluation as the holy grail of public relations. It is time this predictable, Pavlovian reaction ceased. Evaluation should not be seen as a legendary, mythical, intangible, unattainable mystery. PR practitioners need to stop hiding behind excuses or poor practices and accept evaluation as normal operating practice.

**ACTION POINT**

- Batchelor (1938) notes the Roosevelt administration monitored changes in political attitudes to assess the reception of its publicity activities. He observes the Works Progress Administration achieved 'great local publicity' (p. 212) but little coverage of its real objective to put unemployed men back to work; this misunderstanding became a 'political liability'. A revision of the communications policy altered the emphasis of media materials increasing favourable editorial coverage from 10 to over 40 per cent.

- The in-house PR operation of the Bell Telephone System was cited as typical of large-scale business in monitoring and responding to critical letters published in local newspapers to correct inaccurate allegations.

*These simple examples illustrate early practical use of monitoring and adaptation to achieve specific outcomes.*

■ Why might evaluation have been viewed as difficult in subsequent years?

■ What impact does resistance to evaluation have on the reputation of PR practitioners?

Watson (2011) demonstrates evaluation has a long history with social science methods evident in the 1920s and 1930s. Indeed, he notes a full circle (with 'new' techniques echoing those in use almost a century ago) following decades of resistance by practitioners. The prevailing attitude has been that evaluation is difficult and the real measure of success is a happy client.

Since the 1990s, evaluation has been taken more seriously, although Gregory and White (2008) note progress has been slow. Momentum was gained by the *PR Week* Proof Campaign in 1998 (which urged 10 per cent of budgets be allocated to research and evaluation) and the joint industry PRE-fix initiative, which published a Research and Evaluation Toolkit. However, Pieczka (2006) notes this enthusiasm didn't last owing to economic constraints.

Interest in evaluation has been revived with the publication of the *Barcelona Declaration of Research Principles* (2010), which stressed:

- Goal setting and measurement are essential.
- Media measurement requires quantity and quality.
- AVEs are not the value of public relations.
- Social media can and should be measured.

## ADVERTISING VALUE EQUIVALENT (AVE)

AVE involves calculating a financial figure for media coverage on the basis of what this would have cost if bought as advertising. Published advertising rates are used to produce a financial measure for the number of column centimetres achieved by media relations activities. McKeone (1995) states AVEs 'represent an early effort to assign spurious monetary values to media relations activities'. Research by AMEC (2011) found the majority of PR practitioners (55 per cent) use AVE measures.

There are many reasons why this approach is inappropriate:

- Advertisers do not evaluate the success of their work by what it costs; they use recall, attitude and behavioural change measures.

- Multipliers of three to seven times (McKeone 1995) applied on the basis that positive media endorsement or even general editorial coverage is more 'valuable' than advertising are not justified or proven by research.

- AVE values public relations on the basis of fluctuating advertising rates.

- AVE does not accommodate brief mentions or neutral/negative coverage, let alone where PR practitioners have acted to ensure negative coverage is not published.

- AVE does not allow for publications without advertising.

- AVE does not apply to broadcast or online media.

- AVE may be counter-productive as some short pieces of coverage can be very influential, where a large article, may not be read.

Media coverage can be evaluated in ways other than AVE. Simply checks are the relevance of media in which coverage is obtained. Content analysis can be used to check whether aspects of the campaign's narrative have been used, and identify any negative aspects (which can be addressed going forwards). More importantly, surveys and other forms of research (Chapter 5) need to be undertaken to test the effectiveness of media coverage. The cost of this should be built into the budget.

■ Why do you think this method has proven to be popular in PR?

■ Which of the above arguments do you find most influential in arguing against its continued use?

■ PR Award programmes are increasingly banning AVE measurements; what impact do you think this may have on their use?

- Measuring outcomes is preferred to measuring media results.
- Business (organisational) results can and should be measured where possible.
- Transparency and replicability are paramount to sound measurement.

In 2011, the 3rd European Summit on Measurement identified the following top priorities:

- developing global standards for social media measurement;
- further education of the PR profession;
- new work on the ROI (return on investment) of public relations.

## Return on investment

Watson and Zerfass (2011: 11) observe that although the term ROI is commonly used in PR practice and literature, it reflects a 'fuzzy concept'. They argue:

the complexity of communication processes and their role in business inter-actions means it is not possible to calculate Return on Investment in financial terms. Consequently, public relations practitioners should refrain from using the term in order to keep their vocabulary compatible with the overall management world.

## A hierarchy of effects approach

Dr David Rockland, partner and head of global research at Ketchum Pleon, commenting (Rockland 2011) on recent developments in evaluation said:

The reality is there is no simple, easy, perfect or single metric to measure PR. It really depends on what you are trying to accomplish with a PR program as to what you in turn measure. So the idea we're behind is that PR has a whole load of different uses and effects – one could be selling a product or a brand, another could be measuring a company's reputation, another could be dealing with an issue or crisis, another is employee retention and so on. For each of those there is a recommended series of metrics depending on what you are trying to do.

Figure 10.1 illustrates the recommended grid approach that emerged from the 3rd summit. It plots PR activity, output and outcome measurement for different communications/marketing stages: awareness, knowledge/understanding, interest/consideration, support/preference and action. This reflects the hierarchy of effects perspective which asserts that people move through a linear sequence of steps (Chapter 7). As such, it can be critiqued as reflecting a simplistic understanding of public psychology (Chapter 6).

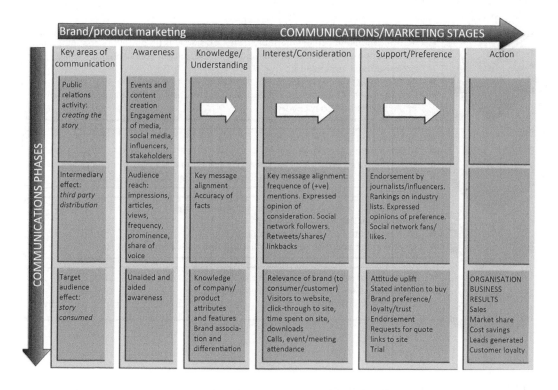

**FIGURE 10.1** Overview of the Valid Metrics Framework proposed by AMEC (2011)

# PRE-EMPTIVE, FORMATIVE AND SUMMATIVE EVALUATION

Pre-emptive evaluation involves assessment of campaign plans prior to implementation. This is an important stage to check feasibility and assess risks. As a reflective process, pre-emptive evaluation helps anticipate problems or issues. Chapter 13 considers risk assessment in detail with useful checklists in the Appendix on pp. 349–353.

Formative evaluation is undertaken during implementation of a campaign. It encourages reflection and adjustment of the plan. Specific stages or milestones may be set as points when formative evaluation takes place. Alternatively, feedback loops may offer continuous evaluation. Care needs to be taken in interpreting the significance of information at this point in the plan.

Summative evaluation takes place at the end of a campaign or when a major component has been completed. It involves robust consideration of all aspects undertaken to date.

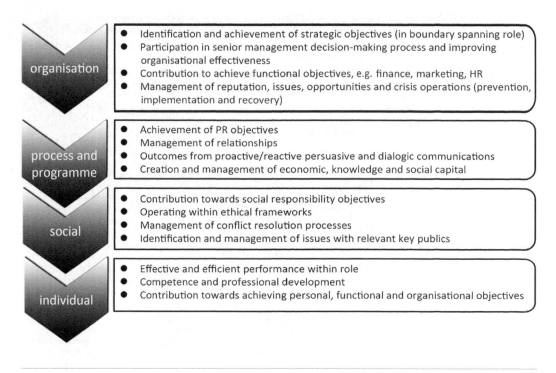

**organisation**
- Identification and achievement of strategic objectives (in boundary spanning role)
- Participation in senior management decision-making process and improving organisational effectiveness
- Contribution to achieve functional objectives, e.g. finance, marketing, HR
- Management of reputation, issues, opportunities and crisis operations (prevention, implementation and recovery)

**process and programme**
- Achievement of PR objectives
- Management of relationships
- Outcomes from proactive/reactive persuasive and dialogic communications
- Creation and management of economic, knowledge and social capital

**social**
- Contribution towards social responsibility objectives
- Operating within ethical frameworks
- Management of conflict resolution processes
- Identification and management of issues with relevant key publics

**individual**
- Effective and efficient performance within role
- Competence and professional development
- Contribution towards achieving personal, functional and organisational objectives

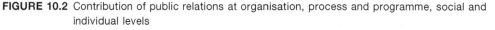

**FIGURE 10.2** Contribution of public relations at organisation, process and programme, social and individual levels

Pre-emptive, formative and summative evaluation can be applied to task and outcome objectives. CIPR claims PR's contribution can be determined at organisation, process and programme, social and individual levels. These approaches are illustrated in Figure 10.2.

Pre-emptive evaluation involves assessment of campaign plans prior to implementation. This should check validity and risk within the planning process as well as reviewing the actions within the campaign. If insurance is required to minimise the impact of any risk, this needs to be included in the campaign budget. A brief risk assessment should be included in campaign proposals and ongoing management reports.

The research stage of planning (Chapter 1) should provide foresight as well as insight. This suggests an iterative approach with research undertaking into plans prior to their implementation. Such information is useful in supporting recommendations and enabling adjustments. Different options can be proposed, tested and reviewed.

# Task/process evaluation

Chapter 7 distinguished task/process and outcome objectives. This same approach is required for evaluation. Measures assessing, for example, whether or not a Twitter account was set up, press releases distributed or an annual report delivered to schedule, do not reflect the effect of the action taken.

Pickton and Broderick (2005: 357) identify evaluation of tasks should consider:

- efficiency – doing things right
- effectiveness – doing the right things
- economy – doing things within a specified budget.

These present operational measures that can be useful when assessing the performance of processes, suppliers, the PR function or individual team members. Similarly, Eiró-Gomes and Duarte (2008) focus primarily on functional aspects of evaluating PR activities:

- conceptualisation and design
- implementation
- impact and efficiency.

A comprehensive post-campaign review offers a summative assessment opportunity. Findings may suggest action that needs to be taken, for example, to inform future plans or suggest development needs for team members. Reviews provide useful research within the PRISM approach (Chapter 5).

Performance also needs to be monitored during the execution of activities. This formative review is important to identify any problems or issues where remedial action can avoid incidents or crisis situations (Chapter 13). Pre-emptive evaluation pulls this assessment forward prior to implementation.

# Outcome evaluation

To demonstrate effectiveness of a campaign, the results specified in outcome objectives must be achieved. Figures 7.2 and 7.3 outline levels of objectives and relevant measures. Relevant outcomes are:

- knowledge – evaluating awareness, knowledge and understanding
- predisposition – evaluating attitudes and opinions
- behavioural – evaluating what people do
- relationship – evaluating mutual understanding and co-orientation
- reputation – evaluating trust and other relevant dimensions.

Methods of research to set benchmark objectives before a campaign is undertaken are considered in Chapters 5, 6 and 7. The same approaches should be used for formative and summative assessment.

# REVIEW AGAINST MANAGEMENT OBJECTIVES

MBO is proposed as way of improving the effectiveness of management (Chapter 7). Achievement of campaign outcomes can be linked to objectives for the PR function and individual team members enabling review within the organisation's appraisal system. Similarly, management of external suppliers, including PR consultancies, includes assessment of results, alongside evaluation of processes and the relationship with the organisation. Evaluation can also consider the value of resources invested in the campaign.

Any evaluation provides a snapshot in time and may need to be followed up to consider any long term impact. It is essential for a campaign to demonstrate internal integrity, which requires recognition that the sum of the individual parts add up to a compelling solution to the issue the organisation faces. This means a Gestalt approach to evaluation, assessing campaigns holistically as well as reviewing individual aspects.

If the PR campaign is integrated with activities of other disciplines such as marketing or human resource, it may be difficult to isolate the impact of particular activities. Nevertheless, suitable research and evaluation must be undertaken so the overall campaign can be assessed and any change in knowledge, attitude and behaviour of the target publics identified. Agreement on evaluation and reporting measures with other functions is important.

At the organisational level, evaluation needs to demonstrate PR activities represent a strategically valuable use of resources; contributing towards the wider objectives of the organisation. Evaluation can also indicate compliance with the organisational culture, mission/vision and overall aims.

Other management in the organisation should understand the value of a PR campaign and, where feasible, integrate activities or outcomes into their operations. For example, quotes from media coverage can be used within marketing campaigns (with permission). Indeed, in many cases, to achieve a strategic difference, the PR campaign must involve early discussion with other functions and be prepared to tackle any operational or other aspects of management that either caused the issue to occur or are acting as barriers to achieving change. Reporting on such processes can be included within evaluation reports.

# EVALUATION METHODS

The first step in evaluation is to determine the methods that need to be used for formative and summative assessment of progress against the stated campaign objectives (Chapters 5, 6 and 7). In addition, a variety of computer programmes and specialist agencies offer means of adding a scientific perspective to the challenge of evaluation.

The evaluation methodology used should be included in the campaign proposal, with details of ongoing and key stage assessment as well as final evaluation of results at the natural end of the campaign. If a programme of activity is ongoing, recommendations should be made for regular points at which measurement can be undertaken as part of the continuous PR management and planning cycle.

The methodology needs to identify how key lessons from the campaign will be learned and how remedial action can be undertaken should plans not proceed as predicted or other factors and issues arise.

Setting clear, SMART, objectives, makes it much easier to evaluate PR campaigns (Chapter 7). The value of the initial research (Chapters 5 and 6) is underpinned by an ability to revisit it to identify significant change as a result of the programme undertaken.

Evaluation may be undertaken within the PR function or by employing external experts who will assess campaigns using measures that may reflect industry standards, competitive perspectives or tailored for the client's specific purposes.

Evaluation should focus on the effect on the receiver:

- Output – what messages went out and who did they reach?
- Outtake – to what extent is the audience aware of the information sent out, what do they understand/recall and what do they feel about it?
- Outcome – to what degree did the PR activities change the opinion, behaviour and attitudes of audiences?

**READING POINT**

There are several leading authorities on measurement and evaluation. Their work offers an expert and detailed perspective. For example:

Lindenmann: *Guidelines for Measuring the Effectiveness of PR Programs and Activities* (2003).

Watson and Noble: *Evaluating Public Relations: a best practice guide to public relations* (2007).

Paine: *Measuring Public Relationships* (2007a), *Measure what Matters* (2011a), http://kdpaine.blogs.com/themeasurementstandard/ (2011b).

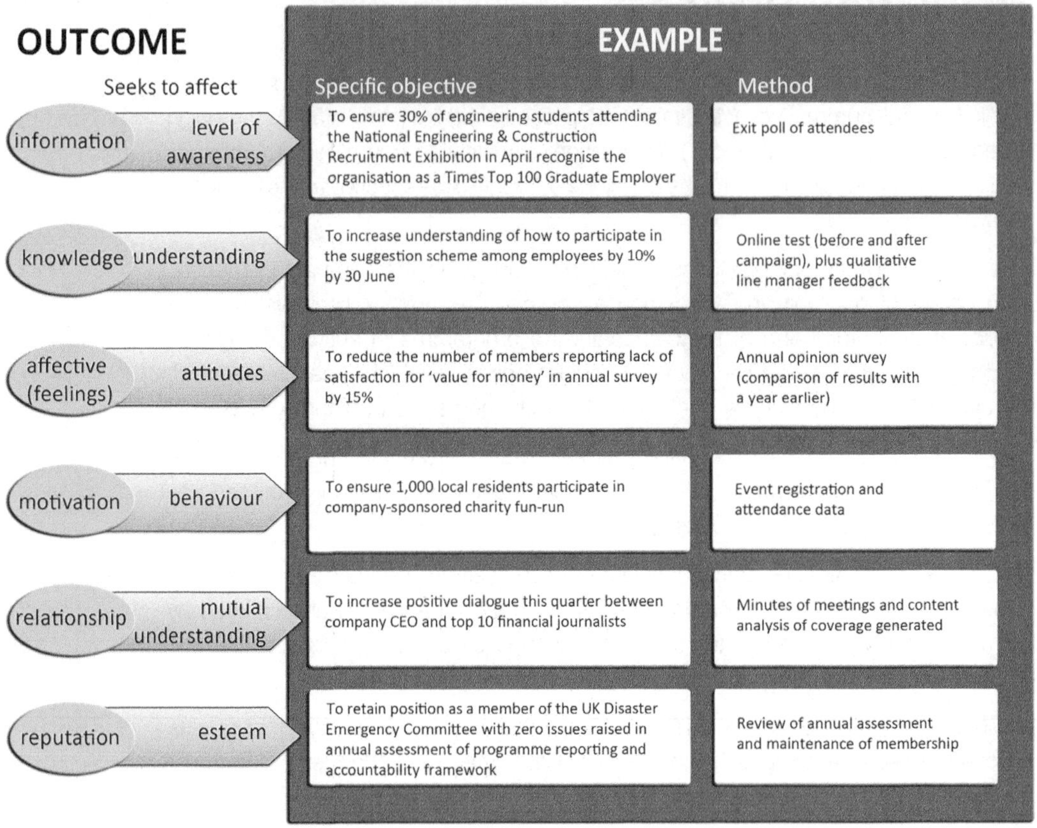

**FIGURE 10.3** Linking evaluation methods to objectives

This approach highlights the importance of what was achieved by the campaign rather than what was done in implementing it. Figure 10.3 provides information on several possible evaluation methods linking them to various objectives considered in Chapter 7. Monitoring and evaluating of digital public relations is considered in Chapter 16.

The cost of all evaluation needs to be included in the budget for the campaign, with human resources also considered (Chapter 9).

One final word on evaluation is to remember the Pareto Principle. In 1906, Italian economist Vilfredo Pareto created a mathematical formula that purports 20 per cent of something is always responsible for 80 per cent of the results (Gronstedt and Caywood 2011). Applying this to public relations activities, Gronstedt and Caywood claim, '20 per cent of all journalists account for 80 per cent of the media coverage of the company, and 20 per cent of all shareholders own 80 per cent of the company. The critical few are, in most cases, the most cost-effective group to

Evaluation is a frequent discussion point among PR practitioners using social networks such as LinkedIn. Members of the CIPR group have discussed alternative measures to AVE with a thread focusing on qualitative methods of evaluation.

One suggestion was the Media Relations Rating Points (MRP) developed by the Canadian Public Relations Society (http://mrpdata.com/). It facilitates analysis of print, broadcast and online coverage by criteria such as tone and cost-per-contact. This method can be incorporated into evaluation by specialist media analysis companies.

The Valid Metrics framework proposed by the International Association for the Measurement and Evaluation of Communication was also mentioned (see Figure 10.1). Similarly, a guide from the UK government's Central Office for Information was referenced. However, this did not include any measures that considered the impact of media coverage.

As well as the focus of such discussion remaining primarily on media relations, there is little recognition of the value of evaluation against objectives, or the range of qualitative methods discussed in Chapter 6. It does indicate how interest in evaluation is not being matched by an understanding of research principles and methodologies.

It is notable that there does not seem to be a research and evaluation specialism within the field of public relations. There are a few individual consultants and organisations providing expert understanding and propriety services. However, unlike marketing, an internal specialism has not become a common feature of many organisations' in-house PR function. A pragmatic option may be to extend the remit of existing research operations. This could include assessment of matters under the responsibility of public relations such as relationships with stakeholders and publics (rather than the traditional customer or staff research), issues and reputation. It would also be useful to see greater focus on research and evaluation as skill sets within PR, with qualifications and training courses reflecting the importance of this area. If PR is to fulfil its potential as a strategic function, based on a knowledge management competency, greater investment in this area is required within organisations, by PR bodies and from individual practitioners.

- What skills do you have in research and evaluation?
- How have you learned about these topics and what challenges do you face in practice?
- Do you agree that greater focus on this aspect is required within PR and what action could you take to improve your own knowledge and skills?

target with communications.' Whether or not this is true, it indicates the importance of prioritising efforts throughout the planning process and suggests evaluation should identify the key elements that have contributed most to the end results.

## END POINT

Although evaluation has been considered an important aspect of PR practice for a century, debate about methods and challenges continues to hamper the use of methods that would help inform activities and demonstrate the value of PR operations. It is important to include pre-emptive, formative and summative assessment within the planning process to ensure an iterative approach helps to review and refine practices. An outcome-oriented approach is recommended based on evaluation against objectives. Evaluation can also be used to assess the planning process itself and contribute towards performance reviews of in-house PR functions, practitioners and consultancies. Development of a specialism in research and evaluation of public relations is recommended rather than reliance on external providers. This would demonstrate a commitment to integrating this key aspect throughout the PR function, its operations and its contribution to the knowledge base of the organisation.

# Outro

*Heather Yaxley*

Part II presents a considered approach to public relations strategic planning. It reflects a pragmatic perspective, encouraging flexibility, a proactive stance and adaptation to particular circumstances.

Nevertheless, some PR practitioners may reject the concept of planning in favour of intuition, instinct and imagination. Like Apple's Steve Jobs (Isaacson 2011), they may believe in their own insight to guide decision-making. Others may reflect another of Jobs' characteristics, a stubborn, perfectionist nature, displaying a tendency to micro-manage rather than benefit from the expert deployment of resources that a dynamic planning process offers.

There are certainly times when research and analysis will not be helpful or possible, particularly within a short-timeframe. Decision-making may require an immediate response. Indeed, Gladwell (2005) argues snap judgements can be more effective than caution and deliberation. What underpins this instinctive capability may be experience, expertise, knowledge, or the reverse: an ability to avoid existing preconceptions and previous practices.

Ultimately, decision-making is subjective, particularly in public relations, where recommendations are frequently a matter of opinion. Sometimes, we just know the right thing to do to achieve the best outcome without a formal planning process. But instincts can be wrong.

Neither is planning an exact science, no matter how carefully it is undertaken. Making a decision involves taking a risk (Chapter 13) and many people, and their employers, are risk-averse or reluctant to expose themselves to unchartered waters. A professional approach to planning reduces the risk of errors of judgement and reflects responsibility, particularly when it involves documented evidence as required by quality management systems or in crisis response situations.

Being a maverick may seem appealing, but PR practitioners need to ensure their counsel is understood, valued and accepted. This means management has to trust and agree to what is being recommended. Planning accommodates those who require evidence as well as those who are looking for creative solutions. When it is necessary to challenge prevailing views or present counterintuitive ideas, planning helps justify any argument being made.

Ultimately, we need to remember, as Sutherland (1992: 3) contends, 'people are very much less rational than is commonly thought'. This applies as much to PR practitioners and those involved in the planning process as the publics they seek to engage. Planning foregrounds rational thinking; it is predicated on a positivist view of the world as behaving in predictable ways. In reality, we live in a messy, fuzzy, ever-changing world. Chance, human nature and capriciousness can scupper the best laid plans.

Planning may seem unethical, particularly when used to achieve persuasive objectives or where there is an imbalance in the financial or political power between the organisation and publics. However, a considered approach enables PR practitioners to adopt an ethical decision-making framework within planning processes. In relation to strategic public relations, planning offers a set of essential tools that can be used wisely.

# Part III

# Corporate communications

# Introduction

*Heather Yaxley*

This section considers a number of specialist areas of communications undertaken by organisations. It aims to provide insight particularly for those without expert knowledge or experience, but should also prove thought-provoking for practitioners who are familiar with the individual areas.

While termed Corporate Communications, the section does not exclusively focus on corporations – that is, the contents are relevant for those working in the public and not-for-profit sectors as well as a wide variety of private sector organisations. Likewise, it is not exclusively concerned with communications as it includes a wider remit for public relations in terms of building relationships and planning activities.

The six chapters within this section focus on areas that reach across a number of stakeholder groups (see Part IV). They also draw on considerations of public relations (see Part I) and a planned approach (see Part II).

Chapter 11: Brand management – examines this much-used term from a PR perspective, while linking to marketing and also good practice. It concludes with consideration of how to rescue a tarnished brand.

Chapter 12: Effective media relations – covers what many consider to be the heart of PR operations. It reviews the role of the media, basic principles, writing effective media relations and the impact of developing technology.

Chapter 13: Risk, incidents, issues and crisis management – tackles topics that are unlucky for some. It considers risk management in respect of identifying areas of negative influence in relation to a variety of organisations and scenarios. The chapter also looks at developing competencies, plans, processes and procedures to anticipate and react to incidents, issues and crisis situations.

Chapter 14: Corporate social responsibility – considers issues relating to this important aspect of reputation management including the practitioner's role, cause-related marketing and integrating CSR into organisation's operational management.

Chapter 15: International considerations – looks at a number of aspects of the global practice of public relations. This includes views on cultural differences and questions to address when operating across international boundaries.

Chapter 16: Digital public relations – takes a practical look at emerging technologies and how practitioners can keep ahead of developments from a personal and organisational perspective. It also tackles issues relating to building virtual communities, monitoring and evaluation.

Together these chapters provide many of the most important tools required by PR practitioners working in a contemporary, changing corporate communications environment.

# CHAPTER 11

# Brand management

## *Alison Theaker*

There has been much discussion about what constitutes corporate identity and corporate image and the difference between these two concepts.

## CHECK POINT

This chapter starts with suggested definitions for these two terms, and then

- defines branding;
- examines the concept of the corporate brand;
- explores Balmer's concept of corporate marketing;
- questions the various elements of good corporate branding practice;
- looks at two examples of corporate branding;
- discusses how an organisation can rescue a tarnished brand.

There is no established definition of corporate identity, although Balmer (2001) suggests: 'The mix of elements which gives organisations their distinctiveness: the foundation of business identities.' He goes on to define these elements as 'culture . . . strategy, structure, history, business activities and market scope'. Image on the other hand is more difficult. Balmer (2001) feels that the creation of a positive image is an objective of effectively managing a business identity and that the term 'corporate reputation' is more useful. The latter he defines as 'the enduring perception held of an organisation held by an individual, group or network'. Bernstein (1984) goes further when he says that image 'cannot be manufactured . . . [it] can only be perceived'. It would seem that identity is to do with the things that can be controlled within an organisation, whereas image is the 'net result of the interaction of all the experiences, beliefs, feeling, knowledge and impressions that people have about a company' (Worcester, 1980, in Bernstein 1984: 40). Wood and Somerville (2012) sum this up: 'corporate identity is what the organisation communicates (either intentionally or unintentionally) via various cues, whereas its image is how its publics actually view it. An image is a perception and exists only in the mind of the receiver'. We will see that consistency is held to be vitally important for a successful identity, but that a company may have many different images among its stakeholders.

# BRANDING

A brand is the value of a name of a product or company and affects people's buying behaviour. It is often called an intangible asset, although strong brands enable corporations to add price premiums, such as Heinz baked beans, which currently retail for 68p against a supermarket's own label at 24p. In some cases, the company name is the brand, such as Virgin, Sony or Kodak. Association with a corporate brand like this may affect consumer decisions. In others, the brand names are well known, such as Fairy Liquid, but the parent company less so, such as Unilever or Procter & Gamble. Companies may produce different brands, which may compete in the marketplace and can be thought of as a cluster of values that promise a particular experience.

'Nobody in the world ever bought anything on price alone,' states L.D. Young (2006). Young quotes a blind test of Heinz ketchup against an own-label brand, where 71 per cent of consumers preferred the own label. However, when they saw the label, 68 per cent preferred the Heinz ketchup.

With the market saturated with new brands that can hardly be distinguished from each other, brand loyalty has declined. Consumers are tending to buy whatever is on offer, so that sales promotions and coupons have become more important in buying decisions (Belch and Belch 2001: 528).

Naomi Klein feels that 'the role of branding has been changing, particularly in the last fifteen years . . . the brand itself has increasingly become the product'. Thus 'Nike was about "sport", not shoes; Microsoft about "communications", not software' (Klein 2000). Companies are now projecting their brand onto many different products. Klein links this increase in branding activity with the tendency of multinationals to shift actual production away from where the goods are bought. She quotes the protests in Paris and Seattle, where rioters attacked McDonald's and Starbucks, as evidence of a backlash against global brands, where brands were seen as the embodiment of exploitation.

Branding means everything that surrounds a company's offerings, and both rational and emotional elements underpin the most enduring brands.

Al and Laura Ries, having written *The 22 Immutable Laws of Branding*, turned their attention to public relations in 2002 with the controversially titled *The Fall of Advertising and the Rise of PR*. They state: 'You can't launch a new brand with advertising because [it] has no credibility . . . You can launch new brands only with . . . public relations.' They also redefine advertising's role as brand maintenance, and public relations' as brand building (Ries and Ries 2002: xi, 266).

Using an existing brand name to promote a new product is referred to as a brand extension, transferring brand values onto new products. Thus Richard Branson has diversified into air travel, insurance, train travel, weddings and skin care using the same Virgin name and brand as his original record stores. Keller and Aaker (2003) indicated that using an existing brand in this way directly benefited the acceptance of new products by consumers.

Corporate Branding (2011) put forward the brand triangle as a way of defining the characteristics of a brand. Functional values – they suggest that this might be responsibility for the Co-op Bank; belief in respecting children's rights for UNICEF; innovation for Tesco – are combined with emotional values – concern, integrity, concern for employees – to produce a corporate promised experience. They also warn that stakeholders select between brands based on a small number of characteristics, so that it is best to form the brand promise from only two or three values.

## Corporate branding

Palotta (2011) says:

> Brand is your strategy . . . calls to action . . . customer service . . . the way you speak . . . the whole array of your communication tools . . . your user interface . . . your people . . . your facilities . . . your logo and visuals too . . . every inter-action anyone is every going to have with you, no matter how small.

Hunt (2011) quotes Bhargava who says, 'We all want to do business with people we like.' Core attributes of likeability are honesty, simplicity and being human.

A corporate brand encompasses a name and the perceived qualities or personality attached to it. Knox and Bickerton (2003) define it as: 'A corporate brand is the visual, verbal and behavioural expression of an organisation's unique business model.' Balmer (2001) suggests that the corporate brand is a mix of 'cultural, intricate, tangible and ethereal elements'.

Davis (2004) refers to three kinds of corporate brand. An attribute brand refers to beliefs about functional attributes associated with the name – is it reliable? Marks and Spencer relies on perceptions of quality, whatever product they are selling.

An aspirational brand might recall the enviable lifestyles of buyers. A Rolex watch or Lexus car suggests that the owner is successful. An experiential brand plays on emotions and other associations. Virgin encompasses innovation and value for money. The corporate brand should be portrayed as a unified image by both the marketing and PR functions.

Moloney (2006) suggests public relations is the distribution system for the corporate brand, presenting the ideal of the organisation for its own advantage. Keller and Aaker (2003) noted that corporate marketing activity can provide a direct marketing benefit by building on a strong corporate brand, rather than using a new brand name.

Moloney (2006) warns that brands attract public attention, which may not always be welcome. Brands such as McDonald's have non-intended meanings, connected to popular culture. He also questions whether the paradigm of two-way symmetrical communication applies to corporate brandings, stating that the construction of the brand is asymmetrical and assumes acceptance by others. Thus brands can have both positive and negative connotations.

## BRAND MANAGEMENT

Knox and Bickerton (2003) add 'competitive landscape' to the normal trilogy of vision, culture and image to set the context of corporate brand management. They also stress the need to look at the current image of the organisation and compare it with the future competition, and do the same with current culture and future vision.

They build on Van Riel's (1995) concept of common starting points (CSPs) as the central values which form the underpinning of corporate communication and Knox and Maklan's 1998 framework (Knox and Bickerton 2003) for brand positioning. This sets out four elements:

- organisation attributes – purpose, commitments and values, or what it exists to do, what's important and what guides its actions;
- performance benefits – products and services: what it does and what it delivers;
- portfolio benefits – product brands and customer: the outward faces of an organisation and who it serves;
- network benefits – contacts and mechanisms: networks and how they are used.

This brand position then needs to be consolidated and communicated to both internal and external audiences in a consistent way. At this point, the business processes can then be reviewed to check that they are aligned with the brand

# CORPORATE MARKETING

John Balmer (Balmer and Greyser 2006) distilled his own corporate marketing structure into six elements. These six Cs are:

- CHARACTER encompasses the organisation's philosophy and ethics, what it stands for and how it undertakes its activities, as well as its product, price, place, performance and positioning. Thus most of the general marketing elements are clumped together to make one entity that distinguishes it from another.

- CULTURE is Balmer's take on personality, and how employees feel about the company they work for. This provides the context for staff to engage with each other and customers.

- COMMUNICATION includes promotion, advertising, PR, all the communication channels used by an organisation to all its stakeholders. He also adds in word-of-mouth and media commentary. This could also be related to corporate identity.

- CONSTITUENCIES recognises that customers may belong to many stakeholder groups, and that organisational success and 'license to operate' depends on meeting groups' expectations.

- CONCEPTUALISATIONS includes the perception of the organisation by its stakeholders. This could include the concept of corporate image.

- COVENANT embodies the promise underpinning the corporate brand and the experience its stakeholders have.

Balmer's co-author, Stephen Greyser, suggested three types of relationship in the market. His original three models were:

- MANIPULATIVE where marketers would force consumers' choices, persuading them to buy their products and may even have acted as the consumer's adversary.

- TRANSACTIONAL relationships started to see more balance between marketers and consumers, with the goal of true consumer choice, marketers working in partnership with their customers.

- SERVICE model relationships tended to give more power to the consumer; marketers became their servant and aimed to cater for their needs.

Greyser (Balmer and Greyser 2006) then added on a fourth model:

- CORPORATE gives sovereignty to consumers and other stakeholders, broadening the emphasis from simply customers. The organisation has to balance a range of needs, and profits are not the only focus. This links with the idea of CSR discussed later in Chapter 14.

Balmer and Greyser (2006) then put forward the idea that corporate identity, branding, communication and reputation should all be integrated under the umbrella of corporate marketing.

How useful is this idea in the real world? It certainly tries to simplify the elements of branding, and also suggests that attention be paid top more stakeholders than simply customers. However, it appears to have a narrow focus on public relations as simply one element of Communication.

position. They also recommend brand conditioning, or the need to 'review [the] corporate brand on a continuous basis'. This ensures that the brand benefits continue to be linked to customer needs.

Van Riel (1995) offered one of the most useful models of managing corporate identity. He suggested that examining current image and comparing it to desired image should be the first step. If there was a gap between the two, then he put forward eight steps to address it. Starting with analysing the problem and ending with evaluation, the model includes researching current positioning, external image and competitive marketing analysis and feeding the answers back into the corporate identity mix. This mix is made up of personality, behaviour, communication and symbolism.

**TALKING POINT**

There are several suggestions for lists of ingredients that create good corporate branding practice. Goodman (2010) gives five:

1   Use the same images, logos and writing style across all communication channels for strong brand recognition.
2   Actively manage the people who represent your brand.
3   Separate the personal from the professional on social media.
4   Combine different communication channels to tell the brand story.
5   Monitor social media and customer review websites.

She suggests that a brand differentiates a business from its competition and thus good communication is vital.

Daye and Van Auken (2008) put forward ten steps:

1   The CEO needs to lead brand strategy, backed by the management team.

2  Each company should build its own model of branding, linked to its business strategy.

3  Stakeholders should be involved in devising the strategy, including the customers.

4  Use the corporate brand to advance the company vision, involving all employees. Internal efforts are 50 per cent of making a successful corporate brand.

5  Exploit new technology.

6  Empower people to become ambassadors. Training employees in the brand vision enables them to have a wider impact on family, friends and many others.

7  Create the right delivery system, so that customers' expectations are met and even exceeded.

8  Communicate consistent, clear and relevant messages that are concise and easy to comprehend.

9  Measure the brand performance to see how much value it adds.

10  Evaluate and adjust strategy on a regular basis. While vision, identity, personality and values should not often change, other elements should be monitored.

MacLeod (2011) suggests that core elements of a good reputation are like ABC:

- Advocacy – endorsements from employees and customers create trust.
- Behaviour – communications is about stimulating a desired response and behaviour from stakeholders.
- Coherence – there must be a match between values, communications and action.

Wood and Somerville (2012) stress that research is key to managing corporate identity. Senior management and stakeholders' views should be sought, and an audit of whether the corporate identity matches the communication of the desired image.

Are there any others that you might add?

Examine the case studies presented below to see what elements of these checklists were met.

# A BRANDING JOURNEY ... *WITH PLYMOUTH UNIVERSITY*

The new 'with Plymouth University' brand captures the institution's pioneering spirit, its collaborative approach to working, and its forward-thinking community. Instead of a static logo, the new identity can be tailored and used to communicate directly with different audiences. By putting the message in the hands of the communicator, it opens up new possibilities.

The finished article tells only a fraction of the story, however, as to how and why the university embarked upon this journey to rebrand after nineteen years. The process of rebranding, after nineteen years with its old logo, took eighteen months, and drew upon the talents and energy of students, staff and stakeholders to define the values at the heart of the university's identity.

**FIGURE 11.1** Plymouth University old logo

The branding project team, which comprised both academic staff with industry experience and professional services members, established a set of guiding principles. These included a commitment to make evidence-based decisions; to harness internal resources and expertise wherever possible; to create a holistic brand that would encompass tone of voice, HR processes, induction events, etc. and that there would be minimal expenditure during the roll-out – the project had to be cost neutral.

The first action was to gather evidence to establish whether the university's corporate identity was still fit for purpose. Using the market research skills of undergraduate and postgraduate business studies students, they established that there was a discrepancy between the way the university was perceived and the message it conveyed through its logo. They also learned:

- 54.8 per cent of students did not like the logo, and 70.6 per cent said the brand needed to be modernised.

- Among teachers, there was a 100 per cent rejection of the current logo, with 87.5 per cent agreeing to modernisation of the brand.
- In the business population, 60 per cent did not like it, and 80 per cent wanted a change.

Concurrently the project team was also conducting research into what people did like about the university itself. They approached 30,000 people and asked them to provide five words that summed up the institution. From the 5,000 people who responded, providing a pool of 25,000 words, certain themes and consistencies were immediately apparent.

Through a series of workshops and focus groups involving people from both inside and outside the university, these ideas and words were refined and distilled down to a set of values. They were:

- expert
- connected
- creative
- spirited
- empowering.

The project team specified that any design agency that was to work with the university had to be connected with it in some way. Two agencies emerged as frontrunners. Between them, they had four Plymouth graduates working as directors, ensuring that their connection to the university was evident at the very top.

The university asked the two if they would collaborate in an enterprising partnership. They were engaged to create a compelling, effective and inclusive brand identity, one which reflected the university's 'real-world' approach. The litmus test applied at every milestone was:

- Are we creating something groundbreaking?
- Does it reflect our collective power?
- Does it communicate with our stakeholders?

The agencies pitched two approaches. The first was an evolutionary approach, which took the most memorable elements of the existing brand and created a refreshed identity. The other took to its heart the aim of the university for people to say they were proud to be associated with the institution. From that, the importance of the word 'with' was evident. This would change the sentence 'I am studying mathematics at the University of Plymouth' to 'I am studying mathematics with Plymouth University'.

It was suggested that 'with Plymouth University' became not only the brand, but also the basis of a new identity that could communicate different messages.

- Pioneer with Plymouth University.
- Endless possibilities with Plymouth University.
- Succeed with Plymouth University.

The two versions were taken to key stakeholders for testing, all of whom backed the radical approach, and plans for the roll-out commenced. Staff engagement sessions were held. For reasons of cost and sustainability, it was agreed that existing marketing collateral would continue in use until existing stocks were used up. In addition, by drawing upon internal expertise for the formulation of the strategy, and student resources for market research and testing, rather than engaging external agencies, the university had calculated it had made significant savings.

**FIGURE 11.2** Plymouth University new logo

Finally, after an eighteen-month journey, which had examined the values of the institution, the new Plymouth University brand was unveiled at the Vice-Chancellor's Public Address in 2011.

*Andrew Merrington, Press and PR Manager, Plymouth University*

*Andrew Merrington was a journalist at a Midlands-based press agency. He then moved into internal communications with Capital One and Experian, and now works in media relations in the higher education sector. With around 30,000 students, including those studying at its partner FE colleges throughout the South West, Plymouth is one of the largest universities in the UK.*

# DEVON AIR AMBULANCE TRUST: BRANDING THE SKY

The Devon Air Ambulance Trust (DAAT) is the charity that raises the funds to keep Devon's two air ambulances airborne. Costing in the region of £4.5 million annually, and independent of Government and National Lottery funding, this means that every penny comes from the community, businesses and friends of Devon.

Devon Air Ambulance Trust

www.daat.org

Registered Charity No: 1077998
Company No: 3855746

**FIGURE 11.3** Devon Air Ambulance Trust logo

This is the DAAT agreed form of words to be used in response to any request from a publication or media source for information about the charity. DAAT operates for ten hours a day from two bases, in Exeter and North Devon. Devon is the only county to have two air ambulances, a response to the characteristics of Devon and the distance which needs to be travelled to get casualties to the nearest hospital on winding and narrow roads, but also a testament to the support from the people of Devon. Currently the charity is raising the money to purchase a second aircraft to replace its leased helicopter in 2013.

Initially the charity adopted a red livery because that was the colour of its leased craft, but by adding its own blue and white branding elements, the brand has developed into a distinctive marque. DAAT sees its brand as a tree, developing from its roots – its vision to be an outstanding and efficient service relieving sickness and injury – to its fruit – what is achieved, lives saved. In between are the trunk – the core values of community, professionalism and independence; the branches – personality, reliable, friendly reassuring; foliage – corporate identity, signage and livery; and blossom – how the DAAT is experienced, acknowledging volunteers, donors and suppliers.

**FIGURE 11.4** Devon Air Ambulance Trust branding on helicopter

The DAAT has resisted branding its aircraft with a sponsor's name, unlike the London Air Ambulance, which sports the Virgin logo. Virgin paid £192,000 for this privilege in 2009, and the public perception is that Virgin funds the service in London when in fact the majority of funding comes from NHS Trusts. The outcome is that it is hard to get public support. In contrast, the only other organisation's name that the DAAT carries on its own aircraft is that of the BBC Radio Devon Air Ambulance Appeal, a joint fund and awareness-raising campaign between DAAT and BBC Radio Devon. This mention is smaller than DAAT's own branding, which declares 'Founded by the Ceri Thomas Appeal and Funded by the People of Devon'. Thus the DAAT benefits from its links to BBC Radio Devon and keeps its own brand intact.

A comprehensive document listing the brand guidelines has been produced, comprising a guide to producing consistent and creative marketing communications for the DAAT. 'Our marketing communications are a visual expression of our organisation and all it stands for,' says chief executive Helena Holt, 'They set the standard for how we communicate our values and messages to the broad range of people we work with. We have a fantastic brand. Clear, consistent, high-quality communications reinforce our reputation.'

The brand guidelines contain sections on why the brand is so important, and what words should be used to reflect the DAAT's qualities. Key words include: open; transparent; professional; honest; friendly; accountable; integrity; truth. Key phrases are: by and for the people of Devon; independent of Government and National Lottery funding; funded totally by the community, businesses and friends of Devon;

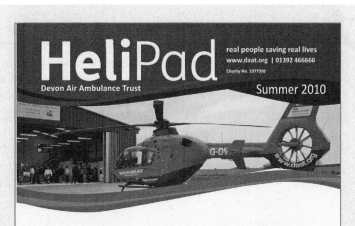

HeliPad

real people saving real lives
www.daat.org  |  01392 466666
Charity No. 1077998

Devon Air Ambulance Trust                    Summer 2010

## Steve Ford Airbase Officially Opened!

### A fantastic new airbase, named after a very special friend

The new Devon Air Ambulance Trust 'Steve Ford' Airbase at Eaglescott Airfield, Umberleigh is now operational. BBC Radio Devon presenter Judi Spiers officially opened the airbase and was joined by the family of pilot Steve Ford, who the base is named after. Steve tragically died in a motorcycle accident on 18th October 2008.

Speaking on behalf of the family wife Julia said 'We have been touched by the many tributes paid to Steve following his death. We are immensely proud that he has been recognised in this way. It's a wonderful lasting tribute to a great man whose life we were privileged to share'.

The airbase took just 5 months to build, and the crew managed to move in just before the snow and cold spell arrived!

Our CEO Heléna Holt said 'There are so many people to thank, without whom this project wouldn't even have taken off the ground. Rok our builders have been great all the way through.'

She added 'We would also like to thank the following for supporting this project - Burdens Building Supplies, Fifields and, of course, Barry Pearson of Eaglescott Airfield, who kindly gifted a long lease of the land.'

IN THIS ISSUE . . .
Patients' Stories, BBC Radio Devon Air Ambulance Appeal plus much more!

**FIGURE 11.5** Devon Air Ambulance Trust Helipad newsletter

real people, saving real lives. The guidelines also include information on the DAAT badge and how it may be used, with examples of full colour and single colour usage, minimum size, the DAAT Helicopter Strip which must be used at the bottom of all corporate documents, pantone references and fonts. Examples are also included of newsletter covers, fundraising posters and images, which can be used from the photo gallery.

Chief executive Helena Holt says,

We have a very strong brand as a well-loved and respected local charity. Of course our two red helicopters are highly visible reminders, instantly recognisable by the majority of people in the county, and we have worked hard to ensure our brand is consistent, from the use of our logo, to the words, images and language we use across the board. An excellent example of how we have used this brand awareness to support a community partnership is the relationship with BBC Radio Devon with whom we have run an extremely successful fundraising campaign over the last year. We identified some significant areas of overlap between our brand values and theirs. We've used visual branding which works for both organisations and both have benefitted from reaching new audiences as a result of the campaign.

# RESCUING A DAMAGED BRAND

O'Rourke (2011) uses the example of Tiger Woods, who lost lucrative sponsorship deals after his extramarital affairs became public knowledge in 2009, as an illustration of how important reputation is to the bottom line. He states that reputation is worth £460 billion of shareholder value to UK FTSE350 firms. Other corporations who have found this out to their cost are BP, whose share price crashed by 50 per cent after the Gulf disaster and News Corporation, whose shares have lost more than 20 per cent of value due to the UK phone hacking scandal. He quotes Echo research, which shows that a 5 per cent increase in reputation will lead to a 1.8 per cent increase in the market cap of a public company.

Discussing which brands had suffered most in the wake of the riots in the UK in 2011, Jo Slatem, MHP Communications deputy head of brands, said that brands could be victims of their own success. 'The more mainstream a brand, the more likely it is to get dragged into these things' (Magee 2011c). Top five tips for dealing with negative associations outside the organisation's control included:

- Assess the brand damage – is it really eroding sales?
- Proceed with caution – don't tell people not to use your brand. This can cause unwanted attention.
- Be prepared – what does your brand enable? Do a people-based risk assessment. What could people do to your brand if they wanted to cause damage?
- Do not overreact – don't accept the blame for what people are doing.
- Be consistent – brands don't change overnight, so stick with your brand messages.

Nick Hindle (2011) was McDonald's UK vice-president for communications and was tasked with dealing with the company's reputational problems after *Fast Food Nation* in 2001 and *Supersize Me* in 2004. Jamie Oliver was also crusading for higher quality food, and McDonald's became associated with obesity. Hindle advocates taking the long view, striking a balance between sales and investing in how the company communicates what it does. Honesty is vital. McDonald's commissioned research to see exactly how much the negative connotations were costing it. Finally, he stresses that advertising is not the answer and that fundamental problems must be fixed to rebuild trust. To do this, McDonald's started by changing their menus to reduce fat, salt and sugar. Journalists and stakeholders were taken to see where core ingredients were sourced, and the company started to communicate that it only used British and Irish beef from 16,000 farms and that all eggs were free range. Restaurants were remodelled with softer lighting and natural materials. Communications had to change and be less defensive.

The company also paid attention to its internal communications and policies. *Fast Food Nation* had introduced the term 'McJob' to mean a dead end job with no prospects. McDonald's challenged this and made it possible for employees to take basic qualifications through the company and became an accredited examination body. They became the biggest provider of apprenticeships in the UK and trained 70,000 volunteers for the London Olympics in 2012.

A website was launched called 'Make up your own mind', where the public were invited to ask questions of the company. CEO Steve Easterbrook took part in a debate with the author of *Fast Food Nation*, Eric Schlosser, live on *BBC Newsnight*. This was followed with discussions on *5Live, Sky,* the *Today* programme and *Tonight with Trevor McDonald.* Journalists from the *Sun* were invited to work shifts in restaurants. Local franchisees were recruited as brand ambassadors and over 100 were trained to be advocates in the regions.

The company experienced nineteen quarters of growth up to April 2011, as well as a twenty point improvement on trust scores since 2006. Customers rose by 80 million in 2009–2010. Even Jamie Oliver said, 'I can't believe I'm telling you that McDonald's UK has come a long way.' All these are 'important milestone[s] on the road back to brand health'.

## END POINT

Brands are made up of a combination of physical attributes and emotional connotations and brand management is a complex business. Having a good corporate brand is not just about having a great logo. So, changing brand perception is not simply a matter of communication but also of examining what the organisation is doing. This makes a compelling argument for the need for public relations practitioners to be involved in corporate strategy, not just in communicating corporate decisions.

# CHAPTER 12

# Effective media relations

*Alison Theaker*

As discussed in Chapter 3, public relations has its origins in the field of media relations. In fact, media relations and public relations are repeatedly used as inter-changeable terms, especially by journalists. The latter often express a knee-jerk antagonistic reaction to public relations – one journalist has even been heard to remark, 'Without PR people, journalists would be the lowest organism in the food chain.' Early practitioners were press agents whose main aim was to gain 'free' press coverage at any cost, and the truth was not allowed to get in the way of a good story. With the development of the internet, practitioners have had to take on board the need for openness and accessibility to companies' affairs.

## CHECK POINT

This chapter will cover

- why use the media to get your message across?
- basic media relations principles;
- how to write good media releases;
- the importance of targeting;
- the impact of developing technology.

# WHY USE THE MEDIA?

One of the reasons why public relations practitioners use media relations to get their message across is the media's role in forming public opinion. Lazarfeld and Katz's (quoted in Wilcox *et al.* 2003: 213) agenda-setting theory puts forward the idea that the media determine what people think about by selecting the stories that go on the front page or are included in nightly television news programmes. For the public relations practitioner, getting something onto the media agenda is the first step. In some situations, the media can also tell people what to think. If people cannot get access to other points of view, they can become dependent on the media's slant on a story. This often happens in a war situation, where limited news is available and often heavily censored by the military. While it is now easier to gain access to different points of view via the internet, most people's information will come from the mass media, leading to a tabloidisation of the issues. On the other hand, if the public relations practitioner for an organisation is the main source of information on a subject, say a new drug or scientific development, it is possible for them to shape the tone of the debate. Framing can also magnify the effect of media dependency. Wilcox *et al.* (2003) cite Tankard and Israel's work analysing the news coverage of the Bosnian war, when 'Ruder-Finn framed the issue as Serb genocide against Bosnian Muslims'. The media picked up on this and started to use emotive phrases such as 'ethnic cleansing'. Lastly, cultivation theory suggests that events in the news are packaged into highlights. Repeated often enough, and given the media's tendency to concentrate on conflict and crisis situations, people get a false view of what is actually happening. Whenever a child abduction hits the news headlines, the media tend to emphasise the number of child molesters who have been released from prison and warn parents about 'stranger danger', rather than concentrate on the facts that most children are harmed by someone they know.

# THE BASICS OF MEDIA RELATIONS

One of the earliest users of this method was Ivy Ledbetter Lee (see also Chapter 3), who in the early 1900s worked for coal operators in Philadelphia threatened with strike action by the United Mine Workers Union. He issued a Declaration of Principles, which stated, 'We aim to supply news . . . Our matter is accurate'. The declaration went on:

> Our plan is, frankly and openly, on behalf of the business concerns and public institutions, to supply to the press and public of the United States prompt and accurate information concerning subjects which it is of value and interest to the public to know about.
>
> (quoted in Grunig and Hunt 1984: 33)

Wragg argues (Bland *et al.* 1996: 66–7) that:

> The purpose of press relations is not to issue press releases, or handle enquiries from journalists, or even to generate a massive pile of press cuttings. The true purpose of press relations is to enhance the reputation of an organisation and its products, and to influence and inform the target audience.

While it is largely of a tactical nature in practice, good media relations can contribute to longer-term strategic objectives, such as:

- improving company or brand image;
- raising and improving media profile;
- changing the attitudes of target audiences (such as customers);
- improving relationships with the community;
- increasing market share;
- influencing government policy at local, national or international level;
- improving communications with investors and their advisers;
- improving industrial relations.

As such, media relations forms part of most strategies in the chapters in Part IV. It is still the activity on which the majority of PR practitioners spend most of their time. In the *PR Census*, general media relations was found to feature in 85 per cent of PR roles, with 21 per cent of practitioners considering it their main task. Nearly half of respondents stated that media relations strategy planning had increased in importance over the previous two years (Gorkana, 2011).

What exactly does media relations consist of? There are a multitude of books and blog posts that deal with the mechanics of contacting the media, how to write press releases in a specific format that conforms to the needs of journalists, and the best ways to target and distribute this information. Most stress the five Ws (who, what, where, when and why), and the need to make the release appropriate to the style and content of the targeted publication or broadcast. Media releases can be supplemented by press conferences, media briefings, exclusive interviews, feature articles and photo opportunities. Advice is also offered on targeting, which is covered later in this chapter.

Hitchins (2003) makes a distinction between 'techniques', used to create media interest and 'tools', which help the process once interest has been created. He includes the following list of tools: news release, press conference, informal media briefing, exclusive interview, media tour, facility visit, as well as online press office, virtual press conference and photo call. These could now be supplemented by streaming video, blog posts, podcasts and the use of social media forums.

Techniques are used by the practitioner to create news, 'turning routine and long-running development into new acts or news pegs'. News vehicles are events created to gain media coverage, planned not spontaneous, and their success is measured solely by how much coverage they obtain. Examples include 'surveys, research reports, media launches, announcements, anniversaries, awareness days, celebrities, awards and publicity stunts'. Linking statements to the current media agenda can also aid coverage. Thus pharmaceutical companies could link news of developments of their products to combat flu or hay fever to the relevant season. This method must be used with care, however, so that organisations are not thought to be capitalising on tragedy. Anecdotally, a media relations practitioner for Kelloggs' Hot Pockets in the USA was thought to have had the bright idea of publicising them immediately after the 11 September 2001 disaster in New York, with the emphasis on the fact that Americans would want to stay at home and eat comfort food that had not been tampered with. Campaigns and special pleading are the third way to frame a message. By appealing to the media's appetite for conflict and confrontation, organisations can emphasise their work to change legislation or fight to preserve the environment. Demonstrations and other stunts provide the media with a visual event to cover. Headlines, slogans and stereotypes can be used to convey the essence of the message quickly and simply. Hitchins quotes a study by the Royal College of Psychiatrists into depression in men across Europe which was called *Men Behaving Sadly*. Finally, selective targeting and tailoring news to specific media interests ensure that priorities are set regarding which media to approach and that their needs dictate public relations activities.

**READING POINT**

Lecturer and blogger Philip Young's chapter in the 4th edition of *The Public Relations Handbook* (2012: 251–272) discusses 'Media relations in the social media age'. He looks at the PR practitioner as a creator of news and how practice has changed with recent developments. He also raises the question of the ethics of media relations.

More information about how to use social media in public relations is given in Chapter 16.

# WRITING THE NEWS RELEASE

A news release is a simple document that sets out as clearly and straightforwardly as possible, information that a journalist could use to write or broadcast a story. Traditional layout rules were drawn from the era of hot metal presses, when releases would be marked up by a sub-editor and sent to a compositor for setting. Originally practitioners were advised to use one side of the paper, double-spaced type, clearly marking the date of issue, the source of the material and further contact details.

Releases are now normally inserted directly into the body of the email. The subject line is used for the headline and provision of contact information should be considered in the same way as in conventional releases. Double-spaced text is no longer used as this increases the need to scroll down and find out the news story.

The cardinal rule of content – always get all the important facts in the first paragraph – was born from the practice of cutting the release from the bottom if space was limited. However, in a world where journalists suffer from information overload, it still serves as a useful way to get their attention when a release may be just one of multiple sources of news. Keeping clichés and 'puff' to a minimum ensures that the story is not buried in irrelevant information that reads like an advert rather than news.

PR practitioners have to learn to spot the story in the release and make sure this is the first thing covered. The subject of a release is almost never the organisation that is sending it out. Countless releases start with the date, which again is rarely the news. It is more likely to be the 'what' of the five Ws, such as a new bank account designed for students, for example. And even then it might be that the account would lead to better degree results because it would enable students to spend less time worrying about their money. The benefits rather than the features of a new product should be emphasised.

Survey results make good news stories, and releases should start with the results, making sure that human interest is to the fore. 'Over 500 jobs have been created in the South East over the last six months, according to a report published today.' Local media need a local slant to a national news story, such as: 'South West businesses are already recovering from the recession, local HR consultancy BestPeople has found.' These stories could be illustrated by the experiences of local job seekers and employers.

To get media coverage the PR practitioner has to supply information that fits the journalist's needs. It may require the practitioner having to tell the client that giving an oversized cheque to a local pre-school is not likely to make national news pages, or maybe even the regional TV news programme. The story must be interesting and specific to the readers, viewers or listeners that the journalist is aiming to capture. Often supplying an interesting picture can garner coverage. Early in my teaching career *PR Week* covered my own use of a local consultancy to update my skills because it was accompanied by a picture of me surrounded by people wearing oversized alligator suits – one of the consultancy's clients was Alcan whose mascot was AliCan. All ten of the mascot suits had happened to be in the office at the time for cleaning. The caption mentioned my employer, Leeds Metropolitan University, the consultancy, BRAHM PR and the client.

Quotes are often used in a release, but have been derided by journalists as often sounding stilted and too much like an advert. Good quotes further the story and are an opportunity to express an opinion. They can also make it look as though the journalist has interviewed someone, even if they did not have time to.

**ACTION POINT**

Using press releases alongside other activities can help to promote a new development at an established organisation. This case study shows how general media releases, exclusives and other promotional tools can be integrated.

# USING MEDIA TO PROMOTE A NEW BRAND

Crealy Rocks is the new brand name for large-scale events and live entertainment at Crealy Great Adventure Parks in Devon and Cornwall. On 13 August 2011, Devon's Crealy hosted its first outdoor concert, headlined by Peter Andre and four support acts for a capacity of 10,000 people.

**FIGURE 12.1** Crealy Rocks logo

This was a new departure for Crealy, which promotes itself as the South West's leading family attraction. The aim of the media campaign was to:

- Create local and regional awareness of the brand Crealy Rocks as a creditable concert venue.
- Encourage individuals to buy concert tickets.
- Engage with key local and regional media and to promote the concert.

Media messages were agreed to be:

- The concert would be the biggest event to take place in the South West this year.
- This was a new development for this well-known family attraction.
- Crealy was supporting the local economy by driving further footfall to the region.

A general press release was sent out in March but Exeter and Mid Devon's leading publication and a key target for local ticket sales, the *Express and Echo* was offered an exclusive the day prior to the official release, which resulted in a front-page news story. A series of competitions were scheduled to appear within print media and online publications within Devon, Cornwall, Somerset and Dorset to win tickets to the event. Tailored editorial accompanied each competition including key messages and event details alongside the Crealy Rocks branding.

A key offer was media time with Peter Andre. Two phone interviews were set up with the *Express and Echo* and Heart FM South West. This resulted in another front-page news story and prime airtime and online coverage.

Alongside this, two days of press and live radio interviews plus live performances in key locations were arranged for the concert's main support act and X Factor semi-finalists, The Reason 4. Not only was positive coverage achieved, but the event PR Manager was able to go out and network with the local media and build further relationships while promoting the Crealy Rocks brand. New media contacts were made and added to Crealy's existing media database including NOVA FM in Somerset and Plymouth FM.

Throughout the campaign a number of news stories were added to the mix. These included updates on ticket sales, additional acts being added to the line up and interview opportunities with the event director regarding the planning and the building of the concert arena. The press team contacted journalists who had already covered Crealy Rocks and offered them exclusives.

Over seventy members of the media attended the concert. They were given media packs including images, editorial and question and answer sheets. Goodie bags were provided containing event memorabilia and signed merchandise from Peter Andre and the support acts. This enabled senior management and members of the PR team to network and build further relationships. Post-event press releases were issued and a photographic database was made available to support concert reviews. This resulted in a number of follow up articles with headlines such as 'Perfect Pete Rocks Crealy's Big Night', 'Pete Rocks Faithful Fans' and 'Crealy Rocks its First Ever Concert'.

While the concert had a capacity of 10,000, final ticket sales were just over 6,000. Although disappointed that full capacity was not reached, the organisers were pleased that the event broke even with 60 per cent of tickets being sold for the first event of its kind held at Crealy.

# Peter promises 'a night to remember' at Crealy

BY RICHARD BIRCH

SINGER and reality TV star Peter Andre has been lined up to take the top slot at a new music event which will be taking place at a Devon attraction.

Devon's Crealy Great Adventure Park will play host to the Crealy Rocks concert in August.

It has been revealed it will be headlined by Peter, supported by X Factor contestants The Reason 4, Paradise Point and two local acts, N.U.M.B and Electric Skies.

Stagecoach South West and Shadow Leisure are supporting the event.

Commenting on headlining the inaugural event, Peter Andre said: "I can't wait to take to the stage at Devon's Crealy as

the South West is a beautiful part of the country.

"I have a loyal following of fans in Devon and I am hoping that a few extra will travel from further afield to see me.

"I will certainly be treating my fans to a great show and am looking forward to giving them a night to remember."

Tickets for the 10,000 capacity concert, which is taking place on Saturday, August 13, go on general sale on April 7, but Crealy Members can buy the first 4,000 tickets from Thursday. Organiser Rod Pearson, managing director of South West attractions company Maximum Fun Ltd, said: "It is brilliant to see our plans come to fruition and we are excited to offer our guests something unique this summer.

"As the area's biggest attraction it's important for us to continually drive visitors to the South West and to support the local economy as much as possible.

"Working with local businesses such as Stagecoach and Shadow Leisure can only guarantee a further boost to the South West economy."

Tickets for Crealy Members can be purchased for £25 per person by visiting the box office at Devon's Crealy Great Adventure Park only, from noon tomorrow until Wednesday, April 6.

General tickets go on sale from 9am on Thursday, April 7, from Ticket Zone by telephoning 01394 234889, or by visiting crealy.co.uk to buy tickets online.

**'LOYAL FOLLOWING':** Peter Andre

**FIGURE 12.2** *Express and Echo* coverage of Crealy Rocks

Crealy Rocks received over 160 news stories in local and regional media including the *Western Morning News*, *Midweek Herald*, *Swindon Advertiser* and the *Cornish Guardian* between March and August 2011. Over ninety minutes of interviews and presenter talk-up of Crealy Rocks was also received on local and regional radio including Heart FM, Plymouth FM, Palm FM in Torquay, Atlantic FM and Pirate FM in Cornwall and NOVA FM in Somerset.

National coverage was also received in *Entertainment News*, *First News*, *News of the World* and Heart FM, plus event listings and columns written by Peter Andre in a selection of celebrity magazines including *New* and *Inside Soap*.

The media relations campaign not only supported the development and awareness of the Crealy Rocks brand, but contributed to the awareness of the Crealy Great Adventure Park brand and helped to keep it in the forefront of the media agenda as the 'South West's leading family attraction'.

*Nicola Ash, Press Office, Crealy Great Adventure Parks*

# THE IMPORTANCE OF TARGETING

The important thing to remember in media relations is that blitzing hundreds of journalists on a press list (however up to date the contact names might be) may hit a few right targets but is likely to miss more and antagonise many. This is probably one of the practices that has fuelled anti-PR feeling among journalists. Journalists are still individuals and have their own singular preferences. One may prefer to have a pitch made by telephone, another may find it irritating.

Journalists have perennially complained about media releases being addressed to the wrong people and poorly targeted. In my 1997 survey (Theaker 2001: 123–126), the majority of journalists felt that too many releases were being sent to them which were not relevant to their publication or programme. The most common complaints were that the information was irrelevant (66 per cent) or not newsworthy (65 per cent). The use of mass email lists has not improved this problem. It is all too tempting to add names to an email media list, especially as it costs nothing to send out. Press offices can now subscribe to services such as Vocus which enable them to search worldwide media lists and classify contacts according to location or subject. Monaghan (2011) suggests that 'blast emails . . . don't work'.

Instead of sending formal media releases by email, journalists are now used to receiving more personalised pitches from PR practitioners. This approach can often result in more in-depth, quality coverage in a few more influential titles. Stateman (2003) quotes Fox 4 News' Jeff Crilley, who says, 'Don't pitch 300 people. Pitch three of the most important journalists you need.'

Each advises that each pitch should be tailored to the recipient. Print media should receive a first paragraph, which could appear in the publication, showing that you have researched the kinds of stories that are covered and the editorial style. The next paragraph should put the story in context and demonstrate why it's newsworthy, and the pitch can finish with a quote.

*PR Week* asked several journalists how many pitches they received and how many were used. Most received 100–150 pitch emails a month and used one or two, although the consumer writer used up to six or seven. Pet hates were faux personalisation (Good morning, hope you're enjoying the sunshine), referring back to the previous week's column (already covered, now looking for the next thing), gimmicks, waffle and irrelevant information. Most wanted timely, concise comment; statistics; exclusive research; case studies that brought the national news agenda to life; and the opportunity for great interviews. Tips included: reading the publication and tailoring the pitch appropriately; being concise and focused; eliminating basic grammar and spelling errors; making sure the PR practitioner knew the pitch inside out and having an interviewee available for comment (Blyth, 2011).

Be careful about attempting to control the content of the coverage, though. *The Guardian* updated its editorial code and included a new clause, which stated that journalists should not agree to promote products in order to secure interviews. This has often been the case in the area of celebrity PR, where access to actors and writers is restricted and depends on them being able to plug their latest book or film. *The Guardian* responded that the clause had been introduced after complaints from readers (Wicks 2011).

Despite these problems a 2011 survey of 500 journalists across fifteen countries found that PR agencies (62 per cent) and corporate spokespeople (59 per cent) are still the top source for news content. In an environment of staff cuts, almost half were having to produce more content and a third were working longer hours, so there was still a need for relevant, targeted information from PR practitioners (Oriella, 2011).

The views of Paul Douglas (Chipchase 2001), then editor of internet title *.net* are still relevant:

> Journalists source newsworthy stories in a number of ways, but the role of the PR agency in setting up interviews, supplying photography and clarifying background information makes an important contribution. Tactics such as the sending of tacky gifts and glossy press packs may fulfil a role in attracting the attention of a journalist, but are no substitution for a clearly written press release that has been tailored to the readers of the publication to which the material is being submitted. Wrongly targeted press releases tend to annoy and reflect badly on a PR agency, as does calling a publication with a possible news story having never read the publication being approached.
>
> Using meaningless phrases in press releases, such as 'the complete internet solution for the cost-conscious SME' in an attempt to sound au fait with the market is unlikely to get a press release noticed. Getting to the point and saying 'a low-cost piece of kit that can benefit many small businesses' is likely to receive a more favourable response.
>
> There is no reason that the internet should do away with the PR function as we know it – it is simply a faster, more efficient way to disseminate inform-ation. Unfortunately, it is sometimes too easy for a PR agency to mass-mail journalists with irrelevant material simply because it can do so at the touch of a button. With or without the internet, there is still a need for talented staff to write releases, liaise with journalists about possible stories and supply additional information or arrange interviews.

## KEEPING UP WITH CHANGE

When I started out in PR in 1980, press releases were typed up, photocopied and sent out in the mail. Little change was noted in a survey I carried out in March 1999. Three hundred questionnaires were sent out to journalists working in the UK national and regional press. At that time, only 21 per cent received over 100 releases.

The following case study shows how targeting information for individual news outlets can bring success.

## TRANSFORMING TRADE RECYCLING INTO MAINSTREAM NEWS FOR TQ RECYCLING

Recycling is a most worthy activity but it tends only to grab the headlines for the wrong reasons. Complaints, complicated systems and council cock-ups are regular mainstream media fodder. Good news stories are harder to find. And trade recycling? Forget it!

I've been working with TQ Recycling since it formed in 2007. Set up in response to the appalling lack of coherent options for local businesses it has been busy transforming trade recycling across south Devon. Most of our news stories had been aimed at the business pages but when TQ built its own recycling plant in 2010, we realised we needed to make trade recycling a mainstream news story.

At our initial planning meeting it became clear the directors wanted TQ's new plant's official opening to meet a plethora of objectives. Not only were they seeking maximum coverage for what the new plant could do, they also needed to acknowledge the role played by TQ's new investors (never a news high point). They needed local government to get excited how the plant could improve domestic recycling but TQ also wanted ordinary people to see what was being achieved on their doorstep.

Getting the media to the launch was not going to be easy as the only day it could take place was Armistice Day (so half the news would be taken up with memorial services) and only at 12 noon. The date was also terrible timing for the region's main business supplement and even the plant's location – being just outside the boundary for two main papers – was a problem.

Then there were the logistics. The plant's machinery (with fantastic names such as ballistic separator and optical laser sorting technology) would be switched on. The noise would be tremendous. On top of any media presence, MD David Newman and Sales Director Stephen Tooke needed to look after some fifty dignitaries and business leaders. The health and safety implications were infinite.

The only way to attract our key media and reach our key stakeholders was to arrange a personalised 'launch' for each, away from the official opening. The business supplement was given an early interview and exclusive commercial details of the plant's capacity and TQ's next steps. We used the visual of a lorry-load of rubbish being whizzed through the plant in minutes to entice TV crews early. Investors cheered as the first load was driven in to the hold. Our photographer recorded the opening, and we sent pictures and individually tailored press releases to the remaining target media.

**FIGURE 12.3** TQ Recycling launch

The result was even better than we'd hoped. TQ had blanket coverage across the regional TV, radio and newspapers including a lengthy appearance on BBC *Spotlight*'s evening news programmes. It was picked up by *Devon Life* and nationally. News articles and video footage are still available on the BBC's website.

For TQ, the coverage delighted their investors and led to a huge number of enquiries, including from several local authorities. The plant is not only running at full capacity but demand is such that phase two of its development has been brought forward.

*Claire Crawley began her PR career in the music industry before moving to the South West and the public sector. She now runs StartPoint PR, which specialises in supporting small local businesses.*

Nearly half (48 per cent) preferred to receive information by mail, as opposed to 15 per cent who preferred email.

The world was changing, though. A Middleberg Euro RSCG survey (Todorova 2002) found that 'for the first time, more journalists favour email . . . than the telephone or a personal visit'. A substantial 61 per cent stated that they prefer email, as against only 4 per cent who still preferred to work with fax sources. However, 51 per cent said that they still preferred to be contacted by phone.

Recent research by Haymarket (Brill 2011) in the charity sector found that 89 per cent of journalists wanted to be contacted by email and 7 per cent by phone.

The use of the internet has affected media relations as journalists are able to obtain information straight from a website rather than waiting for press releases. The internet streamlines every stage of the process – from making proactive contact by email to providing timely material for download.

Momorella and Woodall (2003) listed several elements that could be included in an online newsroom. They suggested a library of archived press releases, background documents, downloadable graphics, a calendar of events, contact information, audio and video and current news to make the journalist's job easier. They also recommended categorising and differentiating releases by subject and importance, not just cataloguing in chronological order, linking releases to related articles.

Haymarket (Brill, 2011) research found that 80 per cent of journalists who write about the not-for-profit sector use organisations' websites mainly to get contact information. Other uses for the website included background information about the charity (74 per cent); background research (60 per cent); statistics (48 per cent) and case studies (25 per cent).

PR practitioners can also use online methods proactively. Back in 1998, Janal recommended:

- look for journalists' queries online
- create a library of press releases
- write articles for online magazines
- create online conferences and seminars.

The advent of social media has also changed the landscape. While in the Haymarket (Brill 2011) survey, only 0.4 per cent of journalists wanted to be sent information through social media, and Oriella (2011) found that 4 per cent were using Twitter, Facebook or blogs as their first source in researching a story, this trend is set to change. Social media enables PR practitioners to form and build relationships with individual journalists and to share useful information. However, practitioners need to understand the protocols of each and be willing to spend time monitoring and responding to conversations. It is not enough to use them as another vehicle for one-way organisation-centred information; social media are more inclusive and generous. Practitioners can share their point of view, but also need to engage with those who comment.

Blogging is another channel that organisations can use to humanise what they are doing. All too often, though, corporate blogs are written by the PR practitioner, while being credited to the CEO. These fake blogs do nothing to enhance the reputation of the organisation or suggest that it is willing to engage in real conversations with its audiences. Practitioners may find it more fruitful to blog as themselves and share their knowledge on a variety of topics.

Celsi (2011) suggests using a variety of methods to send out stories about clients, but using story-telling language. Posting material on an organisation's blog, sending direct messages through Twitter and Facebook, emailing or phoning will all depend on the personal preferences of the journalist you are trying to reach. Knowing these preferences is part of your task as a media relations professional.

Some publications have used social media to determine content. *More* magazine produced an issue in June 2011 that had been written and edited by its Facebook fans. The magazine had higher numbers of followers on Facebook than Twitter, so celebrated its 100,000th fan on the site by offering them a chance to influence magazine content. At the same time, PR practitioners were involved by offering competition prizes and discounts on client products.

## END POINT

This chapter has covered the main elements in contacting the media. While reviewing how the ways in which PR practitioners contact journalists has changed, several of the elements of media relations have remained the same since the early days. Researching the target news outlet, approaching them with stories relevant to their audience, sending journalists information in their preferred format, sending information in a timely fashion, all these elements remain the same whether using hard copy, telephone, email or social media. Media relations will reappear in subsequent case studies as it continues to be the major element of the PR practitioner's role.

# CHAPTER 13

# Risk, incidents, issues and crisis management

*Heather Yaxley*

This chapter provides insight into short- and long-term approaches to respond to negative influences on organisations.

## CHECK POINT

After reading this chapter, you should be able to:

- identify areas of risk and negative influence in relation to a variety of organisations and scenarios;
- develop competencies, plans, processes and procedures to anticipate and react to incidents, issues and crisis situations.

## RISK MANAGEMENT

In the modern risk society (Beck 1992), there are many uncertainties that have potential to impact on organisations as well as publics, communities and wider society affected by their operations. Being able to identify and mitigate such influences is a key aspect of public relations.

The Institute of Risk Management (IRM) specifies risk may feature positive and negative aspects, consideration of which should be central to an organisation's strategic management to ensure its activities provide sustainable value.

IRM recommends formal reporting of risk management to stakeholders, which should detail control methods as well as processes used to identify, monitor, manage and review significant risks. The benefits of formal risk management are advocated as:

- protecting the interest of stakeholders;
- discharging the duties of senior management to direct strategy, build value and monitor organisational performance;
- ensuring management controls are in place and performing adequately.

An organisational risk management policy should be established detailing the processes and procedures in place, specific responsibilities, and compliance within other policy areas (e.g. Health and Safety). Public relations should contribute to such a policy by considering influences on the organisation's reputation and relationships with stakeholders.

## Methodical approach

Understanding the risks facing an organisation requires a methodical, continuous approach, starting with asking three questions (Garrick and Christie 2008):

1 What can go wrong?
2 How likely is that to happen?
3 What are the consequences if it does happen?

Risk analysis enables organisations to implement policies and procedures to increase the likelihood of success, while reducing possible legal, financial and reputational consequences. Such a proactive approach demonstrates responsibility rather than hoping an incident will not occur and being forced to respond after damage has been done.

One challenge of risk analysis is that responding proactively to potential dangers may be costly. It may not be responsible to allocate resources to address risks that have a low probability of occurring. However, potential consequences of such incidents may increase their importance.

Risks may occur in the external environment and/or as a result of strategies the organisation adopts to achieve its aims. Within the decision-making process (Chapter 8), potential risks need to be identified and, if they cannot be avoided, contingency plans devised.

Compliance to a regulatory and governance framework is the minimum response expected from any organisation. Demonstrating accountability through a system of appropriate policies and procedures is the responsibility of strategic and operational management.

A wider perspective to risk management is offered by public relations. It needs to reflect the organisation's values, as well as ethical expectations of, and moral responsibilities towards, key stakeholders. This advocates a responsiveness to enhance the organisation's reputation by engaging with stakeholders and influencers, understanding their particular concerns and ensuring these are considered as part of the risk analysis.

As with issues and crisis management, risk management requires the commitment of senior executives who are responsible for the strategic direction of the organisation. They should ensure proactive risk awareness and management is part of the culture with responsibilities and accountability allocated to individual functions. This underlines the importance of public relations being accepted as part of the strategic management team.

## Risk communications

McComas (2010: 462) states 'effective risk management includes risk communication with affected publics', which she defines as 'a purposeful, iterative exchange of information among individuals, groups and institutions related to the assessment, characterization, and management of risk'. Yaxley (2012b) considers risk communications in detail, highlighting the emphasis placed in contemporary best-practice approaches (Palenchar 2010) on building trust, transparency, respect for others and ongoing communications that acknowledge the uncertainty of risk situations.

A proactive, dialogic approach is accentuated by 'the modern dynamic, complex, 24/7 global communications environment' (Yaxley 2012b: 154) where 'the immediacy and interconnectedness of mobile, online and social media are able to amplify what might otherwise be matters of low or no significance'. The flexibility this necessitates needs to be factored into risk management procedures.

**ACTION POINT**

The UK Health and Safety Executive (www.hse.gov.uk) has developed a five-step approach to risk assessment. It advises adoption of precautions and control measures that are easy to implement. Although specifically considering risks relating to hazards in the workplace, the HSE's advice can be adapted for a public relations risk assessment.

The IRM (www.theirm.org) has developed a risk management standard setting out a best-practice approach against which organisations can assess their own activities.

Action templates based on these recommendations are included in the Appendix (pp. 349–352) to assist with undertaking risk management for an organisation, PR function or specific activities.

**ACTION POINT**

In 2003, confectionary company, Cadbury, launched its 'Get Active' initiative in partnership with the charity Youth Support Trust. The campaign was endorsed by the government sports minister and included funding to support teacher training and increase activity resources within schools.

It featured six stages:

- Training for 5,000 teachers as sports specialists with resource cards and curriculum aids.

- Free unbranded sports kit up to £9 million in value available through a promotional voucher collection scheme.

- A free public activity day at the NEC in Birmingham involving fourteen sports and activities, including the opportunity to run with Olympic champion, Paula Radcliffe.

- Commissioning Paula Radcliffe, Darren Gough and Audley Harrison to be sports ambassadors and highlight the positive aspects of sport and its impact on their lives.

- Employee involvement including community 'adopt a school' fundraising 'token match' and volunteering 'count yourself in'.

- Research in conjunction with Loughborough University studying children's activity levels, interest and response in schools.

Cadbury claimed that 40 per cent of UK schools registered for the programme (with eighteen withdrawing as a result of subsequent media criticism). Over 40,000 hours of activity was recorded by 13,500 children and adults at the Get Active day. Schools were adopted by 264 employees, 160 employees fundraised through sponsorship and 170 volunteered for the Get Active day.

However, the scheme was criticised by media, politicians and the Food Commission for encouraging children to eat large amounts of chocolate in exchange for sports gear. Calculations were made regarding the total fat and calories of all the promotional chocolates and amounts of bars required to obtain sports equipment. For example, acquiring a cricket set would require vouchers from 2,730 bars.

- Use this example to walk through the risk management process to determine whether the negative outcome could have been anticipated and avoided.
- What was the operational risk of this campaign?
- Consider the consequence of removing the promotional product element of the campaign and whether a different approach could have been taken to provide financial and marketing benefits.

In November 2011, *Marketing Week* reported Kraft (which bought Cadbury in 2010) is to launch a new programme in 2012 called Health for Life. Developed with local organisations in Birmingham and the West Midlands, the initiative will focus on improving the health and lifestyle of people and employees in the local area. As part of the UK Government's Responsibility Deal (see Chapter 17), Kraft has pledged to launch community and workplace initiatives to encourage the public to become physically active, as well as reducing salt and fats in its products and improving calorie labelling.

- What risks do you think the new initiative needs to avoid?
- How would you balance the benefits and risks of the Health for Life programme?

## Operational PR risks

A planned approach (see Part II) enables PR activities to be assessed for potential negative outcomes. Contingency plans can be developed to minimise or address areas of risk if they cannot be eliminated.

In some cases, such as organising events, risk may be managed by appointing an external supplier with experience and expertise. A written contract, setting out key responsibilities for risk management, provides legal protection when appointing suppliers, including PR consultancies. It is important to check suppliers maintain professional indemnity and public liability insurance. Specific insurance is advisable for events and campaigns to cover the risk of unexpected, often costly, occurrences.

Senior management may decide the 'opportunity cost' of accepting a risk is worthwhile. This means the benefits of taking action outweigh possible conse-quences, or that the cost (in time and resources) involved in managing a risk is considered better spent undertaking the campaign. In such circumstances, a contingency plan needs to be in place, particularly to manage any possible crisis that could arise.

## INCIDENTS, ISSUES AND CRISIS SITUATIONS

## Incident management

Working in PR requires an adaptive nature, where practitioners are able to consider and accommodate emerging situations. Planned approaches need to allow for changes in circumstances and matters that may affect successful execution. This can be thought of as incident management.

Incidents are generally small issues that occur within everyday activities without affecting the strategic operation of the organisation. For example, travel delays, technical issues, special requests or unexpected changes may affect the success of a planned event. It may be possible to anticipate such incidents and have a back-up plan, although the range of eventualities could make this unfeasible. Consequently, an ability to handle problems is essential. Remaining calm and being able to work out solutions while acting promptly and efficiently are important skills to develop. Building strong relationships with those who can affect the successful delivery of PR programmes will enable solutions to be implemented more readily.

Minor incidents emphasise the importance of ensuring plans and requirements are detailed in writing. Key documentation includes briefing reports, action plans, time-tables, movement schedules, detailed roles and responsibilities, event programmes, records of meetings, media lists, budgets and contracts. These demonstrate a responsible, professional approach and provide a means of ensuring prompt action if a problem occurs. For example, if a venue fails to equip a room as specified, reference to a contract can ensure responsibility for remedying the situation is recognised and resolved immediately. It is also important to document matters arising and solutions implemented in campaign and other reports for future reference.

Although most PR practitioners are unlikely to experience a major crisis situation on the scale of the global problems besetting BP and Toyota in 2010, they will face routine incidents throughout their career. This highlights the need to develop the competency to prepare for, handle and learn from minor incidents in a professional manner.

## Issues management

Unlike an incident, an issue is not simply a problem to be resolved. It is a matter that may present a significant risk or opportunity for the organisation where there is a difference of opinion over the most appropriate action to be taken.

Issues monitoring needs to involve more than a 'surveillance' approach (L'Etang 2008: 86) and should take account of different stakeholder perspectives. Yaxley (2012b: 163–164) advises recognising specific concerns 'enables responses to be developed to meet particular needs or to engage with the most frequently raised aspects of the issue'.

Undertaking a situational analysis (Chapter 5) enables existing or emerging issues to be identified and addressed. This may mean working with other functions on operational responses or implementing appropriate communication strategies (Chapter 8). Trend analysis and scenario forecasting are useful techniques for identifying possible issues although, as with risk management, the likelihood and consequences of such eventualities need to be assessed.

Issues affecting an organisation's licence to operate (Ihlen and van Ruler 2009) may require public affairs or lobbying strategies. For example, organisations may wish

## UNDERSTANDING SOCIETY
## (www.ipsos-mori.com)

The Ipsos MORI Social Research Institute Understanding Society report (Skinner and Mludzinski 2011) reviewed the impact on public opinion of major events. One issue is that economic concerns have become a norm rather than an exception, with one 'watershed finding' noted as people expecting their children to have a lower quality of life than they have enjoyed.

The report compares anger among young people to the global 'Occupy' movement which emerged as grassroots activism in 2011. This can be linked to the Arab Spring uprisings in North Africa, strikes and increased engagement in social media (Chapter 16) to indicate how publics are increasingly active in the real and virtual worlds regarding particular issues.

Environmental issues are also discussed in light of the global economic crisis. Although publics appear to have little interest in pollution/ environmental matters, the report believes this is a long-term matter of concern. This presents a challenge for PR practitioners communicating sustainability and CSR environmental initiatives.

■ Such reports provide a useful context to identify issues affecting organisations – consider the viewpoints expressed in this and similar publications and how they debate matters that could affect your own organisation.

to see issues debated in the public sphere (Chapter 17), where their corporate agenda can contribute towards informing public opinion or policy decisions.

As well as developing plans, processes and procedures to enable early identification and management of issues, PR practitioners need to consider the competencies that enable them to be effective 'boundary-spanners'. Research and analysis is the most obvious skill set required. Another competency is the ability to develop flexible and adaptive strategies (with identification of risk/opportunity factors and resource requirements) that can be agreed by senior management. Traditional communication competencies of PR practitioners are relevant in issues management with regard to determining approaches to inform, persuade or engage stakeholders and publics.

Issues management can be considered as 'opportunity management' (Jaques 2002: 142) or a defensive precursor to crisis management. Two types of issues-related campaigns – social marketing and agenda-setting – are discussed in Chapter 17.

When determining if an issue offers a social marketing opportunity, the dangers of being seen to be promoting special interests rather than acting for the good of the public should be avoided.

Charities, NGOs and groups of active publics, as well as commercial and public sector organisations, use agenda-setting campaigns to raise the profile of issues or stimulate crisis situations to get their voice heard and change public opinion (Bourland-Davis *et al.* 2010).

Another issues management strategy is to form coalitions to co-orientate with others on matters of common concern. Confrontation and civil disobedience are approaches more likely to be found among activist groups than mainstream organisations, which face reputational risks from being seen to act outside the law.

## ACTION POINT

## MOTOR CODES (www.motorcodes.co.uk)

Motor Codes was set up by the motor industry in 2008 to act as the self-regulatory body for the automotive sector. It represented a response to a National Consumer Council (NCC) paper, which claimed shoddy vehicle repair work cost consumers £4 billion a year and called for the automotive industry to obtain full Office of Fair Trading (OFT) approval or be subjected to legislation. The poor image of the service and repair sector was an issue of concern to a wide range of organisations and the solution reflected a coalition strategy (forming Motor Codes) to alter public opinion and improve the industry's reputation. In November 2011, Motor Codes received full OFT approval for its Service and Repair Code following recognition that it had been effective in reducing consumer complaints.

- What are the benefits and drawbacks of co-orienting with other organisations to address issues of mutual concern?
- What role does public relations play in ensuring that such initiatives are a success?

## Crisis management

In September 2011, the British government and the British Standards Institute (BSI) launched the Publicly Accredited Specification (PAS) 200 to help organisations implement systems to detect, prepare for and respond to crisis situations. Building on the existing British Standard in Business Continuity (BS 25999 Parts 1 and 2), PAS 200 provides practical guidance to ensure competence in dealing with crises, including developing a communications strategy.

The full report, PAS 200: Crisis Management – guidance and good practice, is available to purchase from the BSI at www.bsigroup.com.

Although Yaxley (2012b: 168) argues that 'crisis communications is one area where the value of public relations should be indisputable', development of PAS 200 did not involve the industry's professional bodies. Its steering group included representatives from Bank of England, Business Continuity Institute, Leeds University Business School, Thomas Cook, UK Airlines Emergency Planning Group and Visor Consultants.

David Evans, global head of emergency response and crisis management for Petrofac, and a member of the steering group, explains PAS 200 was developed to help senior executives understand what happens when 'inherently abnormal, unstable and complex' events occur (Bovingdon 2011). It details practical steps that organisations can take by providing an 'operational structure'

Rather than presenting a prescriptive solution to every eventuality, PAS 200 acknowledges crisis management occurs in complex and challenging environments. As Edward P. Borodzicz, professor of risk and crisis management at the University of Portsmouth confirms (Bovingdon 2011) there is a 'need to empower the right individuals to break rules to deal with a crisis effectively'.

The recognition of a need for flexibility echoes the argument of Gilpin and Murphy (2008: 5) against 'overly rigid crisis planning procedures'. Yaxley (2012b: 170) supports 'consideration of the actual situation being faced by the particular organisation at a specific time', with public relations 'capable of working as proficiently as possible' rather than being presented as 'controlling the crisis'.

There seems little awareness of PAS 200 among PR practitioners, with no mention in the trade media or by the professional bodies. The specialist reputation strategy and management consultancy, Regester Larkin (2011) has reviewed PAS 200 stating it 'is an interesting addition to knowledge on crisis management and one which should be watched by crisis management globally given the history of BSs being adopted as International Standards (ISOs)'.

The PAS 200 report defines a crisis as presenting 'complex and difficult challenges that may have profound and far-reaching consequences, sometimes irrespective of how successfully they are seen to be managed' (BSI 2011: 7). Significant risk to reputation is seen as one of the consequences of a crisis.

Although incidents and issues have the potential to escalate into a crisis, they are more manageable. As PAS 200 clarifies, it is important to ensure business continuity management alongside crisis management. This is evident in Jaques' circular issues and crisis management relationship model (2010: 442), which presents four areas of effective crisis management:

1   Crisis preparedness:

  - planning processes
  - systems, manuals
  - training, simulations.

2   Crisis prevention:

  - early warning, scanning
  - issues and risk management
  - emergency responses.

3   Crisis event management:

  - crisis recognition
  - system activation/response
  - crisis management.

4   Post-crisis management

  - recovery, business resumption
  - post-crisis issue impacts
  - evaluation, modification.

Business continuity may be considered to include elements that fall within each of the areas of Jaques' model: management of planning processes, system manuals and training simulations; emergency response; system activation/response and business resumption.

PAS 200 not only distinguishes crisis management from operational responses, it argues creative rather than pre-prepared solutions are required when facing a genuine crisis. Similarly, Yaxley (2012b: 171) calls for a 'new approach involving continuous learning', citing Robert and Lajtha (2002: 181), who argue for the need 'to equip key managers with the capabilities, flexibility and confidence to deal with sudden and unexpected problems/events – or shifts in public perception of any such problems/events'.

Another key aspect of PAS 200, which is emphasised by Regester Larkin (2011), is the importance of 'the people and cultural aspects' of crisis management. Appropriate personnel need to be identified and trained prior to involvement in crisis management. When the future of the organisation is at risk, senior executives need to be seen to be managing the crisis. But, as in the case of BP where its CEO and chairman made ill-considered statements during the Gulf oil spill crisis, ensuring executives recognise and reflect professional public relations expertise in their communications is a challenge.

The focus of crisis management training within public relations is primarily on communications, particularly preparation for media interviews. However, a wider perspective is required to encompass relationship building, reputation management and stakeholder communications in all circumstances. This means recognising:

- There are no 'off the record' comments.
- Social media is able to 'amplify what might otherwise be issues of low or no significance' (Yaxley 2012b: 154).
- A reputation that took decades to build can be threatened by a single event.
- Stakeholders and publics form a complex web of interconnections (meaning messages need to be consistent and credible).
- Credibility is subjective to the receiver, but senior executives are increasingly judged on their personality and communicative competence through the lens of broadcast media (which is not as easy to be 'crafted' by public relations experts as written communications).
- Emotional rather than rational judgements come to the fore in crisis situations.
- Media, and public, are increasingly crisis literate and aware of the 'apology phenomenon' (Lazare 2005: 7) of pseudo-apologies – although Yaxley (2012b: 173) claims these may be expected as a form of 'power-rebalance' or entertainment.

PAS 200 identifies four requirements of a crisis management capability:

1 Intellectual: including ability to analyse situations, set strategy, determine options, make decisions and evaluate their impact.

2 Organizational: including structures and processes needed to translate decisions into action and review their impact.

3 Cultural: reflecting willingness of staff to share and support top managers' intentions and policies.

4 Logistical: ability to support solutions by applying the right resources in the right place, at the right time.

## Crisis communications

The planning approach detailed in Part II offers a framework for developing a crisis communications strategy and action plan based on situational analysis, clear objectives and a monitoring and evaluation process.

Effective crisis communication approaches include stakeholder engagement, although Freeman and McVea (2005) go a step further in arguing for stakeholder partnerships. This has the advantage of developing a strong relationship whereby partners not only give an organisation the benefit of doubt (at least initially) in a crisis situation, but act as advocates in extending the reach and credibility of crisis communications.

PAS 200 details five levels of stakeholder engagement:

1   Inform all key stakeholders, including staff, to help dispel myths and rumours and present a positive message about the organisation's ability to deal with a crisis.

2   Monitor constantly for new stakeholders and reactions from known stakeholders to adapt communications strategy as needed.

3   Consult with staff and key stakeholders to disseminate key messages and gain feedback on analysis, alternatives and/or decisions.

4   Involve staff and key stakeholders, where possible, to ensure concerns and aspirations are considered in the decision-making process.

5   Collaborate with key stakeholders to aid decision-making and develop alternative solutions.

Online technologies also need to be incorporated in any crisis communications strategy. In particular, information needs to be available via the organisations' owned or created media, which Yaxley (2012a: 430) explains 'could include a YouTube channel, magazine, podcasts, Twitter accounts, corporate blog and so forth'.

The immediacy of online, social and mobile technology requires prompt consideration of an appropriate response. This does not necessarily involve an instant response to anyone communicating about an incident. It is more important for the organisation to determine a strategic approach, which should include being able to respond proactively and reactively using online and offline communication channels.

## **A PERSONAL PERSPECTIVE ON TOYOTA'S GLOBAL RECALL**

**ACTION POINT**

As corporate communications manager at Toyota GB in the mid-1990s, I was involved in managing routine product and consumer relations issues. Generally, given the company's high rating in the J.D.Power and similar customer satisfaction surveys, the media received few complaints and the company acted professionally and promptly in resolving any cases that were raised with the PR department.

Given my experience with the brand, naturally I followed the global recall situation in 2010 with some interest. Millions of Toyota and Lexus (the company's luxury brand) vehicles were affected by a series of recalls related to claims of accidents reported in the US media. Liker (2011) notes 'this iconic company, synonymous with safety and quality, was vilified by the American press, the government, and expert witnesses to plaintiff lawyers'. He also points out that the official report by the National Highway Transportation Authority (NHTSA) blamed driver error, rather than technical problems, for any reported accidents that it had investigated.

Despite this vindication, the crisis cost the company significant sums in managing the recall, as well as considerable loss of value in its share price. Mittal *et al.* (2010) found 106 of 108 articles in the *Wall Street Journal*, which discussed Toyota during February 2010, were negative to the company, and they found high recognition of the problem among the brand's customers. However, they also found a high level of satisfaction providing 'brand insulation'.

There was considerable criticism of Toyota's handling of the crisis by media and PR commentators, who failed to recognise the realities of managing a fast-moving situation in an increasingly complex world. Normally vehicle recalls are a routine incident where the role of the PR function is small as the customer service function and bodies such as VOSA and the DVLA in the UK are responsible for informing customers.

This is not to downplay the potential seriousness of a vehicle problem and recalls should involve effective monitoring and reporting systems. Communications between car retailers, their service departments, head office customer relations, technical functions and production facilities need to enable issues to be identified early and addressed. When a solution is identified, it will be implemented in terms of manufacturing components or developing software updates. Then, the solution will be communicated (often in a host of languages), parts shipped, training undertaken and work scheduled as and when it suits the customer.

While this process is going on, the PR team will prepare briefing materials; this involves liaising with colleagues around the globe, advising executives, marketing and others on how and what to communicate – which is a constantly moving matter. In some cases, an issue arises via a customer contacting the media, which the PR function will investigate and address, with legal advice where appropriate.

If a recall situation escalates, communications with all stakeholders – from employees to shareholders, politicians to motoring groups, insurance companies to suppliers – will be coordinated, updated and reported so that feedback is used as part of the ongoing process of being clear about what is happening and what needs to be done.

Existing PR plans and everyday tasks will still need to be implemented – or sidelined – as everyone works round the clock to do the best they can in managing the crisis.

Toyota in the UK was proactive with its media and online communications. It used a blog (from the front page of its main website) as well as Twitter. Rather than responding to every post or Tweet (which some critics demanded), priorities need to be determined. Toyota appeared to have decided print and broadcast media had more impact in reaching more viewers and readers, particularly those who are the company's customers.

Liker (2011) identifies 'Toyota's systematic approach to problem solving' as an approach from which the media and government could learn. This logical perspective, however, fails to engage with what Gilpin and Murphy (2008: 4) identify as a 'real-world environment of confusion, unforeseen events, and missing information'. In such circumstances, the PR function at Toyota was faced with acting to resolve an emerging, escalating communications problem in the face of falling share prices, declining sales and potentially long-lasting damage to a hard-earned reputation.

- Were you aware of the Toyota crisis in 2010?
- What is your personal reaction to the above arguments in favour of a flexible, considered approach to crisis management?
- Why do you feel that media and communication commentators are vocal in criticising organisations like Toyota for the management of crisis situations?

## END POINT

Risk management involves strategic management of an organisation in identifying and mitigate uncertainties which impact on its effective operation. The PR function needs to be involved in formal reporting of risk going beyond compliance to consider ethical expectations and moral responsibilities. Risk communications should build trust and acknowledge uncertainty with a dialogic approach.

Incidents, issues and crisis offer different levels of situations faced by PR practitioners, which may represent an opportunity or a threat. When managing incidents, an adaptive nature is important with planning allowing for changes to ensure successful execution of PR activities. Issues management addresses more significant risks, predicated on competencies to undertake ongoing situational analysis and develop particular solutions with the agreement of senior management.

The most serious situations require crisis management with the Publicly Accredited Specification (PAS) 200 offering practical guidance, including ensuring competence in developing a communications strategy. It is recommended that PR practitioners engage with this new initiative which supports a flexible approach to responding in complex and challenging environments.

# CHAPTER 14

# Corporate social responsibility

*Alison Theaker*

As consumers become more demanding, organisations have sought to differentiate themselves. With the use of new technology increasing transparency, one of the elements of differentiation has been to adopt socially responsible methods. How much of this is doing good to be good, or doing good to look good?

## CHECK POINT

In this chapter we will:

- define CSR;
- examine the Virtue Matrix;
- consider the practitioner's role in advising management on CSR;
- look at cause related marketing and how that is different from CSR;
- examine two case studies where CSR is integral to the business.

First, here is a definition of CSR:

> Corporate social responsibility describes the role a company has in society.
> (www.ipr.org.uk/member/PRguides/CSR)

This does not really tell us much about what CSR should look like. In the 1990s, Jerry Wright, Lever Brothers' marketing director, called Persil's support of the Funfit scheme for 3- to 11-year-olds 'enlightened self-interest – a combination of a worthy cause and an opportunity to target heavy detergent users such as the parents of young children' (C. Murphy 1999: 20). Again, an older rationale states:

> An institution's relationship with its neighbours in its community is crucial because these neighbours supply the organisation's workforce, provide an environment that attracts or fails to attract talented personnel, set taxes, provide essential services and can, if angered, impose restraints on the institution or industry.
>
> (Cutlip *et al.* 1985: 393)

This statement disappeared from later editions of Cutlip *et al.* Originally Cutlip seemed to suggest that any such involvement is down to basic self-interest, to enable the company to have an easy life. 'A corporation can gain competitive advantage by having the goodwill of local communities,' agree Werbel and Wortman (2000: 124). These arguments were a reaction to the economist Milton Friedman, who declared that business could not have responsibilities, that only people could have responsibilities (1993). He declared that CSR was a 'fundamentally subversive doctrine,' and that 'there is one and only one social responsibility of business – to . . . increase its profits'.

However, the RSA Inquiry concluded that companies have to earn their 'licence to operate', and CSR was therefore a necessity rather than a luxury. Robert Waterman (quoted in Future Foundation 1998) concluded: 'Companies that set profits as their No. 1 goal are actually less profitable in the long run than people-centred companies.'

Dauncey (1994) devised a scale of 'Shades of Green' to assess how committed an organisation was to being more environmentally friendly. Green Trimmings were just a symbolic nod, a few green products which were marketed more than the unenvironmentally friendly ones. The scale rose through Green Cuffs (basic recycling, turning off lights), Green Clothes (conducting an environmental audit) and Green Body (redesigning the product line to eliminate non-recyclable materials) to Green Brains (having a long-term business plan to achieve sustainability), Green Heart (encouraging social ownership for local offices) and finally Green Soul (overall goals of the organisation consider how they will benefit the planet and pursue higher goals).

Bowd (2005) suggests that a healthy business requires a healthy community and that CSR is generally held to increase profit or improve reputation. The benefits of operating in an ethical manner can include goodwill, customer and staff loyalty and strong stakeholder relationships which can result in a competitive edge. After suffering from a consumer backlash due to publicity about working conditions in factories in the developing world, Gap Inc. (2006 Annual CSR report, mentioned in Bowd 2005) reported that it had revoked approval for seventy supplier factories in violation of their code of vendor contract.

**TABLE 14.1 Enlightenment matrix**

|  |  | Self interest | |
| --- | --- | --- | --- |
|  |  | **High** | **Low** |
| Philanthropy | High | Social responsibility | Pure philanthropy |
|  | Low | Cause related marketing | Enlightened self interest |

Source: Cannon, T. (1992) *Corporate Responsibility*

Moloney (2006) draws a distinction between CSR and philanthropy. While public relations draws attention to CSR activities to enhance an organisation's reputation, this goes against the private altruism of philanthropy. Cannon (1992) set this out in the Enlightenment Matrix above.

This puts social responsibility at the confluence of both philanthropy and self interest. Cannon raises the motivation behind such schemes. Where self interest is low and the main aim is to do good, that would be considered pure philanthropy. So most writers see social responsibility as having benefits for the organisation as well as for the recipients.

Worcester (2007) stated: 'No modern corporation can exist for long, much less thrive, without taking responsibility for its actions.' Every company needs to define who its stakeholders are. Worcester advised that organisations pay attention to ethical consumerism, social reporting, overseas sourcing, community involvement, and the environment.

Being seen as socially responsible is likely to attract sales, reputation, donors and supporters. Moloney (2006) queried whether statements of social responsibility are genuine or 'window dressing'. He quoted research by Christian Aid in 2004 which suggested that companies frequently use such initiatives to defend operations which come in for public criticism.

Davis (2004) pointed out that although the amount spent on CSR rose from £225 million in 1990–1991 to £499 million in 2000–2001 that this represented the same percentage of company profits.

The Labour government's vision in the UK, published in 2004, encouraged businesses to take account of their economic, social and environmental impacts. The Companies Act (2006) obliged listed companies to include a business review in their annual reports. Key performance indicators had to demonstrate the effectiveness of environmental, social and community policies (Gray, 2007).

Research by Price Waterhouse Coopers (www.csreurope.org, 2002) found that 79 per cent of CEOs thought that CSR was vital to their companies, and 71 per cent said they would sacrifice profits in the short term in favour of long-term shareholder value. The London Business School reviewed eighty studies on CSR. Of these, forty-two made a positive impact, nineteen found no link with reputation, fifteen gave mixed results and four were negative. Coverage of CSR activities is certainly increasing. Research undertaken by Echo and presented to the CIPR in 2003 reviewed more than 3,000 articles on CSR published between January 2000 and September 2002.

Yaxley (2011) divides an organisation's stakeholders into different groups. She suggested that focusing on employees, customers and suppliers was simply about survival, while thinking about shareholders and government as well meant that profitability was important. If a company engaged in philanthropy for good causes, this showed that it was considering its community. Social responsibility suggested an agenda which took wider society into account. She listed the expectations of different stakeholder groups.

**TABLE 14.2 Expectations of different stakeholder groups**

| | |
|---|---|
| Customers | Want to buy from companies who share their views |
| Employees | Want to share their values with their organisation |
| Communities | Want jobs and revenue to be created locally as well as environments in which they want to work and live |
| Suppliers | Want to partner with companies with sound business practices and reputations |
| Government | Want business to support its aims for society |
| Media | Want organisations to deliver public expectations |
| Investors | Want to see added value and avoid damaging crises |

**READING POINT**

Martin (2002: 69–75) suggests referring to his Virtue Matrix to assess whether it is worthwhile engaging in a particular activity. He found that consumers, investors and business leaders were all urging corporations to 'remember their obligations to their employees, their communities and the environment, even as they pursue profits for shareholders'. He put forward the view of corporate responsibility as a product, subject to market pressures. By examining the drivers of corporate virtue, he found there were two main elements, compliance and choice. Furthermore, CSR activities could either be instrumental – explicitly enhancing shareholder value – or intrinsic – simply because it was the right thing to do.

Martin then devised his Matrix, with four quadrants. The bottom two he called the civil foundation. This is made up of norms, customs and laws and companies may choose either to observe them or they may have to legally comply with them. Companies operating here do no more than meet society's basic expectations of how they should act. When they move beyond this, this is what Martin calls the frontier. This is above and beyond the call of duty, so to speak. Practices that benefit both society and shareholders are termed strategic and those that benefit society but not shareholders are called structural, because there is a structural barrier to corporate action here. Some actions that start by being in the frontier, such as Prudential Insurance's introduction in 1990 of viatical settlements to allow people with Aids to tap into death benefits in their life insurance to pay medical expenses, create so much goodwill for the companies concerned that others follow suit and this kind of behaviour can migrate to the civil foundation. In the US, only a handful of companies once offered health care benefits to employees' dependents, but because this created so much goodwill, others soon followed and eventually this became included in government regulations.

The upper limit of the civil foundation is therefore not fixed. In strong economies it may move upwards as more social benefits become the norm, but it can shrink if times get hard. Martin also raises the question of international companies who comply with the civil foundation in their area of operation, but not in their home country. Thus Nike complied with local customs in its pay and practices in south-west Asia, but was criticised in the US and Europe because this did not agree with expected standards there.

How does this help an organisation considering its own CSR and what policies to introduce? There will be certain good practices that it will have to comply with, and some that have become accepted as normal in the society in which it is operating. So complying with environmental laws or providing an on-site nursery wins no brownie points. To earn 'public credit' a company has to be in the frontier. Most policies would tend to be strategic, giving some benefit to shareholders as well as society, but Martin makes a compelling case that companies should consider moving into the structural frontier to satisfy their publics.

> No consortium of energy producers had come together to formulate and execute a strategy to reduce greenhouse-gas emissions. Pharmaceutical companies have not yet crafted a plan to halt the worldwide spread of HIV infection. Media companies have failed to take concerted action to stem the tide of vulgar trash that too often passes for children's entertainment . . . the inability or unwillingness to deliver these obvious benefits create a powerful sense that corporations are not doing enough.
>
> (Martin, 2002:72)

# CSR EUROPE: THE EUROPEAN BUSINESS NETWORK FOR CORPORATE SOCIAL RESPONSIBILITY

CSR Europe is the leading European business network for CSR, with around seventy multinational corporations and twenty-eight national partner organisations as members. The organisation was founded in 1995 by senior European business leaders in response to an appeal by the European Commission President Jacques Delors. It has since grown to become an inspiring network of business people working at the very forefront of CSR across Europe and globally.

## The largest CSR network in Europe

CSR Europe's network of national partner organisations brings together twenty-eight membership-based, business-led CSR organisations from twenty-five European countries. In total, the network reaches out to more than 3,000 companies throughout Europe.

## Enterprise 2020

In October 2010, CSR Europe launched a joint Enterprise 2020 initiative to address societal challenges through collaborative action and shape the business contribution to the European Union's Europe 2020 strategy for smart, sustainable and inclusive growth. Since its launch, Enterprise 2020 has become the reference initiative for the ideal company of the future and forms the umbrella for all CSR Europe activities.

## A unique service delivery model

In order to help companies to progress towards Enterprise 2020, CSR Europe has designed a unique service delivery model, which aims to:

1   Support companies in building sustainable competitiveness by providing a platform for innovation and exchange;
    - share and further develop best practice on CSR;
    - benefit from practical research and information services.

2   Foster close cooperation between companies and their stakeholders by exploring new ways of working together to create a sustainable future;
    - cooperate and co-build solutions with stakeholders in several topic platforms;
    - produce tangible results and models which can be shared externally across industries.

3   Strengthen Europe's global leadership on CSR by engaging with EU institutions and a wider range of international players;

- shape European CSR policy development;
- engage with CSR Europe's National and leading global CSR organisations.

CSR Europe's model sets out several elements to sustainable business growth, dealing with climate change, changing demographics, resource scarcity, population growth, global trade, environmental degradation, urbanisation and poverty, education and equality. See: www.csr europe.org/data/files/Marketing/CSR_Europe_overview_and_service_offer.pdf

Should businesses be involved in these areas, or is this the job of governments? What happens if only some organisations get involved, at cost to themselves, and their competitors do not?

What is the role of the PR practitioner in advising management whether to engage in CSR or not? James and Larissa Grunig gave a lecture at the 2010 PRSA International conference where they put forward the view that public relations was about communal relationships between organisations and their stakeholders and that 'we do what we do in the interest of the relationship more than the self interest of the organisation that employs us'. They felt that the developments in social media meant that stakeholders could initiate a conversation with an organisation, and that 'better ways to listen' needed to be put in place.

# CAUSE-RELATED MARKETING: A MORE HONEST APPROACH?

In the Enlightenment Matrix above, cause related marketing (CRM) is high in self interest and low on philanthropy. Sue Adkins (2006) of Business in the Community, states that research shows that '67 per cent of the general public and 42 per cent of business journalists agree that industry and commerce do not pay enough attention to their social responsibilities'. She adds, '83 per cent of the general public feel that it is very or fairly important' that organisations should demonstrate that they are taking their social responsibilities seriously. For Adkins, CRM is a way that companies can differentiate themselves in the marketplace, and that 71 per cent of consumers claimed to be influenced at the point of purchase by this. Consumers are more inclined to purchase a product which is donating a proportion of its price to charity.

CRM is different from CSR in that it is obvious that both parties have a commercial interest in the partnership. While Marks and Spencer's partnership with Breakthrough Breast Cancer raised £1.45 million for the charity, it also raised the company's profile and led to the development of a new product range for those living with or having survived breast cancer.

Adkins warns that CRM, while having clear business benefits in raising consumers' sense of trust in an organisation and its products, must not be undertaken lightly. If it seems like a bolt-on rather than related to business values, such schemes can backfire. In 2000, she said, 'CRM isn't about offering buy this and 10p goes to that – there has to be a greater marketing mix to build awareness and secure emotional engagement and loyalty' (Brabbs, 2000). Cadburys received much criticism for its Get Active scheme, where children could save wrappers to exchange for sports equipment for their schools. This caused a backlash when the media scorned how much chocolate a child would have to eat to claim a football. While Cadburys denied that it was designed to boost sales and that the people collecting vouchers were families and the wider community, it phased out the wrapper collection part of the initiative (Williamson, 2004).

There are only a few charities that could afford to work without corporate support. Wall (2000) quotes Stephen Lee, former head of ICFM, the professional body of fundraisers, as saying: '[CRM] is a con. It's a mechanism dreamed up by business to promote business, with very strong rhetoric about partnership which is usually absolute rubbish'. Lee recommends a formal, written policy and advises caution in forming relationships to avoid alienating private donors. Few charities have such a policy, but simply follow the guidelines of the Charity Commission.

Brabbs (2000) quotes Colin Buckingham of Research International as saying, 'CRM has a real impact on consumer behaviour. People reward companies with increased usage and loyalty'.

The two case studies chosen illustrate organisations where it would be hard to separate the social responsibility element from the business itself. Both have taken social responsibility to heart as part of their mission and business values.

## ACTION POINT

## LOVING THE BEACH

The Venus Company was founded in 1995 by Michael and Louisa Smith and Lee Porter. The first café was opened at Blackpool Sands in South Devon. The three founders wanted to create a business to encompass their interest in environmental issues, but also bring the professionalism of High Street catering to the beach setting. They wanted to create a brand known for both quality and corporate responsibility. At the same time they had clear business objectives to establish market leadership in the UK as the greenest beach café and shop operator. They wanted to achieve double-digit sales growth and 10 per cent pre-tax profit, growing organically from internal funding.

Venus achieved 15 per cent growth from 2001 to 2007, and although a poor season led to a drop to only 4 per cent in 2008, double-digit growth was resumed in 2009.

From 2001–2006, over £30,000 was raised in support of local green lanes heritage conservation, from 500,000 customers opting to pay 5p on a cup of tea or chocolate flake. Venus also collects 5p from every filter coffee to send to the Children of Sumatra Aceh (where the coffee comes from) to pay for six to eight cleft palate and harelip operations each year.

The company strengthened its relationship with the Devon Wildlife Trust from a wildlife survey in 1997 to corporate membership in 2003 and in 2006, setting up the Venus Beach Wildlife Fund with the Trusts in Devon and Cornwall. Since 2007, the VBWF has enabled over 250 primary school pupils from local schools to visit a Venus beach and learn about marine wildlife and conservation. From 2006 to 2011, customers' donations of five pence from each cup of tea and chocolate flake raised another £30,000. Other activities have included litter picks by Venus staff and rockpool rambles with DWT staff. A free Build a Bird Box event is held each year at Blackpool Sands during National Bird Week. A free activity book supplied with kids' meals increases awareness of the sea and shoreline and gives environmental messages to 10,000 children each year.

Venus has increased its local and organic food and drink products from nineteen to forty-three since 2004, and over 90 per cent of food and drink products are produced in the South West, predominately Devon and Cornwall. Suppliers are chosen for their environmental and ethical values. Wall mounted maps promote the local provenance of food and drink at each café. 'Both locals and visitors want to eat local food,' says Michael Smith. Venus also recruits and trains local management and seasonal staff wherever possible.

Michael Smith is President of the Wheels4Bigbury Beach project which loans beach accessible wheelchairs to visitors. Michael also gives his time to transfer his sustainable business knowledge at national and regional level through attending meetings and giving conference presentations and in helping others develop bids to attract regional and European funding. He has been involved with South Hams Food and Drink Association since 2004, and since becoming chairman has encouraged its development into Devon Food and Drink in 2008.

Joint promotions with other like-minded businesses such as Riverford Farms reach additional audiences.

The company has reduced its use of promotional literature since 2007, from 130,000 leaflets to 3,000 special 'Loving the Beach' information packs distributed to targeted green, self-catering accomodation, hotels and holiday parks.

Venus has entered and won numerous awards, including the Queen's Award for Enterprise: Sustainable Development in 2010; Gold Enjoy England for Excellence – National Sustainable Tourism in 2009; Gold Sustainable Tourism Excellence for South West England in 2008. These awards help to raise the profile of the organisation nationally. 'They also help us to benchmark our achievements against our mission to be the greenest café in the market,' adds Michael.

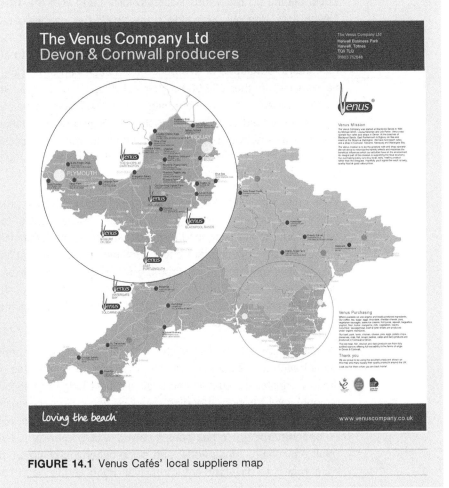

**FIGURE 14.1** Venus Cafés' local suppliers map

Repeat visits are high and research has shown that 99 per cent of customers rate the Venus experience as outstanding or above average. 'Having sustainable development at the core of our operating philosophy is instrumental in creating the Venus difference,' says Michael.

In 2011 Venus launched a fully compostable hot drink cup and lid. The lids, which had previously accounted for almost 9 per cent of Venus' non-recyclable waste, are now made from a biopolymer made of natural plant sugars, which compost in sixty to ninety days. The sugar is taken from corn grown for industrial use and the production of the biopolymer uses 60 per cent less greenhouse gases and 50 per cent less non-renewable energy than traditional polymers. Michael explains:

> We used media relations to tell the story of the cup. It does cost more than traditional polymer lined disposable cups. We wanted to demonstrate to customers that by looking after the beach, we were looking after their enjoyment of our cafe locations, and felt that this was the best way to get the message across.

**FIGURE 14.2** The new Venus biodegradeable cup

Venus uses consultancy Actuate Marketing as their out-of-house marketing department. Managing Director Dave Pearce said:

> The best thing about working with Venus is being able to get involved in the decision-making process on brand development, positioning and marketing communications. We're able to put forward our ideas and offer a different perspective on problems or opportunities. They were our first client in September 2009.
>
> The introduction of the Venus Riders Family SUP Championships back in 2010 has been one of the most successful campaigns to

**FIGURE 14.3** Venus Riders competition at Blackpool Sands

date. With the aim of putting Blackpool Sands on the map as THE place for stand-up paddleboarding (SUP), Venus introduced a free, family-oriented competition to introduce locals and holidaymakers alike to the joys of SUP. A combination of press releases and media visits, email marketing, advertising and the Venus website resulted in over 100 competitors taking part in the first championship. Not only did this raise awareness of the competition but it also reinforced the Venus Riders brand (the water sports arm of the Venus umbrella).

The creation of the 'Friends of Venus' database has been a key aspect of the marketing development. In the eighteen months since the new Venus website has been launched, almost 3,000 people have signed up to receive emails about the latest news and offers from Venus.

The launch of the new cup helped to reinforce to customers and the media that Venus are continuously improving their commitment to sustainability. Being one of the first users of these cups in the UK, it shows that Venus are at the cutting edge of sustainable innovations. Not only will it allow Venus customers to help look after the environment, it will also educate the wider population on what alternatives are available and will hopefully encourage them to seek the same environmental awareness and commitment from other cafe and restaurant chains.

*Venus Cafes are at Blackpool Sands, East Portlemouth, Bigbury on Sea in Devon, and Tolcarne and Watergate Bay in Cornwall. There is also a Venus Cafe at Dartington in Devon.*

**ACTION POINT**

## PENNYWELL FARM: DEVON'S FRIENDLIEST DAY OUT

Pennywell Farm celebrated its twenty-first birthday in 2010. It was the first farm attraction in the UK to introduce a real hands-on experience with animals and to offer activities every half hour. This formula has been repeated at farm attractions all over the country.

Pennywell's target market is families with children up to age eleven. School groups, play groups, church groups and family organisations are also targeted.

CSR is intrinsic to the organisation. Pennywell endeavours to be completely sustainable. Visitors are made aware of their environment so that they can take away the essence of the Pennywell ethos and have an impact on the world they live in.

The environmental policy is on display as well as a responsibly visitor charter. A wind charger plays nursery rhymes for younger visitors. A second turbine has been installed on the top of Pennywell Tower where information is also displayed about the views and the thinking behind the turbines. Solar panels provide hot water in the barns and a low energy electrical system has been installed. Energy efficient lighting is used throughout the site and the newest buildings have been designed to make use of natural light. Solar lighting is also used in the car park and Pennywell is on a green energy tariff.

Rain is collected from the barn roves and used to flush the toilets. As Pennywell has no mains water, this has been invaluable. Ponds are filled with run-off water from the car parks which is filtered through reed beds to remove any oil. Taps have been changed to compression taps to save water, especially as the farm had to deal with increased demand for hand washing following *E. coli* issues at farm attractions.

All glass, cardboard, paper, printer inks and cooking oils are collected and recycled. Individual milk and sugar packs are no longer used in the café to save waste. Shredded paper is used in animal bedding and fluorescent bulbs are taken to a recycling centre. Animal manure is taken to a neighbouring farm for use as fertiliser. Out-of-date fruit and vegetables from the local Co-op are collected for use as food for tortoises.

A wildlife audit was carried out and the resulting report is on show to visitors, encouraging them to look out for wildlife on site. Green Shoots is a scheme that encourages visitors to learn about planting seeds and taking cuttings.

Despite talking to local providers, no public transport is available to the farm. Pennywell has registered with Car Share Devon to encourage visitors to have 'car full' days out. There is a staff car share scheme and mobile homes have been set up near the site to provide staff accommodation and reduce the need for them to travel to work by car. Visitors who cycle to Pennywell receive a 50 per cent discount on admission. There are plans to extend the tractor and trailer ride to Buckfastleigh to collect visitors from train and bus.

Visitor reaction is good – 72 per cent said that the environmental responsibility encouraged them to visit. The farm has won several awards, including a gold award in the Green Tourism Scheme from 2002–2009, and the Best Green Business in the South West in 2009.

Pennywell has reduced its production of printed promotional materials and shifted to the use of emails and an online newsletter. The website is linked in with Facebook to communicate with regular visitors. A dedicated page on the website emphasises the environmental initiatives. Several media relations stories stress the socially responsible nature of the farm's visitor offer.

**FIGURE 14.4** Winners of the Pennywell Green School Award

Other initiatives include supporting a youth worker in the local village and working with the SeedSowers charity in Plymouth. Numerous community events are supported with the offer of free tickets as raffle prizes. Future plans include the development of a Living Larder at the farm to demonstrate the relationship between farming and food.

'It's all about building our relationships with our staff, our community and our customers,' says Managing Director Chris Murray.

The Green School Award was launched in 2008 and open to primary schools across Devon. Chris Murray is one of the judges, along with environmental expert Dr Alan Peacock of the University of Exeter and environmental consultant Tom Hill. Five categories cover: green transport – how does the school encourage walking to school or other green transport; local products and services – does the school source local goods; recycling – how the school deals with litter and keeping waste to a minimum; energy efficiency – what measures are in place; innovation – what unique ideas have been introduced? The winning school won a laptop computer. The award received 120 entries, and the prizes were presented by Nic Baker. St Michael's Primary School in Kingsteignton was chosen for the school's innovative work in promoting high levels of environmental awareness and encouraging the children to develop a passion and understanding of their environment. Widespread press coverage resulted across the region.

Chris Murray's Christian beliefs underpin his commitment to social responsibility: 'We consider we have a duty of care towards the environment and our fellow man. This is the only truly win-win strategy for the business and for the planet. A day at Pennywell lasts a lifetime.'

## END POINT

CSR is often quoted as one of the major issues that PR will have to deal with in the future. This is not just about communicating what an organisation does to be sustainable, but advising organisations on how to increase their credentials and earn their 'licence to operate'. This chapter has shown several models to evaluate CSR policies and presented two case studies where CSR cannot be separated from the mission and values of the business. Public relations is the function that is most involved with communicating with key stakeholders and is therefore in the best position to find out their views and expectations of how an organisation should interact with its environment.

# CHAPTER 15

# International considerations

*Alison Theaker*

Globalisation and the challenges of operating in a diverse world have been on the agenda for the practice of public relations for some time. Here we have a look at some useful writing on cultural differences and some case studies to illustrate how practitioners tailor their communications when dealing with different global groups.

## CHECK POINT

This chapter covers:

- how several writers have attempted to map cultures;
- thoughts about how organisations operate globally;
- does PR follow development or lead it?
- case studies where communications had to be changed in different environments;
- the global PR community.

Public relations is growing across the world. Moss and DeSanto (2002: 3) found 150 national and regional PR associations with a total of 137,000 members. In China alone, there were 100,000 practitioners, with another 450,000 students of the discipline. Even then they said, 'One of the key challenges for practitioners and students of PR . . . will be to become more conversant with how PR is understood and practised around the world' in order to develop communication programmes that span national boundaries (2002: 6). Falconi (2003) estimated that there were 3 million individuals in the global PR community, 400,000 of whom were in Europe.

Heath (2001b) stated that practitioners would need to examine behavioural and communication theories, the mass media, interpersonal communications, research methods, markets and public policy arenas as cultural differences could make or break successful campaigns.

Wakefield (2001) felt that international PR (IPR) is similar to domestic work in that it is strategic, dealing with media relations and promotions. PR practitioners will still communicate with targeted publics, deal with issues and crises, and develop community relations.

By 2005, the Ford Vice President of Communications declared at the ICCO summit: 'There is no such thing as local, globalisation is a reality.' However, the CEO of Weber Shandwick was equally forthright when he said that 'All PR is local' (Crush 2005).

# DEFINING INTERNATIONAL AND GLOBAL PR

Szondi (2006) makes the distinction between global PR, which he defines as the internationalisation of the profession, and IPR, which is the 'planning and implementation of programmes involving two or more countries'. He also suggests that IPR can be preparative (cultivating the environment), situational (dealing with a single issue or situation) or promotional (supporting global marketing).

Only 5 per cent of countries have a homogenous culture (Jandt, 2004). Post-communist Russia contains 148 million people from 100 nationalities, living across eleven time zones. In countries with high levels of immigration such as Australia and the US, it was assumed that children of immigrants would simply assimilate. But learning the language of the host country can take three generations. Moreover, while people learn the dominant culture and language they do not lose their original one. Teaching in the US, I found that of the 30 students in my Masters class on Global PR who were American, all had another culture they related to and often spoke another language at home.

Cultural background of targeted publics can change which media channels practitioners should use. In the US, the highest usage of the internet is among Asian-Americans, as 60.4 per cent use this medium, compared to 39.8 per cent of blacks and 31.6 per cent of Hispanics. A successful health campaign to target the black community used churches and engaged pastors to launch the African-American diabetes programme (Billingsley, 2002).

Asian cultures are also different. Clarke (2000) outlined the differences between the religious, royalist culture of the Thais; the assertive, workaholic culture of Hong

Kong; the international sophistication of Singapore; and the heavily restricted media in Japan.

## MAPPING CULTURES

Several writers have tried to list characteristics of different cultures and put them into groups and themes. Sebenius (2002: 80–81) offers eleven things which people need to find out when dealing with a different culture:

1   Greetings – how do people greet and address each other? What role do business cards play?
2   Formality – will I be expected to dress and interact formally or informally?
3   Gifts – are gifts exchanged? What is appropriate?
4   Touching – what are the attitudes towards contact?
5   Eye contact – should this be direct?
6   Deportment – how should I carry myself?
7   Emotions – is it rude, embarrassing or usual to display emotions?
8   Silence – awkward or expected? Insulting or respectful?
9   Eating – what are proper manners? Are certain foods not allowed?
10  Body language – are certain gestures expected or offensive?
11  Punctuality – should I be on time or are schedules fluid?

Anthropologist Edward Hall's *Silent Language* from 1960 suggested variables that may drive behaviour:

- Relationships – if the focus is on relationships, deals arise from already developed relationships. If it is on the deal, relationships develop after it has been agreed.
- Communication – whether indirect, high context with non-verbal cues or direct and low context. In the US, communication should be to the point, whereas in China people like very detailed data.
- Time – monochronic or polychronic? Anglo-Saxon schedules are fixed, people do one thing at a time. Latin schedules are fluid, interruptions are common, interpersonal relationships take precedence.
- Space – moving too close in some cultures produces discomfort, and in others, backing away may convey disdain. (Sebenius, 2002)

Hofstede (Schneider and Barsoux 2003: 87–91) built on Hall's *Silent Language*. Based on an employee opinion survey of 116,000 IBM employees in the 1960s, across forty different countries, he identified four value dimensions. Power distance is the extent to which unequal distribution of power is accepted. Uncertainty avoidance refers to society's discomfort with uncertainty and preference for stability. Individualism/collectivism looks at the individual or group focus and masculine/ feminine reveals the bias towards masculine assertiveness and competitiveness as against feminine nurturing, quality of life and relationships. On studying Asian cultures, a fifth dimension appeared, referred to as long-term orientation, reverence for persistence, thrift and patience. A table of rankings was produced for each country, showing that the US ranked most highly in individualism and Japan was the most masculine culture. Arab countries were less masculine oriented than both of them. Greece was ranked highest in uncertainty avoidance and Malaysia in power distance. High power distance is reflected in more levels of hierarchy and centralised decision-making. High uncertainty avoidance results in more rules and procedures and risk avoidance. High collectivist organisations prefer group decision-making. High masculinity rates task accomplishment higher than social relationships. The rankings were then translated into country clusters: Anglo, Nordic, Latin and Asian.

While actions can be copied, understanding is more difficult. In Britain and the US, a contract is a document that should be adhered to once signed. In Japan, it is a starting document that can be modified as needed. In South America, it is regarded as an ideal that is unlikely to be achieved but which is signed to avoid argument.

Marx (2001: 47–57) suggests that there is no right or wrong, but that in order to be effective, people must adapt their methods of doing business according to the cultural context.

Stevens suggested (Schneider and Barsoux 2003: 92–93) the following cultural profiles:

- Anglo/Nordic: village market. Decentralised, entrepreneurial, flexible, delegation, informal personal communication. Output control.
- Asian: tribe or family. Centralised, paternalistic, strong social roles, personal relationships. Social control.
- Germanic: well-oiled machine. Decentralised decision-making. Narrow span of control, compartmentalised, throughput control. Efficiency.
- Latin: traditional bureaucracy. Centralised decision-making, less delegation, pyramid of people, elitist. Input control.

Selmer, in 1998, added a Viking form of management, with decentralised decision-making, emphasis on consensus and avoiding conflict, informal channels of communication and long-range objectives. These cultural preferences affect how information circulates and is shared. In French companies, the flow of information between groups is limited, as information is a source of power and not easily given away. In Sweden, communication patterns are much more open and informal, whereas information sharing is not widely practised in Russia, especially with outsiders in case of misinterpretation.

**Living in another culture is a valuable experience. But how do people from other cultures rate their experience in the UK? Here is an anecdotal account from someone who has worked and lived in the UK.**

German students and employees of UK companies often underline the similarities between the German and British culture. Undoubtedly, the British drinking culture and social life of British pubs is the most apparent difference between the two. While Germans distinguish between formal and informal greeting, it is easier to warm towards colleagues and business partners in English.

International students from Asia and Africa talk about cultural differences, as well as the language barrier. The structure of organisations in Asia is more autocratic with predominantly vertical working relationships. Asian people are often surprised about the democratic group status within British organisations, as they observe people arguing over mission and direction without consulting their managers or supervisors. Students from Tunisia on work placements refer to the decentralised structures and dynamic working relationships, effective decision-making and problem-solving process in British organisations. Contrary to the often more autocratic and one-way communication approach in Asia and Africa, international students notice the two- or three-way communication flow in many European companies. Particularly, students from Vietnam asserted their admiration for UK law and how working conditions and personal rights are protected by the British system. At the same time, they also concluded that the implementation of new strategies and corporate change is often more complicated in the UK, as many organisations in Asia, apart from China and Japan, are not as restricted in their environmental and ecological conduct than companies in Europe or North America. Organisations in Africa and East Asia, for example Thailand and Vietnam, do not pay a lot of attention to teamwork and collaboration. International students often find studying and working in the UK more comfortable than in their home countries. Nonetheless, students and employees from Thailand and Vietnam asserted that it was a long process adapting to the corporate climate of British organisations. Despite the pressure from middle and senior managers within organisational power cultures in Vietnam and Thailand, colleagues usually work in a very non-competitive and relaxed corporate climate. However, most students and employees regard their work in the British culture as an invaluable and highly beneficial experience.

*Dirk Heimpold is currently studying for an MSc at Oxford Brookes University. He has also studied in the UK at undergraduate level and worked in his home culture in Germany and in the US.*

In Japanese companies, intensive and extensive discussion is encouraged at all levels (Schneider and Barsoux 2003: 92–93).

Ransom (2011) shared her own views of what makes a successful multicultural campaign, but this related mainly to an exhortation to research attitudes to products and services and avoid stereotypes. Payne (2011) started by warning about differences in language and steering clear of brand names which could be misinterpreted. He quoted the Ford Pinto's launch in Brazil, where the name means 'small male genitals'.

So we can see that there is no universal 'best practice', and no short cuts to simply doing thorough research into the different cultures of targeted publics.

**TALKING POINT**

## DOES PR FOLLOW OR LEAD DEVELOPMENT?

Sriramesh and Verčič (2009) relate the development of public relations to three elements in the infrastructure of a particular country. They feel that public relations thrives on public opinion, and so is most developed in democratic systems. It is most common in developed countries, where suppliers have to compete for public attention, approval and support. Activism, which provides opportunities for public relations in putting both sides of the case, is unlikely to be high if the bulk of the populace are more concerned about where their next meal is coming from. In addition, in developing countries, the media may reach only a small, homogenous group because of illiteracy and poverty. Thus practitioners may have to adapt to using traditional and indigenous media.

However, the most sustained rapid economic growth in the past fifty years has occurred in China. This has also led to an increase in PR revenues, to US$740 million in 2005. PR has an important role in introducing foreign brands to China as well as helping Chinese brands raise their visibility on the global stage (Gray 2006b).

In addition, Africa is a vast and untapped market of 800 million people across fifty-three states. These countries vary enormously in wealth, although the average share of GDP is US$684, compared to US$780 in China and US$440 in India. Gyroscope developed an Africa Communications Index (ACI), examining range and reach of media, the existence of a professional PR body and the ease of access to trained staff. Countries most developed according to the ACI are South Africa and Egypt, with the lowest scores earned by Mozambique and Ethiopia. Wells (2006) suggested that countries could not develop without an effective communications industry.

The events of the 'Arab Spring' in 2011 have changed the political map in the Middle East and Northern Africa. Many of these political movements were sparked by single incidents, communicated by individuals via social media. Public relations cannot be said to have had a hand in these changes, and indeed PR consultancies have more often come under fire for representing the previous regimes to the West. While Lerbinger (2001) stated that 'The essence of PR is cultural context', it seems that most public relations practice in developing countries is geared towards preserving the status quo. This raises the question of whether PR really is intrinsically in the public interest or is irretrievably wedded to corporate and governmental reputation.

**ACTION POINT**

**Taking account of different cultures is integral to the success of global projects. This can be a lengthy process.**

## *NATIONAL GEOGRAPHIC*'S GENOGRAPHIC PROJECT

In 2005, I joined *National Geographic* along with a newly created team of international scientists and IBM researchers to develop and launch a flagship scientific effort to trace the history of humankind using DNA as a study tool, over 60,000 years.

It was a huge undertaking; the scientific consortium was asking big questions through their research: 'Where do you really come from? And how did you get to where you live today?' Using cutting-edge genetic and computational technologies to analyse historical patterns found in DNA from participants around the world to better understand our human genetic roots, *National Geographic* would aim to tell the broader story: we are all related.

The three main components of the five-year project were to invite indigenous and traditional peoples to learn about the project and provide their genetic information to our researchers; to invite the general public to join in by purchasing a Genographic Project Public Participation kit; and to use proceeds from kit sales to fund the Genographic Legacy Fund which supports indigenous educational and revitalisation projects. Genographic is anonymous, non-medical, non-profit and all results are placed in the public domain following scientific peer publication.

It was and is a huge project with a mass of multiple-layered internal and public communicating for many audiences across the world – and most particularly in explaining the project and its regionally approved ethical frameworks with locally accountable review boards to interested indigenous and traditional peoples – people who historically have not been well-respected by some scientists. Much of what we did differently was in how we thought about how we wanted to work; collaboration is the touchstone of every major phase of the outreach. Much of what we changed was in how we learned from the communities about how to talk with them.

Before any trip is planned, researchers at each of the regional centres around the world reach out first with local collaborators and leaders in individual communities not just to explain the Genographic Project, but also to better understand how and if those communities are interested in learning about their migratory history, before any other planning takes place. This work is relationship building. It is structured and transparent and it takes the time that it takes. At the same time it is truly iterative, in that we will follow and adapt to feedback and better practice as advised – all communities are unique.

Actual contribution of DNA takes place only when consultation – which may take weeks and months – is complete, and there is both collective and individual interest in participating. All consent is based on the principle of free, prior and informed consent (both written and oral). Individuals own the rights to their own samples and can withdraw from the study at any time and ask for their data to be removed from the database. This right extends to communities where the consent has been communal in character. The generic, non-individualised research generated by the project is meant to be shared; the Genographic Project research centres release the resulting genetic data (on an anonymous and aggregate basis) into the public domain to promote further research. The genetic data is not patented.

The collaborative relationship continues into the results phase of the analysis. The researchers work with the communities to determine if, when, and how they are interested in sharing the collective information from the analysis of the group's genetic data. Researchers will then go back to the communities to talk through the results and the stories around them and hear more from the communities. We are very clear in presentation from the beginning that we are offering an additional understanding around peoples' and communities' origin stories, not seeking to replace them.

**FIGURE 15.1** Dr Spencer Wells, *National Geographic* Explorer and Director of the Genographic Project and Middle East/North African Principal Investigator Pierre Zalloua talk with leaders in Gouro, Chad, about the Genographic Project

Most of what we knew back in 2005 about anthropological genetics was based on DNA samples donated by approximately 10,000 indigenous and traditional people from around the world. While this information gave us a broad view of the patterns of human migration, it represented just a small sample of humanity's genetic diversity. The project is still underway and new data has already helped support mapping of world migratory patterns dating back some 150,000 years and fill in the huge gaps in our knowledge of humankind's migratory history.

Today, the language of DNA and genetic anthropology is more familiar to many of us than a decade ago, and many of the ethical and privacy issues are more clearly understood by the global community.

## Impact

- Published 25 papers in leading scientific journals with more manuscripts in development.

- Approximately 500,000 indigenous and public participants from over 130 countries – around 420,000 kits have been sold – so far.

- To date, granted over $1.5 million from kit sales to revitalisation and educational Legacy Fund projects around the world.

- Educational program integrated via online lesson plans and swabbing events in universities and schools.

- E-newsletter subscriber base of 60,000+, annual global exhibits and speaking events.

- User-generated content – migration stories from the public make up part of *National Geographic*'s award-winning website.

Widely seen as a genuinely successful, informative and 'real-time' scientific engagement initiative, Genographic continues into the next phase . . .

*Lucie McNeil is a Vice President in National Geographic's Explorer Programs and Strategic Initiatives, based in Washington DC. She began her career in communications as a student in the first year of Leeds Metropolitan University's four-year public relations degree, graduating to work in the British Government as a media advisor for various departments including the Prime Minister's, and later as Director of News and Public Affairs at Harvard University.*

*For more information about the Genographic Project:*
*https://genographic.nationalgeographic.com/genographic/index.html*

**ACTION POINT**

**Sometimes the first step is to make sure that the organisation is associated with something of relevance to a target audience.**

## RAISING AWARENESS WITH DIVERSE AUDIENCES

The Music of Black Origin (MOBO) Awards was inspired by Kanya King MBE back in 1996. The awards entered their seventeenth successful year in 2011. The British equivalent of the US Grammy Awards, MOBO attracts substantial international media coverage from the announcement of the nominations in August through to the 'live' transmission of the awards show in September on BBC TV and re-broadcast by MTV Base in Africa and the Caribbean as well as other TV networks.

One of the most successful brand partnerships in its history was with Western Union, the world's largest personal money transfer business, which was the headline sponsor for the MOBO Awards at Wembley Arena in 2007. Western Union saw sponsorship of MOBO as a primary communication channel to reach black and minority ethnic (BME) audiences and make an emotional impact with them.

The MOBO Awards 2007 was screened on BBC1, BBC3 and MTV Base to an audience of over 3 million across numerous countries. Western Union's logo appeared during 36.4 per cent of the MTV Base highlights show and for 7.9 per cent of the BBC3 ninety-minute live broadcast. Other communication vehicles included Western Union's 'Back to Roots' on myspace.com, which had 40 million unique viewers. A ticket giveaway with Metro newspaper was seen by 500,000 readers and 5,000 tickets were distributed. An e-flyer featuring the Western Union logo was sent to over 100,000 people and 30,000 MOBO magazines were featured in HMV stores nationwide. As well as distributing 25,000 flyers in London, Western Union had a branded float in the Notting Hill Carnival, visible to over 1 million people. In addition, 250 posters were situated in over 200 London Underground stations, reaching over 3 million travellers each day.

*Ardi Kolah works with a large number of organisations in helping to connect with diverse audiences.*

**READING POINT**

For those working internationally, management literature provides some good overviews of different cultural considerations. Jandt's (2009) 6th edition of *An Introduction to Intercultural Communication* is a good place to start. *Management Across Cultures: challenges and strategies* (Steers *et al.* 2010) sets out some general themes that global organisations need to deal with and suggests come strategies for cross-cultural communication. Moss *et al.* (2010) offer descriptions of a variety of PR campaigns in *Public Relations Cases*.

In their 2010 lecture to the PRSA International Conference, James and Larissa Grunig put forward a suggestion that there should be generic principles of public relations that would apply internationally, and specific applications which would then be carried out by people familiar with the local culture. They felt that the financial problems of the West had pushed sustainability up the agenda, and that this had increased the need for PR to be a strategic management functions in organisations (Grunig and Grunig 2010). Read more about CSR in Chapter 14.

## A SNAPSHOT FROM BULGARIA

Nelly Benova of Apeiron Communication in Sofia conducted a study to look at how PR practice in Bulgaria fitted with Grunig's four PR Models (see Chapter 3). She also looked at whether practice reflected a more technical or managerial role (see Chapter 2). She found that there had been a shift from a mainly one-way press agentry approach since previous surveys in 1999 towards a more two-way approach, with the symmetrical and asymmetrical models scoring highest (Benova 2010).

Nelly also found that the Personal Influence model of PR was favoured, with relationship building being very important for Bulgarian PR practice. Long-term relationships were imperative for effective PR, suggesting that Bulgaria was closer to an Eastern culture of communication. In crisis situations, practitioners tended to rely on their interpersonal relationships with key figures.

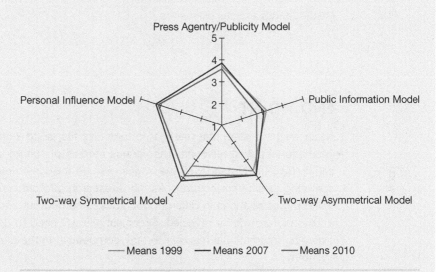

**FIGURE 15.2A** Different models of PR

She also examined cultural dimensions against Hofstede's suggested characteristics. She found high power distance, collectivism and masculinity and lower tolerance of uncertainty and suggested that this was related to the authoritarian organisational culture which was prevalent in Bulgaria under the communist regime. Despite the political changes in 1989, authoritarian values are still prevalent in organisations. She offered PR practitioners as transforming agents to encourage a more participative culture.

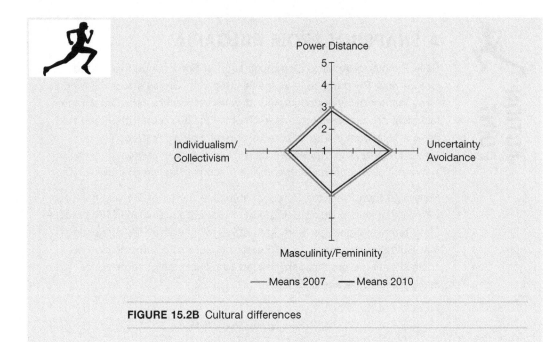

**FIGURE 15.2B** Cultural differences

# END POINT

Again we have seen that there is no 'one size fits all' to working in
international public relations. The various models of cultural awareness
can help to understand why messages may be misconstrued when
operating in different cultures. As more research into different ways of
doing public relations in different countries is carried out and published,
a fuller picture will be revealed. Organisations will need to deal with the
emerging international markets to stay competitive in the global
economy.

CHAPTER 16

# Digital public relations

*Heather Yaxley*

This chapter takes a practical look at emerging technologies and how practitioners can keep ahead of developments from a personal and organisational perspective.

## CHECK POINT

At the end of this chapter, you will be able to:

- adopt strategies to engage with digital technologies as an individual PR practitioner and on behalf of organisations;
- understand benefits of building virtual communities;
- consider issues involved in monitoring and evaluating digital public relations.

Convergence of technologies enables multi-media delivery of information, increasingly via mobile devices, within a 24/7 global communications environment. Duhé (2007: 57) envisages this online environment as a 'conduit for transparency and complexity' that necessitates a flexibility of response she believes resonates with PR practitioners.

Those who equate management with control are likely to perceive recent changes as a threat rather than an opportunity for corporate communications. The immediacy and interconnectedness of mobile, online and social media presents a challenge to those familiar, and comfortable, with a journalist-focused, 9–5 approach to PR based on practices established over many decades.

The open, complex system of online communications supports a move from a linear model of transmitting messages. Instead, information is exchanged, and even jointly constructed in real time within networks of participants.

At the same time, problems, mistakes and misunderstandings can be exposed and, hopefully, resolved, in the glassbox of online communications (where everything can potentially be accessed by anyone). This signifies a shift away from private conversations (e.g. between PR practitioners and professional journalists) to public discussion, assertion and disagreement among friends and foes of the organisation, with or without participation of its PR representatives.

## DIGITAL PR STRATEGIES

The evolution of new technologies affects PR practitioners as much as organisations. Today individuals can easily 'add, change and share content with others' (Phillips and Young 2009: 103) enabling anyone (potentially) to manage a personal presence online, without being particularly computer literate.

Competency with new technology is viewed by Theaker (2007) as a requirement for everyone working in PR, although Eyrich et al. (2008: 413) found practitioners were 'slower to integrate more technologically complicated tools' (p. 413).

## Personal adoption strategies

Rogers' diffusion process provides a useful framework for considering adoption of emerging online technologies. Diffusion is 'the process by which an innovation is communicated through certain channels over time among the members of a social system' (Rogers 2003:11).

Rogers also presents five types of adopters (innovators, early adopters, early majority, late majority, laggards) that can be applied to PR practitioners' engagement with digital PR. Innovators of emerging digital technologies within the PR community welcome change and may be less concerned with immediate financial returns. They engage with others at the leading edge of technological developments but may form a clique that is suspicious of those perceived as too commercial in outlook. Monitoring innovators is useful in keeping up to date with the latest technologies.

Early adopters tend to be more influential than innovators. They adopt technologies once they have been tested and proven of value. Early adopters promote technologies by writing articles in trade media, advocating through PR networks (professional bodies and so forth), running training courses and demonstrating the value and ease of adoption. This opinion leader strategy has benefits of credibility, influence and, potentially, rewards in terms of reputation and business opportunities.

UK-based, Neville Hobson has been involved in social media communications since 2002. He researches new communication technologies and speaks at conferences. He blogs (www.neville hobson.com) and co-presents the For Immediate Release podcast with Shel Holtz (www.forimmediaterelease.biz). Neville features in lists of online influencers e.g. AdAge Power 150, Cision Top 10 UK Public Relations Blogs and PR Week Power Players of Social Media UK. He can be found on Twitter at: www.twitter.com/jangles, as well as in LinkedIn and Google+.

As a prolific user of social media, Neville is an interesting person to follow regarding new technology trends. He connects with other opinion leaders and describes himself as an early adopter rather than an innovator.

- Research Neville's online presence and assess what he has discussed recently to understand the behaviour of someone interested in emerging technologies.

- Consider what is involved in keeping ahead of developments in this ever-changing field.

- Do you agree that Neville is an early adopter rather than an innovator?

The gap between innovators and those who follow can be seen in views towards technologies. Innovators envisage a beneficial aim for the internet as a place 'fostering conversation and connection between people' (Levine 2009: 25) with those who followed seen as contributing towards the 'commercialization of cyberspace' (Curran and Seaton 2003: 235). Those adopting technologies later in the diffusion process are more likely to look at its commercial potential, reflecting the 'aggressive, competitive, hyperbolic, selling mind-set' of marketing (Hutton 2010: 510).

Rogers' early majority recognise advantages of developments but need them to have been widely reported and be simple to use. Once adoption becomes normal practice, the late majority follows, either voluntarily or by force of expectation. Laggards may be in denial over the benefits of such developments, or lack skills and knowledge. One perceived barrier in engaging with technology is age (Prensky 2001). Kitchen and Panopoulos (2010: 226) suggest organisations may fail to develop the skills of more experienced PR practitioners in favour of employing 'young well-informed, technologically sophisticated professionals'.

Emerging technologies reflect a disruption of traditional PR practice, necessitating a continuous, long-term process of adoption (Kitchen and Panopoulos 2010). Practices that start as innovative become the norm. Organisations may initially offer training in technologies, which soon become expected skills. Those starting careers in PR increasingly will bring experience with social media, although their competencies may reflect personal rather than professional use.

This highlights two key areas where PR practitioners need to develop personal strategies in relation to social media use:

1    willingness to identify and adopt emerging technologies for professional PR purposes as innovators, early adopters or early majority practitioners;

2    inclusion of digital PR within career plans; specialist technical roles may reflect opportunities echoing the traditional craft perspective of PR, which could act as a barrier to moving into management roles.

Holmes (2007) presciently observed the PR industry needs candidates who 'possess rare and perhaps even contradictory qualities' such as the good judgement that comes with age and experience alongside knowledge of new media opportunities.

## Learning strategies

Self-efficacy ('the conviction that one can successfully execute the behaviour required to produce the outcome', Bandura 1977: 79) is particularly relevant for older practitioners who may not believe they are capable of understanding, utilising or managing digital technologies. Gangadharbatla (2008) identifies internet self-efficacy as a key factor in influencing adoption of social networking, alongside a need to belong and collective self-esteem. Communities of practice (Wenger and Snyder 2000) within social networking sites (particularly LinkedIn) enable practitioners to share experiences and engage in debate about technologies. However, without the initial confidence or skill to join such communities, practitioners may not be in a position to benefit from this peer-group learning.

Noor Al-Deen and Hendricks (2011: 133) clarify 'social media provides the opportunity to interact with and contribute to the knowledge being created and disseminated'. One benefit is learning within the environment being studied, which could be beneficial to younger practitioners familiar with technologies, but not how they can be used within PR. However, participation online is public and mistakes can gain a high profile. Bridgen (2011) also observes the blurring of PR practitioners' professional and personal identities online as an issue.

It can be difficult to determine the validity of this informal process of learning. Practitioners should consider the veracity of information gained, and reflect on their experiences by keeping a training diary to monitor skills and knowledge development.

As well as self-efficacy and peer-group support, practitioners can draw on a range of texts and courses or use experts to implement social media activities. These learning strategies tend to be more appropriate for those who are early-to-late majority adopters of new technology with innovators preferring to experiment and learn by doing.

**ACTION POINT**

Toronto-based public relations and communication management specialist, Judy Gombita advocates Twitter chats as a good way of engaging with social media:

> I've been a regular and active Twitter chat participant for approximately two years. Solo PR (#solopr) founded by Kellye Crane is one of the most vibrant, targeted 'community-oriented' chats in the Twitterverse. Its accessible and friendly human engagement continues to generate relevance and resonance.

Judy claims that beyond camaraderie, PR participants in Twitter chats report tangible business benefits, new skills, and networking contacts around the world. She quotes Alan Stevens as saying Twitter chats help him in

> finding out new insights, connecting with fellow professionals around the globe [and] crowdsourcing PR – not a new idea, but it's still tremendously productive and great fun, too. Also good to see that PR issues are the same worldwide and have similar solutions.

Judy argues Twitter chats can lead to enhanced profile and opportunities, including the possibility of influence (see: http://blog. commpro.biz/prcafe/digital-pr/digital-pr-teasing-out-the-potential-of-twitter-chats-part-i/).

Twitter chats are regular open discussions taking place at a particular time on specified topics. A chat is given a hashtag (e.g. #solopr), enabling users to follow and participate in discussion. A Google document details regular chat times and topics (https://docs.google. com/spreadsheet/ccc?key=0AhisaMy5TGiwcnVhejNHWnZIT3NvWFVPT3 Q4NkIzQVE&hl=en). Using TweetChat (http://tweetchat.com/) is an easy way to focus on a particular chat.

SoloPR is a Twitter community of small business PR, marketing and communications practitioners that takes place on Wednesdays from 6–7 p.m. GMT.

- Use the hashtag #solopr to monitor and participate in a discussion.
- What have you discovered from this TweetChat?
- What are the benefits and drawbacks of this as a way of learning more about social media?

## Organisational strategies

Lansons Communications published the first-ever UK Social Media Census in 2011 revealing 61 per cent of UK adults use social media. An infographic by web design company, Go-Gulf.com, 'In 60 Seconds', reveals the extraordinary volume of online activity every minute (Go-Gulf 2011), much of which is generated by organisations.

A survey by Altimeter (2011) of 144 global US corporations with over 1,000 employees revealed they employed an average of eleven people within their, primarily cross-functional, social media team. Grunig and Grunig (2010) have argued against creating a specialist function, while Altimeter believes a core team is required for coordination purposes, although its form will change going forwards.

Despite considerable discussion of the need for organisations to develop a social media – or digital PR – strategy, there is a lack of clarity over what this may involve. One complication is the cross-functional nature of the online environment and determining the optimum approach for individual organisations. Yaxley (2012a: 417) considers 'a holistic organisational approach enables a wide range of perspectives and skills to be involved in the process and ensures greater support for the resulting strategy'.

As with any other strategy (see Part II), the starting point needs to be the overall purpose and aims of the organisation, and in turn, how its communications and

**ACTION POINT**

The Content Marketing Institute and MarketingProfs undertook its second annual B2B survey in 2011. Although mentioning strategies, its focus was on adoption of tactics by organisations (primarily US based). It found social media tools were used by 74 per cent of respondents (5 per cent lower than a year earlier), with the professional services sector leading adoption. Brand awareness is stated as organisations' primary objective, which they evaluate by measuring web traffic. The report claims the biggest challenge faced is 'producing the kind of content that engages prospects and customers'.

This study suggests organisations focus on tactics with a mismatch between their needs and the approaches being undertaken. It shows little consideration of the complexity and interconnectedness of online behaviour. For example, the relationship between search engines, social media and online news channels is not investigated.

- Why do you think organisations focus on tactics rather than strategy for their digital communications?
- What is the main difference in achieving engagement rather than awareness?
- Does this reflect a need for a PR rather than a marketing focus online?

PR strategies contribute towards achieving those objectives. Organisations should also consider their adoption strategy (as above), with social media presence diffusing at different rates within individual countries and sectors.

This chapter does not set out to detail how to set up and use existing and emerging social media technologies that can be undertaken by following guidance in online help centres (for example: Twitter – http://support.twitter.com). Likewise, any attempts to present 'best practice' are fraught with dangers as accepted normal behaviour online is subject to change and interpretation. For example, the mantra of openness and engagement can be countered by examples of when keeping silent and allowing an issue to quietly dispel is a better approach.

# FUTURE TECHNOLOGIES

Predicting the next big thing is always fraught with danger – especially within a printed text, but here are three areas PR practitioners should consider:

## Google Plus

Google+ launched in June 2011 by invitation only for its first three months; by the year end it had 62 million users. Allen (2011) claimed a quarter of users joined in December and forecast the site could have 400 million users by the end of 2012 thanks to the use of Android smartphones accelerating take up. In comparison, Facebook had 800 million users at the end of 2011.

The real advantage of Google+ is as the hub of an online Google experience. This means integration of Google search, Gmail, Reader, Maps, Blogger, YouTube and other products and services. Google+ offered businesses and brands the opportunity to set up accounts in November 2011 with the promise of improved search engine results. Its launch partners included: CNN, Fox News, Pepsi, Toyota, Barcelona Football Club and Save the Children. Bright Edge (2011) reported that within a week of launch, 61 per cent of the top 100 US brands had Google+ pages (93 per cent of this group have Facebook pages).

It is probably too early to tell how Google+ will be used by PR practitioners, let alone how it is integrated into organisations' wider communication strategies. Nevertheless, early adopters are working out how organisations can engage with Google+ over the next year.

## 24/7 multi-media PR

Social media increase the need for PR practitioners to be competent in multi-media, reducing the traditional reliance on writing skills. Bailey (2009) explains although broadcast media have been around for a century, PR practitioners remain focused on press relations. A shift is required towards skills involved in creating graphics, images, video and audio communications. Although execution of such materials may be outsourced to specialists, the PR practitioner needs to be multi-media literate to produce briefs and manage holistic, integrated communications programmes.

The *PR Census* (Gorkana 2011) emphasised the long-hour working culture of public relations. Social media use has further blurred personal and professional boundaries (Bridgen 2011) meaning practitioners could be viewed as working 24/7. Mobile phone technology increases the expectations, and pressures to respond to email, calls and social media updates round the clock. At present, engagement 'out of hours' seems to be mainly voluntary, but this will need to be addressed by policies that either formally recognise a need for a 24/7 PR function or establish regulations regarding expectations on engagement.

It is important for organisations to develop policies regarding social media usage. This includes considering legacy issues, which occur, for example, when PR practitioners change roles within organisations or moving elsewhere. The issue of whether connections and content is the property of the organisation or the individual need to be determined before problems arise.

**ACTION POINT**

In December 2011, Volkswagen confirmed an agreement with its German employee works council that the company's email server will not send messages to those with company BlackBerry smartphones more than 30 minutes outside an employee's shift period. This limitation does not extend to senior management and employees not employed within trade union-negotiated contracts. The FT (2011) reported the move reflected 'a growing awareness in Germany of the risks of employee "burn-out"'.

■ What impact could such restrictions have on PR practitioners?

■ Do you recognise concerns of 'burn out' as a result of increased use of smartphones?

## Gamification

Continuing the themes of integration and mobile access, PR practitioners are advised to understand the trend of gamification (defined as 'the use of game design elements in non-game contexts', Deterding *et al.* 2011: 2). The use of gaming concepts helps increase engagement and loyalty (Zichermann and Cunningham 2011).

Gartner (2011) claims over 70 per cent of Global 2000 organisations will have at least one gamified application by 2015. It cites the example of Idea Street, which is a UK public sector social collaboration platform including game mechanics. *The*

*Guardian* (2011) reports the implementation of over sixty ideas, predicted to save £20 million by 2014–15, by 6,000 Department of Works and Pensions staff using Idea Street.

Considering the relevance of gamification for public relations, Richard Edelman (2011) highlights the importance of a number of factors:

- social currency – participants' ability to showcase achievements and encourage additional social interaction;
- universality – appealing beyond teenagers as gamification, driven by growth in smartphone ownership, increasingly dominates popular culture globally;
- motivation – success of gamification is increased when there is an existing level of intrinsic motivation to comply;
- rewards – can be developed and tailored to level of interaction;
- employee engagement – rewards are viewed as particularly useful in encouraging internal collaboration and improvements in performance;
- longevity – gamification creates continued interaction, extending PR activities beyond a focus on achieving interest in a single incident;
- impact – social games create peer pressure which encourages behavioural change.

## BUILDING VIRTUAL COMMUNITIES

One key argument in favour of engagement in digital PR is that it enables interactivity and two-way communications (Morris and Goldsworthy 2012). In particular, social media suggests that organisations can build virtual communities comprising stakeholders, publics and, ideally, advocates. At the same time, communities are able to form in social media to oppose organisations, reinforcing the need to understand relationship building, networking and group behaviour.

There is a difference between establishing a social media presence and ensuring an organisation engages a relevant online community. The vast majority of LinkedIn and Facebook groups established by organisations either fail to engage, or do so only temporarily (e.g. they may attract 'likes' but little discussion or interaction from supporters). Many organisations fail to understand the opportunity to build communities and adopt a publicity (one-way broadcast) approach to using social media.

This perspective of emerging technologies emphasises a relationship-building strategy for digital PR, rather than focusing on generating publicity via online tools. As such, organisations are advised to be open to the views of others, listen to what they are saying, and engage carefully and respectfully.

## SUCCESSFUL ENGAGEMENT

Coca-Cola has over 36 million people 'liking' its Facebook page at the start of 2012 (growing from 22 million at the end of 2010). The site was created by two fans who were unable to locate an official Coca-Cola page on Facebook. This site was subsequently 'adopted' by the brand. It encourages fans to establish and upload content, with the site moderated by its founders. Coca-Cola uses an approach of 4Rs for its online strategy: reviewing, responding, recording and redirecting. Natalie Johnson, digital communications manager says, 'We believe that we don't own our brands', explaining that Coca-Cola participates online where its customers are already present.

Lady Gaga has 'paved a path for stars and brands to get inventive with the ways they use digital and social media to promote themselves and connect with fans' (Hernandez 2011). She calls her fans Little Monsters, sharing with them a common bond of feeling outside mainstream culture. Social media landmarks achieved by Gaga include 1 billion views on YouTube and being the first to acquire 10 million Facebook fans and Twitter followers. As well as her role as Polaroid's Creative Director, Gaga has formed partnerships with companies including Zynga for the game GagaVille, Starbucks, HBO, iTunes and Amazon Cloud Player. Aladenoye (2011) notes lessons PR practitioners can learn from Lady Gaga:

- Acknowledge your fans.
- Establish partnerships that are an authentic extension of your brand.
- Produce content that resonates with fans.
- Ask for help.

Hernandez (2011) further adds:

- Build momentum with elements of surprise along the way.
- Integrate all channels to promote a single brand identity and message.
- Encourage fans, remind them to tell your story and never forget to thank them.
- Give people something to love.

## MUMSNET

Discussion on the Mumsnet online community forum in November 2011 questioned why someone who appeared to be a UK government representative had commented on an earlier thread. Several Mumsnet members were uncomfortable with their opinions being monitored, leading to an official Mumsnet response that the poster had been advised not to participate on discussion boards but to contact the head office to engage with the site.

Writing about the debate on her blog, PR practitioner, Kelly Quigley-Hicks (2011) says: 'The general consensus was that organisations and politicians being upfront about their motives and identities – and going through official site channels – is OK, but simply posting into ongoing threads is a bit creepy.'

Why do you feel members of Mumsnet may be unhappy about PR representatives commenting on forums? What does this tell us about privacy and openness in relation to digital PR?

# MONITORING AND EVALUATION

Monitoring social media is possible using a variety of technologies:

- RSS feeds: deliver email notifications e.g. when Google picks up keywords, updates from your favourite blogs (and comments on them), and monitor online media coverage.

- Social media dashboard: for example, Tweetdeck and Hootsuite are offered in free or subscription versions, via online access using a computer or mobile device. They enable easy, real-time monitoring and updating of Twitter, Facebook and other social media sites, hashtags and keywords.

- Social media influence measurement: for example: Klout, Kred and Peer Index use algorithms to allocate an influence rating to social media presence across different networks. These measures have been subject to criticism and continue to refine their methodology.

- Social media statistics: social media sites and dashboards provide raw data such as number of followers, likes, posts, comments, shares, inclusion on lists, etc. Beware of statistical manipulation, for example, 'reach', which is achieved by adding the number of people who could potentially read a post or Tweet.

- Social media reporting services: many of the traditional media monitoring companies (e.g. Metrica) have developed social media tools. Other specialist

The online PR community is helpful in offering debate and suggestions on what works well and what may be best to avoid. Yaxley *et al.* (2011) at the PR Conversations blog (www.prconversations.com) presented guidance in using Twitter for public relations events. One key area relates to evaluating its use, where TweetChat software programs can capture a transcript of all live Tweets, including statistics of number of Tweets, number of participants and number of impressions. Although many of the measures can be deceptive (confusing 'impression' with 'view'), it is helpful to have some data to analyse and use as a benchmark for measurement. For example, Archivist is a Microsoft-owned platform, which saves and analyses Tweets.

■ Have you used social media at an event, or seen it promoted in pre-event materials?

■ What value do you think this provides and how could it help achieve the organisation's objectives for a PR activity?

■ How could this be evaluated?

Paine's paper (2007b) *How to Measure Social Media Relations: the more things change, the more they remain the same*, emphasises the importance of setting objectives to evaluate outputs, outtakes and outcomes (see Chapter 10). It relates outcomes to impact on behaviour and relationships, as well as financial measures. Outtakes include social capital and social networking with outputs related to attention. When considering an organisation's reputation on social media sites controlled by others, she recommends content analysis as a method of analysis, to be connected to reputational characteristics.

In many ways, despite the title of this paper and its linkage to evaluation theory, it appears dated owing to developments in social media technology over the past five years. However, Powell *et al.* (2011) note that although social media activity is readily measurable it can be difficult to isolate what is valuable from the amount of data available or to determine useful insights. They also note difficulties caused by changes in the technological underpinnings of systems that deliver social media metrics, as well as a lack of searchable, historical data in some cases. As well as raw data, systems may provide an interpretation function with inbuilt analytics. These may be proprietary however, and lack easy comparison to other metrics. Sentiment, tone and influence are among the terms claimed as measures of social media activity. These are subjective and therefore open to interpretation.

services are also available, e.g. Alterian. Another example is Radian6 which was bought by Salesforce in 2011. This means the original service that enabled client organisations to monitor and analyse large volumes of social media content is being developed to offer insights into the impact of campaigns in real time.

Resource needs to be devoted to monitoring and evaluation. Although this can be undertaken in-house (particularly useful in ensuring prompt response to any emerging issues), specialist services are recommended for large-scale assessment. Measuring social media may seem easy with various metrics and data readily available. Owyang (2011) writes: 'Companies are frequently misguided by relying on fan and follower count as the primary measurement for their social media investments, instead they must focus on the outcomes of these fans and followers.' Determining the required outcomes should be considered when developing a social media strategy.

Evaluating social media activity is a developing area, but still flawed particularly in relation to interpreting raw data which is available. Claims to be able to determine return on investment are unproven and lack real value in accounting terms.

## END POINT

PR practitioners need to consider whether they, and the organisations they work with, require strategies to engage with digital technologies as innovators, early adopters or early majority users. There are risks and benefits associated with early involvement. Self-efficacy and communities of practice are recommended as ways for individuals to improve their knowledge and skills in social media.

Social media offer opportunities for two-way communications including building virtual communities. However, this requires an approach which eschews a publicity model in favour of relationship building with publics, who are treated with respect.

Although tools exist to support monitoring of social media activity, there are problems associated with evaluating digital public relations owing to the subjective nature of interpreting the vast volumes of data available. Nevertheless, setting objectives and focusing on outcomes is recommended rather than simply counting statistics.

# Part IV

# Stakeholder engagement

# Introduction

*Alison Theaker*

This final section looks at different sectors of public relations. The chapters in this section look at different stakeholder groups and show the different ways of engaging with an organisation's stakeholders, with insights from a variety of practitioners working in the field.

A 'stakeholder' is a more specific term than a 'public', but both are hard to define. Publics tend to relate to issues. They grow up around issues of concern, such as wanting to be more 'green' in how they choose products, parents' groups and consumer activists. The same person may be a member of several publics. Grunig and Hunt (1984: 160) define four kinds of publics:

- publics active on all issues;
- publics apathetic on all issues;
- publics active only on an issue or small number of issues that involve nearly everyone in the population;
- publics active only on a single issue.

Stakeholders are essentially anyone who can affect or be affected by an organisation. Burkitt and Ashton (in Wood 2012: 113) explain that 'many interest groups may be said to have a "stake" in certain activities . . . these stakes should be recognised by those whose actions impinge upon them'. The concept of stakeholders was taken to heart by the New Labour government in the UK. Rather than simply focusing on shareholders, businesses were encouraged and in some ways forced to have concern for other groups in society, such as their community, employees, competitors, the media, customers and suppliers.

Sometimes, the two terms are used interchangeably, so how do we tell the difference? Grunig and Repper (1992: 124) suggest that 'Publics form when stakeholders recognise . . . consequences (of the actions of an organisation) and organise to do something about it.' A 'public' seems to be distinguished by the recognition of a problem, although we can see from Grunig's own model above that some publics are deemed to be passive.

How are these concepts helpful to the practitioner? Rather than waiting for publics to form around issues, PR practitioners could be investigating and identifying stakeholders, and thinking ahead to how they may be affected by the organisation. Cornelissen (2008: 51–57) sets out ways of mapping different stakeholder groups, helping practitioners prioritise which groups should be communicated with. He goes on to distinguish whether awareness and understanding is the objective of these communications, or involvement and commitment. Awareness could be achieved by sending out newsletters, whereas involvement and commitment require consultation and collective problem solving. This shows the development from stakeholder management to stakeholder collaboration, where it is more important to build long-term relationships.

Political relations provides an understanding of public affairs and government relations, for both those seeking to engage in the process and those working in it. Links between public affairs, the media and lobbying organisations are examined. Public opinion and the role of political bloggers are considered. Restrictions on those working in government and those targeting it are discussed alongside a debate on codes and regulation.

Financial and investor relations provides an overview of the role that financial PR plays in society and the nature of communications with key stakeholders and influencers. Some of the basic tools such as annual reports and shareholder meetings are set out. Finally how recent developments in this area to improve corporate governance has impacted on PR's role is considered.

Internal communications studies one of the most important groups of stakeholders. As well as examples of good practice in the field, this chapter covers the importance of good internal communications and the goals of employee communications. The qualities needed to be a good practitioner in this field are set out. Business to business provides an understanding of working with, and for, organisations where there is a focus on engaging other organisations as the primary public. Community relations sets out the activities which could be included in a good programme to engage with an organisation's neighbours and distinguishes it from cause-related marketing. Consumer PR gives an insight into working in one of the biggest sectors in PR, looking at working with the marketing function and the role of creativity in the face of ever changing channels of communication.

CHAPTER 17

# Political relations

*Heather Yaxley*

This chapter provides an understanding of public affairs and government relations. It includes a particular focus on recent developments impacting on issues-related campaigns, monitoring public opinion and ethical considerations.

## CHECK POINT

At the end of this chapter, you should be able to:

- outline the purpose of public affairs and government relations within local, national, regional and international contexts;
- understand approaches to initiate issues-related campaigns, monitor public opinion and engage with the political process;
- recognise limitations on political relations activities, particularly in respect of ethical considerations.

## PUBLIC AFFAIRS AND GOVERNMENT RELATIONS

There are two sides to political public relations. The first is public affairs, which Moloney (2009) explains enables organisations and groups to talk with each other and government, both publicly and privately, about public policy. The other is use of PR by government organisations, such as central government departments, local authorities, public sector entities (e.g. NHS, education establishments and emergency services), executive agencies and non-departmental government bodies. These institutions have a legal and moral duty to 'inform the population and the media about policy decisions and issues affecting everyone in society' (Yeomans 2009: 578).

It is common for government bodies to work with non-governmental organisations (NGOs), charities and commercial concerns. For example, the UK government body, the Food Standards Agency engaged with a wide range of industry organisations, charities and other NGOs as part of its campaign to reduce salt consumption.

This practice highlights how political access is more readily available to some sectors of society. Those with money and/or influence are able, often through employment of specialist public affairs advisors, to use private means of communication. In contrast, less powerful members of society may struggle to get their voice heard, particularly if they are not articulate, media savvy or conversant in political procedures.

There are also concerns about financial links in politics. For example, in the UK there are traditionally close ties between businesses and the Conservative party, and unions and the Labour party. Such financial arrangements may present opportunities to influence policy decisions.

## Influencing political decisions

Attempts to shape politics date back centuries with Ancient Greece acknowledged as pioneering the Western political tradition (Cartledge 2009). Britain has a long

**TALKING POINT**

In 2011, the UK government established the Public Health Responsibility Deal 'to tap into the potential for businesses and other organisations to improve public health and tackle health inequalities through their influence over food, alcohol, physical activity and health in the workplace'. The government believed requiring commercial partners to pledge action would be faster and more effective than adopting a regulatory strategy. Although recognising the importance of government working with industry and business, several high-profile organisations, including Diabetes UK and the British Heart Foundation, resigned from participation. Critics claimed there was insufficient monitoring of business pledges, which were also felt to lack ambition, and the House of Commons Health Committee Twelfth Report stated 'those with a financial interest must not be allowed to set the agenda for health improvement'.

What are the benefits and drawbacks of such partnership initiatives? How do you think concerns over political influence could be avoided?

history of successful political campaigning. For example, social reformists in the eighteenth century included the anti-slavery movement and Quakers such as Elizabeth Fry who campaigned to improve prison conditions.

Today, organisations involved in influencing political decisions include political parties, think tanks/advocacy organisations, trade unions, interest groups (who lobby on particular topics or causes), religious bodies, charities, NGOs, academics and pressure groups. In addition, commercial concerns, either independently or through trade bodies, engage in the political process. Alliances may be formed to help build a strong case for a cause and increase pressure on policy-makers. (See Fair Fuel UK Action Point on pp. 250–251.)

The term lobbying indicates 'direct attempts to influence legislative and regulatory decisions in government' (Cutlip *et al*. 2000). Somerville and Ramsey (2012: 47) cite Milbraith's fifty-year-old definition that highlights lobbying is undertaken by 'someone other than a citizen acting on his own behalf'. They recommend (p. 48) a wider perspective on lobbying than direct advocacy, including 'monitoring and intelligence gathering' using media relations, 'building relationships and coordinating activities with other actors engaged in pursuing the same interest or promoting the same cause'.

Harrison (2011) claims lobbying in the UK is a £2 billion industry. Pejorative use of the term portrays lobbyists as working for any cause if paid enough and a belief that lobbying involves secret or underhand approaches, such as providing gifts or favours.

The professional lobbyist (working in-house or for a specialist consultancy) is likely to have worked within politics and have a relevant university degree. Non-professionals may develop skills and knowledge to undertake lobbying activities. For example, celebrity chef Jamie Oliver has championed improved funding for school dinners over recent years.

Building relationships with political influencers is the role of an organisation's public affairs function (or its appointed consultancy). Organisations, groups and individuals have a right, within certain parameters, to attempt to influence the actions of governments, which have a direct or indirect impact on them and the environment in which they operate.

Lobbying can be defensive (to avoid legislation) or offensive (to press for action) as organisations seek to shape opinion before government policy or regulation is agreed, or to secure amendments to existing legislation.

Those involved in lobbying supply four things according to Moloney (2000):

1   information concerning policy development
2   administrative support
3   policy advice
4   access to policy-makers.

Lobbying is directed at decision-makers (such as portfolio holders (e.g. ministers), elected members, executive staff or their representatives) or those who are directly able to influence them. This applies across all levels of government from local to international. The EU for example is the target of citizen and professional lobbying activities. Almost 5,000 lobbyists are listed in the voluntary Transparency Register (which is jointly operated by the European Commission and European Parliament) or transferring to it from the previous register.

## Legislative process

Political structures and processes vary from country to country and within different levels of government. Knowledge of how relevant decisions are made is essential. Specialists in public affairs and lobbying have relevant contacts, previous experience and keep up to date on developments in the political arena.

The legislative process generally goes from initiation (deciding to act on some matter) to consultation (seeking views) and formulation (shaping laws). A law may then be enacted – in the UK parliament (Westminster) passing through various stages (in the House of Commons and House of Lords), and concluding by Royal Assent. Passed laws are enforced to ensure compliance.

Individuals and organisations can influence law making at a number of points. The UK government regularly launches public consultations that follow the Cabinet Office's code of practice. In terms of legislation enacted at Westminster, influence may be sought through participation in think tanks, green papers, white papers, party manifestos, the Queen's speech, Acts and Bills. Other opportunities to present a position include: electronic petitions, Private Members' bills (proposed/championed by an individual Member of Parliament), reaction to events (for example calling publicly for legislation), issues emerging with existing laws, rulings by the Supreme Court and other legal precedents (case law).

## Public sector PR

The first political consultants were employed by governments in the US and UK as speech writers, press secretaries and event organisers in the 1830s. L'Etang (2004) places the historical foundation of British public relations in the political sector, with members of the National Association of Local Government Officers (NALGO) seeking public understanding for government administration in the early twentieth century.

In the UK, government employees (civil servants) provide non-political communications functions, but increasingly work alongside researchers and advisers representing political parties or individual politicians. PR practitioners work at all levels of government. These each have specific roles of influence and authority which may include passing laws (legislate) and raising revenues (taxation).

The public sector includes a number of organisations which, in recent years, have become more open to engagement and hence the employment of strategic public

# REGISTER OF LOBBYISTS

There has been considerable debate in the UK regarding the necessity to establish a mandatory statutory register for lobbyists, with government due to legislate in 2012. The UK Public Affairs Council was established in 2010 by the CIPR, PRCA and APPC (Association of Professional Political Consultants). Its purpose is to address the lobbying industry's reputation with voluntary self-regulation for those professionally engaged in public affairs. The initiative has been subject to criticism from within the industry and PRCA withdrew from UKPAC in December 2011.

In December 2011, the Bureau of Investigative Journalism published a report of an undercover investigation of the lobbying industry. Reporters, posing as agents for the cotton industry and government of Uzbekistan (which has a reputation for human rights violations and child labour) contacted ten London lobbying firms. Two consultancies refused to take the business, but one, Bell Pottinger, agreed to a meeting at which it was said to have boasted of its ability to manipulate online coverage and access within the UK government.

One major aspect of a statutory register would be transparency regarding consultancies' clients and employees, who may have personal relationships influential contacts.

Arguments against a statutory register include:

* difficulty in defining those involved in lobbying;
* focus has been primarily on lobbying agencies, meaning corporate in-house lobbyists, SMEs, trade associations, charities, NGOs, legal firms, auditors, management consultants and think tanks may not be expected to disclose their activities;
* extensive administration required to monitor and report all political contact;
* issues involved in determining what activities need to be disclosed;
* distinguishing contact made with individuals in their personal rather than professional context;
* concerns over publication of sensitive client or industry information;
* concerns over calls to publish financial details of lobbying activities;
* issues involved in verifying accuracy of reported information.

Supporters cite that effective registers exist in the US, Canada and Australia.

**TALKING POINT**

## UK CABINET OFFICE PUBLIC CONSULTATION CODE OF PRACTICE (www.direct.gov.uk)

All consultation documents follow the Cabinet Office's code of practice. These guidelines help ensure a common public consultation standard across government. When government consults it must:

- build a realistic timeframe for the consultation, allowing plenty of time for each stage of the process;

- be clear as to who is being consulted, about what and for what specific purpose;

- ensure that the document is as simple and concise as possible. It should include a summary and clearly set out the questions it wishes to address;

- always distribute documents as widely as possible, using electronic means (but not at the exclusion of others);

- make sure all responses are carefully and open-mindedly analysed, and the results made widely available, with an account of the views expressed and the reasons for decisions finally taken.

A list of public consultations can be searched at http://consultations. direct.gov.uk/ by keyword, organisation, status or date to access the documentation and process of public consultation.

relations functions (rather than simply press offices). These include police and fire authorities, health sector organisations, educational bodies, the armed forces, executive agencies and non-departmental public bodies. Somerville and Ramsey (2012) report the significant cost of government communications in the UK, noting the Department of Health, for example, had a budget for communications of £52.2 million in 2007/2008.

Wakeman (2012) states public sector PR operates in a complex stakeholder landscape. Internal communications is a key responsibility with almost 6 million employees (ONS 2011). Many public sector bodies are large, complicated institutions, frequently facing change (not least owing to government policy decisions). Challenges include the diverse nature of employees, who may have different language skills or lack access to online communications.

Media relations is another important role of PR practitioners working in the public sector as a means of reaching large numbers of stakeholders. Somerville and Ramsey (2012) outline how government communications have been carefully managed in recent years, particularly to privilege specific views rather than reflect the wider public interest. Techniques used to announce political ideas, policies and initiatives are reminiscent of the launch of new products, indicating a press agentry or publicity model of PR (Grunig and Hunt 1984), which raises concerns about ethics, accountability and truth.

Public sector PR keeps the public informed on policy decisions and other initiatives. It is also used to influence attitudes and behaviour as part of ensuring policies are implemented or social problems are addressed. This may involve public information campaigns or social marketing initiatives (see p. 247). Another duty is to respond to requests under the Freedom of Information Act (FOIA) introduced in 2005 to increase the accountability of public sector bodies.

PR practitioners in the public sector tread a difficult line in seeking to be independent of political influence. Their role may be considered to be working in the public interest, although they are communicating initiatives to meet objectives determined by those who were elected or appointed within a political process.

Government organisations need to communicate with other public sector bodies, particularly where partnership initiatives are involved. There has been some concern regarding public sector bodies seeking to lobby central government. However, it is

## ACTION POINT

## CODE OF RECOMMENDED PRACTICE ON LOCAL AUTHORITY PUBLICITY

Since April 2011, any local authority communication, in whatever form, addressed to the public or a section of the public, has to comply with the publicity code, which is structured into seven principles. It requires council publicity to be:

- lawful
- cost effective
- objective
- even-handed
- appropriate
- having regard to equality and diversity
- issued with care during periods of heightened sensitivity.

The code states even-handedness addresses concerns regarding political issues, such as ensuring 'publicity about the council does not seek to affect support for a single councillor or group'. Likewise, appropriate use of publicity details, 'local authorities should refrain from retaining the services of lobbyists' as well as ensuring publication of council newsletters does not cause 'unfair competition with local newspapers' by being issued no more than four times a year.

**READING POINT**

■ The *Public Relations Handbook* (Theaker 2012) contains detailed chapters on public relations and politics (by Somerville and Ramsey) and public sector public relations (by Wakeman).

important to ensure two-way rather than simply top-down communications throughout government and the public sector.

Public sector PR practitioners are required increasingly to work in partnership with counterparts in the commercial and not-for-profit sectors. Such activities range from publicity and public information campaigns, to crisis preparedness and issues management. In addition, internal communications frequently require engaging employees of private organisations delivering public services.

Private-public sector joint ventures may reflect a sensible use of expertise or available resources. Alternatively, they may have other objectives, such as to increase the credibility of government information campaigns. For example, the Department of Health paid the British Heart Foundation £4 million for the high-profile 'Give up before you clog up' anti-smoking campaign in January 2004, which enabled it to be positioned as a charity health message rather than a government 'nanny state' initiative. In other cases, the commercial sector may work with government to avoid legislation. For example, the Drinkaware Trust, a partnership between the UK government and the Portman Group (the social responsibility body for alcohol producers) has public awareness, understanding and behavioural objectives for responsible alcohol consumption, with campaign activity funded by the drinks industry.

## ISSUES-RELATED CAMPAIGNS, PUBLIC OPINION AND THE POLITICAL PROCESS

Issues-related campaigns involve raising a matter of concern (opportunity or threat) for debate in the public sphere, which is a concept originated in the 1960s by Habermas. Burkart (2009: 142) explains that the public sphere 'comes into existence when citizens communicate, either face to face or through letters, journals, and newspapers and other mass media in order to express their opinions about matters of general interest, and to subject these opinions to rational discussion'.

Moloney (2000: 150) claims the 'persuasive sphere has replaced the public sphere', where conflicting interests participate equally and outcomes are determined by the majority after careful consideration. Public relations is used to present a particular case by virtue of reason, rather than emotion, which Moloney (2000) argues would be manipulative. The idea of a level playing field is unrealistic however, as government, and those employing professional public relations services, have greater access to the persuasive sphere. Indeed, Moloney states that government can 'declare its view to be the public interest and so close off discussion on a matter'.

One type of issues-related campaign involves social marketing, which aims 'to influence the voluntary behavior of target audiences to improve their personal welfare and that of the society of which they are a part' (Andreasen 1994: 110). Such initiatives are positioned as acting in the public good, although L'Etang (2008) distinguishes between pro-health government campaigns and pseudo-health education involving the promotion of special interests around an issue. An example of a pro-health campaign is the Kill Jill donor initiative (pp. 10–12). Andreasen (2006) criticises many social marketing campaigns for failing to understand the needs of publics, the benefits they want and the barriers that need to be overcome.

A second type of issues-related campaign involves agenda setting, which Martinelli (2011: 40) relates to 'Cohen's (1963) belief that the media tell us not what to think, but what to think about'. Szondi (2009: 123) outlines the tripolar model of agendas: the media agenda, which affects the public agenda, and the policy agenda involving 'pressure groups and political actors'. He also cites Watson's (2003) addition of the corporate agenda and proposition of a 'dynamic, and often imbalanced, relationship between the public, policy, corporate and media agenda'.

The development of social media challenges and extends this agenda setting model as detailed in Figure 17.1.

Social media contribute towards fragmentation by which the traditional influencers have less influence over the public agenda. At the same time, social media channels:

- offer a new arena in which debate is able to take place;
- act as an influencer on the public, media, policy and corporate agendas;
- provide a global, 24/7 dynamic environment in which legacy, current and emerging issues are discussed.

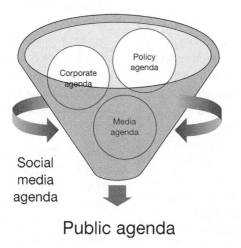

**FIGURE 17.1** Dynamic agenda setting model incorporating social media

The situational theory of publics (Grunig and Hunt 1984) can also be considered in the context of online communications. Recognition of problems can be facilitated, constraints on participation lowered, personal involvement increased, information seeking and information processing made easier, and opportunities presented for publics to form around single, multiple and hot (salient) issues.

In addition to providing a place where anyone can engage in an online public sphere (provided they have access and ability to do so), digital developments have created new influencers and opinion leaders. These include bloggers such as Guido Fawkes (http://order-order.com/) who describes himself as 'a campaigning journalist who publishes via a website'.

## Public opinion

In political public relations the concept of public opinion is used to reflect an overall consensus or an aggregation of individual views. It may be considered the outcome of debate in the public sphere or a statistical result obtained from opinion surveys. The opinion of individuals or vox pop interviews may also be used to illustrate or support a particular perspective. Someone's opinion may be the outcome of considered reflection or expressed as an immediate reaction to a topic. Opinions may be sought from a wide number of people, a representative sample, or from those with personal experience or expertise on an issue.

Public opinion may be used to inform decision-making or within the dynamic agenda setting model illustrated in Figure 17.1. This means the concept of public opinion may reflect the interests of corporates, pressure groups, political actors or the media, that is, those with money and/or influence in society.

Politicians and other decision-makers may be swayed to take action on the basis of acceptance by a majority of people as expressed by public opinion. This may not reflect minority views, which research by Noelle-Neumann (1933, cited by L'Etang 2008) indicates are suppressed by peer pressure, resulting in a spiral of silence.

L'Etang (2008: 100) highlights public opinion is 'dynamic, fluid and a *shape-shifter*' indicating that it is subject to change and so requires ongoing monitoring and evaluation. Public opinion is researched primarily through commercial surveys commissioned by various organisations. Price (1992) identifies this

**READING POINT**

■ Price (1992) provides a review of the literature on public opinion offering an insightful introduction to the topic. The websites of research companies, such as MORI and yougov.co.uk are a useful resource for reviewing published reports commissioned by public relations practitioners working for a variety of organisations.

research plays a role in public debate. Understanding the research brief, methodology employed and process of analysing and interpreting results is important in determining the validity of any survey. However, these matters are often ignored in favour of selective headline results. Detailed analysis of opinion research may be more useful than focusing on averages or totals. Likewise other methods, such as content analysis, observation or depth interviews may be more appropriate for understanding an issue (see Part II).

# Engaging in the political process

Details on getting involved in the Westminster political process can be found at the website: www.parliament.uk. This site also provides information on parliamentary business, arranging visits and free training for organisations wishing to know more about the work of Parliament.

Online information can also be referenced for local authorities, and other public sector bodies, including the devolved regional administrations:

- Scotland: http://home.scotland.gov.uk/home
- Wales: www.assemblywales.org
- Northern Ireland: www.niassembly.gov.uk.

In addition, social media enable the public, and PR practitioners, to engage with these organisations and keep up to date with news. PR practitioners should further research the political landscape by monitoring online and offline media for:

- speeches, leaks and 'flyers' to test public opinion;
- reports of think tanks and other influential groups;
- political discussion at a local, regional, national and international level;
- opinion poll results;
- statements and draft documents issued by government, politicians (especially those who have special interests), select committees and so forth.

Research should form part of a formal situational analysis (see Chapter 5) which enables trends, issues and opportunities to be identified. Similarly, if specific campaigns are determined to be a relevant strategic response, a range of tactics can be considered (see Figure 17.2).

Many of these techniques can be carried out using digital public relations methods (see Chapter 16), which extend the reach of political public relations enabling wider coalitions to be sought to address issues of common concern.

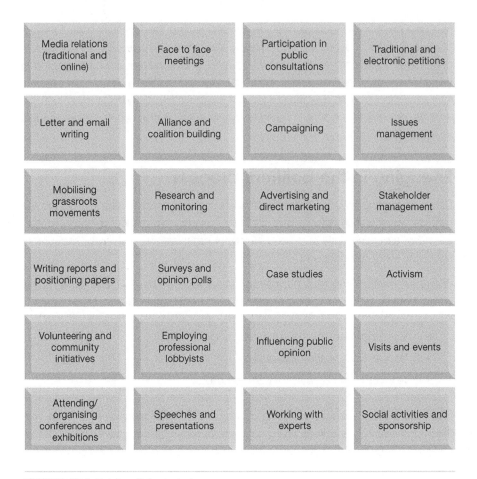

| | | | |
| --- | --- | --- | --- |
| Media relations (traditional and online) | Face to face meetings | Participation in public consultations | Traditional and electronic petitions |
| Letter and email writing | Alliance and coalition building | Campaigning | Issues management |
| Mobilising grassroots movements | Research and monitoring | Advertising and direct marketing | Stakeholder management |
| Writing reports and positioning papers | Surveys and opinion polls | Case studies | Activism |
| Volunteering and community initiatives | Employing professional lobbyists | Influencing public opinion | Visits and events |
| Attending/ organising conferences and exhibitions | Speeches and presentations | Working with experts | Social activities and sponsorship |

FIGURE 17.2 Public affairs techniques

## FAIR FUEL UK (www.fairfueluk.com/)

**ACTION POINT**

The Fair Fuel UK campaign was established in March 2011 to lobby for a reduction in vehicle fuel taxation by Peter Carroll, whose company, Why Not Campaign Ltd, previously ran the Ghurkha Justice Campaign resulting in a change in the law.

Recent developments in technology, which alongside moves to open up government since the late 1990s, have changed the way that Parliament works in terms of engaging in the political process. This means new tools are available to raise issues with MPs who are keen to show they are listening and responding to the public following the 2010 expenses scandal.

An integrated, planned approach was used in the Fair Fuel UK campaign. In particular, opportunities to raise the issue with MPs enabled those interested in the topic to be identified. Fair Fuel UK claims over 150 parliamentarians supported its campaign, which involved a range of tactics including:

- Motoring journalist, Quentin Willson fronted the campaign, providing a recognisable spokesperson. Quentin wrote a blog and regular newspaper features on the campaign.

- Traditional and social media activities (including Twitter, LinkedIn and Facebook) were used to communicate ongoing developments and engage with supporters.

- Stunts were used to mixed effect. Unveiling a banner outside the Houses of Parliament, depicting a graphic of a fuel tanker showing the proportion of fuel cost accounted for by tax, achieved good media coverage. Dragging a truck with no fuel to Parliament to indicate the implications of rising costs did not.

- A website and other technology were used to facilitate and monitor participation by individuals and organisations in the campaign.

- Emails were sent to individual MPs by grassroots supporters of the campaign (these were tailored to reflect specific local or other interests rather than being standardised mass mailings).

- Support for the campaign was provided by motoring organisation the RAC and two trade bodies, the Road Haulage Association and Freight Transport Association. Organisations backing the campaign raised the issue with their stakeholders and through other PR activities.

- Radio, television and print media interviews were undertaken by Peter Carroll to coincide with Parliamentary debates.

- A Westminster Hall debate was secured by Robert Halfon, MP. These enable MPs to enter ballots to raise local or national issues and receive a response from a government Minister.

- An e-petition calling for planned fuel duty increases to be scrapped and for a mechanism to stabilise prices at the pumps, attracted 135,000 supporters, making it eligible for debate in the House of Commons.

- The Backbench Business Committee scheduled a debate in the House of Commons on 15 November and passed a motion asking the Government to 'consider the feasibility' of price stabilisation.

- In his Autumn Statement to Parliament on 29 November, the Chancellor of the Exchequer cancelled a planned fuel duty rise in January 2012 and reduced a promised rise for August 2012.

Fair Fuel UK has welcomed this outcome, but is committed to continuing the campaign.

## LIMITATIONS ON POLITICAL RELATIONS ACTIVITIES

Ethical concerns about political public relations have been considered throughout this chapter. These matters also arise in the context of a government review of the regulatory framework supporting the communications sector, which is in consultation prior to a draft bill expected by mid-2013. The UK government also established the Leveson enquiry in the wake of the *News of the World* phone hacking scandal, to examine the culture, practices and ethics of the media, with a particular focus on the relationship of the press with the public, police and politicians.

Pieczka (2006: 323) observes 'personal ties to powerful individuals can only help' in a career in political PR. The issue of relationships in political PR relates to the notion of 'revolving doors' (L'Etang 2004: 128) within what is 'referred to as the circuit of power, that is a network of prestigious jobs in the media, public relations and politics' (Pieczka 2006: 325). For example, in November 2011 the *Daily Mail* wrote: 'A former breakfast TV presenter was at the centre of a conflict of interest row last night after moving from a high-powered Whitehall job to a lucrative position with Asda, which worked with her on a Government campaign.' *PR Week* noted the appointment required clearance by the Cabinet Office.

Although most examples of journalists entering PR practice are not seen as controversial, one exception was the appointment of former *News of the World* editor, Andy Coulson as Conservative Party communications director and then director of communications for Prime Minister David Cameron. Allegations of his involvement in phone hacking at the now defunct newspaper caused embarrassment and led to Coulson's resignation. He subsequently established a private PR consultancy.

Economic cuts affecting public sector PR and high-profile government campaigns emphasise the importance of evaluation and determining value. Budget constraints have led to reductions in the size of internal teams and fewer projects undertaken by external consultancies. The government announced the Central Office of Information (COI), which had provided communication activities since 1946, would be closed on 31 March 2012. Its final annual report stated government departments had reduced in-house communications staff by around a quarter and cut budgets by around a half since June 2010.

In contrast, the Pearlfinders Index identified public affairs and lobbying as strong development areas for 2012. Here, campaigns must also deliver beneficial outcomes, which may need to go beyond legislative change. Yaxley (2012b) discussed how a road safety campaign had led to introduction of the New Drivers Act in 1997. However, its intended outcome of reducing accidents among young drivers has not been achieved, indeed owing to the introduction of speed cameras, young drivers are more likely to be driving without a licence or insurance.

In addition to the ethicalness and effectiveness of political public relations activities, digital developments reflect a third area of limitations. Although felt by government to offer a cost-effective method for increasing access and engagement, many sections of society (especially the elderly and less well off) remain excluded from such communications. Sweetser (2011: 308) argues governments need to understand 'how citizens use and are impacted by digital political messages on a daily basis' and reflect 'the level of transparency and ethical vigour needed to be successful in digital communications'. Without investment in the resources and systems required to respond to increased public engagement, political communication will fail to deliver on the potential presented by digital public relations.

**READING POINT**

Strömbäck and Kiousis (2011) argue that political public relations is an emerging field as far as research and theoretical development and linkage to other related disciplines, such as political science, are concerned. They offer a definition (p. 8):

Political public relations is the management process by which an organisation or individual actor for political purposes, through purposeful communication and action, seeks to influence and to establish, build, and maintain beneficial relationships and reputations with its key publics to help support its mission and achieve its goals.

As editors of *Political Public Relations: principles and applications*, Strömbäck and Kiousis set out to connect scholars from different disciplines to provide a missing theoretical and empirical context. The academic underpinning of this book draws on a range of public relations areas including issues and crisis management as well as persuasive and relationship theories. Hence, the practices and principles elsewhere in *The PR Toolkit* will prove useful for those seeking to engage in political PR.

# END POINT

Public affairs and lobbying are undertaken by various organisations, groups and individuals either directly or by employing specialist consultancy services. The aim is to influence public opinion and policy decisions using public or private communications. This raises concerns about privileged access for those with money and/or influence in society.

Public relations practitioners working for government and public sector organisations seek to inform, persuade and engage the population and the media in policy decisions and issues affecting everyone in society.

Issues-related campaigns may use social marketing or agenda-setting strategies. The development of a social media agenda extends and challenges debate beyond existing media, policy, corporate and public agendas.

Limitations on political relations activities include ethical considerations, the impact of economic constraints and the emergence of new technologies.

CHAPTER 18

# Financial and investor relations

*Heather Yaxley*

This chapter provides an overview of the role that financial PR plays in society and the nature of communications with key stakeholders and influencers. It considers the impact of the global economic crisis, alongside emerging trends and corporate governance issues.

## CHECK POINT

At the end of this chapter, you should be able to:

- understand the role of financial PR and the nature of communications with key stakeholders and influencers;
- identify the key components of financial communications, including annual reports and shareholder meetings;
- consider the impact of the global economic crisis on financial PR, particularly in respect of corporate governance.

## ROLE OF FINANCIAL PR

Financial public relations is 'one of the most profitable and highly paid sectors of the PR industry' (Phillimore 2012: 311). The problem with this approach is that it reinforces an image of financial matters as complex, mysterious and beyond the mathematical abilities of many PR practitioners (Fleet 2006). Presented as a specialist function playing 'a fundamentally important role in any modern listed business' (Bowd 2009: 465) a focus on financial matters appears to be separate from other areas of corporate public relations, and the preserve of those with expertise in the stock market and its operations.

There are three reasons why this is inappropriate:

1   For public relations to be recognised as playing a strategic role within the dominant coalition (whether or not that means having a seat on the board), the senior practitioner must understand the financial operations of the organisation.

2   An ability to discuss key financial metrics is essential for PR practitioners to be able to engage equally with other senior managers, particularly the financial director.

3   Financial public relations should be applied to all organisations rather than the narrow perspective of those who focus on communications, relationship building and reputation management with stock market investors and those who influence their opinions.

Financial performance is of relevance to a wide range of stakeholders, including internal and political, and concentrating on investor relations ignores the importance of these other interested and influential parties. Indeed, there is a complex web of influence on the financial performance of any organisation which increasingly crosses international boundaries and reacts to the opinions of those with little direct contact with the financial markets.

There were 994 companies with shares listed on the main market of the London Stock Exchange in November 2011. Two-thirds of these had a market value more than £50 million, with 20 per cent valued at less than £35 million. The AIM listed 1,150 companies in November 2011; 23 per cent valued at over £50 million and 57 per cent under £25 million. AIM is the London Stock Exchange's international market for smaller growing companies. A wide range of businesses including early stage and venture capital backed, as well as more established companies, join AIM seeking access to growth capital.

These listed companies represent a small fraction of the 4.5 million private sector businesses operating in the UK (BIS 2011). Many of these may be subsidiaries of multinational or international companies whose shares are listed in other countries. This means their investor relations activities will focus primarily on those countries, despite the increasing interconnection of the behaviour of global stock markets.

Organisations operating in the private sector that are not publicly listed, as well as those in the not-for-profit and public sectors, will each need to communicate to their relevant stakeholders regarding financial performance. Financial reporting is undertaken in one form or another by most if not all organisations. For example,

TALKING POINT

Bowd (2009: 466) identifies three categories of stakeholder for publicly listed companies:

1    national and international regulators of the exchange of money;

2    those who exchange money (institutional and private shareholders, private client brokers, and investment and merchant banks);

3    those who influence or communicate about the exchange of money (analysts, financial and business media, regional media in major cities, broadcast and online media, wire services and trade media).

In addition to the importance of existing shareholders, Phillimore (2012: 315) notes potential and past shareholders as investors and identifies institutional shareholders include 'pension funds, insurance companies and investment banks'. He also details new capital sources (hedge funds, private equity and venture capital) as innovations over the last two decades.

If you work for a publicly listed company, identify the organisation's stakeholders falling into these three groups. If you work for any other type of organisation, identify who controls the money it requires to manage its operations. In the case of a public sector body, this may be the government or tax payers. For a charity, grants and donations from the public may be the main source of income.

details of financial operations will be required by a small business requesting a bank loan while charities need to present an annual report to relevant stakeholders.

Public relations may be involved in ensuring that organisations establish and maintain a reputation for financial probity, producing an informed narrative in annual reports, or communicating financial results with key publics.

## Financial PR practice

The starting point for understanding the role of financial PR in respect of an individual organisation is its relevant regulatory framework. This will cover its establishment, operation, reporting requirements and controls on matters such as mergers and acquisitions. Regulations vary across countries. In the UK, the Financial Services Authority (FSA) is the regulator of the financial services industry.

As with other sectors considered in *The PR Toolkit*, competence in media relations is important, particularly for those working with specialist financial broadcast, print and online journalists. Chapters 12 and 16 provide guidance on media relations and online PR respectively. Journalists specialising in financial reporting should be

cognisant with the language and operations of the sector in detail. However, pressures on the media mean that non-specialists may also be covering financial matters (particularly around major announcements). In addition, financial matters may be communicated by the media to non-specialist audiences. This means an understanding of relevant terminology is required, alongside an ability to communicate financial matters in everyday language.

Financial public relations for publicly listed companies is primarily undertaken in the UK by specialist consultancies, often working with internal corporate or financial affairs functions. External expertise is useful as financial PR consultancies have established relationships with media and influencers alongside relevant experience and specialist knowledge of the financial sector, its processes, terminology and key players. Phillimore (2012: 312) reports the major financial PR consultancies also 'provide government relations and regulatory support'. Regardless of whether an organisation uses internal and/or external financial PR support, it needs to work alongside the finance director and other relevant board members.

## Shareholder activism

Issues and crisis management are important in relation to financial affairs. Knowledge of shareholders and their interests is an important aspect of a strategic situational analysis (Chapter 5). This was apparent when, in 2006, British Airways faced a crisis after banning a check-in employee from displaying a cross over her uniform. The *Daily Mail* reported 'condemnation from an overwhelming alliance of Cabinet ministers, 100 MPs, 20 Church of England bishops and, finally, the Archbishop of Canterbury' who 'threatened to sell the Church of England's £6.6 million holding of BA shares' forcing the company to back-down on its policy.

Companies may also face challenges from activist shareholders. Individuals or pressure and interest groups may purchase shares in order to protest about behaviour of companies they find socially unacceptable. Alternatively, existing shareholders may become active publics in response to strategic changes about which they feel strongly.

## GREENPEACE ACTIVISM

In April 2010, thirty Greenpeace 'orang-utans' appeared outside Nestlé's AGM campaigning for the company to address concerns regarding the Indonesian rainforest. Inside the meeting activists abseiled from the ceiling before unfurling two large banners stating 'Nestlé – give orang-utans a break', a play on the slogan of the company's Kit-Kat chocolate bar. A presentation was also made to shareholders. Greenpeace claimed to 'want shareholders to use their influence to change Nestlé's policies and stop using palm oil and pulp and paper products from destroyed rainforests and carbon-rich peatlands'.

This action was part of an integrated campaign which included 200,000 people sending emails or calling Nestlé, and a website (www.greenpeace.org/kitkat) featuring a video which was watched over 1.5 million times. Two months after the start of the campaign, Nestlé announced a new policy committing to identify and exclude companies from its supply chain that own or manage 'high-risk plantations or farms linked to deforestation'.

What are the benefits and drawbacks of an activist campaign targeting shareholders? How does mobilising the public online contribute to persuading an organisation to alter an existing strategy?

Activist shareholders may develop high-profile public relations campaigns, including disrupting AGMs with stunts or raising motions against the incumbent directors.

## PR FOR FINANCIAL BODIES

In addition to considering financial communications with an organisation's stake-holders, it is worth reflecting on the role of PR within financial bodies. Customers of banks and other financial institutions may be thought of in relation to consumer PR (Chapter 22) although the importance of financial decision-making is different to the products which are primarily the focus of consumer PR campaigns.

The financial sector has been high profile as a result of the economic problems of the last few years. This has encompassed issues and crisis management as well as a strategic need to rebuild trust and reputation in the financial sector and specific institutions.

The Elaboration Likelihood Model (ELM) (Petty and Cacioppo 1986, cited by Larson 2004) detailed two routes for processing information that have relevance for financial communications. The central route of processing requires careful consideration of

ACTION POINT

Technical language is commonplace in communicating financial terms, conditions and product information to the public. The Plain English Campaign claims to have worked with financial organisations to improve the information they produce and has awarded its Crystal Mark as a seal of approval for the clarity of a financial documentation.

Nevertheless, it reports examples of financial jargon such as:

> Our view of the High Yield market remains constructive. However, interest rates appear to be a headwind. High yield has lower duration than most fixed income products, but it is being impacted, nevertheless. The current environment is negatively influenced by technicals more than fundamentals. We continue to see default rates decline which is benefited by an improving economy.

- Do you understand this paragraph?
- Why do you think financial organisations in particular use jargon that obfuscates the message being communicated?
- Look for documents containing the Crystal Mark and consider whether they use 'everyday' English and meet the other criteria specified at: www.plainenglish.co.uk/crystal-mark/about-the-crystal-mark/the-crystal-mark-standard.html.

information and is normally associated with rational information that may require the receiver to engage in a high amount of elaboration. This would seem to apply to financial information. However, if people are not motivated to engage in thinking in depth about such matters (and jargon is one barrier to them doing so), then they will not be making judgements on the basis of in-depth understanding of materials. In such cases, they will be likely to engage in peripheral processing, i.e. low elaboration, in making decisions on the basis of heuristics (mental shortcuts) which tend to relate to more superficial or emotional aspects of communication.

Ironically, the UK government appointed a celebrity, Carol Vorderman (known for presenting the television quiz show, *Countdown*) as chair of its task force on the standard of maths in schools. This is a common technique for peripheral processing of messages. Further reflecting the ELM distinction, the task force report recommended separating theoretical maths from practical, real-world applications such as personal finance decision-making.

## FINANCIAL COMMUNICATIONS

Bowd (2009) cites Grummer's observation that most aspects of financial communication that are legally required to be produced are issued according to a calendar:

- Interim results (half-year results in the UK) – providing a financial account of performance over the previous six months and expectations for the second half of the year in a chairman's report.

- Preliminary results – the first opportunity for financial audiences to gauge whether performance matches expectations.

- A profits warning statement – may be issued prior to releasing either of the above results if performance is notably below expectations. This can be framed to reduce the impact of the published figures with the aim of preventing a lowering of share price, reduced confidence and negative impact on reputation of the organisation's performance.

- Annual report and accounts – provides an in-depth account of the reporting year's financial results with further information felt to be of relevance and interest to financial stakeholders. There has been a move towards Triple Bottom Line reporting covering social responsibility and environmental performance alongside the financials. This is being superseded by Integrated Reporting (see below).

- Annual general meeting (AGM) – offers an opportunity for shareholders (individual or institutional) to ask questions of the company's management; although few investors tend to attend such meetings having voted in advance by postal ballot.

## Annual reports

The preliminary report provides a shortened version of the full annual report, which must reach stakeholders no later than four months after the company's financial year end (Phillimore 2012). Financial results are issued via one of the approved regulatory wire services to ensure that the release of such sensitive information is coordinated to be available to all investors simultaneously.

Although the numeric data, which is included in financial reports, is audited for accuracy, the company tends to position its results to highlight key aspects and influence media reporting and public opinion regarding its performance.

Surma (2006: 58) analysed narratives in CSR reports written to inform stakeholders of performance in this area. She identified PR practitioners tended to create narratives that only served the interests of the organisation and did not provide 'a voice' for less powerful stakeholders. Fekrat et al. (1996: 178) cite a Financial Times (15 April 1992) article stating a similar view: '[environmental reporting] exhibits the glossy hand of the public relations experts.' This approach to generating a one-sided, persuasive narrative is likely to be found also in the text accompanying financial reports.

The counter side of this perspective is that annual reports present an opportunity to present a favourable image of the organisation. This is useful as the 'glossy' annual report will be published on the company's website where it acts as 'a marketing tool and can be used to introduce the business not only to potential investors, but also to potential customers' (Phillimore 2012: 321).

## Shareholder meetings

The primary formal shareholder meeting is the annual general meeting (AGM) held each year. It is a legal requirement for public limited companies (PLCs) to hold an AGM within six months of their financial year end. The meeting may be held either at the company's head office or another suitable venue. The AGM offers an opportunity for shareholders to ask direct questions of the company's senior management. At the AGM, the annual report needs to be formally accepted, directors re-elected and auditors appointed. The company may use the opportunity to make a presentation on the results and plans for the year ahead.

Private companies legally do not need to hold an AGM (unless their Articles of Association specify otherwise). Guidance on AGM and other meetings for charities can be found at: www.charitycommission.gov.uk.

In relation to an AGM:

- Written notice must be sent to directors and shareholders twenty-one days in advance for public companies with traded shares (fourteen days' notice for private companies, unless the articles state otherwise). If 95 per cent of shareholders agree (90 per cent for private companies), shorter notice can be provided.
- Copies of the company's accounts do not need to be sent to shareholders prior to the AGM, but must be sent before filing with the registrar of companies.
- Ordinary resolutions can be passed by a simple majority with special resolutions (which must be filed at Companies House: www.companies house.gov.uk) requiring at least three-quarters of those eligible to vote in favour.

## Other financial issues

Specialist advice or expertise is involved in managing PR around several other types of activities:

- Flotations: This is when an organisation decides to have its shares listed on the stock exchange. Formally known as an Initial Public Offering (IPO), a broker and corporate financier will be appointed to manage the technicalities and marketing of the offering to institutional investors (Phillimore 2012). PR support helps handle media relations and reputation management during the process.

- Mergers and acquisitions/divestments: Companies may consider merging or acquiring/divestment of another company as part of a growth/consolidation strategy. Johnson et al. (2005) state the number of acquisitions tripled during the 1990s, with many involving cross-border deals.

  Johnson et al. (2005: 351) note that 'in the majority of cases' flotation 'leads to poor performance or even serious financial difficulties'. They suggest, as an alternative, organisations may form strategic alliances where resources and activities are shared as a joint venture; although around half of these are said to fail.

- Hostile takeovers: may be launched when the directors of one company resist the advances of another. These can be complicated and very bad-tempered with PR representatives of both sides engaging in a war of words through the media, analysts or direct with stakeholders.

These strategic moves require corporate PR expertise alongside financial PR in order to engage all stakeholders, particularly employees. They are also subject to supervision and regulation by the independent Panel on Takeovers and Mergers (www.thetakeoverpanel.org.uk/). An in-depth enquiry could also be undertaken into a merger by the Competition Commission (www.competition-commission.org.uk/), another independent public body.

Governments may decide to float or deregulate public-sector organisations to become public listed companies. In the 1980s, the Conservative government privatised British Telecom and British Gas (a record £5.6 billion flotation), with more than forty UK state-owned businesses employing 600,000 workers switching to private ownership while Margaret Thatcher was Prime Minister (Groom and Pfeifer 2011). The current UK coalition government has passed legislation paving the way to privatise the Royal Mail.

**READING POINT**

Annual reports, company press releases, corporate videos and other communications can be located for hundreds of companies at the *Financial Times* Company Content Hub (http://markets.ft.com/research/Markets/Company-Content).

Company websites should also contain information relevant to shareholders, which Phillimore (2012) advises may include webcasts and presentations as well as feeds to enable updates to be received by interested parties.

# GLOBAL ECONOMIC IMPACTS

Since the economic crisis began in the final quarter of 2008, global markets have been volatile with share prices falling and rising rapidly and frequently. This indicates a crisis of confidence where an established, long-term reputation is no guarantee of a stable share price for any organisation. Major issues in 2011 affecting global stock markets have included the Japanese earthquake, tsunami and Fukushima nuclear reactor meltdown and financial instability in the Eurozone (particularly relating to debt problems in Greece and Italy). Governments have had to act to prevent major collapses in stock markets, meaning that political and financial issues have been closely linked.

Financial insecurity looks certain to continue for a few years, with austerity measures by governments and companies creating issues that require strategic public relations management to avoid negative reputational impacts. Charities and other organisations in the not-for-profit and public sectors, alongside SMEs will continue to be affected by the economic downturn.

## Corporate governance

A counterbalance to concerns about the ongoing economic crisis is support for improved corporate governance regulation. Johnson et al. (2005: 165) define governance strategy as describing 'whom the organisation is there to serve and how the purposes and priorities of the organisation should be decided'.

Current initiatives to improve the corporate governance of companies include:

- Integrated reporting: The International Integrated Reporting Council (www. theiirc.org) has been established 'to create a globally accepted integrated reporting framework which brings together financial, environmental, social and governance information in a clear, concise, consistent and comparable format.' A discussion paper was published in September 2011.

- King Report III: This South African initiative aims to lead governance reporting internationally with a focus on annual reporting of how a company has affected, both positively and negatively, the economic life of the community in which it operates. Emphasis is required on how the company will enhance the positive aspects and eliminate or ameliorate possible negative impacts. Steyn (2011) argues this move to undertake integrated reporting as a 'holistic and integrated representation of the company's performance in terms of both its finances and its sustainability' presents a strategic opportunity for public relations.

# END POINT

Financial public relations should be considered from a wider perspective than a specialist focus on investor and shareholder relations. This recommendation emphasises the need for all PR practitioners to engage with the financial operation of organisations in order to work at a strategic level.

Stakeholder activism and PR for financial organisations also need to be included within the scope of financial public relations. Traditional financial relations activities operate to a calendar of activities including annual general meetings and publication of financial results, which are also relevant for non-listed companies.

The impact of the global economic crisis continues to challenge PR operations, not least in maintaining confidence and reputation management. It also raises the issue of corporate governance and initiatives to develop integrated reporting which has the potential to enhance PR's strategic role in organisations.

# CHAPTER 19

# Internal communications

*Alison Theaker*

One of the most important groups of stakeholders is a company's employees. Organisational rhetoric may declare 'our people are our most important resource', but while companies can survive without taking the needs of their workforce into account, an informed workforce is more likely to be productive.

## CHECK POINT

This chapter will examine:

- the importance of good internal communications;
- goals of employee communications;
- using the cultural web;
- the qualities needed to be a good practitioner in this field;
- suggestions for best practice.

## WHY IS INTERNAL COMMUNICATIONS IMPORTANT?

Quirke (1995) declared, 'research shows that for all the millions spent on internal communications over the past ten years, employee satisfaction has barely improved'. Recent surveys seem to show this is still the case. Crystal Interactive (2006) suggested that 67 per cent of employees were unhappy with communication within their company. This led to increased staff churn at a cost of £943 per employee per year. Morton (2006) also suggested that 'organisations with highly favourable employee attitudes have significantly better financial performance'. Their survey across the US, UK, Australia and China found that only 33 per cent of employees were happy with the quality of internal communications. Workers wanted more frequent and engaging communications and better information on how to do their jobs. The most popular forms of communication were contact with their immediate supervisors and meetings.

Watson Wyatt (2006) found that companies with effective communication were more likely to have higher market share and the best organisations had shareholder returns more than 50 per cent higher than the worst. They concluded: 'Effective communication is the lifeblood of successful organisations.'

Crystal Interactive (2006) found that companies with a low level of engagement saw profits fall by 1.38 per cent, while those with above average engagement saw a rise of 2.06 per cent. Gallup estimated that disengaged workers cost US business US$270–343 billion per year (Melcrum 2005).

Communication can flow downwards from senior directors and management to workers, upwards from the shop floor, and between groups and individuals. Some routes may work well, others may be blocked. When communication does not work, the grapevine steps in to fill the gap. Problems can arise if the grapevine is seen as more reliable than information sent by management.

# THE GOALS OF EMPLOYEE COMMUNICATION

Most literature in this area stresses that good communication leads to better staff performance, emphasising the needs of the organisation. As we saw in the chapter on CSR, doing good is again a way of serving the company's self-interest. Cutlip *et al.* (2000: 289) say, 'the goals of employee communication are to identify, establish and maintain mutually beneficial relationships between the organisation and the employees on whom its success or failure depends.'

Management often try to show an interest in employees' concerns by organising attitude surveys and suggestion schemes. But if there is no response to this information, employees may be more dissatisfied than before, as their expectations will have been raised. The best communications are about something more than simply telling employees information that they need to know.

# INTERNAL COMMUNICATION METHODS

It is also important that techniques match the needs of employees. It is no longer good enough to rely on a few dated techniques, such as noticeboards, memos and company newsletters. Employees expect more interactive media such as meetings, forums, video conferences, email, intranets and social media. When a company starts up, few people may be involved and communication can be informal. As it grows, more formal methods may have to be introduced. This can lead to more bureaucracy and slower responses.

Different methods will be used depending on the company's objectives for its internal communication programme. If the goal is simply awareness, noticeboards, memos, annual reports for employees and email may be sufficient. If understanding is needed, more feedback and information tailored to a specific group must be added. Roadshows, video conferencing and presentations to groups will start to allow interaction and participation. If employees' support is sought, their acceptance of company objectives is necessary and business forums and training events can be added. Later in this chapter, the increasing use of electronic methods is also discussed.

Involvement needs dialogue rather than one-way communication. Team meetings and feedback forums encourage employees to share their opinions. If commitment to a new strategy is needed, employees must feel a sense of ownership and involvement in developing that strategy. Interaction, team problem-solving sessions, forums and talkback sessions could work here. Management must demonstrate willingness to listen and accept feedback.

Hendrix (1995) set out a variety of impact objectives, such as:

- to increase employee knowledge of organisational activities and policies;
- to enhance favourable employee attitudes towards the organisation;
- to receive more employee feedback.

Output objectives could be:

- to recognise employee accomplishments in employee communications;
- to distribute communications on a weekly basis;
- to schedule interpersonal communication between management and a specific employee group each month.

Once objectives have been set, appropriate techniques can be selected, from noticeboards, displays, telephone hotlines, payslip inserts, internal television, videos, meetings, teleconferences, newsletters, direct mail, leaflets and email. Evaluating success of different methods will help lessons to be learnt for the future.

Quirke (2001) suggested that the way to demonstrate the value of internal communications was to make the link between business problems already on the agenda. Problems such as: low retention of customers; high cost of customer acquisition; high cost base; need for greater internal collaboration; need to stimulate greater

Ingenium (2009) emphasises that 'the pivot point for transformative employee communications is culture', and that this may need attention before any internal communications strategy is designed. Johnson *et al.* (2005: 201–203) suggest a cultural web to examine the culture of an organisation. They pose questions around six areas:

- Stories: What core beliefs are reflected? Who are the heroes and villains? What norms do mavericks deviate from?

- Rituals and routines: Which are emphasised? What behaviour do routines encourage?

- Control systems: What is monitored? Is there an emphasis on reward or punishment?

- Organisational structures: How flat or hierarchical are the structures? Do they encourage collaboration or competition?

- Power structures: How is power distributed?

- Symbols: What status symbols are there? Do particular symbols represent the organisation?

- Overall: What is the dominant culture? How easy is this to change?

It is no good trying to introduce two-way communication methods if the company is very formal with a rigid hierarchy. If only compliant behaviour is rewarded, then employees will not be willing to become visible by suggesting innovative ideas.

- Using Johnson and Scholes' headings, can you define the culture of the organisation that you work in?

- Does it encourage participation? Are employees opinions valued?

- How involved are the staff in the success of the company?

- Do the communication methods used match the needs of employees?

- How does the language used reflect the attitude of management to employees?

- What are the elements of 'the way we do things around here'?

cross-selling and customer service; falling market share; increased cost of administration; high employee turnover could all be 'points of pain' for a business. He also advised that the problem had to concern the internal client. 'If [they] do not feel something is a problem, nothing that is done . . . will feel like a solution.' He points out that internal communication can only increase staff retention if that is a problem. While IT organisations may need to keep their staff because of shortage of skills, a retailer may accept the seasonal migration of young shop assistants.

Watson Wyatt (2006) set eight points for effective communication:

1    helping employees understand the business;

2    providing employees with financial information and objectives;

3    exhibiting strong leadership by management;

4    aligning employees' actions with customer needs;

5    educating employees about organisational culture and values;

6    explaining new programmes and policies;

7    integrating new employees;

8    providing employees with information on their rewards programmes.

Quirke (2001) adds that communicators can add value most by:

- improving the quality of information – clearer messages written in shorter, plainer language;

- improving the capacity of existing communication channels, e.g. by using face-to-face meeting time for more than information exchange;

- reducing the amount of information going out by limiting number of producers and limiting access to communication channels;

- stopping central production and becoming an adviser to help managers achieve their objectives.

## SKILLS NEEDED IN INTERNAL COMMUNICATIONS

Dewhurst and Fitzpatrick (2007) set out twelve categories of competencies for internal communicators (see Table 19.1). Their framework can then be used in personal career planning and development, or in devising specifications for specific roles. Several qualifications have also been developed which have addressed IC as a specialism.

**TABLE 19.1  Competencies for internal communicators**

| Competency | Definition |
| --- | --- |
| Building effective relationships | Developing and maintaining relationships that inspire trust and respect. Building a network and being able to influence others to make things happen. |
| Business focus | Having a clear understanding of the business issues and using communication to help solve organisational problems and achieve organisational objectives. |
| Consulting and coaching | Recommending appropriate solutions to customers; helping others to make informed decisions; building people's communications competence. |
| Cross functional awareness | Understanding the different contributions from other disciplines and working with colleagues from across the organisation to achieve better results. |
| Craft (writing and design) | Using and developing the right mix of practical communication abilities (e.g. writing and design management) to hold the confidence of peers and colleagues. |
| Developing other communications | Helping other communicators build their communications competence and develop their careers. |
| Innovation and creativity | Looking for new ways of working, exploring best practice and delivering original and imaginative approaches to communication problems. |
| Listening | Conducting research and managing mechanisms for gathering feedback and employee reaction. |
| Making it happen | Turning plans into successfully implemented actions. |
| Planning | Planning communication programmes and operations, evaluating results. |
| Specialist | Having specific subject matter expertise in a specialist area. |
| Vision and standards | Defining or applying a consistent approach to communication and maintaining professional and ethical standards. |

Source: Used by permission of Sue Dewhurst and Liam FitzPatrick

**READING POINT**

■ Liam FitzPatrick's chapter in *The Public Relations Handbook* (Theaker 2012) contains more insights from his work in internal communications around the world.

# DEVELOPMENTS IN EMPLOYEE ENGAGEMENT

Smythe (2004) defines engagement as 'the degree to which participants identify with the need or opportunity behind a decision'. He lists four conditions for successful engagement:

- The right people must be involved in any project.
- Leaders and employees must be invited to participate.
- Self-discovery should be encouraged rather than just telling people what to do.
- There must be value for the organisation and its members.

Organisations have various motives to try and increase engagement. Employees need to feel they are taking an active part. Smythe sets out four approaches:

1   Instructional. Telling the many what has been decided by the few. This can result in employees becoming spectators. Methods include cascade briefings and newsletters.

2   Selling to the many what has been decided by the few. Employees may become compliant collaborators. This approach would involve more entertainment and some attempts to collect ideas and create a sense of involvement. Employees could participate in workshops to understand the reasons behind the change.

3   Involving people as individuals. Giving them time to apply change to their own work. The aim is for employees to become willing collaborators. Web-based consultation and learning could be used, local task groups and councils might encourage employees to see the gaps between their workplace performance and the desired change and a corporate 'university' could equip people with the skills they will need.

4   Co-creation. Working with those who will add value in the decision-making, resulting in personally committed reformers. Business simulation games could set real challenges, employee involvement must be seen to influence the agenda and workshops could be used to identify priority areas to change or develop.

Smythe proposes that any of the four methods may be appropriate, depending on the circumstances.

Melcrum's engagement survey (2005) showed that while 48 per cent of organisations had carried out an engagement survey, more than a quarter had no way of evaluating the degree of engagement within their organisations.

**TALKING POINT**

## IS INTERNAL COMMUNICATIONS DEAD?

Ferrabee (2010) posted the following thoughts:

> It wasn't that long ago I was explaining to clients where 'internal communications' came from. It was a 'discipline', it came from the business realisation that people were a key part of their asset portfolio . . . and now that we had driven down supply costs, making people more efficient had to do with Internal Communications. But it's been at least five years since we first started moving away from the term 'internal communications'. Two years ago we abandoned it altogether. Why?
>
> Because it is explicitly incorrect. Internal communications is seen (and too often performed) as a task akin to managing the plumbing or electricity. You stand at the top and turn on the tap and/or flip the switch. On and off. Off and on. The information flows down. If it doesn't make it to every corner of the building you go and investigate. And that is how many executives understand it. Certainly that is how many Internal Communications roles are staffed.
>
> Social media is just one example of how this isn't working, but there are others. Recent safety issues are a better example: you don't get safety by decree. Engagement presents more problems. However the fundamental issue is this: Internal Communications as generally practiced cannot and does not help the business to succeed. In fact, it may be doing the opposite.'

David Ferrabee's comments gave rise to a response from Arun Sudhaman (2010), raising the question of whether most internal communications amounted to little more than vanity publishing programmes. Stuart Smith (2010) of Hill and Knowlton felt that internal communications was vital for employees to make an emotional connection with the company they worked for. He suggested that employees needed to be entertained as well as informed, to encourage them to give 'that extra 10 per cent effort'.

This seems to be returning to the origins of employee communications, where magazines were full of tales of employee achievements, and 'hatched, matched and dispatched' accounts of babies born, marriages and those who had left the company.

However, research by the Institute of Internal Communications (2005) had claimed that 'The United Kingdom would be up to £50 billion a year better off if organisations made a greater effort to communicate with their employees'. Psychologist Laura Godwin's research had found that not engaging staff had resulted in 'higher staff turnover; higher absence levels; poorer performance; a breakdown in customer relationships and satisfaction; and significant costs and missed revenue opportunities'. In addition, she suggested that 'communication is the most significant factor in maximising the potential of employees'.

So what is causing this disconnect between the power of good internal communications and the commitment of management to use it properly? What examples of good internal communications have you experienced in your career?

## USING NEW TECHNOLOGY

More organisations are developing their own intranet. Instead of publishing news-letters, information can be made available on an internal website, accessed by password. It can be particularly useful for multinational companies, as everyone can receive information simultaneously. It also means that information can be dissemi-nated rapidly, rather than producing it in printed form.

The key is to manage information so that it can be accessed quickly. Access to PCs must be addressed. Shift workers on a production line may not have dedicated computers and managers may have to be persuaded to allow them the time off from their workstations to check the intranet on a communal computer.

Public relations practitioners have to adjust too, as every employee can be a communicator. Communication must constantly be updated. The PR function has to work with human resources and information technology departments to make sure that the intranet works for everyone and that conflicting information is not posted.

An intranet means staff cannot be passive and wait for information to be sent to them, they need to be encouraged to regularly access communication, otherwise a 'Why wasn't I told that?' syndrome develops.

Working in a large organisation, I found that so many staff announcements were posted that there was a constant tension to try and keep information on the front page of the intranet. Even though all announcements were listed in the archive, employees were unwilling to scroll down to access them. Mass emails were regularly abused by senior management, with non-essential information being sent to all staff, leading to a kind of 'cry wolf' effect.

Crystal Interactive (2006) found that many companies host corporate blogs, where the CEO posts an online diary and employees can add comments. Melcrum's survey of internal communication (2005) found that 23 per cent of companies were planning to introduce blogs as part of their strategy. For this to be successful, the CEO must write it themselves rather than simply rely on anodyne comments written by the PR function. Otherwise it becomes seen as a 'clog' (corporate blog) or worse, a 'flog' (fake blog).

Melcrum also found that only half of employees were able to feed back ideas to the CEO. Of these, 5 per cent found that the CEO never responded. Thus the upward communication ability of new technologies was not being exploited.

Gray (2004) suggested that one reason why expenditure on internal communications has made so little difference to employee satisfaction is that the wrong methods have been used. He found that what was most likely to increase satisfaction was communication from senior management and the CEO. Other methods which were highly rated were upward communication and management listening, consultation and involvement. Methods which had little effect included company newsletters, road shows, emails and the intranet.

Quirke (2001) warned against getting the balance between 'high tech and high touch' wrong. He set out three things that businesses were trying to do with their communication:

- provide information and make it accessible;
- demonstrate leadership and give people direction;
- build a sense of community, belonging and collaboration.

He felt that an intranet can only achieve the first of these, and that 'Face-to-face communication . . . is vital for retaining staff'.

Rozwell (2010) addresses organisations' concerns about letting their employees 'speak freely' on social media. She feels that managers can be given the skills needed to confront employees who may post negative comments. Posting on social media can be addressed in the same way as advising employees on appropriate style of dress. 'Blogs, Tweets and comments should let the individual's personality emerge,' yet they must be advised of the business ramifications of what they say.

Hurd (2010) goes further to suggest that a good social media policy could be beneficial to a company. By auditing the employees who are already using these tools, they can be encouraged to adapt their skills to create business results. He advises that this can have benefits in customer care and sales: 'If you can enable 5 per cent of your employee base to effectively use social media for the good of the company – you have recaptured an enormous company asset.'

The human touch is still the most effective when it comes to engagement and motivation. Tyler (2011) gives an account of successful communication at LOFT, where the fact that managers asked their store team the simple question, 'How are you?' at the start of every shift made employees feel that they mattered and were valued as a person. Gallup research had indicated that improving recognition and leveraging employee strengths were key to engagement. Tyler quotes a manager at Ann Taylor as saying, 'They say business isn't personal, but it is.'

## BEST PRACTICE

There is no shortage of advice available suggesting best practice in internal communication. Ingenium (2009) declares that communications must be 'map[ped] tightly to employees' needs and interests'. Any programme must have demonstrable buy-in from top management and be adequately resourced.

McNamara (2011) states that 'effective internal communications start with . . . basic skills in listening, speaking, questioning and sharing feedback,' and that 'effective meeting skills can go a long way toward ensuring effective communications'. He gives a detailed list of downward and upward communication methods, from giving all employees a handbook, job description and organisation chart to holding regular staff and team meetings and making sure that management acts on feedback.

The following case studies show how organisations have developed their internal communications based on clear objectives both for the company and for their employees and illustrate how successful strategies can lead to wide-ranging business benefits.

**ACTION POINT**

## DOING THE RIGHT THING

### The Severn Trent way: case study

Severn Trent Plc is a leading FTSE 100 company that focuses on the provision, removal and treatment of water in the UK and internationally.

The company refreshed its code of conduct in 2011, in partnership with Radley Yeldar, one of Europe's leading communications consultancies and experts in ethical business practice. The updated code needed to continue to provide a common and consistent framework for responsible business practices and set out the standards employees need to follow in their day-to-day activities. As part of the refresh, a strategy was developed for engaging over 8,000 employees internationally with the new code, as the company wanted to make sure it did not just become a booklet that ended up at the bottom of employees' drawers.

### Bringing it to life

The new code was given an approachable title: 'Doing the right thing the Severn Trent way'. It was then brought to life with engaging, inclusive language, for example 'Standing up for what's right' was the

**FIGURE 19.1** Doing the Right Thing – Severn Trent's internal communication programme

title of the whistleblowing section. Translatability had to be considered throughout as several language versions had to be published for the company's global internal audience. Each section was concise and maximised white space as well as imagery to make the pages inviting.

## Making it real

The code featured photographs of employees from across the business to help all employees identify with it. Each section opened with an example of a real employee dilemma to give it authenticity and to help employees feel joint ownership of the issues being addressed. This was followed by Severn Trent's position on the issue, an outline of the company's principles and a list of relevant company policies.

## Engaging key influencers early

The Severn Trent board was involved throughout the development of the code, which ensured management buy-in at the very top, right from the outset. Each director assigned a senior manager in a position of influence in his or her team to be a champion for the code during the roll-out.

## Embedding it in the business

A pilot was carried out with representatives across the business to test the effectiveness of the code and the engagement activities surrounding it. Appropriate adjustments were then made prior to launch to maximise impact.

Face-to-face communication between managers and their teams formed a core part of the engagement strategy when it launched. Managers knew how best to reach their teams, whether co-located in a single office or based out in the field. They were also able to address issues on the spot. Other tools were then used to reinforce the message:

Phase 1 – Getting managers on board: The champions were used to get managers on board as it was crucial that they understood and bought into the messages they were communicating. Managers were given an advance copy of the code and an implementation guide to help them prepare to engage their teams.

Phase 2 – Creating employee awareness: Managers were given an awareness presentation to deliver, to ensure consistent messages were delivered across the business. Copies of the new code were also handed out. A DVD was also shown, to help bring employees' ethical dilemmas to life. Managers were also given activities and a deck of 'dilemma cards', again based on real employee scenarios, to help stimulate discussion, with worksheets to encourage teams to actively participate. Finally, to wrap up each session, teams filled out 'commitment forms' to help cement learning.

Phase 3 – Training to embed behaviours: Soon after the awareness sessions, employees were given access to a digital e-learning tool, designed to help reinforce the principles and enable them to understand the outcomes and consequences of different ethical choices.

Phase 4 – Keeping it alive: A regular slot for the code was introduced to the company's monthly Team Talk to enable managers to continue discussing pre-set, relevant topics face-to-face with their teams, in order to keep the door to dialogue open. New starters will also be introduced to the code in their inductions so that the principles are instilled from their first day. The code was made available in the governance area of the corporate website so it would remain accessible to employees, with or without intranet access, such as field workers. Finally, managers and employees were provided with a channel to feed their views on the code or the communication surrounding it back to the company, to enable engagement to be continually optimised. The code is also being used as a springboard for other communication campaigns and to form employee award categories.

*With thanks to Loretta Smith (Deputy Head of Internal Communication) and Helen Davies (Head of Internal Communication) at Severn Trent Water and Radley Yeldar.*

**ACTION POINT**

## COMMUNICATIONS SHAPING THE CHANGE AGENDA AT MAERSK OIL

Driving change is never easy when things are going well. Although Maersk Oil (MO) is successful today, the longer term outlook for the oil industry is less good. The future for MO means growing out of its home lands in the North Sea and Qatar and adapting to new market conditions and technology.

The company faced the particular challenge of developing new ways of working and adopting fresh thinking around its relations with stakeholders and sharing expertise internally. Essentially the business needed to move from a situation where its operations had been very stable and predictable for decades to one where there would be a great deal of uncertainty and an entrepreneurial mindset as it learnt to work in new areas.

MO was clear that communications would be central in shaping change. Communicators were part of the core team driving the transformation with the remit to 'engage' rather just 'tell' the change story.

Crucially, MO's executives wanted local leaders to deliver change; within a year managers had to be turned from observers to advocates.

The communications team set out to mix traditional tools such as road shows, intranet articles, videos and posters with face-to-face techniques such as stakeholder mapping, presentation training and conferences. A campaign was developed that managed to secure the continual involvement of the most senior leaders.

The CEO has taken to blogging, communication staff are invited to senior team meetings and executives have taken on a taxing schedule of site visits and contributions to the intranet. And they have been willing to experiment with new tools and ideas such as interactive video, a remodelling of the intranet and the creation of new types of open fora.

Working with limited resources the Communications Director concentrated on making sure his team were close to the programme manager driving the change. Comms was designated as one of the workstreams for the transformation programme and the CEO was centrally involved. A heavy emphasis was placed on getting senior leaders to demonstrably sponsor change – tactics included the public signing of a change manifesto and a road show visiting sites around the world.

Core to the campaign was the gathering of data through focus groups and a rolling survey. This empowered the communications team as the authority on employee sentiment.

Survey data reports high levels of engagement: 88 per cent of staff say that they understand the company's direction – 14 points higher than the year before, 80 per cent agree with priorities for change, 75 per cent voiced optimism about the changes, and 69 per cent registered confidence in the leadership's ability to deliver the change.

*Liam FitzPatrick, Head of Practice, Bell Pottinger Change and Internal Communications*

**ACTION POINT**

# FRESHFIELDS BRUCKHAUS DERINGER LLP: OLYMPIC INSPIRATION

The HR and communications team at City law firm Freshfields was tasked with generating pride in the firm and inspiring a sense of excitement and international patriotism around its involvement with the London 2012 Olympic and Paralympic Games as the official legal

**FIGURE 19.2** Freshfields staff training with Paralympic athlete

services provider. As well as a once-in-a-lifetime event, the firm wanted to provide employees with an interesting and engaging way to speak about the scope and scale of the services offered by Freshfields.

The relationship with the Games was seen as a chance to achieve a common sense of purpose throughout the business and to leave a lasting legacy within the firm. Three major milestone events were held:

1   Lord Sebastian Coe announced our sponsorship in 2009.

2   In 2010, a lunch was attended by Cultural Olympiad director Ruth Mackenzie, and a trapeze artist gave a breathtaking performance that inspired staff; at 500 days to go, a *Question Time* style panel event included Karren Brady and James Cracknell, offering their thoughts on the true legacy of the Games.

**FIGURE 19.3** Trapeze artist at Freshfields' launch of their 2012 internal communications programme

3   In addition, regular Olympic Park tours gave employees the chance to see how work was progressing on the site. A new London 2012 visual identity, including motivational imagery and messaging, was introduced. Online internal communications on the London 2012 social networking intranet, Gateway London 2012, encouraged discussions and information-sharing about the office-wide sports and cultural programme. London 2010 and 2011 marathon training was arranged with Richard Whitehead, one of three ambassador athletes. The London 2012 mascots came to the office for a staff children's party. The annual internal London festival featured *A Question of Sport* and a fascinating Q and A session with Phil Lane, chief executive of ParalympicsGB. In May 2011, Freshfields hosted the

London 2012 Partners sitting volleyball tournament, encouraging staff members to engage with Paralympic sport. A summer carnival was held for all London employees in July 2011 where employees had the chance to meet past and present Olympians and try out unusual Olympic and Paralympic sports, as well as enjoy an evening of music, dancing and food in a carnival atmosphere. Over 700 staff attended, representing almost 40 per cent of staff in the London office. From August 2011, staff had the chance to attend various test events as London prepared to host the Games as team-bonding exercises.

'London 2012 has helped us engage with more than 75 per cent of London employees,' says Programme Manager Phillippa Piper. In January 2011, Freshfields undertook the first independent employee engagement survey to track the success of the London 2012 project. The results were:

- 90 per cent of staff intended to get involved in the Games to some extent;

- 76 per cent were advocates (talking positively to clients, friends and family about it);

- 72 per cent felt more positive about the firm as a result of the sponsorship;

- 81 per cent were proud of Freshfields' involvement.

Similar surveys were held every six months until September 2012 to fine-tune the campaign and track progress.

Other factors demonstrating the success of the programme:

- 1,300 people out of a total population of 1,700 registered with, and regularly used, Gateway London 2012.

- Milestone events attracted between 500 and 600 attendees, compared with an average attendance of 300 at previous internal events. More than 100 staff children attended the mascot party.

- There was a 21 per cent increase in hours volunteered in the community in 2009/2010, and this increased further in 2011/2012.

- Employees were actively engaged in the project and the legacy of the project will affect how people work together and how the firm is viewed (both internally and externally) for a long time into the future.

- The London 2012 'story' was incorporated in the wider communications strategy and client-facing and recruitment materials – such as the annual review, external website and UK graduate recruitment.

# END POINT

Despite Ferrabee's opinion, it seems that internal communications is certainly very much alive. The key points are to make sure that any cultural issues are taken into account before new internal communications initiatives are introduced. In addition, the methods used must be led by the requirements of the employees themselves. The examples provided show that as well as having beneficial effects on staff commitment to the organisation, good internal communications can have wide ranging effects on relationships with other stakeholders.

# CHAPTER 20

# Business to business

*Heather Yaxley*

This chapter provides an understanding of working with, and for, organisations where there is a focus on engaging other organisations as the primary public. Expert insight is included along with examples of business to business (B2B) public relations in practice.

## CHECK POINT

At the end of this chapter, you should be able to:

- identify the characteristics of B2B public relations;
- understand the importance of decision-makers, relationship building and networking;
- determine appropriate B2B public relations approaches.

## CHARACTERISTICS OF B2B PUBLIC RELATIONS

Within the B2B sector, organisations are the focus of public relations activities. Traditionally, PR in this sector is viewed as supporting sales and marketing although it may attain other goals such as reputation building, thought leadership, securing financial support, participation in industry bodies, crisis management and enacting social responsibility strategies.

Fill (2002: 376–377) states: 'The effectiveness of public relations in a B2B context should not be underestimated,' stressing its role in providing 'credibility and richness to an organisation's communications'.

B2B communication generally involves a defined number of contacts (sometimes identified individually) with whom organisations seek to develop relationships (for example as key accounts).

Organisational behaviour can be complex, with many individuals and functions involved in building relationships and making decisions. PR practitioners need to understand varying needs within organisations. For example, three main buying motives can be identified:

1   General consumption – goods and services used in the organisation's general operations. For example: office furniture, stationery, insurance, public relations and other professional services.

2   Resourcing production – goods and services used by the organisation's in producing its own products and services. For example: raw materials, components, manufacturing equipment.

3   Resale/retail – goods and services which are sold onto other businesses or consumers as part of a marketing channel. For example: franchise, online or shop outlets.

B2B PR may be undertaken by in-house practitioners, and the sector is the primary client base for many consultancies and independent practitioners.

The commercial business sector is dominated by small and medium enterprises (SMEs: defined as employing 0–49 and 50–249 people respectively). UK government statistics (BIS 2011) show SMEs accounted for 99.9 per cent of an estimated 4.5 million private sector businesses in the UK at the start of 2011. They represent 58.8 per cent of the 23.4 million employed in the private sector and 48.8 per cent of an estimated £3,100 billion private sector turnover. In the first decade of the twenty-first century, the number of SMEs increased by almost one-third, while the number of large private sector businesses fell from 7,200 to 6,300.

Research by Moss et al. (2003: 207) suggested SMEs 'may have a rather limited, and at times, naïve understanding of the concept of public relations'. Indeed, communications activities (including PR) tend to be undertaken by non-specialist personnel as part of their other duties in smaller organisations, although a minority of SMEs do employ external agency support.

Some industries are dominated by SMEs (particularly the service sector) while others (e.g. financial and insurance) feature a greater number of large organisations. Construction is the largest industry sector accounting for a fifth of UK private enterprises, with 13.3 per cent involved in professional, scientific and technical activities and 10.7 per cent in the wholesale and retail trade and repair sector.

B2B is not restricted to private enterprises, but includes inter-organisational com-munications in the public and not-for-profit sectors. According to the Government Procurement Service, the UK government spends around £230 billion a year, while the Charity Commission reports 161,500 registered charities in the UK with an annual income of over £55 billion.

Organisations increasingly establish alliances, networks or partnerships in their B2B operations. For example, they may form joint ventures, develop private–public sector initiatives or with charities and non-government organisations, address industry issues as members of trade bodies or act as virtual organisations. Com-munications and collaborative PR activities are necessary between the partners in such concerns.

**TALKING POINT**

The Star Alliance network comprises twenty-seven airlines working together for joint procurement and co-ordinated client services. Members also collaborate on the Biosphere connections CSR initiative, which offers travel support to environmental organisations. This includes a multi-media campaign developed in association with *National Geographic*. Mini-documentaries highlighting five supported projects can be seen via the *National Geographic* television channel and its website, the Star Alliance website and its Facebook and YouTube sites, and through the communication channels of the member airlines, including their in-flight entertainment systems, websites and social media presence.

Consider where inter-organisational communications are required in this example? What are the benefits and drawbacks of undertaking a CSR initiative involving all members of Star Alliance?

Modern, 24/7 global environments have resulted in ever more complex arrangements and interactions between organisations as well as with their stakeholders. Where connections are of strategic importance, they require personal communications to build long-term, close relationships (e.g. between key account managers and corporate clients).

This discussion highlights three main characteristics of B2B PR:

1   engagement with stakeholders and publics on the basis of their occupation;
2   communications support relationship building between employees of the client and target organisations;
3   importance of inter-organisational influencers and communication channels (including trade media).

**ACTION POINT**

Safety and Health Expo is Europe's leading annual event for the health and safety industry. It attracts around 18,000 professional visitors who are 'looking to source new suppliers, network with colleagues and hear leading industry speakers discuss the most pressing issues of the day'. As well as innovations from exhibiting manufacturers, distributors and suppliers, the Expo offers sponsorship opportunities, and a programme of presentations, demonstrations, debates and expert workshops. Editorial coverage and a press office function around the Expo extend the reach to the wider Safety and Health sector.

## Occupational considerations

B2B communications are essentially one organisation engaging with another for the purpose of their mutual interest. In these exchange relationships (Grunig *et al.* 2002), organisations adopt roles, for example as buyer and seller. Relevant procedures need to be understood, such as whether there is a formal procurement process involving purchasing and accounts departments. This perspective presents an objective consideration of information exchange between organisations.

In reality people do business with people. Grunig *et al.* (2002: 552) note: 'Relationships often begin as exchanges and then develop into communal relationships as they mature. At other times, public relations professionals may need to build a communal relationship with a public before an exchange can occur.' This indicates the added-value subjectivity of human relationships, such as mutual respect.

Individuals within organisations reflect their occupational roles. For example, a fleet manager has responsibility for an organisation's company vehicle operations and needs to maintain expert knowledge of the latest models, legislative and political developments, financing options and so forth by contact with representatives of vehicle manufacturers, trade media, attending exhibitions, etc. In this example, politicians will also be key influencers as they determine tax rates and other economic constraints which impact on the choice of vehicle offered to employees.

Organisational culture is important. For example, the tradition with Japanese companies is to develop long-term relationships, while other organisations may stipulate annual renegotiation of accounts.

Blyth (2006) reports individuals employed by organisations act rationally and emotionally when making decisions. He notes organisations are generally risk-averse and use procedures and hierarchical responsibilities to reduce risk, particularly for costly purchases. Senior executives will be involved with major decisions with junior personnel having responsibility for more routine or repetitive purchases.

## Supporting communications and relationship building

PR practitioners develop communication materials and organise attendance at events to support B2B relationship building. There are dozens of industry conferences and exhibitions held in the UK and overseas each year, with other events organised for a specific purpose, possibly by the organisation itself to engage potential B2B clients.

It is important to have a clear brief from the relevant function (e.g. sales and marketing) in order to determine the most appropriate way in which PR can provide assistance (see Chapter 7).

In addition, practitioners may engage directly with other organisations, probably to liaise with their PR function in order to develop mutually-beneficial opportunities. For example, this could involve producing a case study that could be used on an organisation's website or blog, as a direct mail piece, in a conference presentation or within an annual report.

## Inter-organisational influencers and communications channels

Securing media coverage is traditionally important in B2B PR. This involves engaging with specialist media for particular occupations or industries. Smith (2012: 373) confirms that 'effective targeting is essential' enabling appropriate trade titles, exhibitions or other channels to be identified as influencers for B2B PR campaigns.

The three Rs apply to B2B media planning: reach, relevance and reputation. A publication may be chosen because it reaches 100 per cent of the target audience (for example, the *Veterinary Times* is distributed by name to all veterinary surgeons and nurses in the UK). It is also important to establish the relevance and reputation of a publication with the target audience. Too often, trade publications remain unread in their plastic wrapper. A checklist of factors to consider in media planning is included in the Appendix.

Other B2B influencers include relevant academics, industry experts, trade bodies, politicians, consultants, celebrities and personal contacts (including colleagues, family and friends). Mapping techniques are useful to analyse potential influencers so PR activities can be developed to engage with, or utilise these influencers as appropriate (see Chapter 5).

There is an old adage in the IT industry that no-one ever got fired for buying IBM, showing how decisions may follow accepted practice in an industry. Alternatively, organisations may avoid suppliers who work with their competitors.

Inter-organisational communications channels do not always involve a direct route. Figure 20.1 illustrates how intermediary organisations may complicate the

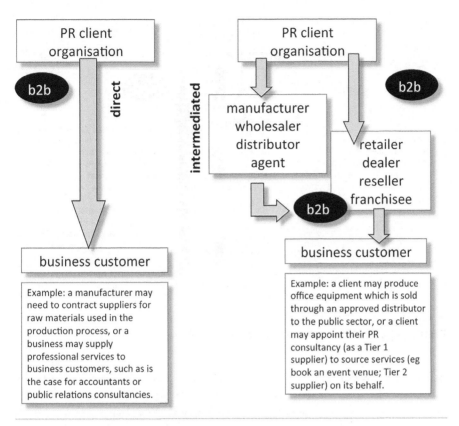

**FIGURE 20.1** Comparison of direct and intermediated business to business communication process

**ACTION POINT**

Foxconn Technology is the world's largest maker of electronic components. Its clients include many well-known companies, such as Nokia and Apple. Businesses purchasing computer or mobile phone equipment may be unaware of this, but could be concerned by controversies relating to treatment of Foxconn employees (with nine deaths reported at one Chinese facility in 2010). Such issues can impact other organisations in the supply chain, with calls to boycott Apple products the most high-profile reaction to exposure of issues within Foxconn factories.

Similarly, companies with indirect links to Huntington Life Sciences (HLS), which tests pharmaceutical, agricultural and veterinary products on laboratory animals, have been targeted by Stop Huntingdon Animal Cruelty. In 2011, AstraZeneca Pharmaceuticals (a customer of HLS) and BlackRock, its largest corporate investor, took legal action in Los Angeles claiming the extreme activist group had harassed their employees.

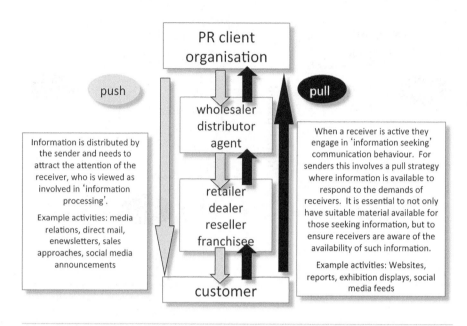

**FIGURE 20.2** Push and pull communications processes

communications process. Money *et al*. (2010) found that partnerships can enhance reputation of the participants with stakeholders. However, partnerships can also generate issues or crisis situations that can impact on reputation and require PR action.

These examples illustrate how issues affecting one organisation can lead to crisis management for its business customers and their stakeholders.

Where there are intermediaries in the process, public relations activities may be used to communicate direct with the end user as well as, or instead of, communicating with the intermediary. Such communications need to fulfil the need for both push and pull communications strategies (Figure 20.2).

When organisations recognise a specific need, they are likely to engage in information-seeking behaviour (pull communications) and also process information that comes (is pushed) their way. For example, attendance at an exhibition may be initiated to seek information on particular products, or an article in a trade publication will be of particular interest.

Equally important are communications with existing contacts within the B2B sector, where understanding, loyalty and long-term relationships are important to manage.

One area where public relations may be involved in supporting ongoing relationships is through corporate hospitality around sponsorship activities. For example, Ford Motor Company, as an official partner of the UEFA Champions League, hosts business customers at games around Europe.

# ROLE OF DECISION-MAKERS

The decision-making process in the B2B sector may involve several steps and requires understanding of the needs of those holding different roles (Figure 20.3). These may be different people or functions in larger organisations.

Organisations may have detailed procurement procedures to manage costs, ensure consistency of approach, control order and invoicing processes or reduce risk of favouritism or unethical purchasing practices. Specific duties may be specified within the decision-making unit. When developing B2B PR initiatives, it is important to be clear which stage of the decision-making process is being targeted, and the responsibilities of the people who are involved at that point.

## Relationship building and networking

At the heart of B2B communications are personal relationships, even within the constraints of formal procurement processes. PR is able to support sales teams who proactively build relationships with prospective and existing clients, by developing a range of communications materials, initiating activities (such as attendance at exhibitions), building an opinion leadership position, generating media coverage, and engaging with third-party influencers (for example, experts in a particular industry).

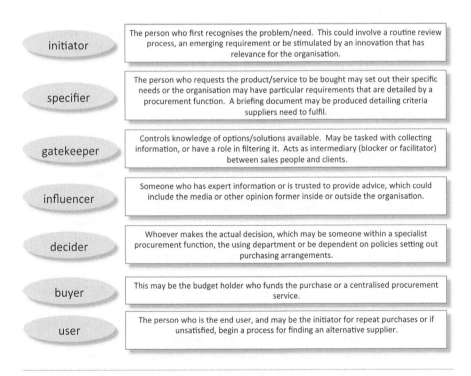

initiator — The person who first recognises the problem/need. This could involve a routine review process, an emerging requirement or be stimulated by an innovation that has relevance for the organisation.

specifier — The person who requests the product/service to be bought may set out their specific needs or the organisation may have particular requirements that are detailed by a procurement function. A briefing document may be produced detailing criteria suppliers need to fulfil.

gatekeeper — Controls knowledge of options/solutions available. May be tasked with collecting information, or have a role in filtering it. Acts as intermediary (blocker or facilitator) between sales people and clients.

influencer — Someone who has expert information or is trusted to provide advice, which could include the media or other opinion former inside or outside the organisation.

decider — Whoever makes the actual decision, which may be someone within a specialist procurement function, the using department or be dependent on policies setting out purchasing arrangements.

buyer — This may be the budget holder who funds the purchase or a centralised procurement service.

user — The person who is the end user, and may be the initiator for repeat purchases or if unsatisfied, begin a process for finding an alternative supplier.

**FIGURE 20.3** Decision-making roles

Advice from sales colleagues is required to ensure PR communications reach the right people at the right time with the right message. They should know if there is a particular time during the year when organisations undertake procurement decisions, probably tied into a formal budget cycle.

Organisations needing to establish new relationships require prospecting activities to generate leads. The promotion of new products and services via PR tactics can be useful in reaching new clients.

Maintaining relationships is equally, if not more important. PR tactics can be used to ensure the client's expertise remains top of mind or to inoculate against the prospecting tactics used by competitors.

Relationships will be required with other inter-organisational stakeholders to achieve corporate B2B objectives. These are considered elsewhere in the *The PR Toolkit*, but may include, for example, managing relationships with providers of finance, professional services, trade organisations, local and national government bodies, and community groups.

**ACTION POINT**

*Richard Gotch, specialist in B2B communications and founder of award-winning PR agency Market Engineering (www.marketengineering.co.uk/):*

Q:  What are the main objectives for PR in a B2B context?

A:  At the heart of most B2B campaigns is the need to generate sales leads, but other objectives are communicating with investors and potential investors, recruitment, supporting the sales process, managing reputation and building brands. The objective of PR is to help the directors achieve their commercial goals, which may involve any or all of these.

Q:  Do you consider the decision-making unit when developing campaigns?

A:  Segmentation is critical, but it isn't always about the people who make the buying decisions. There is a network of publics affecting the success of a business, from unions to politicians to financial markets. Each one requires specific information to help form appropriate opinions. Identification of these publics, aligned with a desired outcome, allows the development of activities that support the business objectives.

As an example, we recently helped a publicly listed client win an Investor Relations Society award for the most improved annual report. The key was to move their approach from 'this is what we would like to tell the investors' to one based on an analysis of how investors make their decisions. This allowed us to understand what information they would like to receive, which was then presented in a compelling way.

Q: How is the approach for B2B markets different to consumer PR?

A: The B2B market can be more complicated as the decision to award high value contracts may be influenced by specialists in purchasing, manufacturing, logistics, brand management and a host of others disciplines, each with their own objectives and evaluation criteria.

To support the sales process, we have to use appropriate messages to build a realistic, educated understanding that answers any reservations and emphasises the benefits in relevant terms.

Q: What are the communications challenges involved in communicating complex issues to businesses – and how do you work with clients to address these?

A: One of the biggest challenges is to encourage clients to think about who influences the success of their business and define the knowledge of the business those people have, including good and bad aspects. We then think through what realistic and honest understanding we would like them to have to support the business objectives.

When thinking about the sales process, this includes a clear view of the client's points of differentiation, and often involves challenging their initial assumptions. Addressing communications to tightly defined target audiences simplifies delivery because you know exactly what will interest that audience and what you would like to tell them.

Q: What is your advice to ensure coverage obtained in trade titles delivers real value to clients?

A: Media coverage will only deliver value if it changes people's opinions in a way that leads them towards relevant action. The article is not the end result, but the delivery mechanism for messages. Yes, trade publications can be the most important, but audiences also read national newspapers, online titles and consumer magazines, some of which have almost a cult following in certain sectors.

Q. How do you determine this value?

A. Some of our multinational clients use market studies, which provide outstanding insight but are expensive and can be difficult to separate out the influence of any particular activity. As a day-to-day measure for media relations, we count the number of key messages delivered per thousand head of each target audience. It isn't 'closed loop' but does focus attention on getting the basics absolutely right and provides a quick, low-cost indicator that can be used for continuous improvement.

Q: The B2B sector is an expert one in which the clients and buyers are likely to be specialists in their subject area – do you feel PR practitioners need to reflect similar expertise and what are the challenges in doing so?

A:  Specialisation really helps, particularly because the solution often requires an understanding of how the industry is structured. Without this, it is difficult to accurately define the target audiences or to facilitate appropriate key-message development. The media is also more highly segmented than is apparent from outside the industry.

For example, there is no such thing as 'an engineering magazine'. Some focus on advanced engineering, some on applications engineering, some on technology transfer and so on. The challenge is to understand which is appropriate to your objective, then to find and develop a story that will appeal to the editor. Pitching is also easier if you are a subject specialist. It's always useful to be able to discuss the story and its context with the editor in sufficient detail to help to shape it into something that fits with editorial plans.

Q:  Do you feel reputation building or opinion leadership can be used within B2B PR?

A:  Both are central to good B2B communications, especially where the range of factors affecting the success of the business – and the success of the sales process – can be complex. For example, engineers dislike risk and purchasing specialists value stability. For a supplier an ability to deliver reliably to a manufacturing line in a small time window can be as important as having the right product features. Reputation involves a belief that the company has proven ability to give strength to 'the complete product offering': always much more than just the product itself. It's about trust, just as a brand is about trust.

Thought leadership is an excellent way of establishing a dialogue by showing that the company makes a useful contribution. It helps small companies punch above their weight and gives investors, customers and staff confidence that the business is led by the best people. A skilful thought-leader can be quoted alongside the industry's global players, providing immediate credibility.

Q:  What are your views on the range of tactics that can be used in B2B PR, such as exhibitions, case studies, facility visits, white papers, surveys, use of experts or celebrities?

A:  There is a role for all of these, although they have to be carefully selected based on return on investment, and supported by a range of complementary communications activities to ensure that the last drop of value is squeezed from them. Using celebrities is interesting in a B2B market where the personality may be the programme director for a new car or the stylist for a new train.

Q:  What have been your highlights in establishing a respected consultancy specialising in technology and B2B PR?

A:  Our clients include giant US, European and Chinese companies as well as some of the best, most entrepreneurial UK businesses. There are so many different insights, so many different skills and approaches. I find I'm always learning something new.

# PUBLIC RELATIONS APPROACHES TO SUPPORT B2B STRATEGIES

The strategic planning approaches discussed in Part II are relevant to support B2B strategies, although budgets may be small in relation to the impact required and require practitioners to be exceptionally creative. Key activities used B2B public relations are detailed in Table 20.1.

The selection of appropriate approaches depends on the objectives that have been agreed with the client, and may be required to support a specific campaign or ongoing communications.

**TABLE 20.1  B2B PR approaches**

| | |
|---|---|
| **Collateral** | Publicity material such as brochures and sales presentations need to be readily available. White papers and opinion statements can also be developed to provide ongoing opportunities for communications with existing or prospect contacts |
| **Online** | Websites need to provide information relevant to B2B audiences and may include case studies, detailed product specifications, financial reports, company histories, podcasts, video, endorsements and opinion leader papers. Social media presence can also be relevant, particularly LinkedIn, for profile and engagement in groups |
| **Brand** | Brand identity is important in establishing a professional impression and immediate identification of the organisation. Product and service brands can also be developed. Branded merchandise, including clothing, is common in the B2B sector |
| **Mailings** | A wide range of materials, such as newsletters, can be developed for distribution to existing contacts and databases by post or email. Options for download from websites and sign up to feeds or email mailings need to be promoted |
| **Editorial** | Knowledge of print, online and broadcast (where relevant) media is essential along with relationship building with freelance and staff journalists. Stunts and creative ideas may be required. Advertorials and advertising support are normal in some industries |
| **Events** | A wide range of events can be utilised, including exhibitions and conferences or original events can be created, e.g. facility trips and events enabling products/services to be tested or viewed in use. Award events are also useful in B2B PR |
| **Sponsorship** | Sponsorship and corporate hospitality offer opportunities for brand recognition and relationship development. Sports, arts and community programmes are available either 'off the shelf' or created for the organisation |

It is also likely that any B2B PR campaign will need to take account of existing activities within an organisation, and ad-hoc opportunities that arise continuously. This emphasises the importance for developing a programme of activities in partnership with key internal parties (e.g. sales and marketing or specific service areas). Regular reviews of activities and opportunities that emerge enable the plan to be adapted to accommodate changing needs. The client is then able to ensure the programme offers measurable benefits rather than spreading PR support too thin across a range of disparate activities.

**ACTION POINT**

## 'MAKING CHANGE HAPPEN'

## Award-winning campaign for Amnis Limited by Footprint Communications

Amnis (www.amnis.uk.com) specialises in enabling quality and performance improvement in organisations, boosting efficiency and transforming service delivery. It approached Footprint Communications (www.footprint-comms.co.uk/) in 2010 with the objective of building its brand profile through nationwide editorial coverage in order to build awareness, enhance reputation, generate valuable intellectual property and, ultimately, drive new business.

With well-documented public sector cutbacks, Amnis wanted to build on its strength in healthcare and reach additional markets, namely local authorities and housing associations, as well as retail and distribution-focused private sector clients.

The core message recognised clients in both public and private sectors are looking for cost-saving opportunities, increased operational efficiency and enhanced in-house knowledge to equip them for the future.

*1 Initial research and planning*
A media audit and planning phase ensured Footprint targeted the appropriate channels for key decision-makers. This involved researching media contact information, future feature opportunities, as well as appropriate awards, meetings and exhibitions. Footprint prepared and submitted details of a company spokesperson to a media database of expert commentators, supporting journalists looking for expert commentary on specific areas of relevance to Amnis.

*2 Media relations*
Media relations was the backbone of Footprint's work for Amnis, drawing on a number of tactics, including:

- feature submissions
- opinion and commentary
- press phone line
- media meetings.

The campaign coincided with speculation over the coalition government's first Comprehensive Spending Review and wide acknowledgement that spending cuts would put huge pressures on local councils, their contractors and many other organisations, to do more with less. In response, Footprint pitched Amnis commentary pieces to a series of media titles exploring the potential for Lean Management to help with cost efficiencies.

Case studies and white papers were issued using research by Amnis showing, for example, how Lean Management could support approaches to patient safety in the NHS. Face-to-face meetings with key media were arranged in support of this work to develop ideas for feature contributions and opinion pieces that were in line with their editorial agenda.

The client was also counselled on sponsorship, award entries and closer working with industry associations.

3  *Measurement*
Outputs: Enhancing company reputation – Amnis commentary pieces and news stories appeared in a range of public sector media, providing thought-leading input to discussions on a wide range of issues facing local and central government. Building relationships with the industry-leading *Health Service Journal* led to a series of contributed articles by Amnis managing director and regular Amnis content on its online resource centre for practitioners and NHS managers. These case-study led pieces showed how the health sector could implement Lean Management techniques to achieve real results in improving patient care.

A well-received commentary piece in *Housing* followed Amnis' work with a housing association on improving the efficiency of gas safety checks, an issue of some concern in the sector. A further piece in the *Manufacturer* on lean management in the supply chain reached another new target audience.

Outcomes: *Awareness* – offering a niche service, Amnis achieved sixteen quality pieces of coverage across a focused media list reaching the target audience. All coverage reflected Amnis's credentials as a leading expert in quality and performance improvement for a variety of organisations.

*Business generation* – as a reflection of the impact this level of coverage can achieve, Amnis saw a number of immediate benefits including:

- an existing client purchasing a further support programme valued at tens of thousands of pounds;
- four new business enquiries;
- a fifteen-fold increase in people registering for the Amnis newsletter (which itself leads to regular business enquiries);
- an offer from other clients to jointly prepare further high-profile articles.

The importance of the B2B sector to PR practice is increasingly recognised. Both CIPR and PRCA acknowledge best practice and specialist B2B practitioners with specific categories in their annual award programmes. Winning awards is a useful B2B PR technique for consultancies, which can then use this success when pitching for new business or to demonstrate industry leadership to existing clients. Indeed, a consultancy's most important client for B2B PR is itself.

## END POINT

The B2B sector offers considerable potential for demonstrating the strategic value of public relations where it is able to work alongside senior management to develop solutions that support the achievement of key goals. It is not restricted to commercial organisations with inter-organisational communications of importance in the not-for-profit and government sectors.

A range of B2B PR approaches can be utilised to support sales and marketing activities, as well as to achieve other relevant goals. In particular, public relations expertise is vital in managing organisational reputation and key relationships with a variety of stakeholders.

This is critical as organisations are increasingly involved in a complex network of alliances and partnerships with other organisations. B2B PR is able to establish credibility and trust in organisations, but requires an expert understanding of relevant industries, as well as inter-organisational influencers and communication channels, beyond the traditional focus on trade media.

# CHAPTER 21

# Community relations

*Alison Theaker*

Organisations want to have good relationships with the communities they operate in. This could be dealing with people who live next to their factory, or with school or university leavers they may want to recruit.

## CHECK POINT

This chapter will:

- define community relations (CommR);
- list the various activities that could be used in a CommR programme;
- compare CommR with CRM;
- make the case for organisations to be involved with CommR and CRM.

Many think that any community relations programme is down to basic self-interest, to enable the company to have an easy life. 'A corporation can gain competitive advantage by having the goodwill of local communities,' suggest Werbel and Wortman (2000: 124). Bowd (2005) suggests that benefits can include goodwill, customer and staff loyalty. However, the Tomorrow's Company Inquiry, set up by the RSA in 1993, found that in a competitive marketplace, CommR was a necessity rather than a luxury and that companies have to earn their 'licence to operate'.

# DEFINITIONS OF COMMR

Some definitions include:

- providing money or people, or advice, something that may be only indirectly measurable (Graham Savage, Millennium Commission);
- planned investment in the society in which you operate (Ellie Gray, Corporate Development Manager at the Prince's Trust);
- the tactical approach to discharging CSR (Tench 2006).

**READING POINT**

■ CommR is closely related to CSR. You can read more about CSR in Chapter 14.

Harrison (in Kitchen 1997: 129) feels that companies are part of the society in which they operate and need to consider what effect they have. She refers to Peach's model of the impact of business on its environment. The initial level of impact simply covers paying taxes, observing the law and dealing fairly. The second level recognises the need to minimise negative effects and act in the spirit as well as the letter of the law. At the third level the organisation 'sees itself as having a responsibility for a healthy society and accepts the job of helping to remove or alleviate problems'. The third-level company is, however, rare.

# MAPPING THE COMMUNITY

So who might be part of the community? Cutlip *et al.* (1995) draws a power pyramid with the top level consisting of major employers and landowners, the next corporate and commercial executives. Underneath come PR executives and journalists, together with council officials. The bottom layer of the pyramid contains small-business managers and professionals such as ministers, teachers, personnel directors, social workers, accountants and factory managers.

Cutlip *et al.* breaks down the category of 'prime movers' into:

- employees' or members' families;
- the press, radio, TV and commentators;
- clergy, teachers, officials, retailers, union officials and industrialists;
- organisations such as planning commissions, welfare agencies, youth groups, veterans, and cultural, service and political action groups;
- crusaders such as protest groups and dissidents.

Organisations need to investigate which groups in the community are important for them to build relationships with. When opening a new store in a small Devon town where local traders had been vociferous in their opposition, Tesco ensured that it provided a platform for community groups to fundraise in the store. A common complaint was the effect on the amount of parking available, so Tesco made their own car park available for three hours free parking, enabling shoppers to visit the local traders as well as shop in the supermarket. Tesco also became involved in the town's participation in Britain in Bloom by sponsoring flower displays on a roundabout.

# WHAT DO COMMR PROGRAMMES LOOK LIKE?

Cutlip *et al.* (1995: 405–406) lists several kinds of activity:

- The open house: a tour of the facilities of the organisation, enabling large numbers to come onto the premises. Exhibits can give information, and using employees as guides can give them renewed pride in their workplace.

- Special events: ground-breaking for a new building or the completion of one; special seminars linked to the company's products, such as a safe driving school run by a motor manufacturer.

- Using internal newsletters: with the addition of some specific news, the internal publication can be circulated throughout the community to enable a wider knowledge of the company's activities.

- Volunteer activities: encouraging and enabling employees to perform voluntary service for local organisations, including secondment. Some schemes enable employees to do this in work time.

- Funding: sponsoring or donating money to local organisations, whether in cash or kind.

Anglian Water (AW) set up a 'transformation journey project' scheme after privatisation, to encourage creativity and personal growth among employees, so that entrepreneurial people could fill the gaps left after downsizing. Clive Morton of AW lists benefits across the organisation (quoted in O'Malley 1999: 46):

- the PR function is likely to be turned on by the effect on image;

- the CEO, by the view of the board; and the City by 'responsible capitalism';

- customer services will enjoy better feedback; procurement should see better supply-chain links;

- HR people put employee development high on the list.

Davis (2004) adds several possible activities, such as decorating old people's homes, reading aloud to children in local schools, seconding staff to local organisations, raising funds for local causes through sponsorship and direct funding of local events. Other schemes might include providing a venue for a local organisation to hold meetings, contributing trees to landscape schemes, offering work experience to young people and creating bursaries for schools and colleges.

CommR is about improving the quality of life in the local community, so organisations may become involved in environmental clean-ups, recycling, arts programmes and children's activities.

## WHAT WILL WE GET OUT OF COMMR?

This area of corporate activity used to be anecdotally referred to as the 'chairman's wife syndrome', or the support of activity according to whim or personal interest of senior management and their spouses. There are still some examples of this, such as Crealy Theme Parks in Devon and Cornwall. The MD, Angela Wright, heard about play pumps, which use a children's roundabout to pump water from bore holes. While this fits with the Crealy belief that children learn through play, no evaluation or link to visitor numbers has been carried out. However, this does not mean that the programme has no value – the park has raised enough for three pumps to be sent to Africa.

Portway (1995) uses the example of IBM's focus on issue management to determine the kinds of activity the company will support. A community advisory panel has responsibility for the Community Investment Programme, consisting of community leaders and IBM managers. One of the key objectives is 'to promote the morale and motivation of employees', so a location manager in each IBM site is used to channel employee input. Projects focus on education and training, given that the education system needs to equip people with the skills to make the most of IT. Another area is support for people with disabilities, as personal computers can provide them with new opportunities for education and employment.

Wheeler and Sillanpaa (1997: 275) reported: 'In 1993, more than 90 per cent of large companies in the US had a community involvement programme, more than two-thirds allowed time off during work for volunteering and 63 per cent had a community involvement fund.' In the UK in 1995, a survey found that only a third of large companies had a volunteer programme and only 44 per cent of those allowed time off for volunteer activities. Less than two-thirds offered financial support.

However, such schemes are now becoming more widespread. The University of Plymouth began discussions in 2010 with employees to set up a scheme where they could have additional paid leave for one or two days per year to work for a chosen charity. In addition they are asked employees to vote on which local charities should benefit from institution-wide fundraising activities. Links were also made to the volunteering activities carried out by the Students' Union.

# EVALUATING INVOLVEMENT: THE EXCELLENCE MODEL

Several merchant banks in Canary Wharf developed links with local schools (Montagu Smith 2006). Staff from Credit Suisse volunteer to tutor children in reading, maths and IT. Heart of the City was launched in 2000 by the Bank of England, aiming to give children a working adult as a role model. Staff from Merrill Lynch mentor sixth-form students in Tower Hamlets schools. In an era when banks have been heavily criticised, such activities attempt to give them a human face.

The European Foundation for Quality Management (EFQM/BITC) Excellence Model uses a nine-point plan to ensure effective planning, implementation and measurement of CommR.

The Excellence Model has nine principles for successful CommR. The first five are enablers:

* Leadership – do the company leaders create a culture where CommR is an integral part of the organisation?

* Policy and strategy – does the organisation have a clear, focused strategy?

* People – is CommR is used to manage and develop employees at an individual, team and organisation-wide level?

* Partnership and resources – does the organisation allocate sufficient resources, both cash and in kind?

* Processes – are CR activities monitored to create value for stakeholders?

Both an organisation and a prospective charity can use the formula to assess whether the results gained from the partnership make the relationship worthwhile.

The other side of the equation is results, and the four remaining principles are:

* community partner results – whether the needs of the charity are being met;

* people results – what the organisation is achieving in relation to its own employees;

* society results – what the organisation is achieving in the communities in which it operates;

* key performance results – are the organisation's business objectives being met.

The kind of benefits that a charity could offer might include enhancing corporate reputation by association. If the company is reducing staff, affecting the local economy, the partnership can also be used to put something back into the community at the same time. Association with a cause could help influence opinion-formers, so strengthening the company's licence to operate and building customer loyalty. Product sales could be benefited through cause-related marketing, and the association may also contribute to recruitment, staff development and motivation.

■ If you were in the communications team of a national bank, how might you use the Excellence Model to demonstrate the benefits of engaging in a community relations programme?

■ What charities or organisations would you suggest partnering with?

## HOW CAN WE DO IT?

Wheeler and Sillanpaa (1997) suggest that the first thing is to think about the goal of CommR. The next stage is consultation with the community before agreeing objectives. They recommend a constant review of how CommR is working and stress that it should be real, two-way and inclusive. Transparency is vital, in terms of how engagement happens and how it is measured in cash and other values. Grunig and Hunt (1984: 270) state that:

> Most organisations participate in the community because they realise that a strong community helps them to be a stronger organisation. Employees will be more satisfied if they live in a desirable community and better employees can be attracted to work there. Employees working in highly constrained job situations also become more satisfied with their job if the organisation helps them to use their talents in the community.

Murray-Leslie (2007) maintains that successful businesses understand they are interdependent with society, and recommends that organisations adapt their business expertise to engage employees and customers. Tench (2006) states that CommR benefits both parties and makes a link between being a good corporate citizen and having a good reputation and share value, although this is debatable. Laying down a good reputational foundation may help an organisation during a crisis. Encouraging employees to become involved in community may also improve productivity. Other benefits include enhancing reputation, positive press coverage, increased brand awareness and customer loyalty, and increased sales. Tench suggests that such programmes could be evaluated by assessing publicity, getting employee feedback, and measuring the effect on former perceptions.

# BUILDING TRUST WITH COMMUNITIES

## The Environment Agency and the Shaldon risk project

In the early 2000s the Environment Agency realised that its default strategy of decide-announce-defence (DAD) was not the best approach for its major construction projects. The imposition of flood defence schemes and other environmental solutions on local communities could no longer continue.

We set out to counter two widespread myths in the organisational culture, that (i) engaging with communities was expensive and time-consuming; and (ii) it was possible to choose whether or not to work with others. The plan was to shift to an inclusive way of working – engage-deliberate-decide (EDD). By engaging with our customers and building trust with communities and stakeholders right from the start of a project we would be able to agree the solution so our schemes would become less controversial and less time consuming. Ultimately they would be less costly to the public purse.

Having already identified locations with very real tidal risk we chose Shaldon and Ringmore as our EDD pilot and brought in Lindsay Colbourne Associates to work with us.

Shaldon and Ringmore are small linked villages at the mouth of the Teign estuary in Devon. There is a 1.2 kilometre long river frontage along the villages. Homes and businesses were in a low-lying basin behind existing, informal defences with a poor standing of flood protection. If tidal water overtopped the old flood walls houses, shops and other properties would easily flood. This tidal risk was made worse by increased waves during storms and high winds and the impact of climate change. We assessed there was a 1 in 300 chance of tidal flooding in any one year at Shaldon and Ringmore. This flooding would affect up to 418 properties with some under 2 metres of dirty river water.

As there was a lack of historical records or living memory of tidal flooding in the community, residents were initially highly sceptical of the tidal risk and potential need to be defended. Much of the income in the pretty area comes from tourism so business and home owners did not want ugly flood defences spoiling their village.

The building trust process began in October 2005 with a public exhibition setting out the facts about flood risk. We encouraged local people to tell us what they thought about the tidal risk and to let us know whether they wanted us to do anything about it. Surface water and sewer flooding caused more concern to the residents than the possibility of tidal flooding. However, at a public meeting after the exhibition, the community confirmed it did understand the tidal flood risk facing the village and it did want to work with us. The next step was to agree the way of working and a local liaison group was agreed.

Twenty-eight volunteers were selected by the community to represent them on the liaison group. We held the evening meetings in the village using church halls and other rooms including group members' homes. Led by Lindsay Colbourne, the group worked through the detail of the risk, the possible options to reduce the risk and this information was shared with the rest of the local people. The output from the liaison group sessions helped us address the surface water flood concerns and eventually incorporate it into the scheme design. We also brought together highway engineers and the water company to do their bit in tackling the whole flood situation.

Once we all agreed that a tidal defence scheme of flood walls and gates was required, our design engineers developed the outline design. Then members of the liaison group helped to run walking tours in Shaldon and Ringmore to show to the community what was proposed to reduce their tidal flood risk. While 83 per cent of those who made the tours were very positive about the plans and 70 per cent supported them, there was a small but growing number of people expressing concern over the height of the flood walls. We organised drop-in sessions and further walking tours to give them a further chance to discuss their concerns.

At this stage, in the light of new national data on tide levels, we decided to review and subsequently withdrew our planning application for the defences. The review of the proposals resulted in a small reduction to the height of the scheme, making it acceptable to the majority and we successfully reapplied for planning. This was a difficult time for us and we continued to ensure we were upfront and clear about the plans, coaching our staff not to become defensive or dismissive when people challenged them.

It was vital to continue our good relations with the local community during construction of the tidal defences. We appointed an on-site public liaison officer for the duration of the project, who, as an engineer himself, was able to deal with local concerns promptly and consistently.

The project was completed in May 2011 and, once again, we continued to involve the locals by asking them to help us organise the official opening ceremony. The final event was a real celebration of working together including many words of praise and thanks from the local people for their lovely flood walls and gates, and for the way we had involved them.

For our engineers and technical staff engaging in a local community in this way was initially hard work, although the benefits quickly became clear as community understanding of what we were trying to achieve developed and support grew.

The time spent on building trust and relationships at the start of this project has been time very well spent. It has also helped our teams think more about the customers when designing a project that will make a real difference to where people.

We spent around £500,000 on community engagement on this £8.4 million project and the real value of that spend is the application of the learning across our wider business.

The Environment Agency has produced guidelines from the project so that the principles of EDD can be learned and applied by staff in future schemes and affected communities can be involved right from the start.

**This is South Devon | £8.3 million flood defence scheme ready for opening**

**FIGURE 21.1** Environment Agency's Shaldon project

*Bridget Beer (nee Norris) – Bridget joined the National Rivers Authority in 1991 and quickly moved into the PR team progressing into the Environment Agency. She worked across the South West specialising in holistic communications and engagement around contentious issues. In April 2011 she took the lead role in customer engagement at the Flood Forecasting Centre.*

Good CommR programmes help to give employees a reason to be proud of the company, with all the benefits of increased engagement that brings. The following case study shows how the Environment Agency changed its way of dealing with communities where it was developing projects, so that opposition was reduced.

# CAUSE-RELATED MARKETING (CRM)

BITC (Adkins, cited in Theaker 2004: 184) defined CRM as 'a commercial activity by which businesses and charities or causes form a partnership with each other to market an image, product or service, for mutual benefit'. They also described it as 'an increasingly legitimate method for businesses to take on their responsibility to address social issues, and positively affect consumer perceptions of companies'.

Unlike sponsorship, which might include the donation of a one-off amount to a charity, or the provision of equipment to a special-needs school, CRM has a clear profit motive, rather than being part of the company's 'licence to operate'.

## Why is CRM important?

- 98 per cent of consumers are aware of CRM programmes;
- 80 per cent have participated in a CRM scheme;
- 71 per cent claimed to have been influenced in their buying decisions by CRM (Adkins 2006).

## Enlightened self-interest

'Like any other aspect of Lever Fabergé's brand activity plans, we believe CRM programmes have to make sound commercial sense and are firmly grounded in consumer understanding,' said John Ballington (2003). The company supports Comic Relief, and over three years raised more than £1 million for the cause but also raised consumer awareness of their Persil brand. In addition, after using findings from their Family Report research they found that the average infant pupil received only £1.18 arts and crafts funding per year. In 2002 they launched their Get Creative initiative, which involved collecting on-pack tokens that could be redeemed for brushes or face-painting kits. Over 40,000 schools registered in the first two years of the scheme. Illustrating that such schemes must be relevant to the products of the company concerned, Persil was keen to be seen as the brand that cleaned up children's paint-stained clothes!

While a 2001 *Which?* report was critical of the long-running Tesco Computers for Schools scheme, claiming that parents would have to spend £250,000 on their shopping to get enough tokens to provide a computer that cost only £1,000 to buy, the programme provided more than £82 million worth of equipment in its first

# TENANTS BECOME COMMUNICATORS WITH WESTWARD HOUSING GROUP

ACTION POINT

**FIGURE 21.2** Westcountry Communication Group

Taking a truly two-way symmetrical approach, Westward Housing Group has set up Communications Group teams of tenants to produce their own newsletters. While members receive training from the corporate communications team, each group decides on the content, conducts interviews and writes articles, agrees on design and proofreads the newsletters and web pages for their own housing scheme. Regular review meetings are also held for the website and annual report, and terms of reference are written with the members.

The Tarka and Westcountry Housing communications groups each have about 12 members. Westward encourages a proportional representation of age, tenancy type, needs, and location of members. While membership of the team is an unpaid role, Westward funds travel and care costs.

The tone and content of the newsletter aims to be inclusive. The benefits of having publications and online material shaped by tenants are that it means we have communication both by and for residents. This means it is far more likely to result in information that is interesting to, and presented for, the readership in a way they would most like to see it. They know best.

As well as the experience of the group members, the readers, who may be older people living in sheltered schemes or marginalised groups, are encouraged to have broader horizons by seeing the work and activities of their peers.

Features such as 'Your Story' or 'Tenant's Tale' have included moving personal achievement stories, neighbourly tales of kindness and experience of living as a disabled person, ranging through to wartime experiences and having a tattoo done in old age. A social enterprise project for marginalised people to grow and sell plants and another therapeutic enterprise run with clients who learn to re-upholster furniture have also been inspirational showcases.

Residents in the communications group find their confidence to speak out and express their views flourishes as their skills and experience grow. They also interview Westward staff about any changes and share the news in a clear, tenant-focused way. Members say they get a lot of satisfaction from seeing their work in print and are rightly proud of their work.

Mike Smith in the Tarka Communications Group writes a fact-finding column about a different village for each issue and interviews local people about their hobbies. He is always very keen to go out and find stories, despite being immobile part of each month with a crumbling spine.

Seeing a village pantomime celebrated in pictures, or an article about evicting anti-social neighbours has a strengthening impact on the community. A contractor who advertises an apprenticeship vacancy and appoints a resident may be interviewed, as well as the apprentice about how their new role is going.

Westward works with partner organisations that have direct relevance and potential benefit for tenants. They work with the fire service to promote safety and liaise with the police in reporting confidence tricksters or thefts from oil tanks.

Readers in the community can participate in surveys and consultations at residents' events. The annual report is viewed at roadshows, in mobile offices and readers can respond with questions and comments.

Staff also consult residents when producing other publications and send the drafts to the group for checking. This earns them a quality mark known as the customer approved logo.

All staff receive training at induction about the group. Staff who are out and about in the community can be a great source of possible stories to feed back to the teams.

Readership and satisfaction rates are high in annual surveys with the Westcountry newsletter being given as the main source of information for 84 per cent of general needs, 90 per cent of sheltered and 85 per cent of supported customers. Postcards with focused and open comment boxes are sent on each annual report for feedback as to how to improve them in future.

The Tenant Participation Advisory Service (TPAS) has highlighted the Westcountry Housing Communications Group and newsletters as good practice.

We have just made a short film on DVD for new tenants explaining the role of the staff and responsibilities of the customer, using both tenants from the communications group and staff as presenters.

We are looking forward to consulting customers on how they find the new annual report when it is hot off the press at our next major resident involvement events. Communications Group members actually signed their work in the annual report themselves this year – nothing like a bit of pressure!

*Vanessa Gray is Communications Manager for Westward Housing Group and its subsidiaries. She trained and worked as a journalist before moving into PR for an environmental education centre and then an organic farming research and policy group.*

*Westward provides affordable housing and related services across the South West to 7,000 households. It is an exciting, dynamic, pressured role and Vanessa works with an assistant, delivering services to the group's several member organisations in the fields of property development and sales, affordable home ownership, support and care, and of course housing associations.*

twelve years of operation. More than 86 per cent of UK schools registered with the scheme (Williamson, 2004). As funding is set to become even more important for schools such initiatives may become even more common. However, the NUT 2003 conference resolved to campaign against commercialisation in schools, so organ-isations would do well to research guidelines drawn up by ISBA, the Consumers' Association, the Department for Education and Skills and BITC on any programme that targets schools (ibid.).

## A calculated strategy

CRM is a calculated strategy in which everybody wins. The CRM campaign is long-term not short-term, strategic rather than tactical (see also discussion in Chapter 14).

Communication of the programme is an important element and must be handled correctly. Organisations must be upfront about the corporate motives for what they are doing. Consumers expect the company to gain from what they are doing, and if this is fudged they will be suspicious.

Companies and charities must both assess risk when entering into CRM partnerships. Engaging in CRM can lead to a more critical examination of a company's policies. The Red Cross's decision to take £250,000 from Nestlé was reported in January 2000, questioning whether the charity should have taken money from a company that had been involved in unethical promotion of its baby milk products in the developing world (Wall 2000).

The Charity Commission advises that charities should not take money from companies that perpetrate the problem the charity is trying to solve. The Red Cross responded that it had been assured by the WHO that Nestlé was now complying with international law on the marketing of baby milk powder, and should that change the charity reserved the right to end the relationship. Wall (2000) quotes Stephen Lee, former head of ICFM, the professional body of fundraisers, as saying: 'It's a con. It's a mechanism dreamed up by business to promote business, with very strong rhetoric about partnership which is usually absolute rubbish.'

## END POINT

Community relations and cause-related marketing programmes have clear benefits for organisations that carry them out in a planned manner. Successful programmes should be based on a thorough analysis of what both organisation and community might gain and involve the community the organisation is trying to form a relationship with. Groups within the community should be empowered to participate. Any financial benefits of CRM should be clearly set out and the results communicated in an honest and transparent way.

# CHAPTER 22

# Consumer public relations

*Alison Theaker*

Public relations that deals with consumer products has to co-exist and interact with marketing communications.

## CHECK POINT

This chapter looks at one of the most vibrant areas of public relations. It covers:

- the relationship between PR and marketing;
- a definition of consumerism;
- the role of marketing communications;
- consumer buying behaviour;
- keeping customers;
- guerilla PR and stunts.

## MARKETING AND PUBLIC RELATIONS

Public relations in the field of consumer relations is often referred to as marketing communications or marketing PR (MPR). Marketing, as we have seen, is the identification of the needs of consumers and how to satisfy those needs profitably.

PR influences markets by sending persuasive messages to buyers. Moloney suggests that as much as 70 per cent of PR jobs are in the field of MPR (Moloney 2006).

Research by Kitchen found that 15 per cent of marketing budgets were spent on brand PR in the UK and that marketing professionals spent 70 per cent of their time on marketing communications (Bacot 2006).

Marketers tend to see PR as a subordinate part of their armoury of tools while public relations practitioners often see marketing as primarily concerned with selling products to consumers. Belch and Belch (2001: 576) see PR as much more about changing attitudes than promoting specific products.

Public relations and marketing should be corporate allies, working together for common goals. Cutlip *et al.* (2000: 478–9) lists Harris' ten ways that PR can support marketing:

1   building excitement before advertising breaks;
2   creating news about new products;
3   creating news about a new advertising or marketing approach;
4   bringing advertising characters to life by arranging tours and public appearances;
5   extending the reach of marketing by creating links to related charities or campaigns;
6   building personal relationships with consumers;
7   sponsoring events and targeting opinion leaders;
8   communicating new product benefits of existing products;
9   building consumer trust with CSR and CRM;
10  crisis management when products may be at risk or have been sabotaged.

Increased market information results in more informed consumers, but this has resulted in a 'wall of sound'. Moloney (2006) estimates that the average American sees more than 7 million advertisements in his or her lifetime.

Davis (2004) quotes Kotler's 1991 definition of MPR as 'a variety of programmes designed to improve, maintain or protect a company or product image' (and see also the discussion of PR and marketing in Chapter 1).

Willis (2006) suggests that 'many marketing professionals now view PR as an effective way to win over hearts and minds of consumers', and so stimulate sales of products and services. PR techniques are seen as particularly useful in changing attitudes and behaviours of consumers. Media relations can produce third-party endorsement by journalists which is more credible than advertising. Kitchen concluded that 'in the real world, [PR and marketing] need one another', and that MPR helped build relationships between consumers and brands (Jardine, 2006).

Swann (2010) considers that consumer relations involves:

•   supporting marketing communication efforts to build consumer demand for products and services;

- maintaining mutually beneficial and lasting relationships between the organisation and consumer.

She points out that the development of the internet and related technology has had a major impact on this field. Now a disgruntled customer can use a variety of methods to get their viewpoint out to millions of web users. So paying attention to long-term relationships with consumers and activitists is imperative to try and minimise reputational damage.

# CONSUMERISM

Consumerism is 'the idea that consumers should influence the design, quality, service and prices of goods and services provided by commercial enterprises' (Macmillan in Mayer, 1989: 309). Consumerism can also be linked to over-consumption and materialism. The BBC programme *Watchdog* publicises where companies have failed to deliver a good response to complaints. The most influential organisation in this field in the UK is the Consumers' Association. Its magazine, *Which?* also available online, carries reports on a vast range of products to enable consumers to pick the best available in their price range.

Bashford (2011) relates how Dell had to respond to consumer Jeff Jarvis in 2005 when he complained online about his computer being a 'lemon' and signed off with the words, 'Dell sucks. Dell lies. Put that in your Google and smoke it.' Jarvis set out to see whether Dell was listening to social media, but it took the company over a year to really get to grips with consumer complaints. Figures on the web suggest that Dell's market share fell sharply as a result. In 2011, however, Dell was awarded 'most social brand' by Headstream in its Social Brands 100 Report. The company gave Jarvis open access and launched a variety of social media platforms, publishing uncensored customer reviews on its website. Social media specialists were sent to business units to deal with any online issues quickly. Dell also used social media to carry out research and set up a panel of independent experts. It has recently trained over 9,000 employees worldwide to become ambassadors in the online world, responding to key word searches to find customers that may need help. Dell director of communications Stuart Handley said, 'branding today is not about how you present yourself on your website or forum; it's about how others present you.'

# MARKETING COMMUNICATIONS AND INTEGRATED MARKETING COMMUNICATIONS (IMC)

'Marketing communications encompasses any form of communication that contributes to the conversion of a non-customer to a customer, and subsequently to the retention of such custom,' says Hart (1995: 25). Ouwersloot and Duncan (2008) define IMC as 'the processes for planning, executing and monitoring the brand messages that create brand-customer relationships'. They suggest that the IMC perspective ensures that all communication activities relate to the same goals. One outcome is 'synergy . . . the interaction of individual parts in a way that makes the integrated whole greater than the sum of its parts'.

How does PR fit here? Don Schultz coined the phrase 'integrated marketing' in 1993, promoting the value of PR alongside other marketing disciplines (Jardine 2006). The traditional elements of the marketing mix are the four Ps – product, price, place and promotion. Price can indicate good or bad value for money; in some cases, a high price signals quality or prestige. Place means the channels of distribution and the kind of outlet where the product can be obtained – a product will be viewed differently if it is sold on a market stall rather than in a high street department store. Promotion refers to the media and messages used to influence buyer decisions. It is here that PR contributes most, bringing a range of activities that can support and supplement advertising and marketing. The selection of which medium to use to convey the messages will depend on the target market, and the combination of choices made for the most effective communication is often referred to as the 'media mix'. Davis (2004) adds on three more Ps: people (customers, employees), process (involvement of the consumer in production) and physical evidence (making the benefits of products tangible).

The size of the market affects which tactics to use. A group of people who are involved in any decision are often called the buying decision unit, or BDU. If only ten BDUs are to be approached, personal contact may be best. If there are 1,000, direct email, editorial publicity, demonstrations or telephone selling could be added. With 100,000, mass media methods would be best. Now careful and targeted use of social media can extend the reach of consumer PR messages.

The kind of message is the next consideration. A simple message could be conveyed by a poster, but a complex or technical one would need to be presented in the specialist media. Davis (2004) suggests that PR is a more cost-effective alternative to spending on advertising, as advertising alone is not persuasive enough. Moloney (2006) agrees that PR and marketing together are better able to handle promotions across a variety of channels such as media relations, events, sponsorship, exhibitions, roadshows and web-based materials.

Marketing traditionally relied on advertising to reach consumers, but this is becoming less influential with the growth of communication channels. While some companies still find 'pay per click' advertising useful (such as the Old Bag Company, on pp. 321–324) most are finding that they need to use editorial methods and events to get their messages across. Traditional media also work less with younger audiences, who are digital natives. Marketing and public relations can form an effective partnership, producing both digital (website copy and social media ideas) and traditional materials (brochures, newsletters and direct mailers). Websites can now carry video, audio and text, and offer consumers games and other promotional items. Electronic versions of media kits can be made available to journalists (Swann 2010).

Pinsent (2011) relates how lines between functions in organisations are becoming blurred. Whether creating a TV spot, sponsoring a TV show, building a feature story for *BBC Breakfast* or defending the company on BBC *Watchdog*, it is important to ensure that they 'each help tell a consistent story'.

Willis (2006) suggested that PR techniques were 'particularly useful in changing attitudes and behaviours of consumers'.

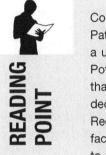

**READING POINT**

Consumer PR can use both informational tactics and emotional appeals. Patricia Swann's 2010 text, *Cases in Public Relations Management* has a useful chapter full of relevant case studies, including how the US Potato Board created an information campaign to counter a perception that potatoes were an unhealthy food choice, causing a 24 per cent decline in consumption in the 1990s. There are accounts of how the Recreation Vehicle Industry Association made the case for RVs in the face of rising fuel prices and how the state of Kansas promoted itself to the outside world to shake off its association with tornadoes and *The Wizard of Oz*. Swann also relates how the budget store Payless Shoesource repositioned itself as high fashion and how Scholastic created interest in the later books in the *Harry Potter* series.

## PUBLIC RELATIONS IN THE LAUNCH PROCESS

'Done well, a launch helps a new product rapidly establish itself among its target users, gain market share and enhance the company's brand position,' says Joan Schneider, CEO of Schneider and Associates, a Boston-based public relations firm with more than twenty years' experience in product launches, 'Done poorly, however, it can negate all the time, money and human capital that went into developing the new product.' With this in mind, Schneider commissioned Boston University to carry out a study into how launches were conducted to identify success factors and help product managers increase their launch success rate.

The survey found that the best launches showed advance planning, with the development of the product occurring one to two years before shipping, along with selecting the advertising agency. Selection of the public relations agency took place ten to twelve months before shipping, with public relations activities starting four to six months before and continuing for at least nine months after the product was on the shelves. The most successful products had benefitted from PR planning to create media coverage to build the brand. The best teams included marketing and brand managers as well as operations, manufacturing or product development. Interestingly, the less senior the overall manager of the team, the better the result. Brand or product managers had a higher success rate than senior marketing personnel or CEOs. In terms of budgets, unsurprisingly those with larger budgets were more likely to succeed, as were those that concentrated on consumer-focused activities rather than trade-focused.

Finally, it was found that the use of public relations activities, such as generating positive consumer and trade press mentions, reviews and retailer interest were seen as having far more impact for highly successful products. 'Considering the amount of time and resources spent on new product development, new products have a surprisingly small window of opportunity during which their fates are sealed,' says Schneider, 'The keys to success are adequate planning and utilising public relations as one of the tools to create a favourable environment.'

## CONSUMER BUYING BEHAVIOUR

The PR practitioner also needs to consider the consumers' buying decisions. Belch and Belch (2001) put forward a basic model of how people make choices:

- problem recognition – motivation
- information search – perception
- alternative evaluation – attitude formation
- purchase decision – integration
- post-purchase evaluation – learning.

The motivation for buying a watch – whether it's to tell the time or to make a fashion statement – will affect whether the consumer focuses on reliability or design. Motivation is often linked to Maslow's hierarchy of needs, which suggests that it is only after basic needs such as food, shelter and sex are satisfied that people can focus on safety, then love and belonging, and finally self-esteem and self-actualisation. Marketers in the developed world assume that the basic needs are met, and may try to associate their products with one of the higher levels. Volvo concentrates on satisfying basic needs for safety in positioning its cars, while BMW focuses on the higher levels of self-esteem and status.

Kotler suggests that stimuli for buying include price, quality, availability, service, style, options and image (Williams 1981: 156). Editorial, advertising, salespeople, friends, family and personal observation can all affect the buyer. Fisk (2004) states that consumers want to be more individualistic, so that product differentiation becomes key.

Another way to influence buying behaviour has been to associate brands with celebrities thought to appeal to the target market. Christian Aid used Ronan Keating for its Trade Justice campaign, aimed at men and women aged 30 to 70 years old, although the majority of its supporters are over 50. Oxfam used Coldplay's Chris Martin and Kaiser Chiefs to raise awareness among 16- to 25-year-olds. Consultancy Entertainment Media Research (EMR) rated artists' popularity by asking a cross-section of 4,500 people to rate their emotional connection to a variety of celebrities. They found that Oxfam's links worked well with their audience, while Christian Aid would have been better to use Kylie Minogue to reach their target demographic (Magee 2007).

# KEEPING CUSTOMERS

Marketing communications is not only concerned with obtaining customers, but with keeping them. Stone (1995: 141) claims that getting back a lost customer costs five times as much as keeping them happy in the first place. L.D. Young (2006) questions this and suggests that sometimes it is cheaper to attract new customers than chase existing ones.

Awareness of consumer needs means paying attention to staff relations, particularly in the retail sector. Brand and corporate reputation can be undermined by a customer's poor experience in a store. Linda Barber of the Institute of Employment Studies found that stores where staff were more satisfied (because they were better managed and looked after) generated a £200,000 increase in sales per month (Murphy, 1999). So, consumer PR needs to link into human resources and internal communications so that their work is not wasted.

Hunter (2011) advises that it is not enough to simply wait until a customer complains, because by that time they may have sent their opinion out via the web to millions of others. She advises that organisations invite feedback rather than passively monitoring comments. In addition, going into the market place where products are sold or delivered and speaking directly to customers can help reveal 'the gap between the brand promise and the consumers' brand reality'. Hunter's consultancy, Unleashed Potential, road tests client's products and visits their premises to see if brands live up to their promises. At the end of the day, however, it is important to use information gathered in these ways to shape both communications and product delivery in the future.

Friend (2011) reveals that, according to YouGov, 41 per cent of people will make a complaint by telephone, 63 per cent by email and 20 per cent by social media. She advises making any complaint from the latter source a private conversation as soon as possible. An apology and a willingness to solve the problem should come first. She too suggests that companies should not 'wait for customers to knock on your door, but go out and find customers who are moaning about you' and offer solutions proactively.

Lowe (2011) reminds us that 'listening did not start with the advent of the social web,' and suggests that consumer PR needs to refocus on consumer needs and 'move away from a "media-centric" approach' back to an appreciation of how information is being communicated from person to person.

## GUERILLA PR AND VIRAL MARKETING

Different techniques have to be used to attract the consumer's attention in order to stand out from the mass of information. Guerilla PR uses stunts and humour to obtain media coverage. Hatfield Galleria invented the protest group the Bargain Liberation Front who protested outside Westminster. This linked into their advertising campaign, 'I'm a Bargain Get Me Out of Here', and to a local radio competition to find the best bargain-hunters. Sales increased by 5 per cent (Blyth 2006). However, stunts should be carefully planned. A cartoon network placed characters on public buildings across the US, but caused widespread panic in Boston when passers-by thought they might be terrorist devices.

Buzz or 'word of mouse' can be created by viral marketing. This involves sending out a video clip and hoping it will be passed on. Sixty hours of video are uploaded to the YouTube website every minute, and more than 3 billion are watched each day (YouTube 2012). T-Mobile's 'Dance' campaign produced a three-minute TV advert. Over 300 dancers were filmed breaking into a seemingly spontaneous dance routine at Liverpool Street station. Travellers' reactions were also incorporated into the film. Similar ads also show spectators filming such stunts on their phones and sending onto friends. The videos can then be posted on YouTube, creating a viral buzz and giving the ad a much greater spread than simply showing on TV.

Consumer PR is the most affected by social media and mobile technology as this allows organisations to speak directly to their customers. Magee (2011a) sees this as an 'opportunity to grab a larger share of marketing budgets . . . [as PR has] a conversational approach'. Morgan (2011) agrees. He says that there will be 'less reliance on journalists and more importance on messaging directly from the brand via owned channels'. Shah (2011) feels that PR's strength in a world with an 'increasingly virtual life' is that it can create 'experiential elements' with live events. Cohen (2011) adds that PR expertise at 'sparking new conversations with consumers' will be important in creating 'virtual word of mouth' through social media.

Mulholland (2011) warns that PR will have to demonstrate that it delivers 'measurable ROI and can genuinely make a difference to a client's business objectives'. You can read more about evaluation in Chapter 10.

## FUTURE TRENDS

Lawrence (2011: 29) gives an account of new ways of reaching customers in the developing world. 'Nestlé is using a floating supermarket to take its products to remote communities in the Amazon. Unilever has a small army of door-to-door vendors selling to low-income villages in India and Africa.' While this may make good commercial sense, and shows an adaptation of traditional marketing methods, selling highly processed food and drink to these communities has been associated with rises in non-communicable diseases such as diabetes, obesity, heart disease and alcoholism. Nestlé and Unilever protest that they are simply giving choices to people and that the sales network is providing job opportunities.

Lloyd (2011) advises consumer PR practitioners to anticipate future trends to be able to stay one step ahead of their competitors. She feels PR practitioners need to 'create ultimate engagement, intimacy and loyalty between brands and their consumers'. She suggests that gaming is a new way to create a more long-lasting relationship. She uses examples such as Braun's Oral B toothbrush that displays a happy face when used properly, and VW and the National Society for Road Safety in Sweden who created a speed camera lottery to reward responsible drivers. Clack (2011) also focuses on the long game, recommending the use of 'behavioural economics . . . [the understanding of] how social, cognitive and emotional factors influence economic decisions'. Clack relates how economist Richard Thaler persuaded 20–30 years olds to start saving for a pension by developing a product that only took contributions from future pay rises.

The following case studies showcase several companies who take a creative approach to relating to their customers.

**ACTION POINT**

## INSPIRATION ON THE BEACH

The Old Bag Company (OBC) was born in 2006 when Sally Hurst was sitting on her local beach in Devon with her five children surrounded by carrier bags and thought she needed a practical beach bag. So she went home and designed one.

Since then the range has grown to include everyday bags, handbags, cool bags, laptop bags, baby changing bags, cosmetic bags, purses and scarves. The main route to market is through retailers, of which there are now over 500 worldwide. Sally still designs every product and is focused on keeping the feel of her company personal and friendly.

There are thousands of bag companies around so it has always been important for the OBC to stand out, not only with their products but as a company. With a good memorable name the personality of the business comes from the children's input. All the ranges are named after Sally's children. Inside every bag is a label with a message from them and on the swing tag they tell you all the latest news. They also are featured in the brochure, all the posters and marketing material giving the product real personality. As the users are predominately women, they love this concept.

**FIGURE 22.1** Sally Hurst's children were the inspiration for her Old Bag range

Entering awards provides the opportunity to raise the profile of the business. As a result of winning Barclays Best Family Business in 2009, Sally was contacted by BBC Radio 4 to take part in a programme featuring small businesses. In 2010, Sally was invited to become a Fellow of the Royal Society of Arts in recognition of her role as an inspirational businesswoman. When she won the National Enterprising Women's Award in 2009, she was approached by Karen Gill MBE, co-founder of Everywoman. She was launching a book called Modern Muse designed to inspire and engage the next generation of female business entrepreneurs by showcasing successful women. Sally was featured in the book, which was launched at a prestigious event in London and covered by the *Guardian* and business sections of *The Times* and *The Daily Telegraph*.

The OBC does not spend money on advertising but works with consultancy Positive PR to promote the brand regionally and nationally. OBC has been covered in *Vogue, Marie Claire, Woman & Home, Best, Pregnancy Baby & You, Condé Nast Traveller, The Daily Telegraph, The Daily Mail, The Sunday Telegraph, The Sunday Times* and on BBC Radio 4, BBC Radio 2, *Big Brother*, ITV *Westcountry* and BBC *Spotlight*. The media exposure highlighted Sally's achievements as a successful businesswoman, which has led to her working with many women's organisations to inspire other women to start their own business. All this exposure gives the brand real credibility and raises brand awareness in a very competitive market. OBC uses this as part of their marketing material with both customers and retailers. Often new business comes from being seen in the media, and hits and orders on the website increase significantly. Positive PR manages media relations, normally related to award wins or product launches, and monitors feature opportunities on women in business and the best beach bags around.

An online presence is key and the home page is as friendly and engaging as possible. 'This is the face of OBC and we want customers to engage immediately,' says Sally. Quick and simple ordering is also important or the potential buyer will lose interest. Web customers and fan club members receive a mailshot every quarter or when there is a promotion. Facebook works well and Google Ad words are used in the early summer and before Christmas. The OBC site can come above the big high street retailers at these times.

Retailers have point of sale boards with their first order, which tells the story of OBC. A Charlotte beach bag is 'dressed' by putting flip-flops in the outside pocket, a bottle of wine and a magazine, and is proven to increase sales. 'We also work with retailers to offer them promotions with our products and we also donate if they are fundraising,' adds Sally:

> We decided to do a Union Jack version of the beach bag, cool bag and purse for the 2012 Jubilee and Olympics, and this has had a tremendous response. A limited edition in the three lines has kept it exclusive. So now we have a very patriotic Old Bag!

The most successful launch was the cool bag, with many new retailers stocking the product, garden centres in particular. It was spotted by the Cook Shop buyer at John Lewis and they will have stocked this product along with a picnic rug Sally designed just for them from spring 2012.

'Having the idea is the easy part,' says Sally,

> Converting that idea into a real product and creating a business to
> market it is the challenge. I always emphasise the story of the
> OBC's beginnings. With vision, determination, passion and a lot of
> hard work, five years on the Old Bag Company is a growing brand.
>     When you phone our office the answer phone message cannot
> fail to make you smile and our ethos is if you can make a potential
> customer smile you are half way there!

**ACTION POINT**

## FOCUSING ON THE PRODUCERS!

Langage Farm was originally just that. In fact it has been a working farm
for over 900 years and was mentioned in the Domesday Book. In 1980,
the farm started to diversify and produce clotted cream. The range of
dairy products produced by Langage Farm now includes: frozen clotted
cream; cream by post; pouring cream; sour cream; crème fraîche; cream
cheese; cottage cheese and yogurt. They also produce a range of luxury
ice creams in forty-five flavours, sorbets, frozen yogurt, ice cream
bombes dipped in Belgian chocolate and ice cream gateau.

Originally the aim was to utilise the milk from the farm's own Jersey and
Guernsey cows. The herd had increased from 40 cows on 100 acres in
1957 to the present day 280 cows on 400 acres. The company now
also support seven Channel Island farms. Langage employ over 50 local
people and have over 1,000 retail customers, with expected turnover in
2012 of £5.5 million.

The company also built its own anaerobic digester plant in 2009 using
food waste to produce 500–600kw to power the dairy plant and feed
back into the national grid. The digester plant also incorporates an
educational centre that hosts visits from local schools, as well as a
demonstration kitchen, which is used in partnership with local master
chefs. The material used in the digester plant becomes fertiliser, which
is then used on the fields to improve the quality of grass and so
increase the yield of the cows.

The marketing of products is distinctive in that a conscious decision
was made to emphasise the real producers of the product – the cows.
Packaging features named cows on the different products, and the
website continues this theme. Mabel welcomes visitors to the website,
and Lulu, Hyacinth and Nora feature on the clotted cream pots. Alice,

**FIGURE 22.2** Langage Farm emphasises the producers of its product

Gina, Emilie and Flo introduce ice cream products. The three members of the management team, Paul Winterton (general manager), James Harvey (business owner) and Gary Jones (AD general manager), all nominate their favourite cow and product on the site.

As well as conventional marketing methods, the company decided to spearhead the campaign to gain Protected Designation of Origin (PDO) status for the Devonshire Cream Tea. The application to DEFRA put forward a proposal that all components (scone, clotted cream and jam) must be produced in Devon to qualify for the name of Devonshire Cream Tea. The campaign was launched in May 2011, and gained widespread coverage from the BBC, *Daily Mail*, *The Daily Telegraph*, *Daily Express* and even the *Londonderry Standard*. Paul Winterton was quoted as saying, 'It's about making sure what people are served is the genuine article. It's also good for the local economy.' The application process could take up to eight years, so the company is set to continue to milk this story.

**ACTION POINT**

## BEST IN SHOW

Falling visitor numbers to agricultural shows over the past few years highlighted a need for The Royal Bath and West Society, organisers of the long-standing annual Bath and West Show, to address the need to both maintain existing visitor levels but also future-proof the show and look to grown new visitor numbers.

JBP PR was appointed to bring a different dimension to the promotion of the Bath and West Show. Specifically with a remit to address:

- how the show can attract more visitors – without being seen to dilute its agricultural foundations;
- exploring new channels for promoting the show;
- boosting advance ticket sales;
- maintaining visitor numbers.

Following a review of all the show's assets, JBP PR set out to:

- build on the show's positioning as 'more than just an agricultural show' – creating an aspirational event that appeals to a broader audience;
- drive pre-show sales by creating reasons to buy;
- promoting advance ticket offers;
- increase the number of overall visitors (in a market where the Highland Show was seeing a reduction in numbers);
- integrate PR effort across all areas of the show.

Positioning the show as more than just an agricultural show, JBP created a targeted programme of activity designed to excite regular visitors and reach out to new relevant audiences. We created exposure for the wide range of activities and features available at the show and focused predominantly on three specific target audience groups: family, food lovers and the country set.

Core to the campaign were four initiatives: a social media campaign, strategic partnership programme, Ladies' Day, Bath and West Banger – a search to find a sausage recipe to be served at the show. All initiatives challenged perceptions about the show being 'just an agricultural show' and provided rich marketing platforms to generate pre-publicity.

However, recognising that media coverage alone would not sell tickets, brokering strategic partnerships with target publications and organisations was also central to JBP's strategy.

**FIGURE 22.3** Ladies' Day at Bath and West Show

The Bath and West Banger was a competition created and launched by JBP six months in advance of the show, the theme of which was to see a new Bath and West themed sausage served at the show. Having researched and identified a regional food producer to partner with – Westaways Sausages – JBP launched a nationwide competition asking for members of the public to create a limited edition sausage flavour that best represented the Bath and West Show.

Buzz about the competition was generated through press coverage and social media channels, which resulted in 325 quality entries. JBP then used various stages of the competition process (appointing a judging panel of local media personalities, announcing the finalists, making the sausage, launching the winning flavour) to engage the media. The winning sausage was a flavour-packed Westcountry pork, Devon farmhouse Cheddar, sweet caramelised onions and dark ale from Bath Ale.

Results included live taster sessions with BBC Radio Bristol, ITV West interview about the making of the winning sausage. This all supported pre-show awareness. Audience reach for this activity across media channels was 2,954,456. As an added bonus in the weeks running up to the show, the winning sausage was sold in selected South West supermarkets. Packaging featured details promoting the show – exposing details about the show to food lovers. During the show, free samples of the Bath and West Banger were made available to visitors. This attracted footfall to the food tent during the show, along with additional media coverage.

Ladies' Day was the second campaign platform devised and implemented by JBP. To generate awareness and front the campaign, local fashion celebrity Gill Cockwell (founder of fashion label Gilly Woo Couture and star of BBC series *Turn Back Time*) was asked to judge a 'best dressed' competition on the day. JBP also identified and secured partnerships with relevant brands, including Neal's Yard, to provide exclusive goodie bags for Ladies' Day ticket holders at no extra cost to the show. JBP launched a competition on Facebook to find a team of fashion scouts who would help find the 'best dressed in show' on Ladies' Day. In total, 120 Ladies' Day tickets were sold, which generated an additional £2,000 worth of income. The Ladies' Day PR campaign reached an audience of 970,000.

JBP research highlighted that many of the target customer groups – foodies, horse lovers, parents – were engaged with Facebook and Twitter social media channels. This steered us to create a specific social media campaign which was launched four months prior to the show. When we started the campaign we had to create a new Facebook page, so started from zero followers. The Bath and West Twitter pages had 750 followers. We contacted every show exhibitor – through their show exhibitor pack – to sign them up to supporting social media activity. This included requesting offers of incentives, prizes and news – all providing JBP with quality content. On a daily basis, JBP interacted with both Twitter and Facebook – posting news about the show's features, competitions and exhibitors' offers. We also retweeted quality content and targeted new followers. During the show, JBP encouraged exhibitors to participate in Tweeting live; this resulted in significant online conversations – a first for the Bath and West Show. Campaign efforts delivered just under 1,000 new Twitter followers, 637 Facebook fans, 400 @ mentions and thirty retweets of show activity.

JBP also brokered strategic partnerships with six organisations and media groups. The most high-profile partnership was with *The Daily Telegraph*. Subscribers to the paper were offered an exclusive '2-4-1' on show tickets in return for four adverts plus a landing page on DailyTelegraph.co.uk for one month. The advertising value alone of this deal was worth £40,000 without taking into consideration the audience reach and the 600 ticket sales generated as a result. JBP arranged partnerships with niche interest/media groups including *Somerset Life*, Moneysavingexpert.com, Neal's Yard Remedies, and Westaways Sausages. These partnerships involved running exclusive ticket offers via member newsletters, websites or editorial coverage.

While press coverage evaluation was important to evaluating the success of the campaign, success was also measured against the objectives laid down by the client at the outset. With several county shows, such as the Highland Show, reporting a decline in visitor numbers in 2010 and 2011, the results more than met the campaign objectives.

## Boost advance ticket sales

- Early advance ticket sales were the highest in six years, 12 per cent up on 2010. The advance ticket sales showed correlation with the pre-show media coverage and activity generated by the Bath and West Banger, social media and Ladies' Day campaigns.
- *The Daily Telegraph* partnership sold 600 tickets.
- Ladies' Day tickets sold 120 tickets and delivered £2,000 worth of additional ticket sales income.

## Maintaining visitor numbers

- Overall visitor numbers to the show were 160,300 visitors, an additional 4,500 visitors compared to the previous year (155,629).

## Expose the show to new audiences

- Total reach of media coverage was just under 11 million (10,753,732) with 129 items of coverage generated.
- Ladies' Day reached a new audience of 970,000 via lifestyle media.
- Bath and West Banger targeted a regional 'foodie' audience of over 2,954,456.

## Establish a national media profile for the show

- *The Daily Telegraph* partnership was worth £40,000 in free advertising.
- Generated editorial coverage across national titles including in *The Daily Telegraph/The Times/Daily Mirror/*BBC online /Heart FM */Somerset Life*.

## Explore new channels for promoting the show

Five strategic partnerships brokered for the show via new channels through networks and contacts:

- Gill Cockwell fashion couture fronted the Ladies' Day campaign free of charge but delivered significant media coverage for the show.

- Westaways Sausages delivered significant media coverage and exposure. They funded the sausage productions and also supported the show through their on-pack promotion across South West retail outlets.

- Neal's Yard sponsored Ladies' Day to the tune of £25 worth of goodies for every Ladies' Day ticket.

- *Life Magazine* Group – negotiated series of double-page spreads about food attractions at the show. This included a promotion offer which delivered 5 per cent of ticket sales.

- Heart FM – supported the campaigns for Ladies' Day and Bath and West Banger, which resulted in high levels of radio exposure and online support through their website.

In total, JBP generated 129 pieces of coverage for the Bath and West Show 2011. Having cancelled their advertising spend in favour of PR, the board of the Bath and West also judged their investment on advertising value equivalent. The total PR value of this press coverage was £120,000.

*Lis Anderson MCIPR, Director, JBP PR and Parliamentary Affairs*

## END POINT

Promoting consumer products is one of the bread-and-butter areas of public relations. PR needs to work with marketing and other communication disciplines to make sure all messages are consistent and coherent. Practitioners also need to keep on top of developments in channels of communication, so that they are reaching customers in their preferred ways. Developments in new technology provide exciting ways to communicate more directly with customers, but it is important not to forget that the best communications always have a human touch.

# Appendix

# PR BRIEF CHECKLIST

☐ Statement of the nature of the issue/opportunity for which a proposal is required

☐ Aims and objectives to be achieved (including baseline data and success criteria)

☐ Background information on the issue, sector and organisation (historical/current)

☐ Profile of the organisation, including vision, mission, values and objectives

☐ Organisational/management structure

☐ Profile of similar/competitive organisations

☐ Operational information relating to the organisation and/or the sector, e.g. details of product/services, stakeholder/customer profiles, unique points of interest, etc.

☐ Information regarding the PR resource (in-house or consultancy, history, size, structure, reporting lines, remit, etc.)

☐ Details of existing PR personnel (responsibilities, competencies, relationships)

☐ Background on previous PR activities, including reviews and results

☐ Profile of stakeholders/publics (historical and current data, plus forecasts) and response requirements in respect of issue/opportunity being addressed

☐ Guide to organisational narrative, messages, culture, style, branding, etc.

☐ Communications audit information including channels, feedback mechanisms

☐ Identification of issues that could affect the implementation of a PR campaign

☐ Information on other communications activities (e.g. advertising) that could impact PR or be integrated with the campaign, including objectives and timings

☐ Nature of the required proposal – format, deadlines, etc.

☐ Resources available (including budget, approved suppliers, in-house resource)

☐ Timeframe for the campaign

☐ Contact details of the client

☐ Information regarding the decision-making process

☐ Details required regarding the consultancy and team members (if appropriate)

# RESEARCH PROPOSAL CHECKLIST

☐ **Background**: brief description of the company, details of the main business issue or problem being addressed, explanation of why research is required and how results will be used

☐ **Outline of any existing research** and explanation of any unusual or specific issues to be aware of when conducting the research

☐ **Details of business and research objectives**: how the research will be used to address a key business issue or objective (and by whom), key information needs (including broad question areas), segmentation needs (audience/country/sector)

☐ **Details of research subjects**: method of defining and characteristics (e.g. of individuals, groups, companies), segmentation approaches, access (e.g. existing database or free/purchased lists), details of subjects to be excluded

☐ **Thoughts on research approach**: need for measurable (quantitative) information, statistical considerations, sampling and analysis requirements, need for in-depth, exploratory (qualitative) information

☐ **Required deliverables**: whether findings will be disseminated through a presentation or debrief workshop (and to whom). Requirements for interim report or executive summary, format required for feedback to support decision-making. Specific outputs (e.g. printed copies of presentations/reports, data tabulations, data files, an online portal to host data, etc.)

☐ **Timing** – key deadlines, cross-sectional vs. longitudinal

☐ **Resources** – budget, existing resources (e.g. research mechanisms), suppliers

☐ **Requirements of the research team** – experience of similar work, qualifications and quality standards, membership of professional bodies, etc.

# ANALYTICAL TOOLS CHECKLIST

**Analysing the situation**

☐ Content analysis of media coverage (traditional and social)

☐ Review of industry/sector: players, reports, positioning statements

☐ Feedback mechanisms

☐ Timeline and history of issue/opportunity

☐ Crisis preparedness: processes, systems, training

☐ Crisis prevention: risk scanning and analysis

☐ Case studies and previous situations: evaluation/reviews

☐ Force field analysis

☐ Scenario/trend forecasting

**Analysing the organisation**

☐ Internal and external data and reports (including media reports)

☐ Reputational and performance rankings

☐ Cultural web

☐ PESTEL/SWOT analysis

☐ Organisational charts

☐ Comparative, competitor and industry reviews

☐ Core competencies

☐ Communications audit

☐ Boston Matrix, Ansoff and other marketing/positioning tools

**Analysing the public**

☐ Stakeholder analysis (including mapping)

☐ Influencer mapping: media, opinion leaders, friends/foes

☐ Segmentation: demographics, geodemographics, lifestage, psychographics and lifestyle

☐ Qualitative insight (e.g. ZMET)

☐ Identification and mapping of publics (situational model)

☐ Identification and analysis of relevant groups (including membership, leadership and influence)

☐ Media usage (information seeking or processing behaviour)

☐ Cognitive research (existing knowledge/understanding)

☐ Balance scorecard and gap analysis

☐ Attitude/opinion research (quantitative and qualitative)

☐ Co-orientation and relationship mapping research

☐ Behavioural data (including loyalty ladders, Rogers' diffusion of innovation, etc.)

☐ Relationship mapping of publics to issue and organisation

# PESTEL CHECKLIST

Audit and analysis undertaken at national, sector, organisation, publics or issue level, covering short-, medium- or long-term perspectives, to identify and gain insight into issues that impact significantly on the organisation and its operations.

**Political factors:**

☐ Local, regional, national, international government policies and plans

☐ Statements issued by relevant institutions and individuals.

☐ Incidents arising that have potential political impact

☐ Bodies and campaigns seeking change in policies

☐ Direct or indirect influences on politicians

☐ Political structure, election process, etc.

**Sources**: Monitoring political communications (e.g. parliament, agenda setting media, social media). Review policy papers by key bodies (think tanks, political parties, NGOs, etc.). Analyse reports from industry bodies, academics and opinion leaders. Opinion research among political stakeholders and relevant publics on issues.

**Economic factors:**

☐ Economic indices (interest rates, taxation, growth data, inflation, exchange rates)

☐ Impact on key resources e.g. labour, disposable incomes, grants/finance

☐ Trends in economic prosperity and confidence of individuals, organisations, society

☐ Controls and influences on economic environment, e.g. political decisions

☐ Internal financial position and pressures

**Sources:** Reports from financial bodies, institutions and analysts, financial media monitoring, announcement of financial data, statistics and indices. Surveys of confidence. Internal financial reports and contacts.

**Socio-cultural:**

☐ Nature and impact of demographic, cultural and social trends (e.g. gender roles, education levels, moral norms, family composition, aging community, etc.)

☐ Health, food and other human considerations

☐ Attitudes towards sector, business, CSR, etc.

☐ Industry trends and competitor actions

☐ Statements released by think tanks, NGOs, charities, etc.

☐ Changing media usage (e.g. fragmentation, convergence)

☐ Interest in issues, civic pluralism, levels of activism, emerging campaigns

**Sources:** Reports from think tanks, NGOs/charities, demographic data, government research. Public opinion surveys. Internal market research data, product development research. Monitoring leading edge media and opinion leaders.

**Technological:**

☐ Communication technologies (including social media)

☐ Working practices and operational technologies

☐ Transport infrastructure, energy and other resources

☐ Security systems (e.g. relating to crisis management, data protection, etc.)

☐ Internal financial position and pressures

☐ Barriers and drivers of change: access, skills, efficacy, cost, ROI

**Sources:** Technology/ news media (traditional and online), websites and forums. Research reports from think-tanks, conferences/exhibitions. Contact with experts and industry leaders. Academic journals/ presentations. Industry publications: newsletters, designer/ engineer reports, information from suppliers and trade bodies.

**Environmental:**

☐ Impact on (and of) natural environment (including biodiversity)

☐ Impact of (and on) local, national, international urban environment – e.g. pollution, congestion, construction and development

☐ Migration, tourism and other human factors

☐ Health considerations, including transmission models

☐ Attitudes towards environmental technologies

☐ Consumer trends (e.g. purchase of 'green' products/services)

☐ Environmental trends, policies and expectations (including social responsibility)

☐ Drivers from legislation, economy, technology or socio-cultural factors

☐  Compliance and reporting requirements

☐  Reports from and about relevant NGOs, charities and activists

**Sources**: Specialist and general media (traditional and online). Research reports, sustainability, CSR and environmental reports, studies and surveys, academic journals and presentations, contact with experts, international conventions.

**Legal:**

☐  Regulatory framework (local, national and international)

☐  Existing and proposed legislation

☐  Influences on legislation (including campaigns)

☐  Processes and opportunity for participation in legislative process

☐  Constraints and consequences on compliance with legal framework

☐  Ethical issues

**Sources**: National archive of UK legislation (www.legislation.gov.uk), media coverage, consultation procedures, monitoring NGO and activist campaigns, statistics and reports, high-profile cases, contact with legal and HR personnel.

# SWOT CHECKLIST

Supports reflection on significance of results from the PESTEL audit or consideration of the internal environment in relation to a particular scenario.

| FACTOR | List relevant factors, e.g. social media |
| --- | --- |
| **INTERNAL ANALYSIS** | |
| **Strengths** | List existing competencies and other advantages |
| **Weaknesses/ Limitations** | List issues relating to potential problems |
| **EXTERNAL ANALYSIS** | |
| **Opportunities** | Identify how this factor presents opportunities |
| **Threats** | Identify how this factor presents risk or other negative outcome |

Example considerations:

| STRENGTHS | WEAKNESSES/LIMITATIONS |
|---|---|
| ☐  Strong financial resources | ☐  Conservative culture |
| ☐  Superior market position | ☐  Outdated products |
| ☐  Industry leading products/services | ☐  High staff turnover |
| ☐  Respected leadership | ☐  Reactive communications |
| **OPPORTUNITIES** | **THREATS** |
| ☐  Emerging markets | ☐  Economic instability |
| ☐  Social changes | ☐  Cultural trends |
| ☐  Access to finance | ☐  Strong competitors |
| ☐  New legislation | ☐  Technological developments |

The SWOT analysis is an evaluative tool that should be based on research and reflection. It involves looking backwards as well as anticipating issues and opportunities. Alongside a risk analysis, it enables action plans to be developed to maximise opportunities and act on strengths or to address weaknesses/limitations and avoid threats.

# COMMUNICATIONS AUDIT CHECKLIST

**Step 1 – Audit plan**

☐  Objective – e.g. to gain feedback, to inform review process, to initiate improvements, to evaluate content, to compare channels, etc.

☐  Method – e.g. content analysis, interviews, focus group or survey, etc.

☐  Framework – identification of assessment criteria, e.g. usability, cost, compliance to style guidelines, recall of key messages

☐  Timetable – e.g. annual/routine process or for a specific purpose

☐  Data analysis – process to review findings and identify recommendations

☐  Outcome – e.g. use by management, to evaluate improvements, etc.

## Step 2 – Identification of communication channels

| Stakeholder/ Channel * | Internal | Local community | Influencers | Trade | Political | Media | Financial | Customers | Public |
|---|---|---|---|---|---|---|---|---|---|
| Marketing | | | | | | | | | |
| Media relations | | | | | | | | | |
| Correspondence | | | | | | | | | |
| Presentations | | | | | | | | | |
| Publications | | | | | | | | | |
| Social media | | | | | | | | | |
| Website | | | | | | | | | |

\* In use, this framework requires further segmentation of stakeholders/publics and also more specific identification of communication channel.

## Step 3 – Assessment of communication channels

| CHANNEL | DETAILS | OBJECTIVE | AUDIT OUTCOME |
|---|---|---|---|
| *For example:* Employee magazine | Monthly (print). Full colour, glossy 24-page<br><br>Produced by external agency | • To increase understanding of company plans<br><br>• To inform staff of business development<br><br>• To improve motivation | Readership survey identifies positive rating by 65% of staff<br><br>Management specify need to cut production cost by 20%<br><br>Content analysis shows 100% compliance with corporate style |

# SEGMENTATION CHECKLIST

| METHOD | CRITERIA |
|---|---|
| **Demographics** | ☐ Personal characteristics: age group, gender, education level, family size, income, occupation, religion, ethnicity, nationality, etc. |
| | ☐ Socio-economic (A,B,C1,C2,D,E) |
| | ☐ Lifestage: newly married, full nest, empty nest, retired, solitary survivor |
| **Geographics** | ☐ Residential, 'drive to work', employment, shopping, etc. |
| | ☐ Level: society, continent, country, region, town, postcode |
| | ☐ Environment: coastal, country, urban, suburban, etc. |
| | ☐ Terminology: Third World, BRIC, Eurozone, EMEA (Europe, Middle East and Africa), etc. |
| | ☐ Market: size, nature, territory (e.g. sales or retail), etc. |
| | ☐ Media: ITV/BBC regions, etc. |
| **Geodemographics** | ☐ ACORN (www.caci.co.uk) |
| | ☐ MOSAIC (www.experian.co.uk) |
| **Stakeholders** | ☐ Bernstein: internal, local, influential groups, trade, government, media, financial, customer, general public |
| | ☐ Intra-stakeholder, e.g. employees: occupation, department, location, grade level, union membership, length of service |
| | ☐ External by issue: economic, socio/political, technological |
| **Behaviour** | ☐ Usage: occasional, high, habitual, etc. |
| | ☐ Technology: silver surfers, baby boomers, Gen X, Gen Y, Net Generation, Mobile Generation |
| | ☐ Sales: prospect, customer, client, supporter, advocate, partner |
| | ☐ Loyalty: hard-core, split, shifting, switchers |
| | ☐ Decision roles: initiator, influencer, decider, buyer, user |
| | ☐ Innovation: innovators, early adopter, early majority, late majority, laggards |
| | ☐ Publics: non, latent, aware, active (single, all, hot issue) |
| | ☐ Information seeking vs. information processing |

| Psychographics | ☐ Attitudes, opinions, beliefs, values, interests, lifestyle, motivations, self-esteem |
| --- | --- |
| | ☐ AIO (attitudes, interests, opinions) |
| | ☐ RISC 8 socio-cultural variables shaping European society: self-development, hedonism, plasticity, vitality, connectivity, ethics, belonging, inertia |
| | ☐ SINUS typology: Basic orientation: Traditional (to preserve), Materialistic (to have). Changing values: Hedonism (to indulge), Post-materialism (to be), Postmodernism (to have, to be and to indulge) |
| | ☐ VALS: innovators, thinkers, achievers, experiencers (all with high level of resources) plus believers, strivers, makers and survivors (with lower resources) |
| Group | ☐ Demographic, geographic, etc. |
| | ☐ Purpose (interest or pressure group), motivation for joining, relationship to organisation, etc. |
| | ☐ Industry sector (UK standard industrial classification) |
| | ☐ Presence: local, national, multinational, international |
| | ☐ Number of employees |
| | ☐ Financial criteria |
| | ☐ Reputation |
| | ☐ Psychographic, behavioural characteristics |

# STAKEHOLDER MAPPING

| | LOW INTEREST | HIGH INTEREST |
| --- | --- | --- |
| LOW POWER | Minimal effort | Keep informed |
| HIGH POWER | Keep satisfied | Key players: keep informed and satisfied |

Groups and/or individuals can be mapped by researching or assessing levels of interest and power.

# TOOLS, TECHNIQUES AND TACTICS CHECKLIST

**Action component**

- ☐ Briefings
- ☐ Meetings
- ☐ Launch events (including openings)
- ☐ Product reviews and demonstrations
- ☐ Facility visits and open events
- ☐ Tours (personal appearances, media interviews, speaking engagements, presentations, roadshow events)
- ☐ Exhibition/conference/convention presence
- ☐ Educational activities (e.g. outreach programmes, school liaison, seminars, 'meet the professionals' events, etc.)
- ☐ Celebrity events (launches, photo-opportunities, parties, other social activities)
- ☐ Awards (launches, short-list, presentation events)
- ☐ Festivals, shows and other community events
- ☐ Webinars and other online events
- ☐ Press conferences
- ☐ Panel and round-table discussions
- ☐ Stunts, pseudo-events and special opportunities (e.g. record-breaking attempts, calendar celebrations – annual, day, week, month, milestones and anniversaries)
- ☐ Contests, quizzes and other promotional activities
- ☐ Fan clubs (real world or virtual, e.g. via social networking)
- ☐ Sponsorship maximisation (e.g. sports, arts, community)
- ☐ Social responsibility activities (e.g. community, charity or fund-raising events)
- ☐ Networking and hospitality activities (social and professional)
- ☐ Experiential occasions, gamification, online presence in virtual worlds, etc.

**Communication component**

- ☐ Corporate identity, branding, style and narrative guidelines
- ☐ Media information (press releases, media kits, feature articles, case studies, etc.)
- ☐ Multimedia resources (including audio/visual materials)
- ☐ Positioning statements, briefing documents, factsheets and Q & A responses
- ☐ Speeches and presentations
- ☐ White papers and opinion leader commentary (e.g. guest blog posts)
- ☐ Annual reports, sustainability and other corporate reports

☐ Educational materials (e.g. student website materials, school resource packs, competitions, etc.)

☐ Email, letters, SMS, invitations and other correspondence

☐ Polls and surveys (traditional and online)

☐ Websites and micro-sites (internal and external)

☐ Apps, QR codes, games and other online/mobile interactivity

☐ Social media (blogs, forums, video, micro-blogging, social networks, photography sites)

☐ Imagery (photographs, graphics, logos)

☐ Visualisations, transmedia story-telling and infographics

☐ Online newsroom

☐ Multimedia press release

☐ Monitoring methods (RSS feeds, searches, dashboards, cuttings analysis, feedback, surveys, sales and other data)

☐ Corporate publications (printed and digital, e.g. books, newsletters, magazines, etc. for various stakeholders, including internal)

☐ Corporate advertising

☐ Brochures, leaflets and other printed collateral

☐ Posters, exhibition materials

☐ Plans, reports, minutes and other management materials

**Support services**

☐ Press release (media information) distribution

☐ Media monitoring services

☐ Media directories

☐ Media training

☐ Multi-media companies

☐ Designers, printers, web designers and other visual crafts

☐ Photographers

☐ Research companies

☐ Event management and sponsorship companies

☐ Specialist PR agencies: consumer, finance, lobbying sector experts, etc.

The tools, techniques and tactics chosen need to be considered within a strategic and creative framework. They should be mapped against time and resource limitations with a rationale decision-making process employed to determine cost-benefit and other reasons for selecting appropriate tools, techniques and tactics.

# DECISION-MAKING GUIDELINES

- ☐ Detail the problem or opportunity where a decision is required

- ☐ Determine risk/likelihood of best/worst case results occurring

- ☐ Specify factors influencing the need for decision-making (what makes this a significant matter outside routine decision-making processes)

- ☐ Identify responsibilities, deadlines and resources available in respect of planning, decision-making, solution implementation and evaluation

- ☐ Collect data on situation, publics/stakeholders and organisation

- ☐ Sort research information – analyse, prioritise, review, edit, identify key factors

- ☐ Visualise the situation and possible consequences – use diagrams (e.g. flow charts) to illustrate impact of decision

- ☐ Quantify the nature of the problem/opportunity where feasible and/or identify specific qualitative impacts (graphical representation of information is helpful)

- ☐ Identify root cause of problems or opportunity, use techniques such as Ishikawa (fishbone) diagram to consider possible causes and effects. List main considerations and continuously ask 'why?' to reach back to possible causes. Use diagram to track results back through a process: i.e. this happens because . . .

- ☐ Determine whether additional research is required (avoid paralysis by analysis)

- ☐ Specify which causes can be addressed

- ☐ Identify possible limitations (e.g. time considerations), risks or bias and stipulate acceptable levels of tolerance

- ☐ Detail assessment criteria – cost-benefit, balanced-scorecard, impact

- ☐ Develop possible solutions or ideas to address the problem/opportunity

- ☐ Determine cost and possible consequences of actions

- ☐ Evaluate possible solutions objectively according to assessment criteria

- ☐ Test viability of preferred 2 or 3 solutions/opportunities

- ☐ Summarise chosen solution succinctly to focus on key deliverables and outcomes

- ☐ Gain agreement from key decision-makers to implement solution (subject to ongoing monitoring and evaluation)

- ☐ Assess decision-making procedures and the selected solution to ensure a continuous, adaptive, circular decision-making process

# STATUS REPORTS

Where feasible, a single page overview should be produced, using visual elements (e.g. infographic approach) to enable key metrics to be assessed immediately. More detail can be presented using tables that update status and help inform and manage resource requirements. For example:

| STATUS REPORT | | | |
|---|---|---|---|
| **Name of project/topic: Launch of product X** | | **Date: 1 June** | |
| Circulation to: JT, MS, DR, JB | | Report prepared by: John Bright | |
| **Task** | **Responsibility** | **Action date** | **Comments** |
| **Writing project launch press release** | Mandy Smith (MS) | 7 June | Success criteria: complete task to required standard by deadline |
| • Research new product features | MS | 31 May (completed) | Liaise with product development (PD) |
| • Draft release for approval | MS | 3 June | Approval from PD and marketing |
| • Finalise release | MS | 7 June | |

# SCHEDULING APPROACH

- ☐ A linear grid (GANTT chart) enables visualisation, planning and implementation of programmes of work

- ☐ Apply critical path analysis to order tasks and determine project duration, sequencing of activities, dependencies and possible problem points

- ☐ A PERT (Project Evaluation and Review Technique) chart can be used to illustrate flow of tasks, determine sequential and parallel activities, identify decision points and note milestones (e.g. critical deadlines, review stages, etc.)

- ☐ Visualise resource requirements by colour coding responsibilities and using a unit measurement to indicate hours or days required

- ☐ Distinguish planning, implementation and evaluation phases

- ☐ Determine an appropriate timeframe: year, month, week, day or hours

- ☐ Prepare one or more grid for the project, task, individual, campaign or annual programme

- ☐ Using technology, e.g. Microsoft Project or a spreadsheet, enables data to be represented in different forms

- ☐ Update the grid frequently – if feasible use online methods (e.g. Google Docs) to enable all participants to report progress

| | WEEK 1 (HOURS) | | | | | WEEK 2 (HOURS) | | | | |
|---|---|---|---|---|---|---|---|---|---|---|
| Task – producing webpage | M | T | W | T | F | M | T | W | T | F |
| Researching content | 8 | | | | | | | | | |
| First draft of content | | 8 | | | | | | | | |
| Approval by manager | | | ▤ | | | | | | | |
| Amend first draft | | | | 2 | | | | | | |
| Get final sign off | | | | | 1 | | | | | |
| Upload onto website | | | | | 1 | 1 | | | | |
| Review web statistics | | | | | | | | .5 | ■ | |
| Prepare report for manager | | | | | | | | | | ■ |

# MOVEMENT SCHEDULE

It is helpful to produce a schedule for the day of an activity (e.g. an event) to help everyone involved to see an overview and personal detail of implementation. An adapted GANTT chart can be used to produce documents for each person showing who is involved in which activity at what time. Another format could plot time and people with activities listed in the body of the table.

# BUDGETING APPROACH

☐ Identify whether a specific budget has been allocated or if a budget needs to be determined based on the recommended course of action

☐ Determine factors affecting budget, e.g. quality standards, time available, brand values, etc.

☐ Specify key budget measures (e.g. delivery on or within budget, break even or profit requirements, savings on previous expenditure, income (sponsorship, attendance, etc.) figures)

☐ List key headings (including administration and incidental costs e.g. postage, telephone, as well as research and evaluation) and determine which need to be included in the budget

☐ Calculate the involvement of in-house resources (within the PR department and other areas) and assess against cost of sourcing externally (cost-benefit analysis)

☐ Identify the external resource requirements (consultancies, freelance, bought in services). Obtain quotations to deliver the required work (to specified deadline)

☐ Detail and cost any skills, knowledge and training needs required to undertake activities

☐ Identify additional bought costs (catering, accommodation, print, etc.)

☐ Distinguish between fixed and variable costs (e.g. venue hire is fixed, catering varies according to the number of attendees)

☐ Indicate any long term requirements relating to the campaign which carry budget implications (cross-over of budget years, inflation considerations, opportunities to negotiate discounts, etc.)

☐ Ensure programme can be delivered within specified or realistic budget. If costs exceed amount, then determine optional elements that can be proposed and removed where possible (clarify benefits and impact of any decisions)

☐ Sanity check whether the stated outcomes can be achieved by an alternate programme at a lower cost and any implications or benefits of different options

☐ Identify budget control measures and how any variance will be addressed (i.e. contingency allowance, need to eliminate aspects or renegotiation terms)

| ITEM | DETAILS OF COSTING | ESTIMATED COST | ACTUAL COST |
|------|--------------------|-----------------|-------------|
|      |                    |                 |             |
|      |                    |                 |             |
|      |                    |                 |             |
| **Total cost** |          |                 |             |
| **Difference** |          |                 |             |

# SUPPLIER BRIEFS

A number of different suppliers may be required when planning a PR campaign, e.g.:

Graphic designers

Proof-readers

Web designers

Event specialists

Printers

Research/evaluation companies

Photographers

Venue providers

Writers

Exhibition designers

Caterers

PR consultancies

All suppliers (even if internal or where there is an established relationship) should be briefed and contracts (detailing requirements and costs) put in place prior to starting a project. These should be in writing rather than verbal agreements or assuming parties are in agreement over essential details.

| | |
|---|---|
| Purpose of brief | |
| Client name | |
| Contact details | |
| Dates | |
| Background | |
| Vision/target messages | |
| Objectives | |
| Target audience | |
| Parameters of project | |
| Approach | |
| Specific tasks | |
| Criteria for success | |
| Timeframe | |
| Budget | |
| Special considerations | |
| Additional information | |

# RISK MANAGEMENT CHECKLIST

This process may be undertaken (adapted as necessary) at the organisational, departmental and/or campaign level by the PR function or an external consultancy.

**STEP 1 – Identify possible areas of risk**

☐ Undertake a risk audit to identify areas that could reasonably be expected to cause an issue (with financial, legal or reputational consequences) in respect of the organisation's operations, the PR function's areas of responsibility and/or campaigns being planned

☐ Identify existing organisational policies, legal requirements, or societal expectations relating to the area where operations could present risk to compliance

☐ Ask stakeholders for their input into areas of concern

☐ Research areas of risk identified by experts (such as professional bodies) where practical guidance on action may be available

☐ Review internal records and external reports (including media and social media) to identify issues that have occurred in the past

☐ Take a long-term perspective to identify issues that may emerge over time as well as more immediate risks

**STEP 2 – Decide who might be affected and how**

☐ Undertake an audit of stakeholders and influencers (see Chapter 6) considering the psychology and requirements of various parties in relation to the identified areas of risk

☐ Map a chain of involvement to show connections between stakeholder groups and influencers where issues could arise from their dynamic engagement

☐ Consider others (e.g. suppliers or competitors) whose actions in relation to the issue could affect stakeholders' perceptions of the organisation

☐ Ask different functions within the organisation to identify their stakeholders and how the area of risk could affect them

**STEP 3 – Evaluate the risks and decide on precautions**

☐ Produce a detailed risk profile for each aspect identified

☐ Specify the probability and possible legal, financial or reputational consequences (threats and opportunities) of the identified areas of risk (using quantitative and qualitative estimates as appropriate)

☐ Highlight risk factors as presenting a high, medium or low level of threat in terms of likelihood of occurrence and potential consequence to produce a 3 x 3 matrix

☐ Rank the identified risks to produce an overall record to inform development of possible precautions or control procedures

☐ Determine (or review) the organisation's established risk criteria in order to determine acceptable levels of cost, benefit, compliance, consequential damage and so forth

☐ Record whether the identified area presents an acceptable level of risk or requires precautionary solutions to be implemented

☐ Determine whether any area risk could be eliminated by implementing simple precautions or controls

☐ Identify what would be considered 'reasonably practical' precautions within the existing regulatory and compliance framework

☐ Review sources of good practice (for example, from existing case studies, such as those presented in *The PR Toolkit*) and compare with the organisation's precautionary measures

☐ Assess existing precautionary or control measures in a test situation and adjust as necessary

☐ Seek to reduce or control the level of risk by adopting different strategies, reducing exposure to the risk, implementing protective procedures

☐ Involve stakeholders in determining the validity of proposed precautions

☐ Review the proposed solutions to ensure they do not introduce additional areas of risk and provide benefits in reduced risk at an acceptable cost

☐ Evaluate the solutions proposed and determine which will be implemented, assigning responsibilities where appropriate

**STEP 4 – Record findings and implement them**

☐ Document the risk assessment procedure and share its results (implementing training where necessary in the process and completion of documentation)

☐ Keep records simple and accessible

☐ Ensure senior management is advised of the most significant risks identified and proposed method of addressing these to obtain their endorsement where appropriate

☐ Demonstrate that a proper check has been undertaken that involved key stakeholders, dealt with the most significant hazards and identified reasonable precautions to reduce the level of risk

☐ Produce a structured assessment of each risk identified covering its scope, nature, probability, and significance, including details of priorities and recommended action

☐ Produce a plan of action that prioritises the most important improvements to be made

☐ Consider temporary solutions, which can be implemented until more reliable, long-term controls are in place

☐ Introduce a process of regular checks to ensure precautions and control measures stay in place

☐ Assign clear responsibilities of who will lead on what action, and by when

☐ Review the plan of action to ensure that action is completed

☐ Identify indicators to ensure early warning for the risks identified as part of an ongoing monitoring process

☐ Integrate the risk assessment, management and reporting process into the organisation's crisis management procedures

☐ Produce a risk management policy which covers the key considerations used in informing the action plan which can be used as a guide for future risk assessment

☐ Ensure risk management procedures are integrated across the organisation to identify areas where PR may be impacted or impact

**STEP 5 – Review the process and update if necessary**

☐ Identify required resources and secure to enable identified issues to be addressed

☐ Establish individual responsibilities for identified risk management within the PR team

☐ Monitor risk indicators to ensure responsiveness and effectiveness of procedures that have been implemented

☐ Establish a process to identify and address additional and new areas of risk that may arise

☐ Undertake a formal regular review (e.g. quarterly or annually) of risk management processes

☐ Identify any areas of change and improvements that can be made

☐ Consider any issues that have arisen, determine the effectiveness of procedures, identify lessons that can be learned and update risk management processes

☐ Ensure that when change occurs or issues arise, the risk assessment and management processes are reviewed and amended as appropriate

☐ Report systematically on the risk management process for the PR function to senior management and, where appropriate, to external stakeholders

☐ Integrate risk management performance into governance processes such as sustainability and responsibility reports

☐ Ensure that risk management based on an adaptive and flexible strategy rather than adherence to procedures and policies is established within the culture of the organisation

# RISK AUDIT

Used to identify areas of risk that could impact on the organisation achieving its objectives:

## Risk identification techniques

Areas of risk can be identified using the following methods:

☐ Management reports

☐ Questionnaires

☐ Industry benchmarks or organisational studies

☐ Scenario forecasting

☐ Stakeholder workshops

☐ Incident investigation

☐ Observational studies

## Risk analysis techniques

Data and information obtained can then be examined using:

☐ SWOT analysis (strengths, weaknesses, opportunities, threats)

☐ PESTEL analysis (political, economic, socio-cultural, technological, environmental and legal issues)

☐ Projection and trend analysis

☐ Flow diagram representation

☐ Critical path analysis

☐ Stakeholder mapping

☐ Option modelling

☐ Decision-making process

# Bibliography

Adkins, S. (2006) 'Putting your marketing where your values are', *Market Leader*, Winter 2006: 2–5.

Aladenoye, A. (2011) 'Lessons we can learn from Lady Gaga', http://blog.ogilvypr.com/2011/04/3-lessons-we-can-learn-from-lady-gaga/ [Accessed: 1 December 2011].

Allen, K. (2010) 'Survey says . . . PR firms (still) the No.1 source for journalists', www.prdaily.com/Main/Articles/Survey_says_PR_firms_still_the_No_1_source_for_jou_8315.aspx# [Accessed 1 December 2011].

Allen, P. (2011) 'Google+ growth accelerating. Passes 62 million users. Adding 625,000 new users per day. Prediction: 400 million users by end of 2012', http://plus.google.com/117388252776312694644/posts/ZcPA5ztMZaj [Accessed: 27 December 2011].

Altimeter (2011) 'How Corporations Should Prioritize Social Business Budgets', www.slideshare.net/jeremiah_owyang/how-corporations-should-prioritize-social-business-budgets [Accessed 1 December 2011].

Ambrose, G. and Harris, P. (2007) *The Visual Dictionary of Fashion Design,* Worthing: AVA Publishing.

AMEC (2011) 'Report gives welcome to Measurement Agenda – but AVEs use still high', http://amecorg.com/2011/07/report-gives-welcome-to-measurement-agenda-but-aves-use-still-high/ [Accessed: 1 December 2011].

Anderson, F.W., Hadley, L., Rockland, D. and Weiner, M. (1999) *Guidelines for Setting Measurable Public Relations Objectives: an update*, Gainesville, FL: Institute for Public Relations.

Andreasen, A.R. (1994) 'Social marketing: its definition and domain', *Journal of Public Policy & Marketing,* 13 (1): 108–114.

Andreasen, A.R. (2006) *Social Marketing in the 21st Century,* London: Sage.

Appleyard, B. (2003) 'PR: the evil art', www.bryanappleyard.com/pr-the-evil-art/ [Accessed: 31 December 2011].

Arrow, C. (2008) 'What is public relations?', www.catherinearrow.com [Accessed 31 January 2010].

Arrow, C. (2009) 'The future practitioner', submission for *Chartered Practitioner*, August. Accessed via www.cipr.org.uk [Accessed 31 January 2010].

Bacot, E. (2006) 'Which way now for PR?', *PR Business*, 13 July: 17–19.

Bailey, R. (2009) 'Media relations', in R. Tench and L. Yeomans (eds) *Exploring Public Relations* (2nd edition), London: FT/Prentice Hall, pp. 295–315.

Baines, P., Egan, J. and Jefkins, F.W. (2004) *Public Relations: contemporary issues and techniques* (3rd edition), Boston: Elsevier/Butterworth-Heineman.

Ballington, J. (2003) 'Marketing society – effective CRM is built in rather than bolted on', *Media Week*, 30 October.

Balmer, J. (2001) 'Corporate identity, corporate branding and corporate marketing', *European Journal of Marketing*, 35 (3/4): 248–291.

Balmer, J.M.T. and Greyser, S.A. (2006) 'Corporate marketing', *European Journal of Marketing*, 40 (7/8): 730–741.

Bandura, A. (1977) 'Self-efficacy: toward a unifying theory of behavioral change', *Psychological Review*, 84 (2): 191–215.

*Barcelona Declaration of Research Principles* (2010) http://amecorg.com/wp-content/uploads/2011/08/Barcelona_Principles_for_PR_Measurement.pdf [Accessed: 1 December 2011].

Bashford, S. (2006) 'Juggling roles', *PR Week*, 6 July, www.prweek.com/uk/features/567711/ [Accessed: 1 December 2011].

Bashford, S. (2011) 'Client view: Stuart Handley, Dell – the listening revamp', *PR Week*, 12 May, www.prweek.com/uk/features/1069439/client-view-stuart-handley-dell-listening-revamp/ [Accessed: 1 December 2011].

Batchelor, B. (1938) *Profitable Public Relations*, New York: Harper & Brothers.

Beck, U. (1992) *Risk Society: towards a new modernity,* trans. Mark Ritter, London: Sage.

Beke, T. (2011) 'Litigation public relations', History of Public Relations Conference, Bournemouth, 6 July.

Belch, G.E. and Belch, M.A. (2001) *Advertising & Promotion*, Irwin: McGraw-Hill.

Benova, N. (2010) *A Snapshot from Bulgaria*, Research Paper, Apeiron Communication.

Bernstein, D. (1984) *Company Image and Reality*, London: Cassell.

Bettinghaus, E.P. and Cody, M.J. (1994) *Persuasive Communication* (5th edition), Belmont, CA: Wadsworth.

Billingsley, L.G. (2002) 'Healthy choices: reaching multicultural audiences', *Tactics*, August: 19.

BIS (2011) 'Business population estimates for the UK and regions', bis.gov.uk/analysis/statistics/business-population-estimates [Accessed: 1 December 2011].

BITC (2006) *Corporate Responsibility Index 2005*, www.bitc.org.uk/crindex, May [Accessed 31 January 2010].

Bland, M., Theaker, A. and Wragg, D. (1996) *Effective Media Relations*, London: Kogan Page/IPR.

Blyth, A. (2006) 'Guerillas in our midst', *PR Business*, 11 May.

Blyth, A. (2011) 'Feature: pitching a story – have I got a story for you', *PR Week,* 14 April, www.prweek.com/uk/features/1065337/ [Accessed: 1 December 2011].

Blythe, J. (2006) *Principles & Practice of Marketing*, London: Thomson Learning.

Bourland-Davis, P.G., Thompson, W. and Brooks, F.E. (2010) 'Activism in the 20th and 21st centuries', in R.L. Heath (ed.) *The Sage Handbook of Public Relations* (2nd edition), London: Sage, pp. 409–420.

Bovingdon, T. (2011) 'New crisis management standard launched', www.rmprofessional. com/rm/pas_200_launch.php [Accessed 1 December 2011].

Bowd, R. (2005) 'Understanding stakeholder and management perceptions of CSR', CIPR Academic Conference, Lincoln, March.

Bowd, R. (2009) 'Financial public relations', in R. Tench and L. Yeomans (eds) *Exploring Public Relations* (2nd edition), London: FT/Prentice Hall, pp. 462–480.

Bowden-Green, T. (2006) 'Public relations – a one way street?', *Profile*, November/December: 12.

Brabbs, C. (2000) 'Is there profit in CRM tie ups?', *Marketing*, 16 November.

Breitman, K.K., Casanova, M.O. and Truszkowski, W. (2007) *Semantic Web: concepts, technologies and applications,* London: Springer-Verlag.

Brettschneider, F. (2008) 'The news media's use of opinion polls', in W. Donsbach and M.W. Traugott (eds) *The Sage Handbook of Public Opinion Research*, London: Sage, pp. 479–486.

Bridgen, L. (2011) 'Emotional labour and the pursuit of the personal brand: public relations practitioners' use of social media', *Journal of Media Practice* 12 (1): 61–76.

Bright Edge (2011) 'Tracking social adoption and trends', www.brightedge.com/social-share-November-2011-GooglePlus [Accessed: 1 December 2011].

Brill, P. (2011) CIPR Diploma Presentation, Bristol, September.

Broom, G.M. (1982) 'A comparison of sex roles in public relations', *Public Relations Review*, 8 (3): 17–22.

Broom, G.M. (2009) *Cutlip and Center's Effective Public Relations* (10th edition), Upper Saddle River, NJ: Pearson.

Broom, G.M. and Dozier, D.M. (1990) *Using Research in Public Relations*, Englewood Cliffs, NJ: Prentice Hall.

BSI (2011) *Crisis Management: guidance and good practice*, London: British Standards Institution.

Budd, J.F. (1994) *A Pragmatic Examination of Ethical Dilemmas in Public Relations*, IPRA Gold Paper, No. 8.

The Bureau of Investigative Journalism (2011) 'PR uncovered: what Bell Pottinger said', www.thebureauinvestigates.com/2011/12/07/pr-uncovered-what-they-said/ [Accessed: 31 December 2011].

Burkart, R. (2009) 'On Habermas: understanding and public relations', in O. Ihlen, B. van Ruler and M. Fredriksson (eds) *Public Relations and Social Theory: key figures and concepts*, Abingdon: Routledge, pp. 141–165.

Bussey, C. (2011) 'Location, location, location', *PR Week,* 28 September, www.prweek.com/uk/news/1095706/Location-location-location/ [Accessed: 1 December 2011].

Cannon, T. (1992) *Corporate Responsibility* (1st edition), London: Pitman Publishing.

Cartledge, P. (2009) *Ancient Greek Political Thought in Practice,* Cambridge: Cambridge University Press.

Cartmell, M. (2011a) 'Profile: Avril Lee, CEO of Ketchum Pleon', *PR Week,* 14 April, www.prweek.com/uk/features/1065332/Profile-Avril-Lee-CEO-Ketchum-Pleon/ [Accessed: 1 December 2011].

Cartmell, M. (2011b) 'PRCA calls for all members to pay interns the National Minimum Wage', *PR Week,* 17 November, www.prweek.com/uk/news/1104372/ [Accessed: 1 December 2011].

Cave, A. (2011) 'From media relations to business strategy', *CorpComms*, September: 23–25.

Celsi, C. (2011) '6 alternatives to sending a press release', *PR Daily*, 5 May.

Centre for Economics and Business Research Ltd. (CEBR) (2005) *PR Today: 48,000 professionals; £36.5 billion turnover. The economic significance of public relations*, www.cipr.co.uk/sites/default/files/CIPR%20full%20report%20-%20November%204% 202005.pdf [Accessed: 16 December 2010].

Chartered Institute of Marketing (2011) www.cim.co.uk/resources/understandingmarket/ definitionmkting.aspx [Accessed 31 December 2011].

Chipchase, J. (2001) 'IT sector public relations', in A. Theaker (ed.), *The Public Relations Handbook*, London: Routledge, pp. 218–238.

Chryssides, G.D. and Kaler, J.H. (1993) *An Introduction to Business Ethics*, London: Chapman and Hall.

CIPR (2009) *Social Media Guidelines*, www.cipr.co.uk/sites/default/files/Social%20Media%20 guidelines.pdf [Accessed 31 December 2010].

CIPR (2010) *State of the PR Profession Benchmarking Survey*, www.cipr.co.uk [Accessed 25 August 2010].

CIPR (2011a) *Social Media Measurement Guidance*, March.

CIPR (2011b) 'CSR Guide', www.cipr.co.uk/member/PRguides/CSR [Accessed 10 July 2011].

CIPR (2011c) 'Research, Planning & Measurement Toolkit', March, www.cipr.co.uk/content/ policy-resources/for-practitioners/research-planning-and-measurement/toolkit [Accessed: 1 December 2011].

Clack, A. (2011) 'Playing the long game', *PR Week,* 12 May, www.prweek.com/uk/news/ 1069444/Alex-Clack-Ogilvy-Playing-long-game [Accessed: 1 December 2011].

Clarke, A. (2000) 'Globalisation – dancing to a new tune', presentation to students at Cardiff University, 12 October.

Cohen, D. (2011) 'Trends in consumer PR in 2010', *PR Week*, 10 June: 25.

Cole, G.A. (2004) *Management Theory and Practice* (6th edition), London: Thomson.

Commission of PR Education (1999) *A Port of Entry*, London: PRSA.

Content Marketing Institute (2011) *2012 B2B Content Marketing Benchmarks, Budgets and Trends*, www.contentmarketinginstitute.com/2011/12/2012-b2b-content-marketing-research/ [Accessed: 31 December 2011].

Cornelissen, J. (2008) *Corporate Communications: a guide to theory and practice*. London: Sage.

Corporate Branding (2011) www.corporatebrandinginfo.com [Accessed 21 November 2011].

Costa, M. (2011) 'How to extend shelf life of your campaign', *Marketing Week*, 13 January: 28–30.

Covey, S.R. (1989) *The Seven Habits of Highly Effective People: restoring the character ethic,* London: Simon & Schuster.

Crush, P. (2005) 'Global PR: what does the world think?', *PR Week*, 9 November, www.prweek.com/uk/features/526852/ [Accessed: 1 December 2011].

Crystal Interactive (2006) 'The human touch', www.crystal-interactive.co.uk [Accessed 4 April 2007].

Csíkszentmihályi, M. and Rochberg-Halton, E. (1981) *The Meaning of Things: domestic symbols and the self*, Cambridge: Cambridge University Press.

CSR Europe (2002) www.csreurope.org/data/files/Marketing/CSR_Europe_overview_and_ service_offer.pdf [Accessed 30 June 2011].

Curran, J. and Seaton, J. (2003) *Power without Responsibility: the press, broadcasting, and new media in Britain*, Abingdon: Routledge.

Cutlip, S.M., Center, A.H. and Broom, G.M. (1985) *Effective Public Relations* (revised 6th edition), Upper Saddle River, NJ: Prentice Hall.

Cutlip, S.M., Center, A.H. and Broom, G.M. (1995) *Effective Public Relations* (7th edition), Upper Saddle River, NJ: Prentice Hall.

Cutlip, S.M., Center, A.H. and Broom, G.M. (2000) *Effective public relations* (8th edition), Upper Saddle River, NJ: Prentice Hall.

Cutlip, S.M., Center, A.H. and Broom, G.M. (2006) *Effective Public Relations* (9th edition), Upper Saddle River, NJ: Pearson Education International.

*Daily Mail* (2006) 'BA backs down over cross ban after storm of criticism', www.daily mail.co.uk/news/article-418498/BA-backs-cross-ban-storm-criticism.html [Accessed: 1 December 2011].

*Daily Record* (2010) 'Transplant mother backs organ donor campaign', www.dailyrecord. co.uk/news/health-news/2010/02/15/transplant-mother-backs-organ-donor-campaign-86908-22044320/ [Accessed 31 December 2011].

Dauncey, G. (1994) 'Shades of Green', *NEF*, No. 30.

Davies, N. (2008) *Flat Earth News*, London: Chatto & Windus.

Davis, A. (2004) *Mastering Public Relations*, London: Palgrave.

Daye, D. and van Auken, B. (2008) '10 steps to successful corporate branding', www. brandingstrategyinsider.com [Accessed 21 November 2011].

Daymon, C. and Holloway, I. (2010) *Qualitative Research Methods in Public Relations and Marketing Communications* (2nd edition), Abingdon: Routledge.

Deterding, S., Khaled, R., Nacke, L. and Dixon, D. (2011) *Gamification: Toward a Definition*, CHI 2011, Gamification Workshop Proceedings, Vancouver, BC, http://hci.usask.ca/uploads/219-02-Deterding,-Khaled,-Nacke,-Dixon.pdf [Accessed: 1 December 2011].

DeSanto, B. and Moss, D. (2004) 'Rediscovering what PR managers do: rethinking the measurement of managerial behaviour in the public relations context', *Journal of Communication Management*, 9 (2): 179–196.

Dewhurst, S. and Fitzpatrick, L. (2007) 'Building a framework for internal communicators', *Strategic Communication Management*, 11 (2), February/March.

Dichter, E. interview with R. Banos (1986) 'Ernest Dichter: Motive Interpreter', *Journal of Advertising Research*, February/March: 15–20.

Digital Market Asia (2011) www.digitalmarket.asia/2011/07/the-age-of-spin-is-now-dead-says-ogilvy-pr-chief/ [Accessed 16 April 2012].

Dozier, D.M. (1992) 'The organisational roles of communicators and public relations practitioners', in J.E. Grunig (ed.) *Excellence in Public Relations and Communications Management*, Hillsdale, NJ: Lawrence Erlbaum.

Dozier, D.M. and Broom, G.M. (1995) 'Evolution of the manager role in public relations practice', *Journal of Public Relations Research*, 7 (1): 3–26.

Dozier, D.M., Grunig, L.A. and Grunig, J.E. (1995) *Manager's Guide to Excellence in Public Relations and Communication Management*, Hillsdale, NJ: Lawrence Erlbaum.

Duhé, S.C. (2007) 'Public relations and complexity thinking in the age of transparency', in S.C. Duhé (ed.) *New Media and Public Relations*, New York: Peter Lang, pp. 57–76.

Edelman, R. (2011) '"Gameification" and public relations', www.edelman.com/speak_up/blog/archives/2011/10/gameification_a.html [Accessed: 1 December 2011].

Edmunds, H. (2000) *The Focus Group Research Handbook*, Lincolnwood, IL: NTC Business Books.

Edwards, L. (2010) 'An exploratory study of the experiences of 'BAME' PR practitioners in the UK industry', ESRC/Leeds Metropolitan University/CIPR.

Egan, J. (2007) *Marketing Communications,* Belmont, CA: Wadsworth, Cengage Learning.

Eiró-Gomes, M. and Duarte, J. (2008) 'The case study as an evaluation tool for public relations', in B. Van Ruler and A.T. Verčič (eds) *Public Relations Metrics: research and evaluation*, Abingdon: Routledge, pp. 235–251.

Elton, L. (1993) 'University teaching: a professional model for quality', in R. Ellis (ed.) *Quality Assurance for University Teaching*, Oxford: Open University Press.

Ewen, S. (1998) *PR! A Social History of Spin*, New York: Basic Books.

Eyrich, N., Padman, M.L. and Sweetser, K.D. (2008) 'PR practitioners use of social media tools and communication technology', *Public Relations Review*, 34(4): 412–414.

Falconi, T.M. (2003) 'Europe – the PR challenge', *Profile*, May: 12–13.

Fawkes, J. (2006) 'Public Relations, Propaganda and the Psychology of Persuasion', in R. Tench and L. Yeomans (eds) *Exploring Public Relations*, Harlow: Prentice Hall.

Fawkes, J. (2012a) 'What is Public Relations?', in A. Theaker (ed.) *The Public Relations Handbook* (4th edition), Abingdon: Routledge, p. 10.

Fawkes, J. (2012b) 'Public relations and communications', in A. Theaker (ed.) *The Public Relations Handbook* (4th edition), Abingdon: Routledge, pp. 21–37.

Fawkes, J. and Tench, R. (2004) 'Does employer resistance to theory threaten the future of public relations? A consideration of research findings, comparing UK practitioner, academic and alumni attitudes to public relations education', International Public Relations Research Symposium, Bled, Slovenia, 11 July 2004.

Fekrat, M.A., Inclan, C. and Petroni, D. (1996) 'Corporate environmental disclosures: competitive disclosure hypothesis using 1991 annual report data', *The International Journal of Accounting,* 31 (2): 175–195.

Ferrabee, D. (2010) www.ableandhow.com [Accessed 31 October 2011].

Festinger, L. (1957) *A Theory of Cognitive Dissonance*, Stanford, CA: Stanford University Press.

Fields, D. and Robbins, D. (2008) *Speaking to Teenagers: how to think about, create, and deliver effective messages*, Grand Rapids, MI: Zondervan.

Fill, C. (2002) *Marketing Communications: contexts, strategies and applications,* London: FT/Prentice Hall.

Fishbein, M. and Ajzen, I. (1980) *Predicting and Changing Behavior: the reasoned action approach*, New York: Psychology Press.

Fisk, P. (2004) 'The Future of Marketing', Annual Cambridge Marketing Lecture, CMC.

Fitzpatrick, K. (2006) 'Baselines for ethical advocacy in the "Marketplace of Ideas"', in K. Fitzpatrick and C. Bornstein (eds) *Ethical Public Relations: responsible advocacy*, Thousand Oaks, CA: Sage, pp. 1–18.

Fitzpatrick, K. and Bronstein, C. (eds) (2006) *Ethical Public Relations: responsible advocacy*, Thousand Oaks, CA: Sage.

Fitzpatrick, L. (2012) 'Internal Communications', in A. Theaker (ed.) *The Public Relations Handbook* (4th edition), Abingdon: Routledge, pp. 273–310.

Fleet, D. (2006) 'Think PR people don't need math? Think again', http://davefleet.com/2009/07/pr-people-math/ [Accessed: 1 December 2011].

Forsyth, D.R. (2009) *Group Dynamics* (5th edition), Belmont, CA: Wadsworth, Cengage Learning.

Free Dictionary (2011) www.thefreedictionary.com/journalism [Accessed 31 October 2011].

Freeman, R.E. and McVea, J. (2005) 'A stakeholder approach to strategic management', in M.A. Hitt, E. Freeman and J.S. Harrison (eds) *Handbook of Strategic Management*, Oxford: Blackwell Publishing, pp. 189–207.

Freitag, A. and Quesinberry Stokes, A. (2009) *Global Public Relations,* Abingdon: Routledge.

Friedman, M. (1993) 'The social responsibility of business is to increase its profits', in Chryssides, G.D. and Kaler, J.H., *An Introduction to Business Ethics*, London: Chapman & Hall.

Friend, R. (2011) 'Keep the customer satisfied', *PR Week*, 12 May, www.prweek.com/uk/features/1069448/rachel-friend-weber-shandwick-keep-customer-satisfied/ [Accessed: 1 December 2011].

Fröhlich, R. and Peters, S.B. (2007) 'PR "bunnies" caught in the agency ghetto? Gender stereotypes, organizational factors, and women's careers in PR agencies', *Journal of Public Relations Research*, 19 (3), 229–254.

*FT* (2011) 'VW gives BlackBerry-wielding workers a silent night', December 22, 2011, www.ft.com/cms/s/0/24b9df80-2c99-11e1-8cca-00144feabdc0.html#axzz1kDFVQD2q [Accessed 31 December 2011].

Fung, V.K.K., Fung, W. and Wind, Y. (2008) *Competing in a Flat World: building enterprises for a borderless world,* Upper Saddle River, NJ: Prentice Hall.

Future Foundation (1998) *The Responsible Organisation*, BT.

Gangadharbatla, H. (2008) 'Facebook me: collective self-esteem, need to belong, and internet self-efficacy as predictors of the igeneration's attitudes toward social networking sites', *Journal of Interactive Advertising*, 8 (2): 5–15.

Garrick, J. and Christie, R.F. (2008) *Quantifying and Controlling Catastrophic Risks*, London: Academic Press.

Garsten, N. (2011) 'Evolution and significance of PR specialisms in contemporary Britain', History of Public Relations Conference, Bournemouth.

Garsten, N. and Howard, J. (2011) 'The evolution and significance of public relations specialisms in contemporary britain (1985–2010)', International History of Public Relations Conference, Bournemouth University, July.

Gartner (2011) 'Gartner says by 2015, more than 50 percent of organisations that manage innovation processes will gamify those processes,' www.gartner.com/it/page.jsp?id=1629214 [Accessed: 1 December 2011].

Gilpin, D.R. and Murphy, P.J. (2008) *Crisis Management in a Complex World*, Oxford: Oxford University Press.

Gladwell, M. (2000) 'The Tipping Point' website, www.gladwell.com/tippingpoint/ [Accessed: 1 December 2011].

Gladwell, M. (2005) *Blink: the power of thinking without thinking,* London: Penguin.

Go-Gulf (2011) '60 Seconds – Things That Happen On Internet Every Sixty Seconds', www.go-gulf.com/blog/60-seconds [Accessed: 1 December 2011].

Goldhaber, G.M. and Krivonos, P.D. (1977) 'The ICA communication audit: process, status, critique', *Journal of Business Communication,* 15 (1): 41–55.

Gombita, J. (2011) 'Digital PR: teasing out the potential of twitter chats (part i)', http://blog.commpro.biz/prcafe/digital-pr/digital-pr-teasing-out-the-potential-of-twitter-chats-part-i/ [Accessed: 1 December 2011].

Goodman, G. (2010) 'Five key ingredients of lasting brands', www.entrepreneur.com [Accessed 21 November 2011].

Gorkana (2011) *2011 PR Census*, *PR Week*/PRCA.

Gray, R. (2004) 'Finding the right direction', *Communication World*, November/December: 26–32.

Gray, R. (2006a) 'Agencies drawn by China's riches', *PR Week*, 21 July, www.prweek. com/uk/news/570225/Feature-Agencies-drawn-Chinas-riches/ [Accessed: 1 December 2011].

Gray, R. (2006b) 'Feature: Time well spent?', *PR Week*, 26 October, www.prweek.com/ uk/news/600215/Feature-Time-spent/ [Accessed: 1 December 2011].

Gray, R. (2007) 'Time to act on CSR', *PR Week*, 21 February, www.prweek.com/uk/features/ 634208/ [Accessed: 1 December 2011].

Green, A. (2007) *Creativity in Public Relations* (3rd edition), London: Kogan Page.

Green, A. (2010) *Creativity in Public Relations* (4th edition), London: Kogan Page.

Greenwood, R.G. (1981) 'Management by objectives as developed by Peter Drucker, assisted by Harold Smiddy', (originally in *Academy of Management Review* 6 (2): 225–30), in J.C. Wood and M.C. Wood (eds) *Peter F. Drucker: critical evaluations in business and management,* volume 1, (2005), pp. 163–174, Abingdon: Routledge.

Gregory, A. (2000) *Planning and Managing Public Relations Campaigns* (2nd edition), London: Kogan Page.

Gregory, A. (2009) 'Public relations as planned communications', in R. Tench and L. Yeomans (eds), *Exploring Public Relations*, London: FT Prentice Hall, pp. 174–197.

Gregory, A. (2012) 'Public relations and management', in A. Theaker (ed.) *The Public Relations Handbook* (4th edition), Abingdon: Routledge, pp. 60–81.

Gregory, A. and White, J. (2008) 'Introducing the Chartered Institute of Public Relations initiative: moving on from talking about evaluation to incorporating it into better management of the practice', in B. Van Ruler and A.T. Verčič (eds) *Public Relations Metrics: research and evaluation*, Abingdon: Routledge, pp. 307–317.

Gregory, H. (2006) 'The grads are back', *PR Week*, 3 November: 24–26.

Gronstedt, A. and Caywood, C.L. (2011) 'Communications research: foundational matters', in Caywood, C.L. (ed.) *The Handbook of Strategic Public Relations and Integrated Marketing Communications* (2nd edition), New York: McGraw-Hill, pp.13–36.

Groom, B. and Pfeifer, S. (2011) 'Privatisation defined Thatcher era', *Financial Times*, www. ft.com/cms/s/0/51ccaa1c-20c2-11e1-816d-00144feabdc0.html#axzz1hCNuwSmH [Accessed: 31 December 2011].

Grunig, J.E. (2001) 'Two-way symmetrical public relations: past, present and future', in R.L. Heath (ed.) *The Handbook of Public Relations*, Thousand Oaks, CA: Sage, pp. 11–30.

Grunig, J.E. (2009) 'Paradigms of global public relations in an age of digitalisation', *PRism*, 6(2), http://praxis.massev.ac.nz/prism on-line iourn.html [Accessed 31 December 2010].

Grunig, J.E. and Grunig, L.A. (2010) 'The Third Annual Grunig Lecture Series: Public Relations Excellence 2010', PRSA International Conference, Washington DC, 17 October, www.instituteforpr.org/files/uploads/Third_Grunig_Lecture_Transcript.pdf [Accessed 31 December 2010].

Grunig, J.E. and Hunt, T. (1984) *Managing Public Relations*, New York: Holt, Rinehart & Winston.

Grunig, J.E. and Repper, F. (1992) 'Strategic management, publics and issues', in J. Grunig (ed.) *Excellence in Public Relations and Communications Management*, Hillsdale, NJ: Lawrence Erlbaum.

Grunig, J.E., Dozier, D.M., Ehling, W.P., Grunig, L.A., Repper, F.C. and White, J. (eds) (1992) *Excellence in Public Relations and Communication Management*, Hillsdale, NJ: Lawrence Erlbaum.

Grunig. L.A., Grunig, J.E. and Dozier, D.M. (2002) *Excellent Public Relations and Effective Organisations: a study of communication management in three countries*, London: Routledge.

*The Guardian* (2011) 'Gamification for the public good', 27 June 2011, www.guardian.co.uk/government-computing-network/2011/jun/27/gamification-principles-public-services-dwp [Accessed: 1 December 2011].

Gurău, C. (2008) 'Integrated online marketing communication: implementation and management', *Journal of Communication Management*, 12 (2): 169–184.

Hampden-Turner, C.M. and Trompenaars, F. (2000) *Building Cross-Cultural Competence*. New Haven, CT: Yale University Press.

Harben, J. (1998) 'The power of storytelling when cultures merge', *Journal of Communication Management*, 3 (1), Winter: 80–87.

Harcup, T. (2007) *The Ethical Journalist*, London: Sage.

Harrison, C. (2011) 'Cleaning up the lobby shop', *CorpComms*, Issue 62, November: 13–17.

Hart, N. (ed.) (1995) *Strategic Public Relations*, London: Macmillan Business Press.

Hazlett, K. (2011a) 'Your career and you', http://kirkhazlett-aprofessorsthought.blogspot.com, 16 January [Accessed 9 May 2011].

Hazlett, K. (2011b) 'Take some you time', http://kirkhazlett-aprofessorsthought.blogspot.com, 25 June [Accessed 26 June 2011].

Heath, R.L. (2001a) 'Shifting foundations: public relations as relationship building', in R.L. Heath (ed.) (2001) *Handbook of Public Relations*, London: Sage, pp. 1–9.

Heath, R.L. (2001b) 'Globalisation – the frontier of multinationalism and cultural diversity', in R.L. Heath (ed.) *Handbook of Public Relations*, London: Sage, pp. 625–628.

Heijden, K. van der (2011) *Scenarios: the art of strategic conversation* (2nd edition), New York: John Wiley and Sons.

Hendler, J. and Berners-Lee, T. (2010), 'From the semantic web to social machines: a research challenge for AI on the World Wide Web', *Artificial Intelligence*, 174 (2): 156–161.

Hendrix, J.A. (1995) *Public Relations Cases* (3rd edition), Belmont, CA: Wadsworth.

Hendrix, J.A. (2006) *Public Relations Cases* (7th edition), Belmont, CA: Wadsworth.

Henry, A. (2008) *Understanding Strategic Management*, Oxford: Oxford University Press.

Hernandez, B.A. (2011) 'How Lady Gaga created a web marketing spectacle for Born This Way', http://mashable.com/2011/05/24/lady-gaga-case-study/ [Accessed: 1 December 2011].

Hill, N. and Alexander, J. (2006) *The Handbook of Customer Satisfaction and Loyalty Measurement* (2nd edition), Aldershot: Gower Publishing Ltd.

Himler, P. (2011) 'PR Redefined', www.forbes.com/sites/peterhimler/2011/11/21/pr-redefined/ [Accessed: 31 December 2011].

Hindle, N. (2011) 'Client view – Nick Hindle, McDonald's: managing the McFightback', *PR Week*, 7 April, www.prweek.com/uk/league_tables/1063766/Client-View—-Nick-Hindle-McDonalds-Managing-McFightback/ [Accessed: 1 December 2011].

Hitchins, J. (2003) 'News from Nowhere', Current Debates in Public Relations Research and Practice, Bournemouth University, 10–12 April.

Holmes, P. (2007) 'A manifesto for the 21st century public relations firm', http://pr20.wordpress.com/2007/05/13/a-manifesto-for-the-21st-century-public-relations-firm/, 13 May [Accessed: 31 December 2010].

Holtzhausen, D.R. (2002) 'Resistance from the margins: the postmodern public relations practitioner as organisational activist', *Journal of Public Relations Research,* 14 (1): 57–84.

Hunt, R. (2011) 'Personality and authenticity', *PR Week*, 14 September, www.prweek.com/uk/league_tables/1089934/ros-hunt-cohn-wolfe-personality-authenticity/ [Accessed: 1 December 2011].

Hunter, S. (2011) 'It's important to listen', *PR Week*, 12 May, www.prweek.com/uk/news/1069447/Sharleen-Hunter-Unleashed-Potential-Its-important-listen/ [Accessed: 1 December 2011].

Hurd, B. (2010) 'Employee social media – risk and reward', http://barryhurd.com [Accessed 13 October 2011].

Hutton, J.G. (1999) 'The definition, dimensions and domain of public relations', *Public Relations Review*, 25 (2): 199–214.

Hutton, J.G. (2010) 'Defining the relationship between public relations and marketing: public relations' most important challenge', in R.L. Heath (ed.) *The Sage Handbook of Public Relations* (2nd edition), London: Sage, pp. 509–522.

Ihlen, O. (2009) 'On Bourdieu: public relations in field struggles', in O. Ihlen, B. van Ruler and M. Fredriksson (eds) *Public Relations and Social Theory: key figures and concepts*, Abingdon: Routledge, pp. 62–82.

Ihlen, O. and van Ruler, B. (2009) 'Introduction: applying social theory to public relations', in O. Ihlen, B. van Ruler and M. Fredriksson (eds) *Public Relations and Social Theory: key figures and concepts*, Abingdon: Routledge, pp. 1–20.

Ingenium (2009) 'Best practices in employee communications and engagement', *Ingenium Communications*, www.resultsmap.com/e/downloads/BestPractices_Employee Communications.pdf [Accessed: 14 July 2011].

Institute of Internal Communications (2005) www.ioic.org.uk/content/training/knowledge-bank/741-internal-communications-makes-the-difference-to-success.html [Accessed 13 October 2011].

The Institute of Practitioners in Advertising (2009) 'How share of voice wins market share', Nielsen and the IPA Databank.

IPA (2010) *Results of the Third IPA Touchpoints Survey*, www.ipa.co.uk/Content/Results-of-third-IPA-TouchPoints-Survey [Accessed 28 January 2011].

IPRA (1990) *Public Relations Education – recommendations and standards*, IPRA Gold Paper No. 7, September.

Isaacson, W. (2011) *Steve Jobs,* London: Little, Brown.

Jahansoozi, J. (2006) 'Relationships, transparency, and evaluation: the implications for public relations', in J. L'Etang and M. Pieczka (eds) *Critical Perspectives in Public Relations*, Mahwah, NJ: Lawrence Erlbaum Associates.

Janal, D. (1998) *Online Marketing Handbook*, London: John Wiley & Sons.

Jandt, F.E. (2004) *An Introduction to Intercultural Communication* (4th edition), London: Sage.

Jandt, F.E. (2009) *An Introduction to Intercultural Communication* (6th edition), London: Sage.

Janis, I.L. (1972) *Victims of Groupthink: a psychological study of foreign-policy decisions and fiascos,* Oxford: Houghton Mifflin.

Jaques, T. (2002) 'Towards a new terminology: optimising the value of issue management', *Journal of Communication Management*, 7 (2): 140–147.

Jaques, T. (2010) 'Embedding issue management: from process to policy', in R.L. Heath (ed.) *The Sage Handbook of Public Relations* (2nd edition), London: Sage, pp. 435–446.

Jardine, A. (2006) 'MPR: the solution to the budget puzzle?', *PR Week*, 15 March, www.prweek.com/uk/features/547179/ [Accessed: 1 December 2011].

John, P., Cotteril, S., Richardson, L., Moseley, A., Stoker, G., Wales, C. and Smith, G. (2008) *Nudge, Nudge, Think, Think: using experiments to change civic behaviour,* London: Bloomsbury.

Johns, B. (2011) 'The 9 things that matter more than GPA', *PR Daily*, 4 May, www.prdaily.com [Accessed 9 May 2011].

Johnson, B. (2007) 'Blogs mark the first 10 years', *Guardian*, 7 April, p. 31.

Johnson, J., Scholes, K. and Whittington, R. (2005) *Exploring Corporate Strategy* (7th edition), Harlow: Pearson Education.

Johnson, J., Scholes, K. and Whittington, R. (2008) *Exploring Corporate Strategy* (8th edition), Harlow: Pearson Education.

Kaba, N. (2001) 'More is socially very appealing', *PR Week*, 24 June, www.prweek.com/uk/features/1076348/more-socially-appealing/ [Accessed: 1 December 2011].

Katz, E. and Lazerfield, P.F. (1995) *Personal Influence*, Glencoe, IL: Free Press.

Keller, K.L. and Aaker, D.A. (2003) 'The impact of corporate marketing on a company's brand extensions', in J. Balmer and S. Greyser (eds) *Revealing the Corporation*, London: Routledge.

Kelly, M. (2011) 'Judging nudging: choice architecture and social norming in health related behaviour change', Wolfson Research Institute Durham University, 8 April, www.dur.ac.uk/resources/wolfson.institute/events/WolfsonDurham080411.pdf [Accessed: 1 December 2011].

Kim, J-N. and Ni, L. (2010) 'Seeing the forest through the trees: the behavioural, strategic management paradigm in public relations and its future', in R.L. Heath (ed.) *The Sage Handbook of Public Relations* (2nd edition), London: Sage, pp. 35–57.

Kitchen, P. (ed.) (1997) *Public Relations, Principles and Practice*, London: International Thomson Business Press.

Kitchen, P.J. and Panopoulos, A. (2010) 'Online public relations: the adoption process and innovation challenge, a Greek example'*, Public Relations Review, 36* (3): 222–229.

Klein, N. (2000) 'Tyranny of the brands', *New Statesman*, 24 January: 25–28.

Knox, S. and Bickerton, D. (2003) 'Six conventions of corporate brand management', *European Journal of Marketing*, 37 (7/8): 998–1016.

Koenig, D.T. (2003) *The Engineer Entrepreneur*, New York: ASME Press.

Kotler, P. and Mindak, W. (1978) 'Marketing and public relations', *Journal of Marketing*, 42 (10): 13–20.

Lansons Communications (2011) *UK Social Media Census,* www.lansonsconversations.com/financial-services/infographic-the-uk-social-media-census-2011/ [Accessed: 1 December 2011].

Larson, C.U. (2004) *Persuasion: Reception and Responsibility* (10th edition), Belmont, CA: Wadsworth.

Lawrence, F. (2011) 'Fat profits: health hangover as big brands woo world's poorest shoppers', *Guardian*, 24 November, p. 29.

Lazare, A. (2005) *On Apology*, US: OUP.

Lerbinger, O. (2001) 'Diversity and global communication require social interactive approach', *Purview*, 8 January.

L'Etang, J. (1996) 'Public relations and corporate responsibility', in J. L'Etang and M. Pieczka (eds) *Critical Perspectives in Public Relations*, London: International Thomson Business Press, pp. 82–105.

L'Etang, J. (2003) 'The myth of the 'ethical guardian': An examination of its origins, potency and illusions', *Journal of Communication Management*, 8 (1): 53–67.

L'Etang, J. (2004) *Public Relations in Britain: a history of the professional practice in the 20th century*, New Jersey: Lawrence Erlbaum.

L'Etang, J. (2006a) 'Corporate responsibility and public relations ethics', in J. L'Etang and M. Pieczka (eds) *Critical Perspectives in Public Relations*, London: International Thomson Business Press.

L'Etang, J. (2006b) 'Public relations as diplomacy', in J. L'Etang and M. Pieczka (eds) *Critical Perspectives in Public Relations*, London: International Thomson Business Press.

L'Etang, J. (2006c) 'Public relations and rhetoric', in J. L'Etang and M. Pieczka (eds) *Critical Perspectives in Public Relations*, London: International Thomson Business Press.

L'Etang, J. (2008) *Public Relations: concepts, practice and critique*, London: Sage.

L'Etang, J. (2009) 'Radical PR – catalyst for change or an aporia?' *Ethical Space*, 6 (2): 13–18.

L'Etang, J. and Pieczka, M. (eds) (2006a) *Critical Perspectives in Public Relations*, International London: Thomson Business Press.

L'Etang, J. and Pieczka, M. (eds) (2006b) *Public Relations, Critical Debates and Contemporary Practice*, Mahwah, NJ: Lawrence Erlbaum.

Levco, J. (2001) 'The key to catching a reporter's eye? Pitch like one', 14 July, www.prdaily.com (members only).

Levine, R. (2009) 'But how does it taste?', in R. Levine, C. Locke, D. Searls and D. Weinberger (eds) *The Cluetrain Manifesto: 10th anniversary edition*, New York: Basic Books, pp. 22–36.

Liker, J.K. (2011) 'Toyota's recall crisis: what have we learned?' http://blogs.hbr.org/cs/2011/02/toyotas_recall_crisis_full_of.html [Accessed: 1 December 2011].

Lindenmann, W.K. (2003) *Guidelines for Measuring the Effectiveness of PR Programs and Activities,* Gainesville, FL: Institute for Public Relations.

Lindenmann, W.K. (2006) *Public Relations Research for Planning and Evaluation*, Gainesville, FL: Institute for Public Relations.

Lloyd, L. (2011) 'Stay ahead of the trend curve', *PR Week*, 12 May, www.prweek.com/uk/features/1069441/louise-lloyd-cirkle-stay-ahead-trend-curve/ [Accessed: 1 December 2011].

Lowe, M. (2011) 'PR must refocus', *PR Week,* 12 May, www.prweek.com/uk/features/1069446/mark-lowe-third-city-consumer-pr-refocus/ [Accessed: 1 December 2011].

McComas, K.A. ( 2010) 'Community engagement and risk management', in R.L. Heath (ed.) *The Sage Handbook of Public Relations* (2nd edition), London: Sage, pp. 461–476.

McCusker, G. (2006a) 'Disastrous times for public relations', *Profile*, March/April, p. 17.

McCusker, G. (2006b) *Public Relations Disasters: talespin – inside stories and lessons learnt*, London: Kogan Page.

McDonald, H. and Harrison, P. (1999) *The Use of Marketing and Public Relations Activities by Performing Arts Presenters*, http://smib.vuw.ac.nz:8081/www/ANZMAC1999/Site/M/McDonald.pdf [Accessed 1 December 2011].

McGrath, C. (2011) 'Early Journalistic and parliamentary references to lobbying and lobbyist in the UK', International History of Public Relations Conference, Bournemouth.

McKeone, D.H. (1995) *Measuring your Media Profile*, Aldershot: Gower Publishing.

McLachlan, H. (2008) 'I don't know about you but I'm no killer', www.scotsman.com/news/i_don_t_know_about_you_but_i_m_no_killer_1_1083658 [Accessed 31 December 2011].

MacLeod, S. (2011) 'The ABC of reputation', *PR Week*, 14 September, www.prweek.com/uk/league_tables/1089936/sandra-macleod-echo-research-abc-reputation/ [Accessed: 1 December 2011].

Macnamara, J. (2005) 'Media content analysis: its uses, benefits and best practice methodology', *Asia Pacific Public Relations Journal*, 6 (1): 1–34.

Macnamara, J. (2007) *The Fork in the Road of Media and Communication Theory and Practice*, June, www.instituteforpr.org/files/uploads/MacnamaraPaper_b.pdf [Accessed 18 November 2011].

Macnamara, J. (2010) *The 21st Century Media (R)evolution: emergent communication practices*, New York: Peter Lang Publishing Inc.

McNamara, C. (2011) *Basics in Internal Organisational Communications*, www.resultsmap.com [Accessed 13 October 2010].

Magee, K. (2007) 'How to pick the best star for the job', *PR Week*, 11 April, www.prweek.com/uk/features/649853/ [Accessed: 1 December 2011].

Magee, K. (2010) 'Measurement: what next for measurement?', *PR Week*, 18 August, www.prweek.com/news/1022935/Measurement-next-measurement/ [Accessed 16 November 2010].

Magee, K. (2011a) 'Top 50 consumer consultancies', *PR Week*, 10 June, http://toppragencies.prweek.co.uk/Consumer-table.aspx [Accessed: 1 December 2011].

Magee, K. (2011b) '5 key skills for the future', *PR Week*, 10 August, www.prweek.com/uk/features/1084292/5-key-skills-future/ [Accessed: 1 December 2011].

Magee, K. (2011c) 'Tarnished brands', *PR Week*, 14 September, www.prweek.com/uk/features/1091797/Tarnished-brands, [Accessed: 1 December 2011].

Martin, R.L. (2002) 'The virtue matrix: calculating the return on corporate responsibility', *Harvard Business Review*, March: 69–75.

Martinelli, D.K. (2011) 'Political public relations: remembering its roots and classics', in J. Strömbäck and S. Kiousis (eds) *Political Public Relations: principles and applications*, Abingdon: Routledge, pp. 33–53.

Marx, E. (2001) *Breaking Through Culture Shock*, London: Nicholas Brealey Publishing.

Mayer, R.N. (1989) *The Consumer Movement: guardians of the marketplace*, Boston: Twayne Publishers.

Melcrum Publishing (2005) *Employee Engagement*, London: Melcrum Publishing.

Miller, D. and Dinan, D. (2008) *A Century of Spin*, London: Pluto.

Mintzberg, H. (1994) *The Rise and Fall of Strategic Planning*, Harlow: Pearson Education.

Mitchie, D. (1998) *The Invisible Persuaders*, London: Bantam Press.

Mittal, V., Sambandam, R., and Dholakia, U.M. (2010) 'Does media coverage of Toyota recalls reflect reality?', http://blogs.hbr.org/research/2010/03/does-media-coverage-of-toyota.html [Accessed: 1 December 2011].

Moffatt, G. (2008) 'Brands influence choice, so why should social marketing not?', http://radaris.co.uk/p/Giles/Moffatt/ [Accessed 1 February 2011 – no longer available in full].

Moloney, K. (2000) *Rethinking Public Relations: the spin and the substance*, Abingdon: Routledge.

Moloney, K. (2006) *Rethinking Public Relations: PR propaganda and democracy* (2nd edition), Abingdon: Routledge.

Moloney, K. (2009) 'Public Affairs', in R. Tench and L. Yeomans (eds) *Exploring Public Relations* (2nd edition), London: FT/Prentice Hall, pp. 441–461.

Momorella, S. and Woodall, I. (2003) 'Tips for an effective online newsroom', *Public Relations Tactics*, May: 6.

Monaghan, B. (2011) '6 ways PR has changed for the better', www.inkhouse.net/six-reasons-pr-has-changed-for-the-better/ [Accessed 1 December 2011].

Monck, A. and Hanley, M. (2008) *Can You Trust the Media?* London: Icon.

Money, K. G., Hillenbrand, C., Day, M. B. and Magnan, G.M. (2010) 'Exploring reputation of B2B partnerships: extending the study of reputation from the perception of single firms to the perception of inter-firm partnerships', *Industrial Marketing Management*, 39 (5): 761–768.

Montagu Smith, N. (2006) 'Giving something back', *CorpComms*, May, pp. 27–31.

Moore, S. (2011) 'Bawdy tittle tattle has always been part of our press – let's not lose it', *The Guardian*, 16 July, p. 39.

Morgan, M. (2011) 'What lies ahead for consumer PR?', *PR Week*, 10 June, http://toppr agencies.prweek.co.uk/Consumer-table.aspx [Accessed: 1 December 2011].

Moriarty, S.E. (1997) 'The Big Idea: creativity in public relations', in C.L. Caywood (ed.) *The Handbook of Strategic Public Relations and Integrated Communications*, New York: McGraw-Hill, pp. 554–563.

Morris, T. and Goldsworthy, S. (2012) *PR Today: the authoritative guide to public relations*, Basingstoke: Palgrave Macmillan.

Morton, J. (2006) 'Internal branding and experiential marketing', www.jackmorton.com, [Accessed 28 November 2006].

Moss, D. and DeSanto, B. (eds) (2002) *Public Relations Cases: international perspectives*, London: Routledge.

Moss, D. and Warnaby G. (1997) 'A strategic perspective for public relations', in P.J. Kitchen (ed.) *Public Relations: principles and practice,* London: Thomson, pp. 43–73.

Moss, D., Ashford, R. and Shani, N. (2003) 'The forgotten sector: uncovering the role of public relations in SMEs', *Journal of Communication Management*, 8 (2): 197–210.

Moss, D., Newman, A. and DeSanto, B. (2004) *Defining and Refining the Core Elements of Management in Public Relations/Corporate Communications Context: what do communication managers do?* 11th International Public Relations Research Symposium, Lake Bled, Slovenia, July 1–4.

Moss, D.A., Newman, A. and DeSanto, B. (2005) 'What do communications managers do? Refining the core elements of management in a public relations/communications context', *Journal of Mass Communication Quarterly*, 82: 873–890.

Moss, D., Powell, M. and DeSanto, B. (2010) *Public Relations Cases*, London: Routledge.

Mulholland, N. (2011) Market watch, *PR Week*, 10 June, http://toppragencies.prweek. co.uk/Consumer-table.aspx [Accessed: 1 December 2011].

Mumsnet (2011) 'Dear mn hq why is a government posting on mn?', www.mumsnet.com/ Talk/site_stuff/1347966-dear-mn-hq-why-is-a-government-department-posting-on-mn?pg=1 [Accessed: 1 December 2011].

Murphy, C. (1999) 'Brand values can build on charity ties', *Marketing Week*, 25 March: 41–42.

Murphy, C. (2011) 'Comms director survey: managing the chatter', *PR Week*, 30 June, www.prweek.com/uk/features/1077605/Comms-Directors-Survey-Managing-chatter [Accessed: 1 December 2011].

Murphy, F. (1999) 'Service with a smile', *The Guardian*, 28 October, pp. 14–15.

Murray, K. (2003) 'Reputation – managing the single greatest risk facing business today', *Journal of Communication Management*, 8 (2): 142–149.

Murray, K. (2006) 'Reputation 2.0', Behind the Spin Conference, College of St Mark and St John, Plymouth, Devon, 8 September.

Murray, K. and White, J. (2004) *CEO Views on Reputation Management: a report on the value of public relations, as perceived by organisational leaders,* London: Chime Communications.

Murray, K. and White, J. (2005) 'CEO views on reputation management', *Journal of Communication Management*, 9 (4): 348–358.

Murray-Leslie, N. (2007) 'Adapting to the concept of social responsibility', *Profile*, January/February, p. 10.

Noor Al-Deen, H.S. and Hendricks, J.A. (2011) *Social Media: usage and impact*, Plymouth: Lexington Books.

NUJ (2011) 'Code of Practice', http://media.gn.apc.org/nujcode.html [Accessed 31 December 2011].

Okun, B. (2011) '3 benefits of earning your accreditation in PR', www.ragan.com/Speechwriting/Articles/3_benefits_of_earning_your_Accreditation_in_PR__43396.aspx [Accessed 1 December 2011].

O'Malley, H. (1999) 'Charity begins at work', *Human Resources*, April: 46–49.

ONS (2011) www.ons.gov.uk/ [Accessed 1 December 2011].

O'Rourke, C. (2011) 'The value of reputation', *PR Week*, 14 September, www.prweek.com/uk/league_tables/1089931/Charlie-ORourke-AlMediaComms-value-reputation/ [Accessed: 1 December 2011].

Oriella (2011) 'The state of journalism in 2011', *Oriella PR Network*, www.oriellaprnetwork.com/sites/default/files/research/Oriella-Digital-Journalism-Study-2011_1.pdf [Accessed: 14 July 2011].

O'Shaughnessy, N. (1996) 'Social propaganda and social marketing: a critical difference?', *European Journal of Marketing*, 30 (10/11): 54–67.

Ouwersloot, H. and Duncan, T. (2008) *Integrated Marketing Communications*, Maidenhead: McGraw Hill.

Owyang, J. (2011) *Data: composition of a corporate social media team*, www.web-strategist.com/blog/2011/12/22/data-composition-of-a-corporate-social-media-team/ [Accessed: 31 December 2011].

Paine, K.D. (2007a) *Measuring Public Relationships: the data-driven communicator's guide to success*, Berlin, NH: K.D. Paine & Partners.

Paine, K.D. (2007b) 'The Measurement Standard', *How to Measure Social Media Relations: the more things change, the more they remain the same*, Gainesville, FL: Institute for Public Relations.

Paine, K.D. (2011a) *Measure what Matters: online tools for understanding customers, social media, engagement, and key relationships*, New York: John Wiley & Sons.

Paine, K.D. (2011b) http://kdpaine.blogs.com/themeasurementstandard [Accessed: 1 December 2011].

Palenchar, M.J. (2010) 'Risk communication', in R.L. Heath (ed.) *The Sage Handbook of Public Relations* (2nd edition), London: Sage, pp. 447–461.

Palotta, D. (2011) 'A logo is not a brand', http://blogs.hbr.org/pallotta/2011/06/a-logo-is-not-a-brand.html [Accessed 1 December 2011].

Parvanta, C., Nelson, D.E., Parvanta, S.A. and Harner, R.N. (2011) *Essentials of Public Health Communication*, London: Jones & Bartlett Publishers.

Payne, N. (2011) *Public Relations across Cultures*, http://allaboutpublicrelations.com [Accessed 15 November 2011].

Pearlfinders Index (2011) *Q3 2011 – PR Highlights,* www.pearlfinders.com/ [Accessed: 1 December 2011].

Penn, M. (2007) *Microtrends*, London: Penguin.

Peter, J.P., Olson, J.C. and Grunert, K.G. (1999) *Consumer Behaviour and Marketing Strategy* (European edition), Maidenhead: McGraw-Hill.

Petty, R.E. and Cacioppo, J.T. (1986) 'The elaboration likelihood model of persuasion', in L. Berkowitz (ed.) *Advances in Experimental Social Psychology*, New York: Academic Press, pp. 123–205.

Pew Research Center (2010) *A Portrait of Generation News*, www.pewresearch.org/millennials [Accessed: 1 December 2011].

Phillimore, M. (2012) 'Financial communications', in A. Theaker (ed.) *The Public Relations Handbook* (4th edition), Abingdon: Routledge, pp. 311–330.

Phillips, D. and Young, P. (2009) *Online Public Relations* (2nd edition), London: Kogan Page.

Pickton, D. and Broderick, A. (2005) *Integrated Marketing Communications* (2nd edition), Harlow: FT/Prentice Hall.

Pieczka, M. (2006) '"Chemistry" and the public relations industry: an exploration of the concept of jurisdiction and issues arising', in J. L'Etang and M. Pieczka (eds) *Public Relations: critical debates and contemporary practice*, Abingdon: Routledge, pp. 303–327.

Pink, D.H. (1998) 'Metaphor Marketing', *Fast Company*, 31 March. www.fastcompany. com/magazine/14/zaltman.html [Accessed: 1 December 2011].

Pinsent, M. (2011) 'Comms lines are blurring', *PR Week US,* 12 May, www.prweek.com/ uk/features/1069445/Mark-Pinsent-Shine-Communications-Comms-lines-blurring/ [Accessed: 1 December 2011].

Portway, S. (1995) 'Corporate social responsibility: the case for active stakeholder management', in N.A. Hart (ed.) *Strategic Public Relations*, London: Macmillan.

Powell, G., Groves, S. and Dimos, J. (2011) *ROI of Social Media: how to improve the return on your social marketing investment*, New York: John Wiley & Sons.

Prensky, M. (2001) 'Digital natives, digital immigrants', from *On the Horizon*, MCB University Press, 9 (5), October 2001, www.marcprensky.com/writing/Prensky%20-%20Digital%20 Natives,%20Digital%20Immigrants%20-%20Part1.pdf [Accessed 31 December 2010].

Price, V. (1992) *Public Opinion,* Newbury Park, CA: Sage.

Public Health Responsibility Deal (2011) www.dh.gov.uk/en/Publichealth/Publichealth responsibilitydeal/index.htm [Accessed: 1 December 2011].

Quigley-Hicks, K. (2011) 'Being sociable on social media', http://kellyquigleyhicks.wordpress. com/2011/11/23/being-social-on-social-media/ [Accessed: 1 December 2011].

Quirke, B. (2001) 'Identifying the real value of communication', *Strategic Communication Management*, February/March.

Quirke, W. (1995) 'Internal communication', in N. Hart (ed) *Strategic Public Relations*, London: Macmillan Business Press, pp. 71–94.

Ransom, C. (2011) 'Launching a multicultural PR campaign', http://aboutpublicrelations.net [Accessed 15 November 2011].

Raz, A.E. (2003) 'The slanted smile factory: emotion management in Tokyo Disneyland', in D.A. Harper, D. Harper and H.M. Lawson (eds) *The Cultural Study of Work,* Lanham, MD: Rowman & Littlefield, pp. 210–227.

Regester Larkin (2011) *PAS 200: 2011 – Crisis Management: guidance and good practice. An assessment*, London: Regester Larkin.

Riel, C.B.M. van (1995) *Principles of Corporate Communication*, London: Prentice Hall.

Riel, C.B.M. van and Balmer, J.M.T. (1997) 'Corporate identity: the concept, its measurement and management', *European Journal of Marketing*, 31 (5/6): 340–355.

Riel, C.B.M. van and Fombrun, C.J. (2007) *Essentials of Corporate Communication*, London: Routledge.

Ries, A. and Ries, L. (2002) *The Fall of Advertising and the Rise of PR*, New York: Harper Business.

Robert, B. and Lajtha, C. (2002) 'A new approach to crisis management', *Journal of Contingencies and Crisis Management,* 10: 181–191.

Rockland, D. (2011) 'A world without advertising value equivalents', Ketchum Pleon, www.ketchum.com/David_Rockland_Barcelona_Principles_A_World_Without_AVEs, [Accessed 1 December 2011].

Rodgers, S., Thorson, E. and Jin, Y. (2008) 'Social science theories of theories of traditional and internet advertising', in D.W. Stacks and M.B. Salwen (eds) *An Integrated Approach to Communication Theory and Research* (2nd edition), Abingdon: Routledge.

Rogers, D. (2007) 'Honesty on display at ethics debate', *PR Week*, 21 February, www.prweek.com/uk/opinion/634571/OPINION-Honesty-display-Ethics-Debate/ [Accessed: 1 December 2011].

Rogers, D. (2011) 'Marketing and media focus: what keeps these guys awake at night', *PR Week,* www.prweek.com/uk/features/1081011/ [Accessed: 1 December 2011].

Rogers, E.M. (2003) *Diffusion of Innovations* (5th edition), New York: New York Free Press.

Royal College of Physicians (2010) 'Passive smoking and children', www.rcplondon.ac.uk/news-media/press-releases/passive-smoking-major-health-hazard-children-says-rcp [Accessed 1 December 2011].

Rozwell, C. (2010) 'Employee expression on social media – red herring or real problem?', http://blogs.gartner.com/carol_rozwell [Accessed 13 October 2011].

Ruler, B. van and Verčič, D. (2002) 'The Bled manifesto on public relations', 9th International Public Relations Research Symposium, Bled, Slovenia, July.

Ruler, B. van, Verčič, D., Butschi, G. and Flodin, B. (2002) 'The European body of knowledge on public relations/communication management: the report of the Delphi research project 2000', *European Association for Public Relations Education and Research*, June 2000.

Ruler, B. van, Verčič, A.T. and Verčič, D. (2008), 'Public relations metrics measurement and evaluation – an overview', in B. van Ruler and A.T. Verčič (eds) *Public Relations Metrics: research and evaluation*, New York: Routledge, pp. 1–18.

Santi, A. (2006) 'Made to measure', *PR Business*, 25 May: 15–17.

Saunders, M., Lewis, P. and Thornhill, A. (2000) *Research Methods for Business Students* (2nd edition), Harlow: FT/Prentice Hall.

Schein, E.H. (1991) 'What is Culture?', in P. Frost, L.F. Moore, M.R. Louis, C.C. Lundberg and J. Martin (eds) *Reframing Organisational Culture,* Newbury Park, CA: Sage, pp. 243–253.

Schneider, J. and Boston University (2001) *New Product Launch Report*, Boston: Schneider & Associates.

Schneider, S.C. and Barsoux, J-L. (2003) *Managing Across Cultures* (2nd edition), London: Prentice Hall.

Sebastian, M. (2011a) '42 more signs you work in PR', *PR Daily*, April 27, www.prdaily.com [Accessed 13 October 2011].

Sebastian, M. (2011b) 'PRSA unveils campaign to redefine public relations', http://prdaily. com/Main/Articles/PRSA_unveils_campaign_to_redefine_public_relations_10112.aspx [Accessed 1 December 2011].

Sebenius, J.K. (2002) 'The hidden challenges of cross-border negotiations', *Harvard Business Review*, March, pp. 76–85.

Seitel, F.P. (1998) *The Practice of Public Relations* (7th edition), Upper Saddle Rivers, NJ: Prentice Hall.

Shah, R. (2011) 'What kind of work are clients asking for?', *PR Week*, 10 June, http://toppragencies.prweek.co.uk/Consumer-table.aspx [Accessed: 1 December 2011].

Shepherd, C. (2011) *From Classroom to Boardroom: an investigation of skills required of PR practitioners,* unpublished dissertation, UCLAN.

Skinner, G. and Mludzinski, T. (2011) 'Understanding society: an extraordinary year', Ipsos MORI Social Research Institute, www.ipsos-mori.com/DownloadPublication/1452_SRI_ Understanding_Society_Winter_2011.pdf [Accessed 1 December 2011].

Smith, L. (2012) 'Business-to-business public relations', in A. Theaker (ed.) *The Public Relations Handbook* (4th edition), Abingdon: Routledge, pp. 370–386.

Smith, R.D. (2005) *Strategic Planning for Public Relations* (2nd edition), Mahwah, NJ: Lawrence Erlbaum Associates.

Smith, S. (2010) 'Death of Internal Communications', www.hillandknowlton.com/content/ exaggerated-reports-death-internal-communications [Accessed 13 October 2011].

Smythe, J. (2004) *Engaging People at Work to Drive Strategy and Change*, unpublished report, McKinsey, 3 November.

Somerville, I. and Ramsey, P. (2012) 'Public relations and politics', in A. Theaker (ed.) *The Public Relations Handbook* (4th edition), Abingdon: Routledge, pp. 38–59.

Springston, J.K. and Keyton, J. (2001) 'Public relations field dynamics', in R.L. Heath (ed.) *The Handbook of Public Relations*, London: Sage, pp. 115–126.

Sriramesh, K. and Verčič, D. (2009) *The Global Public Relations Handbook: theory, research, and practice* (expanded and revised edition), London: Routledge.

Stacey, R.D. (2003) *Strategic Management and Organisational Dynamics: the challenge of complexity* (4th edition), London: Pearson Education.

Stateman, A. (2003) 'A Fox reporter tells all!', *Public Relations Tactics*, May: 15.

Stauber, J. and Rampton, S. (2004) *Toxic Sludge is Good For You*, London: Robinson.

Steers, R.M., Sánchez-Runde, C.J. and Nardon, L. (2010) *Management Across Cultures: challenges and strategies*, Cambridge: Cambridge University Press.

Steyn, B. (2011) 'Integrated reporting and strategic public relations', www.prconversations. com/index.php/2011/11/integrated-reporting-and-strategic-public-relations/ [Accessed: 1 December 2011].

Stockholm Accords (2010) www.globalalliancepr.org/content [Accessed: 19 January 2011].

Stone, N. (1995) *The Management and Practice of Public Relations*, London: Macmillan Business.

Strömbäck, J. and Kiousis. S. (2011) 'Political public relations: defining and mapping an emergent field', in J. Strömbäck and S. Kiousis (eds) *Political Public Relations: principles and applications,* Abingdon: Routledge, pp. 1–32.

Sudhaman, A. (2010) 'Is internal communications dead?' www.holmesreport.com/feature stories-info/9687/Analysis-Is-Internal-Comms-Dead.aspx [Accessed 13 October 2011].

Sung, M. (2007) 'Toward a model of scenario building from a public relations perspective', in E.L. Toth (ed.) *The Future of Excellence in Public Relations and Communication Management: challenges for the next generation,* Mahwah, NJ: Lawrence Erlbaum Associates, pp. 173–198.

Surma, A. (2006) 'Challenging unreliable narrators: writing and public relations', in J. L'Etang and M. Pieczka (eds) *Public Relations: critical debates and contemporary practice,* Abingdon: Routledge, pp. 41–60.

Sutherland, S. (1992) *Irrationality: the enemy within,* London: Constable.

Swann, P. (2010) *Cases in Public Relations Management,* New York: Routledge.

Sweetser, K.D. (2011) 'Digital political public relations', in J. Strömbäck and S. Kiousis (eds) *Political Public Relations: principles and applications,* Abingdon: Routledge, pp. 293–313.

Szondi, G. (2006) 'International context of public relations', in R. Tench and L. Yeomans (eds) *Exploring Public Relations,* London: FT/Prentice Hall, pp. 113–140.

Szondi, G. (2009) 'International context of public relations', in R. Tench and L. Yeomans (eds) *Exploring Public Relations* (2nd edition), London: FT/Prentice Hall, pp. 117–146.

Szondi, G. and Theilmann, R. (2009) 'Research and Evaluation in Public Relations', in R. Tench and L. Yeomans (eds) *Exploring Public Relations* (2nd edition), London: FT/Prentice Hall, pp. 198–221.

Taylor Herring (2009) http://www.taylorherring.com/blog/index.php/2009/01/50-top-publicity-stunts/ [Accessed: 1 December 2011].

Tench, R. (2006) 'Managing community involvement programmes', in R. Tench and L. Yeomans (eds) *Exploring Public Relations* (2nd edition), London: FT/Prentice Hall, pp. 355–375.

Tench, R. and Fawkes, J. (2005) 'Mind the gap, exploring different attitudes to public relations education from employers, academics and alumni', Alan Rawel/CIPR Academic Conference, Lincoln.

Tench, R. and Yeomans, L. (eds) (2006) *Exploring Public Relations,* London: FT/Prentice Hall.

Tench, R. and Yeomans, L (2009) 'What next? Future issues for PR' in Tench and Yeomans (eds) *Exploring Public Relations* (2nd edition), London: FT/Prentice Hall, pp. 633–644.

Thaler, R. and Sunstein, C. (2008), *Nudge: improving decisions about health, wealth and happiness,* New Haven, CT: Yale University Press.

Theaker, A. (2001) *The Public Relations Handbook,* London: Routledge, pp. 123–126.

Theaker, A. (2004) *The Public Relations Handbook* (2nd edition), Abingdon: Routledge.

Theaker, A. (ed.) (2007) *The Public Relations Handbook* (3rd edition), Abingdon: Routledge.

Theaker, A. (ed.) (2012) *The Public Relations Handbook* (4th edition), Abingdon: Routledge.

Todorova, A. (2002) 'Technique: inbox of tricks for sending a pitch', *PR Week US,* 22 July, www.brandrepublic.com/features/153556/ [Accessed: 1 December 2011].

Tyler, J. (2011) 'The Value of Conversations with Employees', *Gallup Management Journal,* 30 June 2011.

University of Liverpool (2004), *Passive Smoking Qualitative Research in Merseyside,* Research Report 99/05, Robinson, J. and Kirkcaldy, A. www.liv.ac.uk/haccru/reports/ps_final_report.pdf [Accessed: 1 December 2011].

Vasquez, G.M. and Taylor, M. (2001) 'Research perspectives on "the public"', in R.L. Heath (ed.) *The Handbook of Public Relations,* London: Sage, pp. 139–154.

Verčič, D. (2004) www.prstudies.com/weblog/2004/06/index.html [Accessed: 31 December 2011].

Wakefield, R.I. (2001) 'Effective public relations in the multinational organisation', in R.L. Heath (ed.) *The Handbook of Public Relations*, Sage, pp. 639–647.

Wakeman, S. (2012) 'Public sector public relations', in A. Theaker (ed.) *The Public Relations Handbook* (4th edition), Abingdon: Routledge, pp. 331–353.

Wall, I. (2000) 'Does your charity take dirty money?', *Big Issue*, 24 January: 19–20.

Walser, M.G. (2004) *Brand Strength: building and testing models based on experiential information,* Wiesbaden: Deutscher Universitats-Verlai.

Watson, J. (2003) *Media Communication: an introduction to theory and process* (2nd edition), London: Palgrave.

Watson, T. (2011) 'The evolution of evaluation – the accelerating march towards the measurement of public relations effectiveness', 2nd International History of Public Relations Conference, http://blogs.bournemouth.ac.uk/historyofpr/proceedings/ [Accessed: 1 December 2011].

Watson, T. and Noble, P. (2007) *Evaluating Public Relations: a best practice guide to public relations*, London: Kogan Page.

Watson, T. and Zerfass, A. (2011) 'Return on investment in public relations: a critique of concepts used by practitioners from communication and management sciences perspectives', *PRism*, 8 (1), www.prismjournal.org/fileadmin/8_1/Watson_Zerfass.pdf [Accessed: 1 December 2011].

Watson Wyatt (2006) 'Effective communication: indicators of financial performance 2005/ 2006', Communication ROI Study, www.watsonwyatt.com [Accessed 31 December 2008].

Wells, T. (2006) 'Africa: a comms sector on the rise', *PR Week*, 10 August, www.prweek. com/uk/analysis/576166/ [Accessed: 1 December 2011].

Wenger, E.C. and Snyder, W.M. (2000) 'Communities of Practice: the organisational frontier', *Harvard Business Review*, January–February: 139–145.

Werbel, J.D. and Wortman, M.S. (2000) 'Strategic philanthropy: responding to negative portrayals of corporate social responsibility', *Corporate Reputation Review*, 3 (2): 124–136.

Wheeler, D. and Sillanpaa, M. (1997) *The Stakeholder Corporation*, London: Pitman Publishing.

White, J. (2000) 'Psychology and public relations', in D. Moss, D, Verčič and G. Warnaby (eds) *Perspectives on Public Relations Research,* London: Routledge, pp. 145–155.

White, J. (2011) PR 2020: 'The Future of Public Relations', Appendix 3, www.cipr.co.uk/ sites/default/files/PR%202020%20Final%20Report_0.pdf [Accessed 16/4/2012].

Wicks, N. (2011) 'Mixed response from agency bosses as Guardian cracks down on PR plugs', *PR Week*, 11 August, http://prweek.co.uk/uk/news/1084250/Mixed-response-agency-bosses-Guardian-cracks-down-PR-plugs/ [Accessed: 1 December 2011].

Wilcox, D.L. and Cameron, G.T. (2006) *Public Relations: strategies and tactics* (8th edition), Boston, MA: Allyn & Bacon.

Wilcox, D.L., Cameron, G.T., Ault, P.H. and Agee, W.K. (2003) *Public Relations, Strategies and Tactics* (7th edition), Boston, MA: Allyn & Bacon.

Williams, K.C. (1981) *Behavioural Aspects of Marketing*, Oxford: Heinemann Professional.

Williamson, L. (2004) 'Cause-related marketing: Back to school', *PR Week*, 16 January, www.prweek.com/uk/news/199861/Cause-related-marketing-Back-school/ [Accessed: 1 December 2011].

Willis, P. (2006) 'Public relations and the consumer', in R. Tench and L. Yeomans (eds) *Exploring Public Relations*, London: FT/Prentice Hall, pp. 409–424.

Windahl, S., Signitzer, B. and Olsen, J.T. (1992) *Using Communication Theory*, London: Sage.

Wood, E. (2012) 'Public Relations and Corporate Communications', in A. Theaker (ed.) *The Public Relations Handbook* (4th edition), Abingdon: Routledge, pp. 107–125.

Wood, E. and Somerville, I. (2012) 'Corporate identity', in Theaker, A. (ed.) *The Public Relations Handbook* (4th edition), Abingdon: Routledge, pp. 126–153.

Woodward, J. (2011) 'Richard Edelman: public relations must evolve or get left behind', *Public Relations Tactics*, 1 July.

Worcester, B. (2007) 'Internet not the be all and end all', *Profile*, May/June: 14.

Wysocki, R.K. (2011) *Effective Project Management: traditional, agile, extreme* (6th edition), Indianopolis, IN: John Wiley & Sons.

Yaxley, H. (2009) *Societal Perspectives*, Green Banana, http://greenbanana.info/career/2011/12/05/the-social-dimension-of-csr/ [Accessed 31 December 2011].

Yaxley, H. (2012a) 'Digital public relations – revolution or evolution?', in A. Theaker (ed.) *The Public Relations Handbook* (4th edition), Abingdon: Routledge, pp. 411–422.

Yaxley, H. (2012b) 'Risk, issues and crisis management', in A. Theaker (ed.) *The Public Relations Handbook* (4th edition), Abingdon: Routledge, pp. 154–174.

Yaxley, H., Gombita, J. and Pirchner, M. (2011) 'Using Twitter for PR events', www.prconversations.com/index.php/2011/08/using-twitter-for-pr-events/ [Accessed: 1 December 2011].

Yeomans, L. (2009) 'Public sector communication and social marketing', in R. Tench and L. Yeomans (eds) *Exploring Public Relations* (2nd edition), London: FT/Prentice Hall, pp. 577–599.

Young, L.D. (2006) 'Urban myths and their disastrous effects on marketing', Annual Cambridge Marketing Lecture, CMC.

Young, P. (2012) 'Media relations in the social media age', in Theaker, A. (ed) *The Public Relations Handbook* (4th edition), Abingdon: Routledge, pp 251–272.

YouTube (2012) 'Statistics', www.youtube.com/t/press_statistics [Accessed 19 April 2012].

Yu, L. (2007) *Introduction to the Semantic Web and Semantic Web Services*, Boca Raton, FL: Chapman & Hall/CRC Press.

Zack, M.H. (2002) 'Developing a knowledge strategy', in C.W. Choo and N. Bontis (eds) *The Strategic Management of Intellectual Capital and Organisational Knowledge*, New York: Oxford University Press, pp. 255–276.

Zerfass, A. (2010) *Levels of Impact and Evaluation*, www.communicationcontrolling.de/en/knowledge/levels-of-impact-and-evaluation.html [Accessed 9 November 2010].

Zerfass, A., Tench, R., Verhoeven, P., Verčič, D. and Moreno, A. (2010) *European Communication Monitor 2010. Status quo and challenges for public relations in Europe. Results of an empirical survey in 46 countries* (chart version), Brussels: EACD, EUPRERA, www.communicationmonitor.eu [Accessed 18 November 2010].

Zichermann, G. and Cunningham, C. (2011) *Gamification by Design: Implementing Game Mechanics in Web and Mobile Apps*, Sebastopol, CA: O'Reilly Media.

# Index